A real HR Head

From one fortune 500 American company, annual revenue reach to 2 billion Chinese division HR head, gone through 7.5 years exciting career, won numbers of awards, finally decided "I want to make a new change"!

When I firmly step out company gate, I shake hands with all the colleagues who send me out, a fond embrace, say goodbye, see the tears filled in their eyes, I thank you for their support and caring to me from my heart deep, can't express by wording, only one wish hide in my heart three years ago: I want to write one book to show what we have done for Company J, share our best practice with public, support HR folks to settle the headache problems, We even discussed where can we get the subsidy? "Can use the prize we won." however we planned this without further proceeding.

On today, I joined another MNC company, aim to the original target: I grew from one clerk, to be CHO of MNC, gone through years of mills, acquired rich experience and the reward from it, all rely on the opportunities granted from others, I shared what I think and what I done without reservation, hope everyone can get the benefit from it, build up HR business to be stronger and stronger.

Content

1. Think as globalize, act as localize 4
2. "The Next Prize" We target it 14
3. Is it HR separation or integration? 22
4. HR how to evaluate HR? HR how to develop HR? 31
5. How to face Boss repeat change? 35
6. How can M&A be? 47
7. Consider People not others before you find location for new site setting 53
8. Digital HR: Not perfect enough, can be more perfect 61
9. Shared Talent across different sites 75
10. We can be EICC Ambassador by organizing female training program 79
11. We show "PIC" project in United Nations 87
12. Being HR Head, your every movement affects the overall situation 93
13. Is it normal for Phrenoplegia/Suicide? 102
14. We just follow someone to strike! 112
15. How to lay off employee? I experienced to be laid off 132
16. After Lay Off, what next? 140
17. International expatriate staff 's caring: All-in-all, sickness and death 148
18. To protect integrity will be more difficulty than complying with integrity? 159
19. Did provide the old bed with the worm to employees to sleep? 185
20. The headache canteen management can be HR awarded score 192
21. In three months went to five provinces only for hiring 100 staffs 198
22. Close to year end, I want to target DL candidates by using "Machine Gun" 207
23. Is the labor agent extort the hard-earned money from dispatching worker? 214
24. Both recruiters & managers need to be trained : How to hire the right people? 226
25. The recruitment of fresh graduates-Fight repeatedly after suffering repeated defeats 239
26. Training essence, can you make it clear? 251
27. We train up hundreds & thousands of engineers by TR & MER trainings 265

28. DL also needs training and career development 277
29. MIT training is not a training program in MIT 284
30. EAP project support hundreds of employees getting educational degrees 295
31. Boss said why is my company losing the money?! 300
32. Annual reviews and annual adjustment: One story in one year 314
33. Talking about performance before payment 332
34. Oh, My God-The Manager pay will be cut 20%? 367
35. Stock grant- God glory ? 391
36. Who want to be Chinese Worker ? 410
37. Happy life beyond 80 422
38. The employee survey just like "Look at the flowers in the flog" 431
39. The unique annual gathering 441
The Word from My Husband 450

1.Think as globalize, act as localize

As MNC HR head there is no doubt that you will encounter more difficulty problems than others.

The first one you must face the pressure and work load push you going forward continually.

The first one HRM coach me in the orientation training named May, she told me:" I have been COMPANY J for more than 10 years, in every day, I asked myself, should I leave my job?" After several years, this HRM passed away from transportation incident.

Marketing colleagues made one joke with me, according to COMPANY J history record, there weren't one HR head could stay in this position last for more than 2 years, not only be fired but also couldn't stand for the work pressure, "Survive ratio really low"! I asked why and kidded with them: "This is all due to I have bad luck, always join the companies at the crisis, predecessors repeat to change, However, I can stabilize the jobs and support the company has at least 3 times revenue grow.

Seeing I wasn't scared, this colleague encouraged me and said, "It will be better after the first half of the year, then you will become addicted. Without such pressure and speed, you will feel unaccustomed."

Without too much saying, in the first half a year without a sleeping earlier than 1 o 'clock go to bed in the morning, you have to be gone through 100 to 200 e-mails per day, There were numbers of meetings in everyday: The highest record 10 meetings a day from morning till midnight, day time in China is the night time in the United States, your priorities unable to adjust will not cope with heavy workload.

You must figure out, how to respond to each key problem, how to respond with the solution quickly and effectively.

In the meeting you must be the first one clear express your point of view, neither to be too sharp words, can't be only know "listen attentively" and follow without questioning, because your boss like to compare you with other countries HR Heads, when they throw out problem they hope they can dug out answer from your mouth, you must think more than your boss.

As for the pressure, you must have your own solutions. Interestingly, I bought myself a small gift at the end of each month to reward myself for passing another month. For this "short and precious two years HR head life time", I must well "Enjoy" it!

No matter how busy I am, I always insist on working out and getting fit. It's not whether I like sports or not, but I must work out to bear the heavy pressure of work. In a multinational company you will see that the more senior the more energetic and cherish every minute, even to open the computer plug in projector before the meeting - your gestures and spend time are under observation of your bosses, you give them impression may be start from this small detail, they can discuss and decide your promotion and your future in a few minutes, the reality is more "skinny" than other companies.

When you are an HR head of a multinational company, the second problem is the language and communication style, as well as the completely inverted thinking mode of understanding employees in other countries.

If you can understand and effectively cope with it, it is already the most value for you to be an HR head of a multinational company.

I graduated from the department of foreigner secretary in Guangzhou foreigner language institute. Before that, the working language used in Hong Kong companies were Chinese. However, I told myself that one day I would go to European and American companies to work. When others speak Chinese, I will write English emails, chat with the foreigner, memorizing words selfishly and desperately, I used an hour reading English aloud in every morning, use post-it note down all the unfamiliar words from HR English magazine I saw, recited one put them into a candy jar, filled in a candy can then filled in another candy jar, etc. I didn't complete the second time recitation but I already received Company J's interview notification, it's my dream company.

After two rounds of interviews, four foreigners were tortured in turn, the whole process was in English. Each interview lasted more than 2 hours, making people sweat.

If I didn't listen to my former boss's advice: She taught me how to list out all the possible questions, learn how to answer them in colloquial English, I wouldn't have been able to get through this fast-track interview that changed my entire career.

When I came to the company, even if all Chinese sat there, I used English to have a meeting. The trouble was how to understand and use English words correctly, instead of only speaking English. At that time, I forced myself to use English write notes. I like to hire the best people, the best people like to stay together.

When I feel that my English is not good or I can't understand my colleagues from different countries speaking different "dialects" English, I would get angry being looked down by the senior management and even being satirized, even in a multinational company. I was once ridiculed by a Singaporean boss for using "Chinglish" to answer questions from customers. At that time, I thought it was ok to answer questions like this. I asked my foreign teacher is there any questions about my answer?

"No problem, but your boss wants you to use a more professional term: 'Healthy check or physical examination' instead of 'body check'." I realized the joke I made.

It's not just about how you make yourself understood in English, but also about understanding what other people are trying to say: Now I am in a new company managing 8 Cambodian plants, every policy should be posted in English, Cambodian, and Chinese three versions, the local government always announce a new policy all in Cambodian, a little misunderstanding on a formula for calculating wages will bring huge loss to the company, even the whole year profit of the company will be used up due to this, so how can I fully communicate with local colleague, translate the provisions accurately, make corresponding comparison, both sides fully understand the local law, fully understand the demands of local employees are important, otherwise you can't carry out work.

Chinese people often work day and night but not efficient, this is the reason why foreign bosses think you are inefficient. In the beginning, I often read and replied to emails late at night and did not spare myself on Sundays. The two previous bosses are Chinese, so they will appreciate your working attitude and kindly remind you to pay attention to work-life balance in the year-end assessment. But then it was the Indian and Singaporean who told you not to take my time off and even gave you an inefficient assessment. I changed my approach. I saved all my evening and weekend emails and sent them out the next working day within one or two minutes on the next day start working time.

Sometimes, you can't imagine why people in this country have such thoughts and actions. It's hard to understand why even Chinese people have reversed thoughts when they go to a foreign country. In Company M, we need to terminate the employees, in China, the employee will be fighting with you, don't want to leave because it's lost a job, but in Cambodia, the employees were more willing to be dismissed immediately, he can get a large amount compensation, start again, you may not hire him regularly, you can hire him to do temporary worker job, you also can drop his salary, when he looked at the others could get compensation, he could stop the work desperately, regardless of his position in high position and so on, in order to get seniority compensation, work one day by one day, live one day by one day, get compensation in an instant spending.

The third problem that multinational companies face - local laws, labor union pressure.

When hired at least 10 regional/national employees in a single branch: e.g. Hong Kong, Macau, Taiwan, Philippines, Vietnam, Cambodia, Singapore, Malaysia, India, France, UK, USA.

As HR head, at least you need to know the individual income tax law, labor law, regulations for transferring in and out, keep close relationship with accountant films, lawyers, the local government departments, as well as local non-governmental association and organization, to make comparison between the national regulations and details, every company system change and execution should balance all the interests and feelings, in that way "The boat will not capsized in the sewer".

In China, we feel that labor law was in favor of employees. The labor union in China is elected by the government, and the labor union of the company under the management of the company. But there are serious differences in foreign countries.

In Cambodia, only five workers are required to join the labor union to set up a labor union within the company. Each company can have numbers of labor unions at the same time. These unions can work against the company. Companies can't lay off employees in a biased way, they can get a minimum wage even if they don't show up for work, even if their workload doesn't meet the minimum standards.

The inconsistency of holiday among different countries has a great impact on the operation. In India, workers can take 20 days of annual leave, dismissal is subject to government approval.

Vietnamese workers do not accept overtime easily.

There is no retirement age in Hong Kong and employees can work until death.

American companies encourage home-based work.

Therefore, how to unify the policies and systems of MNC? You should always respect local laws and regulations and maintain smooth communication with local employees.

Before you draft a policy, ask yourself: why am I making this policy? What behavior does the policy want to regulate? What do you want them to do? If policies and institutions fail to achieve the intended effect of implementation, then policy making is a failure.

Here is a living example: I received an urgent report from the Marketing Department last week, the Cambodian plant was caught by using child labor. This is no small issue: The customer can stop the order at once because of this discovery! Investigation result is the director of the plant admit to use labor casually, salary is measured with piece, the company must pay the salary if the employees done the job no matter how old is the employee.

I really gasped when I heard that! Plant management, HR management is basically out of control, recruitment is out of control, record is out of control, salary is out of control, security is out of control, management structure is out of control.

This kind of out-of-control cannot be continued, so what I need to do immediately take out all the procedure of recruitment and salary payment of the branch plants. Among them, there are at least three different versions, issued at different time and with different approvers. Even one supervisor can approve the recruitment documents for more than 4000 headcount sizing plant. Using different languages, you really don't know what the Chinese and Cambodian languages mean.

We first took a well implemented system plant as the template for modification, translated the regulations into English and Cambodian. We asked the senior management of each factory to look at it. What can't be implemented? Are departments clear about their roles and responsibilities? Repeatedly discussed &

modified before announce to the public, request all the supervisors sign on the policy for confirmation: Any violations in the future, don't use 'Don't know how to do as "Excuse"', let every Chinese supervisor write down the commitment, HR may refuse to pay the salary if break the rules, who to hire who is responsible for the payment. It seems funny, but the problem is that it's Chinese supervisors who are more likely to break the rules.

After that, they should strictly track and compare the personal data of employees' salary with all the data of HR system, clean up all the personnel with problems. The system should be implemented in place, HR internal execution should be reinforced.

How to integrate HR system?

Systems are a constant pain in the heart of HR, especially when it comes to global integration.

First of all, the platform is not unified, each country each plant has its own computer team, do their best to develop their own plant plug-in program, APP, plug-in hardware... , like the game who uses IT technology more advanced and more special, came out a complete analysis report always feel less than perfect, always like women buy clothes -There is always the next one, so the group IT department need to do is to build a unified platform for different plant to building up their own IT building construction   according to "urban planning".

In each plant one change need IT management team help to update the background program for a policy or system or formula slightly modified, , when the group scale constantly expanding, system extends to the different country, IT is more and more difficult to control, the new email account, the password of each system, even outsourcing supplier used password can't be stopped when their employees left, I had this issue fully entangled with IT department by spending nearly two years' time solve it completely. Any permissions used by the system must be connected to HR system. The system will open the permissions for people, the system will automatically delete the permissions for the leaving people. Do not rely on manual work and do not blame for HR.

Regular HR guys "fickle in love" in new systems, because each system always has its bright spots. The Salesman of these systems sells the goods, regardless of how well you use the system. So in the latest round selection of HR system, 100 HR voted on the new system, only me choose to maintain the existing system and modify it, only me did the record the most detailed, I know the new supplier company didn't develop each module, its customer is our biggest competitor even give up to use their new system, both the customer don't want to use or input incorrect information are failure.

A good HR system should have rich experience how to serve peer customers, have a well-developed platform module can be demonstrated on the spot, guarantee for the system at least three years usage, the future development fee of the patch module must be carefully compared.

How to integrate HR system?

Because the global HR system were separated, HR bosses even didn't know important indicators like how many employees did the company have? What were their level? How much was monthly turnover? How many were new hires? How much was the labor costs? How many had OT hours? Absence hours? EICC observation items and so on, why there were so many multinational companies CXO challenging HR don't understand business, have not overall strategy, can't help on decision-making, the root cause is because they can't get first-hand information, senior HR don't know how to show their own project in front of their bosses and provide the suggestion, and don't know how to demonstrates the result of the different definitions in the case of dynamic? A large but not strong HR dept just put there.

It is easier said than done, how to unify HR report format, definition, statistical time, calculation formula, submission time, summary and results generated by various assumptions before the unified system comes out. I did. SVP- the HR boss, showed the HR monthly report I designed in front of all CXO.

Among them, you must have Excel skills, data accumulation capability, understand each indicator, interaction with HR in other countries, understand the problems from the perspective of the boss...

The fourth problem of HR management in multinational companies -- salary cost

Each country's economic and industrial development cannot leave away from the labor cost, why multinational companies invest in China, why today China face the reality of many foreign capital withdrawal, why today Chinese companies also invest to foreign countries, compensation costs rise sharply is harsh reality that the boss faced.

How to objectively evaluate and compare labor costs in different countries?

Minimum wages alone do not reflect full real costs:

For example, the minimum wage in Cambodia is USD170, even add on social security is only USD189, which is only half or even one-third of the minimum wage in China's first-tier cities. No matter how inefficient their workers are, they cannot be less than half of it, can they? Is there a cheaper country than Cambodia? There are a plenty of. Vietnam, Myanmar, Laos, & Indonesia,

Of course, the efficiency and speed of employees, the attitude of employees, and the speed of technicians reflected by education development all need to be considered.

How to manage and analyze the salary and welfare costs of different countries in a company to find a balance?

We adopted the method of simplifying the complex:

No matter which country you come from, we only have localized and oversea dispatching two sets of C&B scheme: localization scheme according to the local employees unified compensation standard to carry out, included on board, promotion, transferring and separate each steps, the only difference is the foreign employees contribute insurance in China, depends on the employees country which has concluded an agreement for abolition contributions, when the employee transferred to other employees, complete the separation process and continue his/her seniority.

If the overseas dispatch scheme is retained, the employee shall follow the unified salary standard of the branch company in his home country, calculate and charge the corresponding cost of the branch company across the border.

In the process of employment, the exchange rate and the life index should be adjusted in a balanced way in every quarter, otherwise, the real income of employees will be unbalanced due to the exchange rate change.

Balance the differences of various benefits with cash as far as possible, return the free choice to the employees, otherwise the management is complicated, heavy loading and unsatisfactory.

The balance between annual tax calculation and employee departure tax should also be the content of frequent communication between countries and plants. A little carelessness will directly lead to the dissatisfaction of employees. Afterwards, the communication between transnational governments is not an easy thing.

2. "The Next Prize" We target it

"You must win the first prize for us" Listening to the instruction from my Singapore boss David, it gave me quite a shock: like the shockwave attacked, never have the feeling like this. It should be the fourth application for the best practice competition in global, the experience was painful: All losses in three matches, never been to the front three! The old saying: "Never do the things more than three time", however, I have done three times, why I can't be front three?!

I felt depressed and came back to HR dept, I swore by myself this time: Scrap it and start all over again, no matter how the result will be, I try it again, no regret any more in the future.

I called all the leaders of dept, reviewed the past three years' painful projects we worked out, compared with the other winning projects, why was our projects going so well but nobody recognizes it?

"Indulge in self-admiration will not be successful, we list out all the projects we done, the list last quite long, investigate the Pros & Cons one by one, everyone is good! This state of "self-absorption" is the most dangerous.

At that moment, one recruiter, Rachel, can speak English frequently, high working efficiency but "Lazy" new generation girl stepped ahead and talked to me: "Cindy, let me try "Buddy Program".

Actually "Buddy program" brought in by me from E company, put in practice successfully in both companies, the positive result showed there, rank No.1 from our listing, hadn't any sample work from brother companies, it will bring out generous remuneration to the global company, especially for the headcount sizing up to 160K! The corp. guys will smell out this unaccountable benefit.

The young are fearless, I like the guy with courage to try and to change. We made the detail plan for campaign:

We need to give one outstanding name to this project, to translate the company cultural "Join COMPANY J, make the difference", after serious brain storm, ""有 伙 伴 就 不 同 ""Join with buddy, make the

difference" The bilingual slogan came out!

We designed one dazzling poster, I hope the audience can see the colorful version instead of black and white version. Thanks for E-book version can show the colorful version.

Why there will be this screen? Because our colleagues experienced the same, join COMPANY J company looks like "Big jump with parachute", you knew it is taking the high risk, who know the undersurface is abyss or plain? Who can stand for "average 2 years survive period"?

There was job list for buddy program, She or he will tell you, how can we survive, the company cultural, people habit, communication style, management organization, the buddy support the new comers identify the job priority, work together with them, become their bosom friend, play fellow. The list will be going through by HR to new comers and their buddy. Three months later, the new comers vote on "The best buddy".

"Buddy Plan" Work Guide

In order to support new comers adapt into new working environment, speedy fit into company cultural, pls assign one buddy provide the guidance to new comers, finish below job items, and share below form to the new comer (Only apply to new employees)

(Before new comer on board) HR inform dept about on-board information->The dept assign Buddy to new comer.

(After new comer on board) Buddy execute the working instruction for one month, share the working instruction to new comer->new comer fill in the feedback, submit the form to HR->HR combine the result and feedback to dept. The form drafted by HR, if there will be any inquiry, pls contact with HRXXX

Buddy Job Content (The job done by Buddy and kick "V" to confirm)

The First Day

- ☐ Pls tell new comer "I am your Buddy, I will help you to adapt company environment and understand company cultural, if any inquiry you have pls find me to clarify. After one month, you should feedback to me and HR.
- ☐ Pls confirm the new comer received dept gift (Flower, pot plant, notion and small hanging), handover welcome card with all dept colleagues' signature.
- ☐ Pls confirm office desk and chair, office stationary, name card be well prepared, to prevent any mess from it, provide the contact point about applying for stationary, computer, desk phone can workable, and apply for the new password for desk phone for the new comer.
- ☐ Tell the basic and useful information, for example: office layout, often used phone number and email usage guidance, how to use copier, fax, printer, where is rest room and WC.
- ☐ Pls introduce the direct supervisor and the major working relations to new comer (Face to face), introduce more to new comers.
- ☐ Let new comers send the personal living photos, self-introduce to the related colleagues.
  Pls have the meals together with the new staffs, talk about home and family issues.
- ☐ Ask him at least one time "what do you want to know about?" "Who do you want to meet?"
- ☐ The other finish jobs_____

In The First Week

- ☐ Pls confirm the dept has one simple introduction on new comer.
- ☐ Pls arrange the new employee meet with the close related colleagues, face to face communication will be the best
- ☐ Pls confirm he received contact list, meet the close work colleagues. Pls confirm there is the new comer contact information on the updated contact list.
- ☐ Pls introduce at least one global recognized employee to new comer, and arrange their meeting.
- ☐ Pls support the communication between new comer with supervisor, work out working plan for new comer (at least in the following one month)
- ☐ Pls arrange the direct supervisor have lunch with new comer (informal meal)
- ☐ Pls invite the new comers have the important meeting, though this meeting has not close relation with new comers, This meeting will provide the important information to new comer, for example: let him know about company environment, people character, organization chart, decision making, etc.
- ☐ Before closing time, ask new comer "How was your day, is there any difficult? Can I help you?" Ask him about tomorrow work plan.
- ☐ Pls encourage the new comer join at least one spare time activity, for example: Write down your dream on the dream wall, Badminton, gym room.
- ☐ Try to understand the family situation of new comers, know about if he arranged family life, is there any difficult for the living, the family member support his job change or not.
- ☐ Pls try to understand his feeling on the company.
- ☐ Pls confirm if he got the name card or not.
- ☐ The other jobs: _____

In The First Month

- ☐ Pls introduce the new staff visit Guangzhou downtown and nearby sight spot.
- ☐ Pls confirm if he finishes orientation training
- ☐ Pls ensure the new comer finish product knowledge, working process training.
- ☐ Pls ask the new comer "what the job you done?" "Who did you communicate?" "What the job plan you made?" If the answer not clear enough, pls feedback to direct supervisor.
- ☐ Pls confirm if the new comer satisfied the job and hope to continue the job, if new comer unsatisfied and want to change the job, pls feedback to his direct supervisor asap.
- ☐ Help the new comer draft the career development direction and plan.
- ☐ Other need to finish jobs:_____

Buddy signature: _____
Date: _____

The new comer feedback (Below column should be filled by new comer)

One month after on board date, you will receive this form, pls fill in it, provide the assessment on your buddy, (Point 5 is the highest score, point 1 is the lowest score, pls kick on "V" specific score. After fill in it, submit the form to HR XXX within 3 days, extension 5658, Thank you! If there will be any complaint, pls contact with Christine Deng, Extension 5848.

1. You buddy complete above items? ☐ Below 50%   ☐ Around 75%   ☐ 90% & above
2. How is the quality for completion ☐ 1   ☐ 2   ☐ 3   ☐ 4   ☐ 5
3. ☐ 1   ☐ 2   ☐ 3   ☐ 4   ☐ 5
   Base on Buddy working quality and quantity, how is your comment score to him?
4. Is there any feedback to your buddy? If yes, pls list out: _____
5. Base on company Buddy plan, is there any advice? If yes, pls list out_____

New comer signature: _____
Date: _____

Remark:
- Buddy Plan process:

There are four stages into this program:

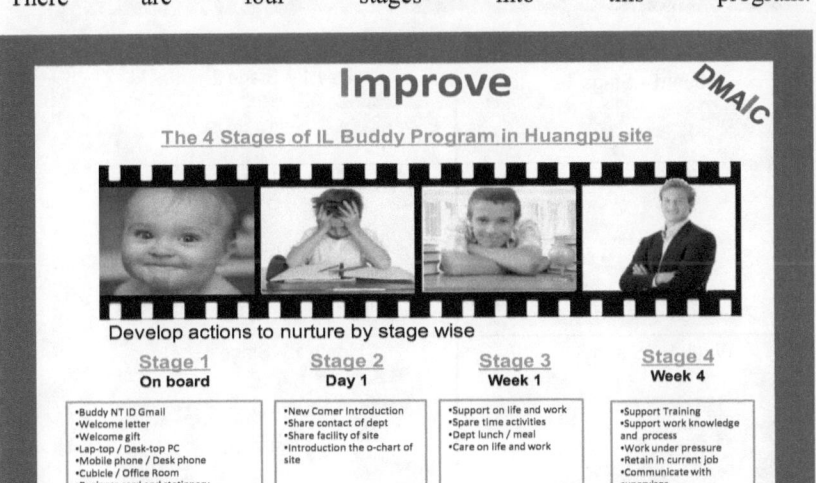

The first stag: The buddy should prepare all the tools for the new comer.

The second stag: The new comer on board, buddy must shake hands with new comers within three minutes, introduce the other colleagues in the dept. Introduce the job responsibility and scope to the new comer, try to use the computer and different systems, start up.

The Third Stag: Complete the orientation training within first week, visit different dept to understand the operation and the contact point for future jobs.

The Forth Stage: After one month, arrange the new comer to have reporting meeting, the new comer present what he have done and achieved in the past one month, answer the dept heads inquiries, accept the assessment then pass the probation. At the same time, HR will send out the survey in highest confidential, understand the new comer comment and feedback on buddy.

In the month end, HR will combine the survey feedback, list out 10% the best buddies, grant the award and medals, the award included two film tickets, BBQ etc, encourage the buddy and new comers support each other continually.

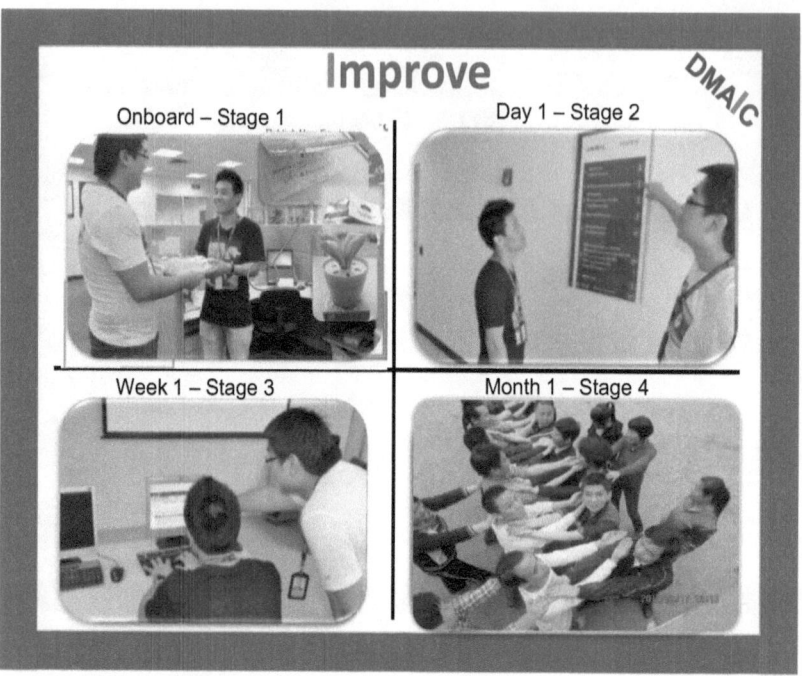

The project target to set up one effective and supportive system, help the new comers adapt the new working environment, fit into the company speedily.

In order to make it as successfully as possible, we visited brother companies, learn from others.

The result for the program obvious: There were 13,000 employees, more than 6000 employees be selected as buddy, new comer turnover rate dropped to 1.8% from 4.23%, reduced 57%. The good feedback from the new comers supported the staff recruitment result, the recruitment period dropped to be 32 days from 76 days, reduced 58%.

In order to present the program in simple and clear way, my boss presented in the meeting personally, gathered all dept managers challenged us one by one, from different direction and presentation style, modified PPT at least 90 times, because of one wording, one sentence, argued to be red face and red neck, unforgivable, My boss even asked me wrote down one word by one word on the white board, changed to be PPT wording and slide.

The first-round competition used phone call plus PPT running, after Rachel completed presentation, followed our several key supporters answered all the judges inquiry, by pass the interference, listened to the judge challenge, avoided the trap, reacted immediately, need the team work, finally we overcome all the difficulties to get the attend ticket to final round competition in American General Company!

The finals closed, the most worrying things happened, like to travel Rachel even went to Malaysia one week before the finals, forgot the presentation from here to there, don't know how to open.

I couldn't forgive this and shouted to her! I asked her to think it over how did we make it successful? How did the manager group support her? If she could remember all these, she would know what should she do.

Rachel is a big girl, she never forgive and continue to practice it by forgetting the meal and the sleeping, I took the video for her, let her know her voice, her pose, proficiency, in the end we threw away the speech draft, I ask her to repeat the presentation in the heart by priority. In order to prevent the jet lag, Rachel changed the night and day working hours, stayed in night to work.

In order to support her, GM arranged one American colleague who won the prize before, flighted to company general office to provide the necessary support to Rachel.

Before the journey, Rachel carried three U dish and placed to different place of luggage, to prevent any lose, I felt I took care of her better than my daughter.

Until the finals completed, I didn't disturb Rachel, Because I was confident on this project, I deeply believed we could win.

Just as our expectation, WE WON!

Afterward, the speed and frequency of winning prize never stop, one by one, continually.

3.Is it HR separation or integration?

I want to separate one HR into two parts, one is BP (Business Partner) part you will take in charge, another part is Share Service Center, HR head quarter in United States General Office is COE (Center of Expert), then HR will be changed to three parts, you can decide which one will you lead, the rest one handover to M, he used to be your subordinate." My Singapore boss said to me, the sentence I will not forget and can't forget in my life.

The reason for why I don't want to dig deeper, I like the sentence showed in Liu Xiaoqing （Chinese Movie Star） autobiography: "Don't trace back too deep, everything will be gone", I was quite impressed by her wordings, it influenced me to write down this book.

I was unfamiliar with HR-BP role, but I am quite familiar with the old saying: "HR is the business partner of company", one competent HR can support the company has high performance, however, the boss recognizes HR contribution in one high performance company? From boss point of view, he is more concern about actual result, can settle the problem in high speed, no matter how self-indulgent, how self-sensation your HR will be.

In this time, my direct boss conspired with Corp HR to bring me and my team as "White Mouse", no guidance no trainings, when we consult with COE team in headquarter in USA, they look us like "Heterotypic HR", astonished why are you asking this strange question from me?

To consult an internal customer, what do you need BP to do? A colleague of BP team wept and speak out the truth: "The head of the department asked me what is BP team doing. I'm busy. You talk to someone else. I seem to be doing nothing but seeing a lot of problems that don't seem to work out.

Our BP team members are full of the most potential in the department and the person who is the most willing to accept change and accept new things. We didn't give up on ourselves, I told them, "No matter where to put me, even if raising a pig, I'm going to fatten the pig otherwise it will not get through my own." BP team Listen to me. All of them have the courage to face "Hard to deal" internal customers, we take the initiative to find an online introduction to BP, that was four years ago in China, very few company HR set up organization like this, we go to participate in foreign training, we can find all the books about BP introduction, we download from the Internet, The understanding of BP learned in books and classes, integrated into PPT, but also a brainstorming method to set their own goals, with the Singapore boss to discuss, but he believes that BP should not play a "bridge" role, but should play the role as a consultant, he felt in the Company J group's COE team away from thousands of miles, Don't play a specific role at all, you just "swim" by yourself. "The boss is always right ", no matter how perfect the theory really to implement you can feel the actual imperfection, this set of theory to convert a functional department into the separation of powers itself there is innate flaw

1. As the Commissioner of the COE team, there is a lack of communication and interaction with internal customers, how to specifically understand the real needs of customers? Relying on the "message" of BP team alone, they do not understand how the internal situation can provide practical solutions?

2. BP team need time to communicate and understand customers for operational requirements, it takes a considerable amount of time to communicate this part of the specific requirements to the COE team, the group COE team faces more than 100 branches around the world, they also have a bunch of CXO at Headquarters to do this project or that project, they clearly told us "we're here for show-show."

3. SSC team itself does the most basic work, the policy of making the most direct solution to the problem, the policy is the most accurate and clear only for the

specific formulation of the person to preach, the actual voice of the customer can be heard, quickly solve the customer's problems.

4. HR function module is divided into three modules more like split HR work step to the station and sub-level, it is actually the opposite to lean production concept: Integrate-remove unnecessary processes and reduce waste, many companies claim to set up a BP and COE team, the real situation is: Some BP to take care of the recruitment, Some have picked up employee relationships, and some have picked up COE specialist centers, compensation and benefits, employee relationships and training, we belong to the latter one.

The internal management heard that BP's role was to support them, all overjoyed, shouting all day about what the value that your HR department creates for the company? What is the value created by your BP team? In fact, this problem does not require customers to ask me, in every day I am asking myself where is my value?

If there is no value, why does it exist? The organization that does not meet the actual needs of the company should indeed be abandoned, only the best HR organization is right for you. No matter how famous human resources godfather recommended it. Even if I was put in the position of that worthless team.

BP is to concentrate on the searching of key talents, retention and development, that is, to do the inventory of talent. Do talent Inventory first one we have to ask ourselves why do we have to do talent inventory? In order to implement the Company's development strategy. So why is it up to them to implement the company's development strategy? What is the company's strategy? What can be done to ensure that they really implement the strategy?

We first understand these problems in order to implement, otherwise all the way to do talent inventory, in the end is what to do?

I'm properly understand the question from the company's manager class thoroughly. It was we first set up BP team, we are entangled can't break through, the three authors to set up this organization: General manager of the company is transferring out, global HR SVP and Asia VP resigned less than two years. Then another took in charge, the general manager of the company, a new officer, begin with a discussion of the HR management organization, he asked very directly, why should a HR have separated into two team? What do BP team do? How do you do BP management key talent? How to put the key talent into the combination of the company's strategy and help the company make money? Still can't forgive "Make money" for the company owner's consistent attributes, this boss with management theory educational background, like to show his qualification.

Immediately thereafter, he asked me to deliver his "MIT-Manager in Training manager retraining" 13 series of courses to all managers and to arrange exams!

"You're going to talk about the" battle for talent, " I've recommended you to read the book before" He said.

I have taught a lot of lessons, whether inside or outside the company, but I have always had my own proposition, the topic of the battle for talent is really a topic of old scum.

He hasn't really recommended the book to me, although we used to be colleagues, he was transferred to other branches and now he's back.

I will go to find the book, in order to well teach the class, talent is important, but did not have a good summary. I found two books named the same: "Talent wars" "war for Talent, when I read word for word, I knew that was not the book he was referring to.

I must ask him again, is that the book you're referring to? Finally, he showed me that it was "the differentiated Workforce talent defense"! Total two different names! But this is really a good book, is the classic of HR classics book I have seen.

The point of view it sets out:

Put the company's strategy first, not people. We should link the ability to promote strategic development to the company's strategy.

1. Find out where the strategy is.
2. Building leadership can take responsibility for making the company successful (every manager HR role)
3. Design the organizational structure of human resources for different companies.
4. Measures for the development of strategic organizations.
5. How is it implemented?

There is a awaken feeling, in order to further understand the company's strategy: Intelligent Factory, Smart factory, to be industrialization 4.0. What is Smart factory exactly, to figure out what is industry 4.0, borrowed back the relevant books read again, what 's Germany Industrialization 4.0? What does Japan's industrialization 4.0? What 's the difference between 4.0 and China's industrialization?

What 're the key talent our company need to implement industry 4.0? I continue to search the Web page, in the end which position can promote intelligence? Can you drive automation? ME, IE, IT?? Why can they? When the problem arrives here, I can't answer it, after all, the technical industry should have specialized, I train to tell the truth, the definition of specific key skills should be the boss and the issue of the key departments.

Teaching played a great role, it not only forced me to understand all the contents of the content thoroughly in a limited period of time, to sort out the structure, to use a beautiful PPT to express, to ask a deep and interesting question, drive the department managers have action after class! Because the next step, my new boss won't forget the managers, he asks them to:

Identify the most critical 10 skills in each business group, why are these skills the most important? How much business can these skills affect? How do we manage these skills?

Who has these skills now? Their positions, all key skills, performance, development potential, payroll, self-development plans, reserve development plans (internal replacements or external recruitment), overall ratings.

HUA Site SME List

Dept.	Area	Q2-Skill Level	SME	Experience (Years)	Join Date	Train up plan	Successor Plan
Quality	IPQE	Green	Anna Yang/ QinHua Zhu	8	2010/08	Join VDA 6.3 training,5 key quality tools---	Emily Chen
	QMS	Green	YukiTu	11	2009/10	1. Explore more in specific audit project to understand more about process and product-Done (Conducted QMS Health Check, Baseline Audit, AOS) 2. If possible, try to lead a workcell	Linka Chen
	NPI	Green	Happy Zhu/ Sally Zhao	10	2012/11		Roy Liu
	IPC	Green	QingHua Zhu	20	1996/10		Sylvia Xiao
	FMEA	Green	Hans Pan / Filippo Huang	11	2011/06		N/A
	SPC	Yellow	Hans Pan/ WeiMin Zeng	11	2011/06	More practice / get more instruction from CK Wong, Quality leadership and communication, influence.---One previous 3rd party trainer was rejected, HR is working on new resource	Anna Yang
	MSA	Yellow	Hans Pan	11	2011/06		
	DOE	Green	Nie Wang	15	2011/		Joshua Tam
	Minitab	Green	Hans Pan	11	2011/06		Anna Yang
	ESD	Yellow	Jiang Xue	6	2010/06	External Trainning--Plan to conduct it in Apr'17	Filippo Huang
	8D	Green	Anna Yang/Black Zeng	8	2010/08		Happy Zhu
	Calibration	Green	MingYing Zhu	17	2006/12		Zhu Heng
	Super OBA (PCBA+Boxbuild)	Green	QingHua Zhu	20	1996/10		Meiying Liang
	Inspection (PCBA-Mfg)	Green	Sylvia Xiao	13	2008/03		Miya Liu
	DCC	Green	Xuelian Liu	19	1996/11		Mingying Zhu
	MES	Green	Weimin Zeng/ Ming Juan Zhu	11	2007/07		N/A

Green	13	81%
Yellow	3	19%
Red	0	0%

Which is responsible for each key process? Are the teaching materials they have written for the department incorporated into the company's central file system? How to teach how to test? How to Practice? How do I update? The plans for the development of these specialist themselves.

Manager level or above in each department to do leadership tests and record results, record all promotions, transferring, achievements and failures in Company J, equipped with the corresponding management tutor give coaching and feedback, record retention.

The key talent in each key technology business unit, the specialist level talent, the management talent file is summarized as the whole factory talent pool map and training map, the general manager quarterly reviews the overall performance of the past quarter and formulates the plan for the new season

HUA Talent summary

	Printer			I&E			Auto		
WCM Assessment Result	7 qualified			7 qualified			1 qualified	2 have gap	2 are low
WCM Successor	Still idendifying potential WOM			No mature successor candidates			2 successor candidates are under developed		
Sector SME Assessment Result	62%	37%	2%	29%	50%	21%	30.43%	39.13%	30.43%
Plant SME Assessment Result	73%						25%		

	WCM/SrWCM	MFG	ME	TE	IE	QE	Purchasing	Planning	IA	SQE	Logistic	HR	IT	Lean	PMO	Total
External Talent Pool	16+1		22	6				23								58
Can Rehire Talent Pool		3	2		1		2	5	1	3		2			1	24

It is too many rounds of "disregard for life and death" arguments and fights that can be to made the rules clear.

First, the boss himself is not willing to confess with HR! Really share the person in his heart!

When I shared the good report with him, he was quite happy, by the time I asked him, when did you share your suggestions and comments on the talents to me, so that I could combine into the whole factory's talent pool map. At that time, he replied coldly: "I have all the assessments on you, all have a record, but I will not share with you, how can I share with you?" "To be a HR always remember the golden rule: To see how the boss do rather than listen to the boss how to say, HR in the boss's mind is a few pounds and two you can see if he respect for HR, so I calmly reply to him: Then we will be other levels and departments of the results of the record to you, you do summary. "Worrying about HR know your boss's secret, let it be.

Vice president has not yet figured out how to do, also disdain on the management class, Quarterly Review the talent pool map with GM, often confused everyone, I really want to "Kill" them, let them wake up thoroughly! Once by once they come back there're still that sentence, your HR help me get it done. "Hold it on! HR can be coordinator (assisting person), but not Leader (project leader)! The key skills and talents in each business group are still to be determined by the general manager and vice president level, if they cannot be determined, find the team to determine together, we adhere to the defensive line!

Each manager is quite hesitate to nominate successor, BP can't speak out the truth: After all these managers still working on their position, they don't like to nominate someone to replace themselves, however, Company J will not provide the promotion to anybody who didn't find out two successors, to train up successor is one assessment index for being one manager.

The training opportunity will be rare, in the past every dept like to self-design training course, teach whatever they like to teach and show whatever they like to show.

In this time General Manager ask for write down the training content by strictly follow the requirement, step by step, must be reviewed by himself, check the quality issue, one by one check and pass through, it was never seen before, only training content spent half a year to complete, we regularly review it on each Thursday, HR learn a lot of professional knowledge from here.

To do talent store take not easy, to do a good BP isn't easy as well, BP team gone through that hard time!

4.HR how to evaluate HR? HR how to develop HR?

HR often make the assessment on others, often discuss how to train up and develop others, how to set company organization chart to be more effective, however, when mention their own, will be "The flower man shows the willow". There is one indicator provided by consultant company in CBM (Compensation & Benefit management) report: In Electronic industry, the prevailing ratio is 100 employees Vs 1.21 HR.

"HR is the most difficulty and suffering dept, "It is your duty to do the good job, your guilty if didn't do the good job." That is what I heard from advises from others when I find out the starting job in HK.

Indeed, in my more than 20 years HR career development, read the countless people, can survive and develop to nowadays, it is rareness. HR develop others develop ourselves, support others support yourself.

I like to involve daily operation, included weekly Gemba Walk, included HR do the Gemba Kaizen, answer the customer question when receiving the customer visit together with marketing dept, provide the suggestion to other depts. Only you know "Three present doctrine" then you can settle the problem on the spot at the first time.

When I work in company E, the boss looks like "going crazy" on lean improvement, however, HR only stand besides, don't know how to support the other depts., don't know how to propaganda lean cultural, even if do it by yourself improvement.

At that time, HR was appointed to do Kaizen improvement. At first, it is a simple "literacy class", know what the means on "Seven kinds of waste", what calls "TAKT Time", What calls "Three present doctrine".

After all, I was appointed to represent HR to do training improvement, at that time, training team separated from HR, in the beginning I took a lot of detours, this one instructed I should walk this way, that one order me to walk that way, in the end, I was totally confused by internal guys, don't know what should do, faced CHO challenge, got a rocket from CHO: "What the chicken project you are making?!", I was thunderstruck, didn't know what to do, afterward, two bosses reviewed my workout one by one, go back again & again, pull down then start again, then pull down again.

Sank in self-melancholy for some time, I suddenly storm waved, how can I make improvement when I didn't clarify what 's wrong on training? I must invite the external assistant, I invited "Experts" who done lean improvement in every BU, ask them take one week figure out N question marks and wastes, come up with way to improve, we found out:

The training method is in flexible;

Too long training lecture notes, not easy to remember;

The waiting time for training and examination is a real waste.

The skill learn can't be used.

No update on the lecture note of the latest motor product.

The motor showed to the new comers is the oldest model not the current motor producing in the production lines.

One day spend for training, one more day still spend on the training after going back to production lines, because the knowledge taught are lagging.

A lot of problems, few people, very little time, we divided 5 team members into three teams, everyone settle two problems, I settle more problems and jobs: Show "What the problems they figured out and how to fix it" to the boss. Thank you for the lean experts, they work out the result and everyone has their own unique solution:

We took the photos, enlarge the image to standardize training methods to teach the workers, use the simplest wordings to explain.

We used jingle, label method shows the defective products to the workers, allow them to touch it, see it, ask the questions, attentively remember it.

We asked the new comers direct to training center to have orientation training, have the test immediately. If failed, retrain them, if still failed, will be treated dismissal.

Arrange the relevant motor sorting training, not to waste the skill and training time, the multi-skill allowance pay to the employees who full use the relevant skills.

The new product trial run should report to training dept for training information update.

There are existing the argue for No.6 to No.7 problems, because it relates to the training team functional transferring problem: The production frontline team members asked why can't split training team into different production lines?

From CHO point of view, he wasn't willing to transfer training team into production, however, why not? I support production dept suggestion from my heart, however, being one member of HR team, I can't say anything, prevent CHO treat me as one Scape Goat! I must be clever enough throw this problem to the big boss to make a noise, my death is coming on this Friday, if I failed, I will be slaughter by following this chicken project, If, If I can be win, who knows? My direct boss suggest I use English, even if my mentor-Company COO asked me to use English one minutes ahead presentation, because they want me to show my qualification in front of big boss, I knew their intention, so I took a deep breath and put my life safety out of consideration, complete the presentation in one attack without any break, the big boss appreciated my presentation nodding while listening, further explain the key points what I presented to the beside CXOs, he is the first one gave the warm applause after my presentation, I am so glad to say thank you repeatedly, at that time, I saw our respective CHO, stand far away and afraid of the big boss will blame him on my failure, in the end, he bluntly said to me:" Good job, and well done." In the second time Gemba Walk, the company already make the final decision to transfer worker training into front line production line, let the new comers' access to the latest, the practical training, get the training result from reducing the waste.

It was well known among internal company even exposed to the same industry that push down training concept and build it up overnight, "Everything is impossible" one unrealistic, nonvalue added dept shouldn't exist. The same principle for our HR people, don't over estimate yourself, when you think you are No.1 in the world, you already going to the down trend, continue to study, continue to make the progress, align with different depts., you will not drop behind. "You didn't develop yourself, who take the responsibility to develop yourself?" This is the most classical management thought I heard in one HR develop HR speech.

5.How to face Boss repeat change?

In Company J 7.5 years, I ever direct reported to 5, dotted line reported to 15 bosses, on average, 1.5 years to change one General Manager, they came from 6 countries. Singaporean, Indian, American...

In every time change the boss, I must introduce the branch companies profiles, Chinese labor law, people profile to new boss, they came from different countries and regions, have different management mission, different values, different character, you have to run with them: Know and understand something without wording.

American like to praise, often said "Great! Well done! Good Job! Fantastic! Perfect!" Strong praise, no stinginess. The foreigner bosses make use of praise.

Singaporean has the high standard, investigate detail, over demanded, most of them came from army.

Indian boss like to talk, like to show, like to present, like to control, there is one illusion, if you see one viper and one Indian on the road, you should kill the Indian rather than viper.

Hong Kong people look important for relationship, like to comment, like to complaint, like to talk.

Inland supervisor looks important on Relationship, Face, Studying, Worship, and Copy, Chinese was rare can be my 1 of 20 parts boss; don't forget I am one of them.

Hired me into Company J is a Malaysian direct supervisor, he had been one QA before, "I need hands on people, do things guy!" He repeats this requirement to headhunter company, in the whole interview process, he said much more than me, let me know how intense competition Company J was facing, the profit only left several points, have to feed more than 100,000 employees, all and all introduced to me, I was wondering: If he want me join or he want me to forgive?" When I describe myself, he kept silent, listen calmly and observed, "I saw the white hairs on your head so I brought you in, I infer that you were aged around 30 years old, the white hairs you already have must be the hard work you done. After hearing how you analysis the problem confirmed what I thought." He said to me, it looks my white hairs saved me." I laughed. This boss is a hardworking boss, mastered the technology and knowledge incomparable, He got the full score on global talent selection, a high rise from QA engineer promoted to GM, however, his character was quite direct, never conceal his "Animosities", offend many people, finally the "Elder brothers" make the excuse for "Lost the biggest customer", submitted a joint letter to Corp, ask for transferring him out of China. I am the only one have the fair well lunch with him, because I admired him work day and night for the company, a solid grasped the technology and knowledge, but I also advised him: Clam down, it will be easier accept by others if you put yourself on their shoes speak to them." However, this boss still left us, joined the most profitable company M as GM.

The second boss is one tall & handsome Singapore boss, amicable, I often call the others as "Brother, Sister" that everyone like to hear and feel warm, because HR work closed with boss, so everyone calls him "Brother Sheetoh", call me "Sister Cindy". This boss should be the most unlucky boss, when he on board not more than 1 month, call me go into his office and said: "Cindy, we have big trouble this time, we are posted by NGO on the website, Corp looking into this very seriously, I was shocked, Oh no, how can NGO things fall on me? This will defect my HR fame! I only heard about Brand N sport wearing company was exposed by NGO about locking the employees into workshop, damage the company reputation and don't know how to close it, it spends a lot to protect the company image. Look at it, more than 10 charges, there were photos and witnesses, hundreds and thousands words looks like "Irrefutable evidence", almost put me and Company J on the international court to shoot. I am undeserved; I only passed probation then deserve this probation examination again?

Sheetoh saw me was frightened, don't know where did the bravery come from, said to me: You and me are new for this company, what the statement in the news weren't made by you and me, what we can do is settle the problem thoroughly and make the good change, we should thanks for this NGO, it is not easy to ask for budget to do some improvement without this report.

Listen to his wordings, I recovered bravely, who ask me to join this "Company J TV Program", the programs were more exciting one by one, more wonderful one by one, only left personal safety out of consideration, face the media bravely, face the customers, face Corp, face the employees, clarify the fact, "Make the good change if there are problems, treat it as encouragement if there aren't problems"

We list out all the problems it mentioned like one essay: Oh, God, 8 big crimes and five small crimes, looks like more crimes compare with "Down with gang of four".

12 hours of standing works: Brutality management, no rest place, deduct labor union fee forcibly, use temp workers, crowded dormitory, no meat meals, no grievance receiving channel.

In the beginning, we thought about how to trace back which employees were poisoning our company in media? Soonest we already forgave this thought, because we have more than 7000 employees, we can't seal their lips, it has been many years before it made, we should focus on root cause:

Within 24 hours, we already check it out what's the fact described in the report? List out the improvement plan, solid evidence, respond to group communication dept.

Use one channel, one standard answer to media & customer, commit "Take serious improvement if there will be, treat it as encouragement if there will not be", post it on the group public webpage, align with marketing dept colleagues answer the customers' inquiry.

It is the most important to identify why were the employees dissatisfy? Let them speak out, let them can see what are we making the change.

We set up numbers of communication channel at first

Hold the tea talk organized by HR and different dept supervisors, listen to the employees' heart.

We post out HR and production front line supervisor and manager phone number, 24 hours take employees' call.

Employee blue box-The union is responsible for collecting, tracking, reporting and resolving, and public feedback; Escalation system-Allow all the employees escalate, bypass the immediate supervisor and report directly to the next level if they feel dissatisfied with the boss job, the next level can or can't settle the problem should respond to the employees in 3 days, the employees can continue to escalate until settle the problem thoroughly.

GM mail box-Sheetoh take in charge of receiving, personally trace back, settle and respond, protect confidentiality.

Integrity hotline-The employees can direct call external third-party professional organization, clarify the problem, submit the problem by professional organization to Corp CXO, CC relevant dept head, limit 3 days must response the initial investigation status, consistently update until the problem settled.

Collect the information from different channels, not only let the employee release their dissatisfaction from their heart, but also provide the advice how to solve the problem, of course, from this know more about deep seated problems. Understand the problem and suggestion, one more brain storm we had, take effective measures:

Cancel the standing work for all the employees: We analyzed If the human body muscle keeps "Tighten" status for the long time, cause the bad impact to the healthy and mood, actually it hasn't much improvement on the efficiency, provide the seat will not waste the space on production line setting.

Whether sitting or standing, we also analyzed how to sit and stand will be more comfortable? This time Sheetoh GM led as one example, he put on the workers' uniform, went to production line, worked together with the workers and chatted with them, that went through several positions, gathered all the managers and said:" You don't know how to make the improvement on production line, make the employee more happy and more efficient, you, yourself, get off your manager uniform take off your badge, go to work in production line for one hour, after that tell me how to make the good change on production line!"

At that time, I was "forced" to "stand" for more than one hour then I knew:

The height setting for the seat is unreasonable, I am 1.68m high, I must lower my head bend my back to work, one hour later I felt the back pain already.

However, the carts busy come and go, I need to repeatedly straight my back allow the carts pass through.

The waiting time for conveyor belt set too slow, the worker waiting time=Time waste etc, even one HR I am, I knew how to take the lean improvement already.

Then we have the flat heeled rubbed mat shoes, standing mat, self-adjusting seat, production conveyor, maternity lounge, feeding room…

The employees mostly concern about their basic need.

Bear the brunt is canteen improvement-canteen management is Admin management basic course, if losing management, lead to the strike at any time, canteen hardware is still very good at that time, however, Admin team didn't manage the supplier in good way, run canteen looks like market stall, dirty, disorderly, and bad, really lost appetite, we take immediate improvement:

We provided one fruit per day to the employees-Doctor away from us.

We guarantee to provide at least 56 dishes in every meal, make the difference in everyday, four seasons, which supplier of three didn't well done their job will be replaced by the new one, one supplier didn't want to leave even threaten "Fight" with us when we replaced it.

Set the canteen reward and punishment system, pay RMB3K for the good feedback from internal employees, enough weight, clean and orderly, saved water and power supplier, vise verse, one tenable complaint will be treated the fine.

Start with various meal supply: Pasta, Hamburger, Congee & Rice stick, Steam, Boiling, Frying, Deep frying, stock with everything.

Strengthen communication, when there will be one new dish announce it to public, send WeChat and mail, stir up the employees' appetite.

The headache problem for HR became my bonus part.

The most difficulty change should be dormitory due to the high cost related, we have more than 2000 rooms accommodated more than 8000 workers, in order to save cost, emptied the dormitory for two years, not enough bed space provide to the new comers when the production expanded and offered to the new comers, I complained operational director to Asia SVP, because he only knew cost saving, not solution can provide, I can't let the employees lie on the ground without one bed to sleep.

Joinder, finally he was terminated by the company.

No happy start for new dormitory opening, but continue complaints we received, because more than 900 of 2000 new dormitory rooms were leaking! Why? The bad construction quality! Even me could break down the water pile by hand, how could the facility dept audit the building quality? Where were their conscience? Water dropped down to the employee head, body and bedding when the employees lie down, how can't the employee complaint? I was sad when I saw these, because my family was poor when I was a girl, the small house was leaking day and night, when storm came, the small storm having into my family house, I fully understood the pain the employees had, I had a good quarrel with facility manager, because he didn't know what he did in the past 40 years in Company J!

I shouldn't let the employee suffer this pain any more, I rolled out all the maintenance budget and show it to Sheetoh, more than RMB900K cost isn't a small amount, occupied 1/20 of net profit! He firmly told to me: "Cindy, we now have the ability to help those who need help, we must use our ability!" After that, he and me persuaded Finance and BU GMs, approved to maintain more than 900 leaky rooms thoroughly.

In order to make employees happy, feel warm, we encourage the employees pick up the brush, paint on the walls in and out of dorm & canteen, you have to admire this new generation employees, from their hands, you can see "The greenery bamboo forest, Brilliant purples and reds Cockaigne, modern and naughty lady dorm, Dream flying fresh graduates" different topics, vigorous, active, dress up the dorm like university campus.

At that time, Sheetoh was particularly excited, he like to lead the customers and visitors to walk around and present, he said: "I feel so proud of what you have make achievement and result."

Working with him, we have to face the underworld gang! Because the company large scale, we have to reject the interest temptation, even if gang 's threat. One time, we rejected the corruption of RMB120K cash canned by milk powder can sent by shipping company.

One more time, we terminated one gangster with triad background without hesitate.

The bravest time, he went to the meeting individually, settle contract conflict with one supplier has black and white background.

He even promised to our subordinates "Shave Bald!" in order to encourage us to achieve the impossible target, in order to see his bald looking, our subordinates work together and achieved impossible target, looks on the reachable target, he touched the hair and joked: "Well, it should be the big lost for me." Finally, he showed the great achievement to CEO and his bald as well.

I suffered 3 times hard scold by him: Once, he asked me to hire in more government relations, I showed him the list who we hired government relatives total more than 30 heads. Talked with him: " It is enough, we can't hire these idlers, he open with a scold, count in the conflict I had with labor union chairman, told me: "We sought the support from government, if we don't hire in one or two guys they recommended, how can we do, I don't need your arrangement, I ask others to arrange it."

At this time, I cried by his scold, in my mind, Company J only accept the capability talents, people rely on their own capability, if they rely on relation, how many capabilities they will have? Which dept accept them? I have to beg the dept heads to accept them, even myself think I shouldn't do that how can I convince the others to do that? After that, I thought what he faced the same situation as me, who would like to do this?

In another time, I followed his subordinate and his secretary to be scold, he blames the driver who picked up his boss, not show the indicator in front of car, and didn't ask someone, only wait in the car, I seldom saw he was so angry, even pounded the table angrily, afterward every driver scared with care.

At the last time, one QA Sr engineer complained QA manager, promoted the subordinate and raised the salary in turn implicitly hint the subordinate "you should know what to do", I told him the fact, he even ask me to trust QA manager not to trust QA Sr engineer, looks like he was under pressure came from his supervisor, because this QA manager recommended by his supervisor to join.

In fact, boss is human, he isn't so special just like you and me, face his boss, have to lower the head when facing the bigshot, also aim the higher position, neither flatter boss to be so high, nor paint him so black, I am the others' boss, I treat my subordinates like my children, although I take care of my subordinates, it doesn't mean they must accept you, your children doesn't obey your instruction you can beat them, turn to your subordinate, can you beat them?

The fourth direct boss is still Singaporean, he listed the top position in the army, treat the others like soldier, everyone must follow his instruction can't say no, his name is David, the same name as god in the bible.

I won the global best practice competition within his tenure, with his personally coaching.

To split HR is his decision, before that he asked me transfer to Chengdu site and promote to next level, I guess it should be the discussion result he had with my previous boss, however, consider my daughter only has 9 years old, need parents' accompany and caring, I gave up this opportunity, stay in Guangzhou site, there is also another reason, Guangzhou site remain course of my struggle, I fully knew what will happen if I stay in Guangzhou site, this boss will test my EQ, see how much pressure I can take. No surprisingly he hired back my subordinate by instructed my dotter line boss secretly, split HR into two parts, ask me responsibility for BP and C&B, till to my subordinate on board, he still questioned me why I didn't arrange his jobs? If I decide to leave the job I can leave. This is the pain I can't endure, a long time I cannot fall sleep, I don't know what the dogma I broke? This subordinate on the job when I joined, I heard about the rumor he takes the "Black Money" from previous company labor agents, nothing he done when he had been my subordinate, why our company hire him back?!

After that I swallow criticism in every day, I asked myself what the job I done on today, afterward, I kept silent, spend my time to study, even read the bible, from bible I learn about life philosophy. I read numbers of specialized and non-specialized books, I am acuminate my knowledge and energy, waiting for one day exploration.

After that he was removed from Guangzhou site due to the violation on supplier selection process, another GM named Steven came on board, in the opening, his secretary asked for resign at first, she even forgave the long seniority of more than 10 years, numbers of GMs she worked close, only one sentence she left: "I can't stand his working attitude, I will go crazy if long time face him." She wasn't the first one told me that. Being HR, I used some chances to remind Steven that someone can't withstand him. He was so angry and responded to me loudly: "I don't need everyone agree with me, I only need the ones who have the same value sense follow me to run."

He is energetic, run on the way not walk in everyday, in every management meeting, he like to comment, he has his management style, he like to have the training with managers, share the management theory for different management master built, after that, occasionally he will check how much you really learned, once he asked me what 's balance score card, I answered his question easily, he was applauded on me. Another time, he asked me what 's career anchor, I didn't hear it clear and ask one question in reply, finally when he heard I don't know what 's it, He said to me unhappily: You are so uneducated HR even don't know what career anchor means." It is not the first time I faced his challenge in front of other managers.

In the last time I can't cut down dept budget by following revenue dropped, he takes me out as bad example to criticize.

Come on, I am getting braver after one by one "fight", I don't know this but I can learn, I can't cut down the cost that company can cut me down.

That I study "career anchor" literature, and learn how to match candidates' character with their jobs, what's 9 kinds of career anchor, being one HR, we should fully know it and fully use this theory, hire the right people put on the right position, assign the job they like to do.

After I learn a lot on career anchor, I was well prepared for his next torture; however, he didn't find me but find the other to ask. He read the book in extremely high speed, In the farewell lunch, I asked him the last question, how did you read one book, how fast did you read one book? How can you remember the book contents?

I spent 1.5 hours for reading one book, if you read much books you will understand that the theory, they mentioned are quite closed, so you should list out the special points it mentioned, remember it, drop down the notes, after certain time, go through it again that you will not forget." I asked "Will it waste your time for dropping down notes?" He said: "Your notes should be recorded by computer, there is special website for reading notes recording." It seems everyone success has their success reason.

I remember that he saw me busy day and night, reminded me "You shouldn't read all the mails, only your boss mails read and settle at the first time, there is not mail more important than your boss mail, in addition, I should divide many bosses' mails into different mail boxes, then you will speed up X times.

He advocated digital platform integration, HR system must support depts. And employees rather than HR, roll out data when there is necessary, his expectation is high, however, the catch-up speed for IT slowly, he changed two IT senior managers for that reason.

He requests our managers remark annual target setting on the first page of daily, often review how many targets accomplished, he review all the achievement and failure in the past one quarter, adjust annual target again, set the whole week schedule in Monday meeting, his schedule is accurate to every 5 minutes as one unit, He thought millions income people should do millions valued jobs.

Boss isn't the god, they have advantage and disadvantage also, I worked with the worst boss was complained by the whole marketing dept which submitted the joint letter ask for the company to get rid of him, I also met the most unlucky boss, who just came on board, already black listed by NGO, also the "Crazy" boss, one more abnormal than another one (My peer dept managers made this "Verdict" on them)! I listen to their comments, not lightheaded comment share without deep digest, stand out to correct misunderstanding if there will be the necessary, not for the boss, for self, for the company.

What I do: "Learn their advantage, find out the shining points from them, they can be your boss there should be something worth you to study, who can you study if you don't study from your boss? The smart subordinates know how to learn and use, I also summarize their shortcoming, their mistake, avoid it.

6.How can M&A be?

Company J Merge & Acquisition expanding in the unprecedented speed, target to find out the profit growth point from M&A, Company J merged Company G successfully, jump to top 3 from No. 6 in the world ranking, took over the most famous handset brand A customer manufactory orders, however, the original Company G big boss in charge of internal management, no matter how the top position redeployment will be, only one result: Nobody listen to your instruction, their real boss is Company G original boss.

This is cultural integration problem, when you have meeting with Company G management, you strongly felt you are living in military, everyone call you "Sir/Madam", you can't freely express your personal opinion, because your boss didn't comment. You cannot open ask why they sell the company, this will touch their dead point, which make them feel you are look down on them.

Although these principles never showed on the M&A "treasure books", however, the predecessor will tell you "You should know it."

Company J acquisition speed up to one month or one quarter target for one company, included plastic, optical, fixture & mould,you would be dazzled.

Once, in a rare opportunity, I asked company top management, what the criteria the company base on to decide whether to buy another company? He answered: Considering the compatibility of the industry is the most important factor, then prospect forecast, when we grow to large enough, have sufficient cash flow, if we still stay in EMS low margin industry, can't build value for the stockholder, inject fresh blood, will easy to become a stagnant company.

One of most unsuccessful acquisition in company V, which seems to be the classic M&A failure case, it is the famous HK electronic company acquainted

American famous telecommunication company, misunderstood that Money can buy everything, hard asset for this be merged company are the first class machineries, and software asset are talent and advanced technology, Who knows three months after acquisition more than 300 telecom experts throw their resign letter by batch continually, finally only left 96 experts, all the R&D projects & machines stopped, it caused the big impact on cash flow of the whole group, even if monthly pay rely on HR dept collect money from here to there.

In company E, experienced twice M&A projects sizing were smaller, all proceed like touch the stone pass through the river, proceed to this step then think about the next step, only several relevant dept heads sit down together, think over what the problems will be, settle immediate problems, if can't settle it, direct ask the boss whether you agree to pay this or that? Set HR structure separately and individually. I was called by HR-VP Bruce went to Shanghai to have one M&A meeting, in the beginning, he emphasized one key point: if the company accepted our acquisition, in order to prevent the following days HR problems, we need to set up one whole set M&V action plan apply to global level, list out M&V all possibility, list out solution.

While Company J successfully acquired Company G, revenue jump from No. 6 to top 3 in the world, however, two companies cultural can't integrate easily, because Taiwan Company admired Paternalistic & Militarization management mechanism, from up to down instruction. It is existing the direct conflict with American company admired freedom and empowerment management style. Company G employees always said we are living in heaven, so in this meeting, allow the guys who living in heaven and hell set the detailed plan for "M&A" projects in future, implement it in a systematic and methodical manner.

At first, we define Acquisition included "Opportunity Identification", "Objective Evaluation", "Transaction management", "Integration" "Performance Evaluation" total five stags.

We set the target and timeline for each stage as the whole plan.

The jobs alignment among different dept.

The cooperation among different functional teams.

Remark milestone for completion of each work.

We simulate the specific screen:

Company J received a recommendation from the investment bank to be confirmed by the acquisition company, welcome us proceed "Opportunity Identification" on them, so we immediately:

One side we kicked off the project, another side proceed "Opportunity identification" on portfolio planning, project planning and internal resources planning, both parties have the initial contact and introduction.

Proceed into "Transaction Management" is the most important process, included "Dual Diligent", "The conclusion of the contract", two steps mayn't be natural transition.

During Dual Diligent:

We must evaluate and finalize the list of inquiries, align with another company contact person.

Arrange M&A resources, team, management & test another company data base, complete C&B comparison and record the good practice, list out the company cultural, risk & findings.

Evaluate the risk link with cost, combine into the whole project to make the holistic evaluation, submit the written report, in person reports risk assessment and amendment recommendation, confirm if the action finalized.

We only described the acquisition situation, because if the acquisition was abandoned, the whole project will be ended.

The agreement on acquisition once signed off, HR must confirm to complete dull diligent, report the actual situation to the shareholder of our company truthfully.

Before transferring into transition management, HR different functional teams should go into role, included:

Compensation & Benefit

Set up the incentive program for acquisition project key persons, investigate new market compensation system and position of each position, compare with existing compensation and benefit system, define how to transfer positions' budget and practice strategy, understand tax law, the third-party employee contract, finance and related dept linkage, formulate C&B position and strategy, confirm the proposal information and prepare the communication.

Personnel system and record management

Confirm the acquisition scope and comply with rules and requirement of different countries, open the key personal system and mail and related system authority, All the data sourcing of all employees' HR information of being acquainted company transfer into general company system, provide the related operator training.

Compliance management

Background checking for the key brick personal, prepare compliance documents and trainings, set up hot line phone system, and contact with labor union, make the amendment on employee handbook, set up internal audit process.

Training and development

Evaluate all the employees' capability, establish training system, conduct the company orientation training, provide how to integrate training instruction.

Talent Planning

Manage Executive level position total cost, control promotion, transferring, and separation, reorganize plan after transition.

Cultural integration

Deep discuss with key management and HR of acquired Company about how their understanding of new company cultural, establish regular communication channel and time table.

All above 6 preparation should be completed before transition.

Now, it is really handover:

On the beginning day, communicate with all the employees in different levels on full scale, allow them fully understand C&B structure change, establish communication and complaint channel.

From the second day to 100 days, M&A team announce the target set for 30 days, 60 days and 100 days, submit report and assessment method.

C&B team

Confirm C&B structure and announcement, set annual review planning, sign the contract with related organization which provided employee benefit.

Personnel system and record management

Check all the data resource connected accuracy and safety, kick on group standardized HR system, check the data report accuracy.

Training

Conduct orientation training on HR of acquired company, provide the mentor for key brick personal management, make assessment on key technology positions and conduct the missing training until all grasped.

Compliance management

Completed training, arrange internal audit, set up primary action.

Talent planning

Use company united recruitment channel and system post recruitment information, utilized recruitment process and use talent searching organization, implement handover plan.

At the scheduled 30 days, 60 days and 90 days assessment stage, M&A project team evaluate the result, if the assessment result is dissatisfied, immediate mobilizes the back stage global resources assist the completion, M&A project team submit the report to all related depts., provide the honest and fair evaluation on good and bad aspects.

From transition 100 days to 365 days, establish relevant central file note saved all the information, organize the closure meeting enable participants learn from it.

It takes 365 days for the Earth to orbit around the sun, M&A project successful completed at the same time.

7.Consider People not others before you find location for new site setting

The establishment of a new plant and M&A another plant is fundamentally different, more time spend on location choose than M&A, whether the business caused conflict is not a factor to consider.

Experienced several new factories setting up, which have been success, failure, failure at the start and success afterward, inner province and outer province, even run to foreigner country to open new plant, my experience worth sharing.

Why to open a new factory this is what every boss must ask himself, because of:

To save labor cost consideration;

The reason for business quota;

Customers and market development;

To improve supply chain;

The cheap land price, vast scope;

Convenient transportation;

Government support effort and preferential policies;

…

The pursuit of interest has relevant reason, to understand the main reason has the close relationship with HR, I often remind boss: "To set a new plant location we should consider the people rather than others at first." "One side of soil and water to raise a person"- the localness works hard, honest & creditable, high efficiency, low cost, good educated, enough manpower, will be more important than anything!

Company M which produce sweater move to Cambodia 19 years ago, After the fight, everything is waiting to be taken up, there isn't quota restriction to any countries export, cheap labor cost, plentiful manpower, my boss look important on this and go along (because none will accomplish with him), he look down when the military flight landed, the localness holding a cannon, with the gun & the big gun barrel in the hand, it scared him, he asked if he can fly back and don't land on there. The streets were full of tanks.

He transferred Chinese and Vietnam technician to Cambodia, move the machines one by one to there, one by one stitch teach workers how to make sweater, as hot weather in the whole year over there, the localness don't know how to make sweater, localness no wearing and no shoes to wear after years of fight force. Many people strip to the waist came to work, finally nobody know how to export, he even run to commercial bureau to tell government servants how to do, at that time 1/5 labor cost compare with China, my boss enjoy "The first one tasted the best soup".

However, the Cambodian government has sharply increased the minimum wage every year, the introduction of labor laws to increase the excessive welfare costs, my boss carelessly released generous reward above local government legal requirement, it is too late for regret: Why my plant cost keep so high? Only several years, many labor-intensive companies closed and relocate to Bangladesh, Myanmar, even move to Africa, does this process sound so familiar?!

Company E compared Zheng Cheng city, Zhongshan city, Qingyuan city, finally choose Beihai city in Guangxi province, the reason is close to sea port, the shipment cost will be low, the close transportation distant spend 6 hours drive to Shenzhen General office, the preparation done before two years, the biggest consideration is sufficient manpower, however, this key company direction was missed from the final decision.

In the beginning we done a survey on more than 30K Shenzhen plant employees, who did come from Guangxi? Which couple came from Guangxi? Only 19 out of 35K heads have the intention relocate to Beihai city of Guangxi province to work, finally we talk with personals, they clearly told us, Beihai people already go out of Beihai to find the job, they have own tourism and aquatic business, few will enter into factories to be worker.

In order to explore, we organized Guangxi recruitment tour, via Guangxi capital city-Nan Ning, visited several technology schools with thousands of students headcount sizing, however, the graduates in technology schools are persons who liked best, the requirement much higher than college graduates, the teacher audaciously ask for commission if we hire one graduate from their school, I lost my confident on Chinese education, the more I numbed, because this is technology school "Unspoken rules" If your company need people you have to pay, what the virtue and morality put aside, hire back the people is the first priority.

After that we hold the special job fair in Beihai development zone recruitment center, booked two floors of whole fair, vowed to "overcome all odds" in order to hire the people back, it is a poor result that only 60 peoples we can hire back no matter from morning to night stick to the booth, more than half is workers, more stay on technician and line leader level. Base on this speed, open the new plant of 2000 headcount at least spend one month, in addition, manpower is one kind of resources, hire more remain few, in the later, you can't expect 60 heads per day hiring speed growth.

In the end, the management in the job fair blame me and said" Even your company didn't confirm to invest here, you hired our Bei Hai people to Shenzhen". I was thinking: "No wonder so many plants you built didn't rent out in your development zone" I report the actual recruitment situation and suggest to change the target location.

After that I resigned, but I heard the company still set up plant over there, because went through southern cities not cheaper rental there would be, more convenient water way-Shipment cost for heavy motor product were quite expensive. After all, my previous colleague called me to collect another city labor cost information and plan to relocate to there, due to Beihai difficulty recruitment, the headcount sizing remains 2000 heads, however, total cost in Shenzhen special economic zone is increasing, does this process sound so familiar?!

Company J has more than 10 M&A projects and set up new plant experience, familiar with setting up new plant, however, fall on the most basic problems: Even if set new plant location not far away two kilometers from Sulphur Acid plant. In everyday, the air filled with Sulphur Acid smell." The discussion I heard from employees. This is the company investigated several projects, a sudden hasty discussion on a finalized project, there wasn't need to do in-depth investigation per top management estimate, didn't involve HR due to two plants and one Asia training center set up and operated more than 10 years, to set up one new plant need to go through N processes, however, the top management only saw the data and the report, no deep investigate, signed off without hesitate, no fly from America to here to take a look, smell it, , when trace back who should take responsibility? Everyone takes means nobody takes the responsibility.

However, the employees' voice is too loud (Although didn't move in yet), the upfront investment (Only renovation cost up to RMB20M) will go into the drain, it is the time for HR & COC team to "Wipe the butt" (Clear up the mess).

First of all, American General office COC management arrived, instructed to suspend all the related projects, wait for the working environment assessment report, the report came out, looks all the Chinese environment report only has one result-"Passed", only the trust we can have, but the most important is employees "Trust" it, so CSR, HR and all new subdivision GM sit down together, by one word one sentence check how to send one note explain the reason and situation, answer the employee inquiry, finally quite down the employees' complaint.

From this exciting overture, HR start our own business on setting up new plant, from that moment, we identified:

It is forbidden to have flame in the building.

The dorm has 100 rooms, can't accommodate more than 2000 heads live in, we need to use more than 20 shuttle buses send the employees from General plant to new plant.

At that time, the road work performs on the only major trunk road last more than five months, the original time spend on the road to work is 15 minutes, finally spend more than 45 minutes to one hour, everyone works in electronic company knew the time unit control accurate to be minute even to second, delay one or two hours will lead to the shipment and product delivery delay.

The industry zone located in deed angle, few passengers pass through, not easy to attract the candidates.

Industry zone has no clinic, no supermarket, and no entertainment facility; belong to "Three abstentions" Zone.

……..

Lacking this or that isn't the big problem, lack caring to the people is the biggest problem, this is Company J principles, so the first thing for HR to do:

Set up new plant HR team, assign the key person for every functional teams;

General plant HR provide on time support until the new team set up and handover smoothly.

Discuss with new plant new general manager and different dept supervisor, ask them share the customer demand, how to plan production plan, deploy manpower in advance.

Set up individual HR management system, one whole set handbook, HR policy, consider the impact to general plant employees in the same region.

Set up regular meeting policy, talk with key members in the team about their concern.

Apply for all the registration and certification to government, sign the new contract with all the service suppliers by using new plant name.

Compare two separated zone C&B difference, included social insurance and housing fund etc., provide the suggestion.

Provide the training to key personals and new employees, expand to other positions, full use general plant trainers' resources.

The contract relation handling for the employees transferred to new plant.

The final one point is the most important point, at least it is the most difficulty what I have to handle case

No.10 clause in labor contract law statement:

The employee is arranged to work in the new employer company from original employer, the seniority of the employee will be combined into new employer seniority. The original employer already paid economic compensation, when the new employer terminates the labor contract, the original employer seniority will not be counted in.

No 33 Clause of labor law "The employer changes the name, the legal representative, principal person or investor etc, doesn't affect the execution of the labor contract.

No. 34 Clause "The employer merge and separation" The employer merge and separation etc., the original labor contract continues to be effective, the employer continues fulfill its right & duty.

No. 35 Clause "The amendment of labor contract" The labor contract stipulated content can be changed base on both party's consensus. Any change should be written down, each party keep one set of changed labor contract.

There is existing the conflict amongst three rules.

The new plant employees will sign the contract with another brother company, although the seniority will continue, if the employees want to make trouble things, want to take the economic compensation (N+1 months' salary) then quit, each stick to their own version, not give up, even if one or two trouble makers provoke, will lead to strike, the normal production will be halted, follow by customer claim for reimbursement.

We rough estimate the lost will be USD500M at least! It will be a millstone around the neck for the new plant when it hasn't the good revenue yet.

How to work it out smoothly? I and GMs of old and new plant repeatedly to weigh, finalized to adopt the "push" "pull" coexistence, gradual transition way:

Push way: After announcement issued three days, ask all the employees who transferred to new plant sign off the new labor contract, the dept head lead and coordinate the contract sign with employees.

Pull way: If the employee temporality unwilling to transfer, want to go back to General plant to work, we try to convince.

Gradual transition:

When there will be vacancies in General plant, the new plant dept accept to release the employees, then the employees can go back to General plant to work. If there isn't vacancy sign the temp contract, stated how long will be transferred from General plant to new plant.

If the employees still insist on resignation rather than signing the new plant contract, we can negotiate to settle the contract by controlling the headcount within minimum scope.

In order to ensure the whole communication process, go smoothly, we talked with major key depts. Included labor bureau, foreign trading bureau, labor union, police bureau, petition office, submit the documents draft by lawyer, stated why we make this decision, how to deal with? How to prevent the risk? What need to seek the government support?

The company General manager gather all dept heads, cascade the communication plan, the skill how to answer, how to deal with contingency situation base on classification, how to coordinate with relevant depts.

When start to communicate

HR will prepare the whole set document, schedule the meeting with dept supervisor, start from the higher grading employee, then to the junior employees to sign off labor contract, answer the inquiry when there will be, if there is inquiry can't answer at once, record it, pass to next employee at first.

In everyday regularly check how many employees already sign off the labor contract, collect the problems, immediately to respond and solve.

The first day completed 90%, the second day completed 95%, the third day completed 98%, only left 60 heads, most of them have the deep morel engagement with General plant and hope to return, we will not force, sign off the transitional contract, step by step transfer them back to general plant when paying attention to the vacancy reserved.

To this, the new plant can move forward by releasing the contract barrier.

8.Digital HR: Not perfect enough, can be more perfect

Company J data collection, assessment and sharing ability is the strongest among the companies I served, one obvious example: After office house 17:30, to 17:35, the output for each production line, defective rate, labor cost for each product is formed as the most key information share report to each dept mail box, they only need to explain rather than challenging the accuracy of the data, because it is generated by SAP global system, the global model is consistently, if there would be mistake, it would be the system security or monitoring problem, would attached by "hacker" within one of million parts of a second.

Although admire the data modernize capability, as one of them, I often struggle continue to learn the new system, the different dept has different system, SAP link with the data processing of every dept, HR responsibility for providing employee personal information, working hour, TM1 is the monthly & quarterly budget system, SRM is material ordering system, CER is fix asset purchasing system, E-gate for product ship in and out control system, Labor & Conduct is EICC management system, E-form system sharing all the forms, JAWS included all the system in, the most dizzying is these system keep to upgrade, break down and rebuild, one system implement, one notice for holding global meeting, three times for morning, afternoon and evening meet different time zone requirement to train up the users, if you can follow up then follow up, if you can't follow up then replay the meeting record, if no record keep then you learn to use it by yourself, if you can't adapt to this new technological times, nobody will bear the consequence for you.

Particular global network conference system WebEx, 7.5 years of which I have experienced from phone, to video, to multi-party call, listen to the record, and respond on time, share your opinion, self-control on own topic, different topic is controlled by different countries toastmaster, you only have one opportunity, nobody can help you in that occasion, nobody will have pity on you, you will be clean out if you fall behind, quite realistic.

As dept head you must bear more than your subordinates, coach them, how to do? The whole group use SuccessFactors install employee performance system, which you do the assessment on your subordinates by using the system, set up annual target, adjust quarterly target, check the subordinates' training record, develop successor plan, trace successor competition improvement situation.

In addition to manage your own team, to conduct periodic quarterly audits on parallel departmental performance, use MES production and quality system to implement QIC quality control, TIC product test, MIC material control, for scoring and tracking completion. At the same time use JOS system, record different dept key performance index, following action and closure situation.

Every dept bear the pressure for this, many people complaint: It isn't the problem for no system control, it is due to too many system, no unified platform, it is difficulty to take the data from different systems and doing repetitive job, group CHO Bruce hate this situation mostly, he wants a simple HR report, Asia using A system A version, Europe using A system B version, American using B system A version, at least three days come out the format, another two or three days come out the result, must pour data from this or that, without good solution, he asked me to design the format, provide to different countries, ask them provide the excel report, however, different countries don't know English, don't know the formula, delay the submission, the inquiries are various, finally three months passed, became more stable, the foreigners like Chinese "Build it up then break it down", ask IT dept redevelop the program, the result came out no much different compare with previous "HR Dash Board", however, each CHO like to rebuilt again.

From that opportunity, Bruce keep the fresh memory on my heartily and close follow up attitude.

Let him unbelievable that in another time I assess SAP SuccessFactors performance, advice Corp HR whether negate it or use the new system Workday, I detailed checked and voted to SAP-success factor when the others all voted on workable, there is necessary to state here I don't have a dime relationship with SAP & Workday two IT companies. At that time Bruce experienced "The painful data collection from global" make him decided to build one HR system, gather HR key persons from each continent, discuss how to select IT system supplier for future coordination.

The assessment from talent searching/on board/Key HR/Performance management/Successor plan/Training & development/Compensation/Report and assessment/Safety/Technical aspect different circle to score, write down the reason for scoring, finding, let supplier response to it together.

I insist on "Don't let go" attitude, because I heard too many supervisors and employees complaint on "SuccessFactors", so I compare with workday system, find out which one is better, which one is worse, one by one list out, if two suppliers will to do investigation in depth, one by one compare what I listed two big systems advantage and disadvantage, that is the real feedback from front line user.

To the final round count total score, I gave SF total score higher than WD, because two systems are imitating each other, consider the fact that only several shining points work day have, but training module didn't develop, I voted continue to develop SuccessFactors.

Finally Corp management board voted continue to use SF system and continue to develop, after I leave Company J not more than 3 months, Bruce instructed someone to communicate with me and request to rehire, let me responsibility for Asia-pacific region SF system continue development, but I like to develop my general management instead of specialized expert, so I politely decline, actually grasp the HR system and seize the direction, that is the competency for HR people.

HR develop digital system must focus on three criteria:

1. Coordinate with company strategy alignment, must figure out one shortcut for internal users to achieve business target achievement.

    The project should be estimated investigation return; IT dept can complete the system development per planning; Adjust the new requirement on new system to meet the business growth capability; Communicate with internal using dept, set the rules and other requirement.

2. With business understanding, provide the information and data to users, answer the question, encourage the new understanding and learning. Included:

    Support internal customer (employee & manager etc) to improve service quality, to achieve the goal original setting;

    Support the reorganization, full use existing IT resources and foundation;

    Support company upgrade to be world class company, attract, retain and develop company manpower asset, correlate business success with people performance.

3. Improve efficiency and speed, can completely change HR people service level, free up more time to do higher value jobs, reduce waste.

Below is HR system integration designed by me and IT dept, based on united port to generate the data, for checking, coordinate with each other, for customer user friendly idea to design.

Recruitment platform:
1. Dept supervisor submit the manpower application from original SuccessFactors system, select the position code from Job grading system, match with dept budget headcount, seek approve, set up profile.
2. Recruitment individual design the company cultural webpage, can update the related webpage in specific websites on time.
3. The applicants can link with SuccessFactors webpage submit applicant information, attach certification scan copy.
4. Recruiter check applicant information and vacancy matching, and background information acceptance status (Check with group intern shared "Forbidden to rejoin company black list", pass through the first-round phone communication and interview, link with SuccessFactors system interview questionnaire, independently complete the examination, the result directly passed to interviewer directly.
5. The interviewer automatically input the comment, transfer to C&B team negotiate salary and onboard date, open the profile after offer successfully.
6. The applicant read and study company introduction by access linkage, included company cultural, policy etc.

    The employee came on board, system achieved one stop service, follow system instruction, the relevant dept help to prepare your seat, computer, office systems installed, open access right, stationary, name card well prepared, Mobil phone/desk phone/gate check opened, dormitory and canteen registered, excluded system order, the process need different depts. online and offline cooperation.
7. The dept buddy welcome you, Company J training plan and completion status link with new comer, welcome note publish by weekly.
8. The supervisor set probation target in a timely manner, identify job capability and organizational chart.

Employee self-service platform

The next 11 main functions, 70 small functions

1. Welcome to join Company J
    1.1. My resume
    1.2. Come on board
        1.2.1. On board instruction
        1.2.2. On board process
    1.3. NTID & mail box
        1.3.1. Get process
        1.3.2. SAP/NTID/Mail box reminder
2. Company family
    2.1. Company introduction
    2.2. Company cultural
    2.3. Company policy
    2.4. Company magazine
    2.5. Notice & Announcement
3. Employee service
    3.1. Dormitory
    3.2. Canteen Introduction
    3.3. Clinic Introduction
    3.4. Post office Introduction
    3.5. Gym Introduction
    3.6. Transportation Introduction
    3.7. Event Highlights
    3.8. EAP Employee Assistant Plan
    3.9. Q&A

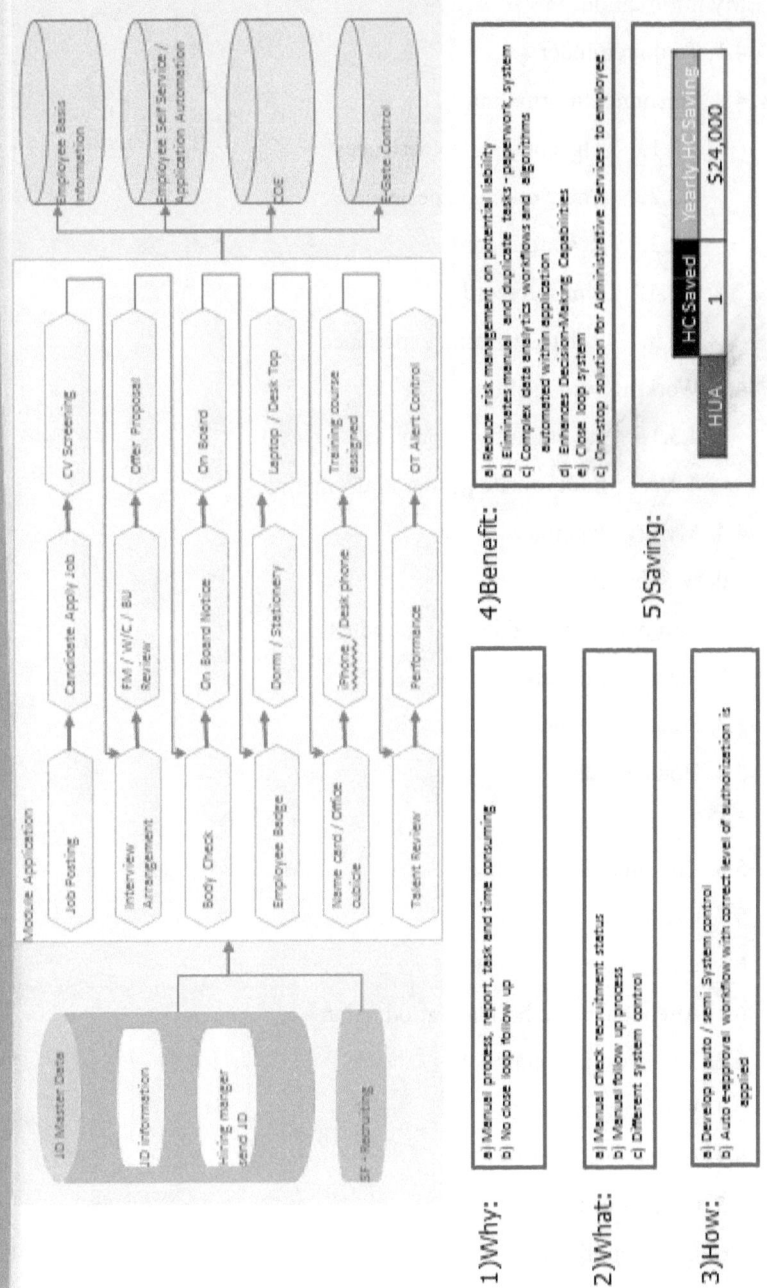

4. My information
    4.1. To do reminder
    4.2. Personnel information
        4.2.1. The company experiences
        4.2.2. The working experience
        4.2.3. Reward record
        4.2.4. Punish record
        4.2.5. Related training experience
    4.3. Working responsibility
        4.3.1. My job information
        4.3.2. Subordinate position information
    4.4. My organization
5. Salary & benefit
    5.1. Compensation and benefit introduction
    5.2. Salary introduction
    5.3. Social insurance
    5.4. Housing fund
    5.5. Tax inquiry
    5.6. Commercial insurance
    5.7. Q&A
6. My attendance
    6.1. Attendance and holiday introduction
    6.2. The latest job natural
    6.3. Working calendar
    6.4. Attendance checking
    6.5. OT application
    6.6. Leave application
    6.7. Special attendance

6.8. Annual leave checking
7. My training
    7.1. Training and development introduction
    7.2. Annual training need
    7.3. Training course
    7.4. Training record
    7.5. Training application
    7.6. Q&A
8. My contract
    8.1. Probation
    8.2. Contract record
    8.3. The reminder for contract expiration
    8.4. The comment on training renewal
9. Company recruitment
    9.1. Recruitment Information
    9.2. Internal recruitment plan
    9.3. Employee recommendation
    9.4. Q&A
10. Communication platform
    10.1. Questionnaire survey
    10.2. Blue Box
    10.3. Review hot topic
11. Separation instruction
    11.1. Separation proceed status
    11.2. Social insurance transferring instruction
    11.3. Housing fund acumination
    11.4. Housing fund transferring instruction
    11.5. Foreigner employee's social insurance acumination

From on board to separation, we can achieve one stop service.

Manage knowledge/Capability platform

Company J on line training courses looks like many stars in the sky, thousands professional training courses, management training courses still buying external consultant training course, everyone can apply for English training if there will

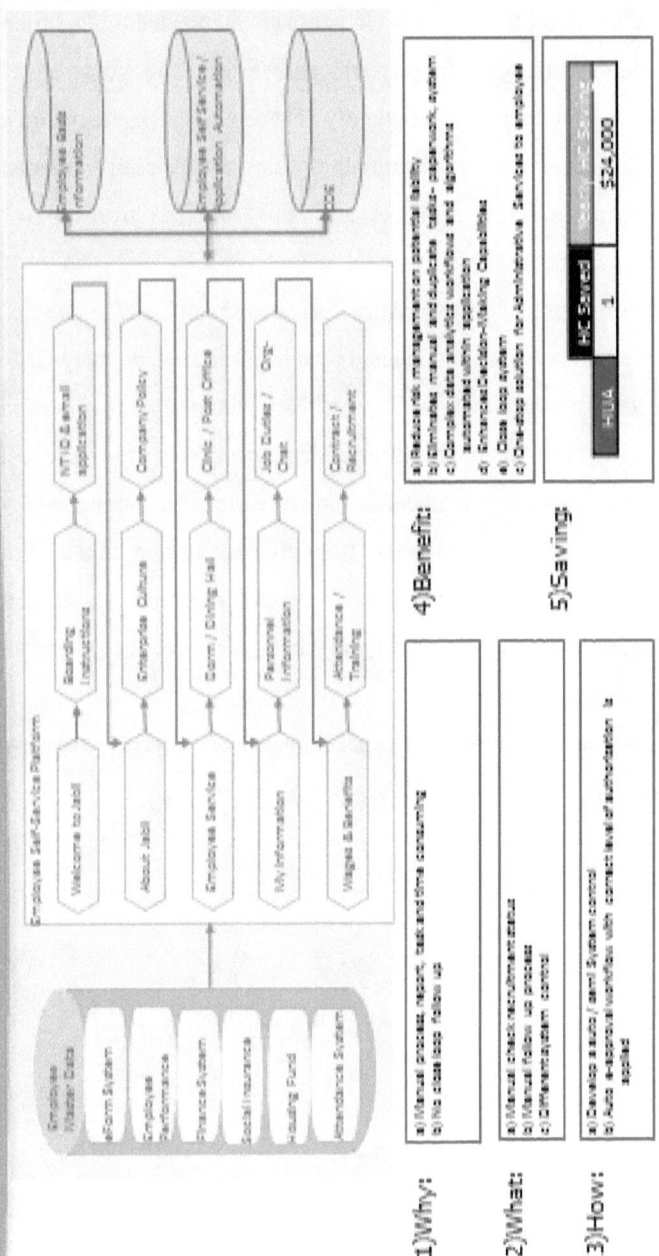

be necessary, don't worry about you learn more but only worry about you don't willing to learn. Corp ask the employee to complete nominated on line training courses. The digital management platform allows the employees select the training base on their function dept, regularly dept expert check, the record kept on line or offline, everyone must go through position certification examination, HR take responsibility to refresh the test bank, the employees pass the examination then can be promoted.

This latest HR management system really dedicated the effort from whole HR and IT team, in addition, we are undaunted by repeat set back, we defy GM and lean team rejection, because there were more than 1000 programs of profitable depts. are queueing up. We defy different dept. cynicism: Your HR system doesn't have a usable one. We are under the pressure came from upper and lower level-because we need to remove the risk from different system linkage, timely delete 50 outdated user account, even if I was treated as "Sinner" challenged by CHO and CTO, how can it be? Do your good job, there wasn't one system failed in my hand, all are successful.

HR digital system meet or above user expectation is difficulty, more are lag the customer expectation.

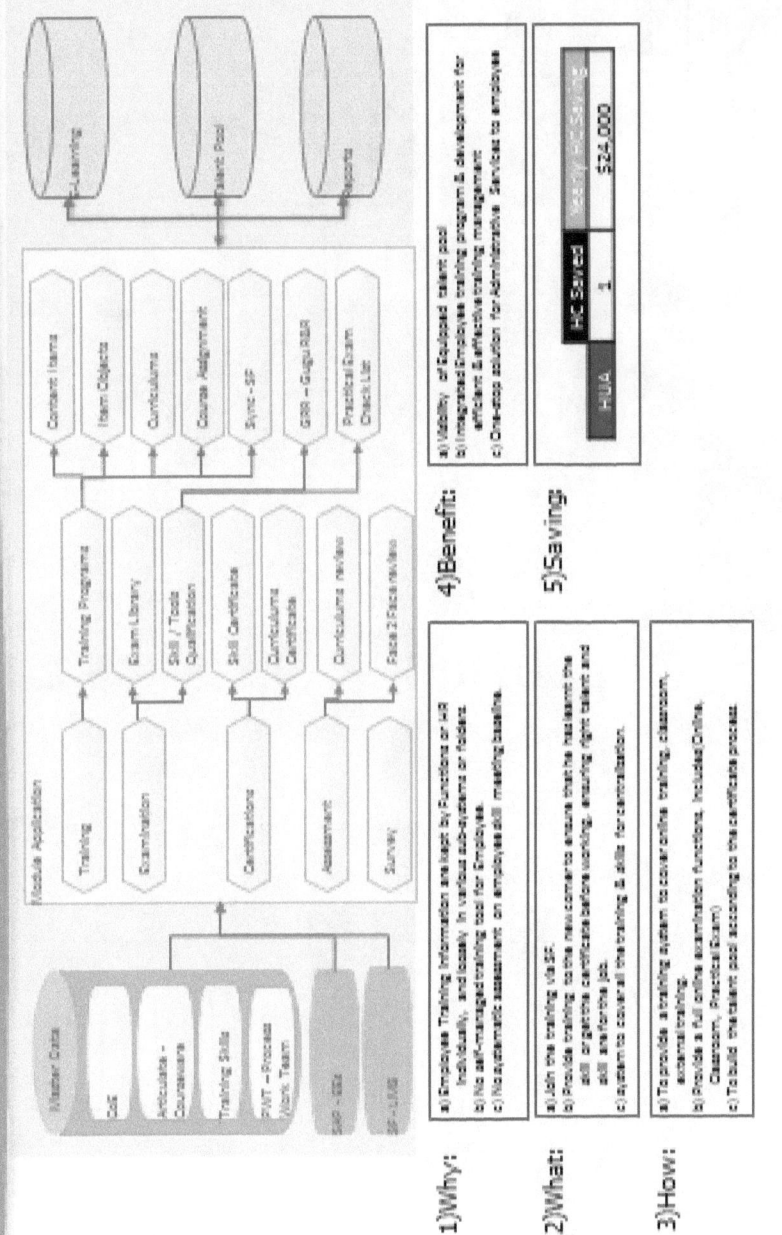

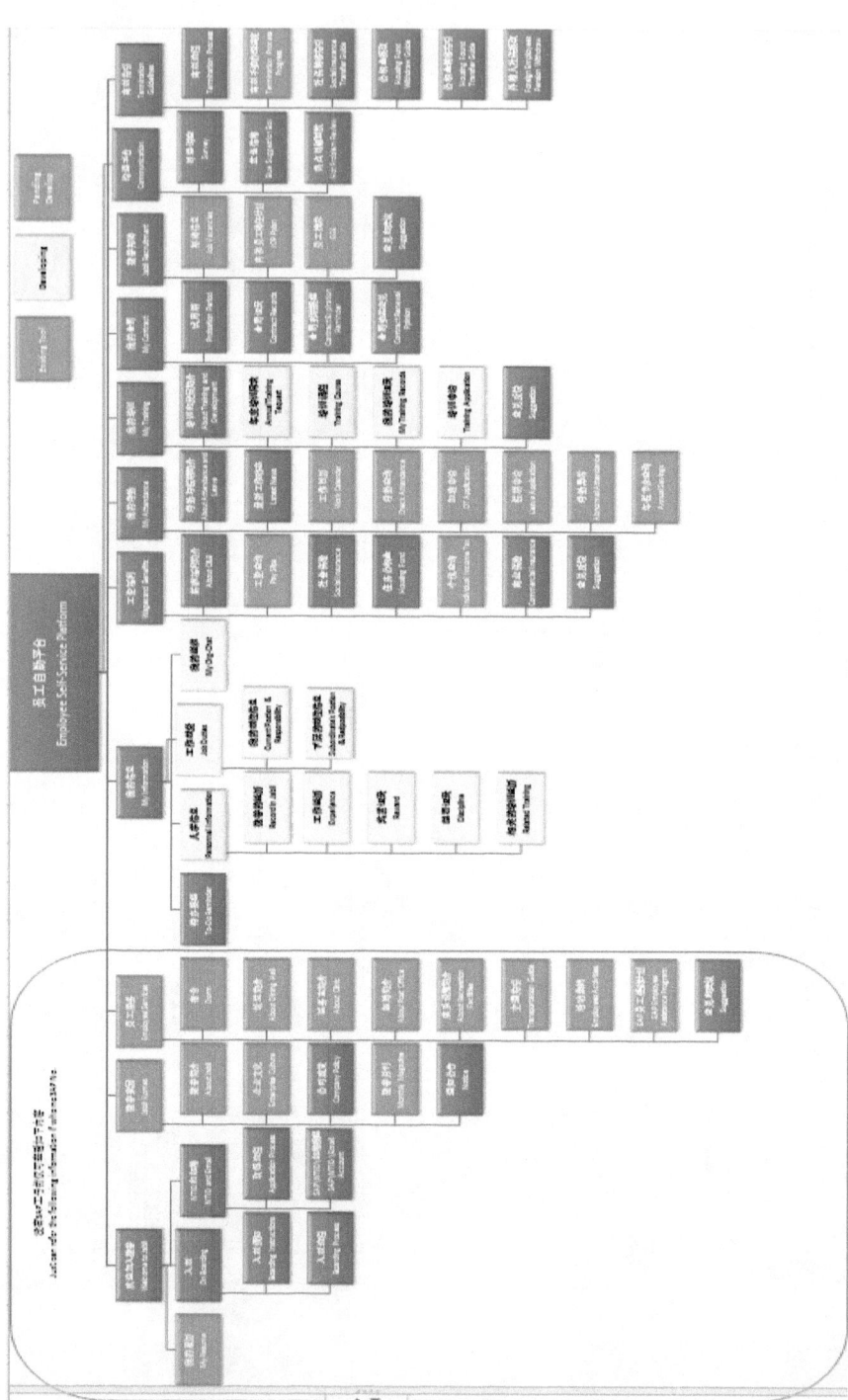

9.Shared Talent across different sites

In EMS business like Company J, different site and different customer had demand fluctuation, their demand up and down in their business throughout the years, there will not be one time the demand will across the broad and flat, there will never be always up, there will be up and down.

In going up & down, at up time, we need to pull in the resources.

At down time, we need to reduce the people, we defined the problem we often face: When revenue drops down, the people become over staffed. When business goes up, the hiring becomes difficult because there are no enough resources to supply at the same time.

This project, when we do the bench mark, we can't find any project or any solution that has been done before, so there is not reference for our bench mark. In our goal, we want to eliminate and minimize the fluctuation. At the same time, we want to take care of our people, on top of that, we need to leverage, and we can normalize the fluctuation better than our brother sites.

In line with Jabil culture, we are looking at not just optimizing talent valued resources. But collaborating with all the sites, that is where the culture is, to find a way to give creative solution to the problems we are facing now. "Shared talent across different sites" project was born.

It costs a lot of money and time to hire & fire.

To lay off people, the company must compensate around more than 150K for surplus group employees, but to hire them back and train them up, invested more than 280K.

At the same time, losing talent, can damage company's image, reflect the daily operation indirect impact we also considered.

To align with 5 sites in China and 2 sites outside of China, consulted their demand, exchange the needs within each other.

From define to control, one quarter we spend but the clear result already came out.

Compared with Asia brother sites, Huangpu revenue down sized, however IL cost% increased, the heavy trend could not sustain business health grow.

The average lead time for hiring one IL takes 41 days, it costs 10k per head.

"How to maximize talent utilization during the revenue fluctuation?" This is our clear target.

One step by one step, one level by one level to access, with four steps we can drive our performance: Select, Match, transfer and track!

The platform we built: Take the Store checking, select the good perform employees to form a mobile force.

Set up an automatic process for select, match, transfer and track, transferring "Smart Factory e-solution" to brother sites, they can implement it automatically. HR is the contact window, network connection with brother sites' FMs & HR team.

"Extra talent store check" "Skill and will matching" "Competency matching" are systematic steps went through for everybody.

One example shows here:

Mark hu is our QA FM, he asked regional QA director Nithia: I have one surplus QE, is there any site that needs support? Then Nithia built up the connection with T-town, 1 week later this QE was already working in T-town to support.

The skill set matching with "R&R", arrange both sites FMs communication, FM communicate with candidates, clarify the job requirement, what the products they are making? What the skill they need? How long for the project support will be? Check the employees' skill, language, willing and expectation, the process is much better than external interview, because it is easier to understand working background information, all are J Companied.

We created the new cross sites transfer procedure, differentiated key steps compare with normal dept to dept transferring procedure.

Now Let the employees tell their stories to you...

Hello, Everyone, I am Civil Liao, production asst manager, I went to Chengdu site to support more than one month, learn a lot from there."

"I came from Eletrolux workcell, Sr Engineer Shen Zhiwen, to me, this is one totally new scope, I need to fully understand on the whole production process of brother site, this is a good learning process, if there will be opportunity, I will to support Vietnam site again.

I am production ME engineer Chui Xiaoxiong, I went to Chengdu site support one month, during support period, I learn about ABC computer production proceed and manufactory process, if there will be opportunity, I hope to support other site again."

"I came from ME dept Xie Yuan Chao, I learn the knowledge about rear assembling during my support period, I am young and hope to visit more sites."

"I came from ME dept Liang Yun Xiong, the support process went through smoothly this time, I like to support the other site."

Yes, I do! Yes, we do! We have 47 employees short support other sites included workcell managers, NPI manager, planning supervisors, QA Sr Engineers covered 7 main depts.

From Guangdong to Chengdu, to Shanghai, to Wuxi, to Wuhan, four provinces they go!

From China to Vietnam, to Hungary they go! They look like "International Rescue & first aid force"!

We created Visual tracker, shared sheet, timely check revenue, staff headcount, surplus pool, matching, hiring, support period, cost status.

Let 's review how much cost saving we got:

More than 460K/quarter saving, changed up trend of IL cost when revenue has a bit jump up.

We saved hiring lead time and training costs for brother sites, they don't need to hire and they don't need to train just bring in!

We consolidated Hard saving + Soft saving – Investment of relocation, saved 679K per quarter!

We made the survey which covered 47 transferred or short support employees, 100% responded to us, 95% satisfied with this program, because 95% employees learned a lot and got the rare working experience across sites, across regions, and across countries.

The most important question we answer: If there will be next opportunity to allow you to support other sites, will you go or not? "Yes, I do" that is most support employees' confirmation to us!

3 key points allow me to emphasize here:

"We shared the talent across country, division, region, site, dept, translating "Embrace Diversity & Collaborate" "one Jabil" culture among 7 sites, 3 countries.

In the following step: We will set up e-tracker system for all brother sites demand and supply information on line sharing.

We will design one- or two-days training to support employees fit into brother sites' culture and environment.

To summarize the achievement for this project:

1. Collaborated and shared talent across 7 sites 3 continents.
2. Huge saving by overcoming the revenue fluctuation normalized IL cost.
3. 47 employees took the challenges, got priceless experience.
4. A sustainable systematic solution can be copied to any other sites.

10. We can be EICC Ambassador by organizing female training program

1. The female worker occupied total headcount 68%;
2. Above 80% female worker under 30 years of age;
3. Above 80% is junior middle school and high school graduate;
4. Above 80% female worker came from the field, far away from hometown;
5. 75% female workers unmarried;
6. 43% employee on board no more than 6 months, worker level turnover rate average 10%;
7. "On time Delivery", "People management", "Promotion Opportunity" these are the most concern problem in our interview with front line female line leaders.

   …

All above data is the result of BSR Non-Government Organization coordinate with our company to conduct female worker training program, that is Dec 2009 after I joined Company J, open invited them to make an employee survey, they got the result from our internal information, the results are so similar? I am referring to the very similar situation of female workers in many large labor-intensive enterprises in China.

This vast, young, doing simple work female workers often faced emotion, family, job, colleagues, and supervisor problem; this is the problem for HR must face, I handled numbers of female workers suicide case, their supervisor management style too simple and brutal, even can't endure heavy loading got psychopathy, at every time, when I handle these cases, I have to suffer humanity and conscience torture, often lose sleeping in several months, the terrible screen often appeared in front of eyes, and the grieved cry repeat heard in my ear, If there is possibility, I bless their soul can rest in heaven, never to be deceived, suffer no more, I hope the living employees learn how to protect yourself, in the face of difficult and brave to survive.

It is in my debut, one day I received the urgent call, I followed the nurse who carried hand frame run to the incident scene, I saw one girl (Later confirmed she was 15 years old at that time) jumped from third floor, grim faced, had low moan, she couldn't speak anything when suffering the unbearable pain, I can't forget that scene.

The ambulance sent her to hospital, I run to her room directly, ask the security following her to handle termination process, understood she was terminated because only one sentence she rebutted to the line leader. She can't accept this fact, jump from balcony, even one sentence already be treated termination?! I was so angrily, want to claim this with production manager! But more urgent is how to get her back asap, I instruct hospital to take rescue for full effort, no matter how much will be, finally we save her back. However, she will lost the ability of having children, and one arm can't raise too high, I called her father came to company from hometown, her father arrived, accompany with her daughter and ask for the compensation repeatedly, open the month ask for RMB600K, at that time RMB600K is really enormous figure, at that time, I don't know follow which clause of labor law to handle this attempted suicide case? Because the new labor law just implemented and no matter which law didn't mention how to handle suicide case. The only thing I can do is check it out follow which law which clause, at the same time, negotiate with her family, I don't want to take this role! Finally reach to RMB150K figure, her father shaves my hand and say thank you to me for the properly handle, then held her daughter 's hand and walked slowly away, that scene also unforgettable in my brain.

After that I call my direct supervisor Alan Tse: "I felt too sad, I seems to be in the wrong line, I acted as executioner, it looks I push her downstairs, I even bargain with her father!" Alan coached me "Don't upset, this is the often thing you have to face as HR, you didn't push her down, you are in accordance with the law and reason to try to solve the matter as satisfactorily as possible."

That was 20 years ago screen, after 20 years later, I experienced case by case, make me deep reflect:

I took one call from production line: One female worker sent the WeChat to line leader, her boyfriend proposed to break up, she want to cut the vein and intent to suicide, We called all the employees in the production line to find her and call the police at once, finally we found out her boyfriend guild us and doctor to their rental apartment, poor girls repeat to cut the waist but it did not cut to the aorta, bind up the wound then come back to life.

Why none love them? None take care of them? Why the others became so cruel to them?

Why they only can use "Dead" to prove their innocent and real love?

Why they don't know protect themselves?

Why they don't know how to protect themselves?

Why 20 years passed, the same situation repeat?

At the right time our customer HP proactive recommends "HER project" to me, why it called HER project instead of "Him" project? My boss Sheetoh asked me, even if male worker no need to be taken care of? Interesting problem.

The head of BSR, who specializes in the promotion of the project, replied: Her project was aimed at low-income women workers, targeted at their physical health, focused on their income and finances, on the subject of respect they should have, asked women who had been tutored to tutor other women workers, let them help each other so that the audience expands rapidly.

At first use 3 to 6 months to popularize the basic training, included:

Module 1: Come on board (Five hours)

1.1 The adaptive capability

1.2 Effective communication

1.3 Pressure and emotional management

Model 2: Be Heathy to work

2.1 Industrial health and safe

2.2 Gender Health

Model 3: Long term development

3.1 Finance and life plan

3.2 Career development

3.3 To be old and learn to be old

Then proceed to next level within 6 months to 12 months

Model 1: Gain new knowledge while reviewing old knowledge.

1.1 Review basic content

1.2 Introduce training content of strengthen section

Module 2: My life

2.1 Health and nutrition

2.2 Female "5 stages" protection

2.3 Harmonious between sex

2.4 Care for the children education

2.5 Financial proposal for workers

Module 3: My work (5 hours)

3.1 Management role identification

3.2 Management quality model

3.3 Management mind map

Module 4: My capability (32 hours)

4.1 Manage migrant worker

4.2 How to manage employees

4.3 How to motivate employees

4.4 Crisis management

Module 5: My management way (12 hours)

5.1 Management difficulties

5.2 Review case

In the beginning it is too slow to have individual trainings to line leaders and outstanding perform employees last for 100 hours, the impact and narrow coverage, later we change the training

1. Combine with orientation training;
2. Talk the key points with employees;
3. Use lunch break time use funny way to talk, because the production line would not allow us to occupy too many working hours;
4. Involve male workers, even if male supervisor to train the workers;
5. Invite local family plan commission to have training;
6. Coordinately organized the big events with BSR, family plan commission, and hospital: Included how to prevent Hep B? How to prevent HIV? Deepen the content of the lecture.
7. Distribute small manual, let them know more, if feel shy to ask and see the photos and read the words.
8. Play the games and get the gifts, let them know how to be "Millionaire"
9. Arrange the top management dialogue on sensitive topics, collect the feedback and follow up.

The project last 12 months, HP customer grant the training certification to us by recognized our effort put on this project.

Then we never stop this training, last more than 5 years, coverage exceed 50K employees accepted this training, which is complete training number.

With this project, we have enhanced the awareness of women workers of self-protection, but also strengthened the awareness of women managers dare to manage, and strengthen the communication between the frontline leaders and subordinates. This is a personal feedback from BSR in-person, as well as a random sampling of staff, interviews with people who have been taught.

Following this project, we took a step further into the "women in Factory" WIF mentoring Project, which aims to improve women's leadership, communication, emotional management, problem-solving skills, help employees find more room for career development.

It included 4 modules

Module 1

1. General introduction and basic investigation
2. Line leader model

Model 2

1. Emotional management
2. New generation management
3. Continue improvement
4. Team building, Time management

Model 3

1. Public speech
2. Confident lady
3. Production workshop

Model 4

1. Investigation summary and graduation

The training module is similar with HER project, the same knowledge it delivering, so we proceed as well.

Due to consistently intention, finally it impressed the WIF project organizer, granted EICC Ambassador Award to us, we eventually were invited to participate American annual meeting to demonstrate what we have done for female workers. After that Company J organized Female activities like a raging fire, "Joules" was born.

Joules' mission is to educate, guide and encourage employees to engage in diverse exchanges and dialogues.

Joules is committed to promoting the business advantage of gender balance, constantly challenging the organizational barriers of the company, working to increase women's performance opportunities in leadership and business operations.

In order to make this project successfully, we found out Group CFO Forbes, because in Finance and HR dept staffs is majority of woman.

We elected the Joules Project ambassadors for each plant to build the team, we advertise through the company's blogs, Chinese blogs and official Weibo and WeChat platforms.

We use Education

1. Explain to employees the importance and strengths of a diverse team and encourage the building of an inclusive environment.
2. Encourage initiatives that contribute to increased flexibility.
   (eg. Balance of life and work, second-generation gender bias, intangible barriers to career development)
3. Meetings and events.
   (eg. International Women's Day or October breast cancer prevention Month)
4. Employee-picked blog stories related to this topic.

We guild them through:

1. Set up a working group under the Steering Committee to build a global mentoring program and implement it.
2. Work with local high schools and engineering schools and business schools to provide funding for girls, including internships and mentoring by employee volunteers for interns.

Through communication and dialogue, we:

Work with local businesses, governments, non-governmental organizations and academia to promote women's interaction and share expertise and experience.

In local employee communication and dialogue, "Success story sharing" attract the most audiences, because we invited Financial Controller-Twinkle, Marketing Senior Manager-Ying to share their successful story, the meeting room was so crowd that nobody can't join any more, the atmosphere compares with music concerts of famous stars.

The hot flush wave above waves, we continue work with BSR to organize "Big hand hold small hand" activity, looking at the children came from thousands of miles even kept a blind view on the parents hands-they can't identify their parents' hands, my heart is trembling, these parents having the jobs away home for the long time, left behind these lonely children, poor parents, poor lonely stay children, I hope I can do something for them.

11.We show "PIC" project in United Nations

Our reason for implementing this project is quite simple: Whether the company pay the disabled employment fund in every year according to the proportion of 1.7% employees X3 social pay ratio, or hire PIC employees equal to the above formula in Company J, we are more willing to hire PIC, because we want to do something for them.

This thinking came from one of our company financial supervisor has one PIC younger sister, from birth her handicapped grading already reach to the severity of "She will fall down by facing a little wind blow", that is what her sister own description, she can't take care of herself, walking like sidle, serious side glance." I and my mother spent our whole life time in order to support her to survive, we can't abandon her, she is also a people, one member of our family!" It is conceivable how much they suffered, she sought the support from company controller Dave-a wise, kindness company top management, can I get my sister to do what she can, to make her self-reliant? Dave answered her firmly: "We can do it if we want to!" so he gave the first serious disabled staff Shelly arranged a new job opportunity:" File the miscellaneous documents in a book", in fact, the job is not a simple repetition of a number of challenges so the staff turnover of this post is large. It supports her to find a new life, but shelly done the job seriously, slowly put a sheet of documents stacked neatly, it never happened lost document, this job saved my sister life, and saved my whole family." Shelly sister filled with tears in her eyes when she mentioned this, she always showed diligence and strong will.

After that, we continually to hire PIC employees:

We hired deaf-mute; how can she understand the job request? You will ask. We even hired her mother in, told the specific job requirement to her mother, let her mother translate to her deaf and mute daughter. Even if for easier communicate with this employee, we contact with Guangzhou local school for deaf and blind, let them send the teacher to teach our internal more than 100 interested supervisors and employees to learn "Common sign language".

Because of this opportunity, we met teacher of the graduate class school of deaf and blind, we invited them come to visit our big model plant, coordinate to hire the fresh graduates. This teacher responded: We welcome you can hire our students, you are one MNC fortune 500 companies, we are afraid that our students can't do the job." I asked her why? She said our students have too many requisitions on the facilities, such as:

1. We need the road for blind, allow them use the stick knock it can define the road block, it should cover all the corners.
2. Change the wash room seats, included office, workshop, canteen, entertainment, public places, even live in dormitory, it requires to change wash basin.
3. Set the "side out" mirror in food supply line in canteen, for the wheel chair employees not need to stand up can see the specific dishes, the table set in canteen need to remove the chairs from it, allow the wheel chair employees sit in have meal there.
4. Remodel elevator, set up elevator where there are stairs, even the keypad in elevator request the rugged key board, convenient for blind employee can touch and identify.
5. Change production channel, ensure production line channel between the two has 1.5meter space, convenient for wheelchair employees pass, it is hard especially for Guangzhou rich land price space.
6. Provide the anti-static wheelchair to all the production wheelchair employees, there should be the space put their common wheelchair there.

...

I budget it: The entire investment exceeded RMB1.6M! I didn't give up, submit the whole assessment report to Sheetoh and let him make the decision.

GM Sheetoh is a kindness people, he used my assessment report to convince another two GMs, three pack decision they make, all of three are kindness people, how can they say no, I am always so lucky to meet the kindness bosses.

But I can't always think about how to spend the money, I need to know how many PIC people I can hire, because Company J is a company concern the efficiency in every minute and every second, We go to the school special for deaf and blind handicapped students, interviewed more than 30 graduates, understand their body status, which part has problem, which part can normally work, we can arrange the working positions accordingly.

We found IE manager, convince every production manager, expect they can consider full use PIC employees in all the available working positions, finally we sought the support from one faith Christianity Mr Yeong, one work-cell manager, we work together to see how to restructure production line that full use these graduates.

This is an interested technical job, we combine with working procedure requirement, if working procedure request left hand work we put left hand healthy employee on it, wheelchair employees will not put into the working position have equipment put under the foot, blind employees will be arranged in the QC position by full use their sensitive hearing, and strong hand awareness…you can learn a lot from this.

In the first day, when these wheelchair, crutched, physical in challenge employees came in to work, the other employees look them with strange eyes, feel why should I work with this kind of employees, because in their deep seated mindset, they were look down one level compare with normal people, when PICs walk close to normal guys by wheelchair and aid stick, the employee looks like seeing the monster, escaped, nobody actively provide the support, actually they need the support, even if they walk one step have to spend more price than normal people, HR hired one employee lost one leg, he install the artificial limb, he responsibility for taking photos for the new comers, in every day, he go here and there, call this or that one to take photos, after work, he came back to dormitory and use heat water for warming the foot, doing the massage for blood flow, he never sue the bitter to me, only the colleague saw it and said to me, he done his job in high speed, perform well consistently.

After one week they joined, asked our company provide the shuttle bus allow them to carry more language back to dormitory, when going out of company gate, they can't go up to shuttle bus, it depends on the driver hug them move into the bus, help them to get the wheelchairs into the bus, but other heathy employees just stand beside and don't know provide the support.

I am disappointed. how can I do? I think it over with HR colleagues, then another well-known HR project created: It named "We are different, we are the same." This topic has correlation with the prior "Join with buddy, make the difference", right?

We organized PIC multi aid team: Encourage them to help each other, share unhappiness, take care of each other.

1. We organized warm heart team by healthy employees, the same dept colleagues, security, and drivers, coach them how to help those in need, in addition to the daily caring when fire incident happen, the first time they should think about PIC employees, one support another to take them to the safety places, send them to hospital when they get sick…this warm heart team colleagues became more and more kindness, even if the internal colleagues need support, but also the old garden, orphanage garden, poor mountainous area children, donate the blood to hospital.

2. We organized PIC employees to show their capability by using different

ways: Singing, dancing, play basketball, running, gym…

Gym room in Company J take in charge by one strong wheelchair employee, he can instruct other employees how to exercise to have the muscled belly and arm. He like to play basketball, the hit rate up to 80%! He like perform, he perform his own story on the stage: When he aged 6 years old he got the poliomyelitis, lost the act ability for his feet, he lost the brave to live, knock himself in the room, however, his character active and slowly accept this fact, join handicapped school, he like singing, when we interviewed him, he even sang the song at once, we need this sunny boy! After he joined our company, he performed outstanding, the colleagues accept him in the short time, make friend with him, push his wheelchair everywhere, afterward he worked as fitness coach, after that he met his girlfriend, after that, he bought one PIC car for himself and drive car come to work, he introduced his own experience on the stage without any reservation. Every audience impressed by his story, all the judges in the annual gathering shave his hands and appreciated for his outstanding performance.

We asked all the bosses should lead as example, contribute their kindness, don't only stay on the mouth, hire as much as possible PIC employees, arrange their job and rest, assign the buddy help PIC employees, with their strong support, we hired more than 200 PIC employees. There is one very interesting story, our recruitment team hired one PIC responsibility for filing, in the process he need to seek bosses approve on the documents, often the boss will challenge this or that, reject to sign on it, however, when this PIC employee rolling his wheelchair go into their office, they said nothing and only sign on it, because they felt embarrassment by holding one PIC waiting for them.

These disabled employees to work are hooping, concentrate, not afraid of hard work, cherish the hard-won job, active, , often provide the good feedback for production lean improvement, in the end their efficiency win top 1 in the whole plant, our boss like to show to the client this model line, in addition, the turnover rate in this model line is "Zero", because no employee is willing to give up the job which makes them proud of.

The beside healthy colleagues slowly change their mind, they say hello to these employees, provide the active support, make friends, even their strong intention impressing the beside employees, PIC employees perform better than healthy man, how can't we do better and better?

We advertise our best practice to various medias, we only want to use this channel call more companies provide more support to these people in need, there is one is TV program chief, you never knew, Why he will take care of PIC propaganda topic, at that time he should more care about "Fast man and fast lady" "Where is my father", more famous public topics! The reason is he has one PIC son, he has one son and one daughter, everyone calls his son "Handicapped man" all day long, that is the most unbearable, so he specially appreciated what we have done for PIC people and call them PIC rather than handicapped man, put our TV report at the golden time, after that recommend the activities about PIC to us.

After that, we are invited by international labor bureau, introduce our best practices to different countries and different famous branding company about we hired large amount PIC employees.

On April 27th, 2016, we are invited by united nation human right organization, went to Geneva, Switzerland, gave 13 minutes speech to 15 countries representatives by presenting what we have done project for PIC employees!

12.Being HR Head, your every movement affects the overall situation

"You are HR Head" your every movement affects the overall situation; this is what labor union chairman who can be called as "Supreme" gave me advise.

The words are quite harsh, but the implication of profound truth: HR is a person's work, up and down in and out should be considered thoughtful, both virile in the soft, and soft in the Virile, say sense wording to the "people", say non sense wording to the "ghost", while debut, I did not put these words in the heart, have suffered a lot of immediate loss.

In before, I said excess wording sentence "Fight to the end" at inappropriate time, result in the employees who was terminated raise their claim compensation cases to arbitration, last more than half a year, I experienced three times sat in "Defendant "seats, was forced to make consensus once by once to the employees, once by once repeat count how much should pay back to the employees, I repeatedly asked myself, I really can "Fight to the end"? The case close to the end, my boss asked me: "What did you learn from this incident? "I still forthright: "I think I didn't say the wrong sentence, now I still fight to the end, I didn't forgive, until defined and settled whole case, actually this case can be settled rely on this previous boss and his boss Paddy gave me the opportunity, without their backbone stand support, or they fired me because I said that sentence, that I really do nothing in the halves, can't fight to the end.

In every time think back, in that time Chinese social, many wage earner already understood use the new labor law to protect their private interest, however, they borrowed my one sentence "Fight to the end" as excuse, even if I said some peaceful wordings to claim down the employees, they may not have so fierce reflection and vowed to fight with the company in the court, after this incident, I repeatedly remind myself: "I must take care of myself when alone, learn to overcome my own anger."

A careless, only two yuan account fee cause utter confusion as to make everybody nervous, this also happened when I debut, did not consider the staff will have any reaction? Open one bank account for the employee, it is for their convenience to take the money from auto machine, from now to see, the cost charge looks unreasonable, RMB2 worth less. At that time, only one announcement I posted out, it was borrowed by the trouble makers as execute again, they used hostile and bold wording to challenge: How can your HR deduct RMB2 from my income? Although RMB2 isn't the big amount but it is our money earn by hard toil, if company decided to pay salary by bank, that should be company bear this cost instead of deduct the money from our pay, whether your HR doing some dirty things with bank and want to save our money into the bank? I remain my open attitude to direct communicate with R&D manager, tried to explain our intention and find out the solution together, however, they doubled the complaint rebuke to me, I felt so sad by listening her reprimand, I asked myself: "Didn't you saw what HR done for you? Do you want to make the mess on the company that show prestige? Who are really think about the employee?" Look back from now on, is there better solution if this case recurrence? If I tried harder to negotiate with bank and waive this service charge? Consider the employee reaction, can company bear this cost? Fully communicate with dept heads, agree to proceed then communicate with the employees together? There is much better solution, depends if I think it over and will to do? If I plan it in advance rather than settle it by myself? I remind myself in the future if any touch employee benefit implementation must consult with employees' feedback then proceeds, I must face the reaction, why don't I face it in advance that can save more time and energy, the barrier can be little.

"I also made the mistake, made more mistake you will know how to settle it in future" This was the experience shared by my previous boss Elvis.

Another Boss Bruce taught me: You should say the right wordings at the right time, Like Chinese old saying: Talk to people, talk to ghost, it doesn't means you haven't integrity, therefore, you speak out but you can't expect the result which you demanded, even more the guys do it for you, so you need to think about how to change the method and let the other can accept your opinion, even sometime, you keep silent much better than speak out, because in that occasion, nobody will protect you, not the one that you want to protect can listen to you, so you became very disadvantaged." He is Company J HR-SVP, I understood what he means, the implication of profound truth, after experienced so much.

I made the third big mistake in company V: dare to contradict the Code of Conduct auditor! Argue OT problem with them.

Company V is the top 1 producer for Educational toys, they often encountered one headache problem: In peak season keep up to OT for catching Christmas order delivery, in the following one or two months all are idle over there, however, it is stipulated that the electronic industry isn't seasonal industry according to Chinese labor law. However, the customer ask the supplier follow CSR strict requirement, at that time, it was the first time to audit Chinese supplier, I am so new for CSR and don't know hit the "Muscle" this time, in the beginning, they only asked for salary record, rejected by me, in my mind, salary is the most confidential information, how can I expose it to auditor so easily? Gave them the first impression I am playing the trick, after repeat communication, my boss authorized me to release employee salary accept the audit, when the auditor opens the payment record, saw OT pay column, start to challenge me: Why are there so many OT hour?" At that time, I count it out one by one exactly; however, I jumped into their "Trap" They wrote it into audit report by much more wordings, gave one "RED light" result to us. What 's the meaning for red light? Stop the order! Marketing manager reminded me splutteringly, I got so and fed up, and questioned the auditor: We OT for on time delivery, we can't follow

Chinese Labor law OT 36 hours, our big company feeding so many employees, they will lose the job without order, what did we arrange OT for? You are so exaggerate your description will make customer stop their order place to us" However, the auditor only know find out the problems and record it, how to survive it is your supplier own problem not his, they just look like "Big Buddha" sat there, our supplier 's life and death has been disregard from their business no matter how I try to convince them to revise their report.

After that I had been rebutted repeatedly by marketing manager and General Manager, I felt vexed, actually they would be clearer than me why arranged so many OT, they didn't stand out and say to auditor, but push me out to explain to auditor, ask me why dare to embarrass with auditor?

The following three months take corrective action period whether I was writing the CAP report or was thinking out various methods in order to pass the re-audit, "The boss and CSR auditor sat each side, the auditor can definitely make the boss grow a century of insight" that is the joke, put this on me-one HR represented boss face the audit, I fully knew what it means.

Finally, I passed the re-audit by settling all the difficulty issues, I summarized one valued experience: Never rebut with auditor, the lost will be yourself, if there were the fact, admit it bravely, even if auditor, they need the job, the audit company need the business, if they haven't any finding in the audit, how to show their prestige?

I respect and learn from my bosses always, never by pass my boss report gossip to his boss, this is the forbidden ground for the bosses, no matter which kind of boss, I maintain the proper distant with my boss, rely on my capability to do my job, whatever sub-regulations never casting me- I never sent one gift to my boss, there were twice opportunities join the celebration parties, to be make fun of saying "I love you" to my boss and call his name. I forgave, because I and my boss, included all the colleagues are brothers and sisters, I like to work together with them, but it doesn't mean I have any relationship with anyone, we should act properly whatever to play game.

To deal with customer relationship, HR involved into it, taken care of, act as supporter, in Company J, HR need to meet with customers, even from start point, marketing colleagues will invite HR Head to join and meet with customers, introduce our company cultural, CSR performance, visit our accommodation, the closer step will get more information about staffing speed and capability, labor cost, compensation and benefit, training etc.

"Customer is our real boss" now the existing company owner told me. So, we take care of customer rather than taking care of customer, what is the customer demand? Quality, Price, Speed, value above price, to achieve can't be settled by one dept alone, it depends on the team. Many managers asked me "How can American Company full use team play spirit? I answered to them:" You see how they serviced the customer you already knew why."

1. The whole year customer visit plan will provide to every dept, operation dept review it every week, arrange actions accordingly.
2. Customer visit, all dept manager and asst manager meet with customers, introduction PPT must be well prepared before three days, recheck and polish by project leader.

2.1. It included every minute plant tour plan, PIC and action plan.

2.2 PPT use the standardized format, letterform and detail explanation, at the same time prepare all the answer for conceivable questions and data demand.

3. Follow by different dept head take relevant responsibility, present PPT and answer the customer questions, lead the customer have the plant tour, HR responsibility for living facility introduction.

The plant tour route, introduction key point updated by HR by quarterly and share with every dept.

The visit route, poster, layout is the job scope for HR ER team, collect the latest information from every dept.

HR update quarterly min salary, labor law, hourly rate updated information with marketing dept, they adjust unit quotation to customer at the first time, protect company profit accordingly.

In addition to engage the customer, HR attempt to have more opportunity to work with customers on code of conduct cooperation, work with H customer on PIC project, energy saving, Hep B and HIV prevention, migrant children projects, apply to join customer A educational subsidy project, customer W female worker training project etc., we shared our best practice with customer, they shared their good projects with us, we support each other and share the achievement.

When there is a big change, to take into account the impact on customers, such as the previous mentioned NGO negative report, HR first time not only think of the impact on their own company reputation, but also you have to take into account the impact on the reputation of customers, to the first time standing in the customer's position to consider how to deal with customer impact. Early to help customers resolve his problems and contradictions, do not bring trouble to customers. Just like now company M we want to cut the last process manpower, we will give H customer the reason and action plan, with their support before implementation, the result is settled the problem calmly.

How to deal with the labor union relationship? The role of the Chairman of the labor union is important.

In Company J, the former union chairman was expelled from the factory for "commit crimes", in China, in the top 500 American company, the process needed zone's labor unions to kick him out.

Then another chairman of the labor union replaced, she is who I met the "best" of the Union chairman, when I joined Company J, she belongs to HR, I have not only thousand to ask myself why leave her in HR? I even join a training course on this topic: "How to get along with the union?" On the surface, we do everything for each other, but inside I extreme dislike her to do nothing, American companies pay attention to human rights, pay attention to the values of equality, allow such "idler" Everywhere "perform"-and making confrontation on the company's decision, against HR, so that can reflect the company "Audit and balance" value? Looking at her mail sent from this or that time, the half with sarcasm half-threatening, you want a round of "straight fist counterattack", but considering the impact and response to the company, as HR does not have enough "Open minded" how do you get along with each department? Besides, she is a half of your subordinates, but the problem is that she did not put HR in the eye, she thinks she should be in the company level parallel with the structure of the Organization, she is only in the "negotiation" with HR every day. If a person with this consciousness exists in the company, many decisions can be made like "Z" font to walk.

What lead to the model strife? One is religion another one is labor union, from both you can understand what the role for labor union play among employees and social conflict, no matter socialism countries or capitalism countries. Now company M is facing more serious problems in 7 satellite companies, these labor union chairmen can be rated as "Gang leader", openly get labor union fee, openly get the benefit from company, in headcount reduction, they insist to get more than employees, I have been the role for "Sweeping house", combine 7 labor unions into one union, let them fight with each other internally, I use labor union to manage the workers, successful or not, you can see my continuation.

Many HR often make a good relationship with the government, the departments HR often work with: Labor Bureau Supervision Brigade, Arbitration Office, court, Foreign Commission, Defense office, Zone office, public security and police station, Homeland Security Bureau ...

I do not know whether I have succeeded in this respect but I have good relationship with the government different depts, so I have accumulated a set of methods.

Because of OT problem, I was treated "to contradict" Labor bureau supervision brigade, they even want to issue the huge amount fine ticket to company V, however, I think it over and over, don't know where did I contradict? I didn't cover OT data, and didn't say in rural way, only show the actual station, put data and problem on the table, however, the team leader thought I only throw the problems to him, they were come for fine, not for solving our problem, so I must correct my attitude, invite foreigner trading dept to coordinate with us, one expensive and delicious food warm reception, claim down the case.

The relationship built from this contradiction case happened.

After the employees' group appeal, my relationship with labor bureau became "Never know each other without fighting", when facing the employees on the court, can't handle it smoothly rely on relationship with which party, rely on the clear understanding of labor law, and full use it, identify both parties stand point, fight back or accept the opposite party opinion, so I put me down, direct consult with judge in the arbitration office, after coming back, study all related clause seriously, finally the whole case settled down, I really understand the "Essential" of labor law, built up the real friendship with big brother in labor bureau, after 5 years I left Dongguan, due to M&A project reason, I have to consult with labor bureau arbitration again, from another end of phone call, the other side asked me" Are you Cindy?" Even after so many years, I forgot them, but they didn't forget me!

Because I acuminated experience how to deal with labor bureau, in Company J, we kept harmonious relationship with labor bureau and high court, if there will be the company visit, they will first arrange to show us, to submit the working report, only mention our company good performance, because we never lead to them disappointed. For our thousands of employees' company, we didn't have one court case happened, if labor bureau didn't pick us up which one will they pick up?

I can use quite direct sentence to cover: Where there is benefit where there will be relationship, without benefit, no relationship has remaining value, even impossible to remain. Keep "close but not too close, far away but not too far away".

The most basic and the most difficult for HR is to self-control EQ, because you need to "In heartless day to dismiss thousands of employees," do the psychological preparation, there are all kinds of employees: someone will yell at you, someone will cry to you, someone will lose their mind walk away, some will intimidate, even use weapons, I have faced the underworld boss: because need to dismiss him. I even need to dismiss my own boss, because no one dares to do it, the task falls on my head only. There is no such experience is easy to get through, in fact, the most uncomfortable is often touch to their own conscience, often physically and mentally tired, during which you can't have personal emotions, must be well-reasoned, watertight, because your every movement affects the overall situation.

13.Is it normal for Phrenoplegia/Suicide?

The question I asked was a bit strange, when the public continued to expose Foxconn's 12-Jumps, 13-Jumps-the employee suicides to the media, they looked at Foxconn with contempt and challenged how serious Foxconn lacked humanized management, it looks like that the same case would never happen to them. In fact, they lack a basic understanding of the causes of mental illness and suicide.

I've dealt with a similar incident, I've handled it a lot, surprised? I have dealt with three cases of suicide and mental illness in five months, at those days I cannot close eyes every day-sleepless nights, is always reflected in the scene of the staff suicide scenes of horror, mental illness employ cannot walk, nipped by our company security into the car, I will never forget that scene, Can you imagine what I've been gone through, I've been gone through intense emotional events earlier than the Foxconn incident 20 years, I did not find the "Buddhist monk of Wutai Mountain" also did not know how to find, but visit Guangzhou Medical College to consult with psychological experts Professor Li, when I put this kind of intense events when the disease to cure, also from that time I learned to analyze the emotional and psychological problems of the staff from the academic aspects, mental illness and suicide cases have its inevitability, the results of the research statistics found that the incidence of mental illness and suicide cases of 200,000 people in the proportion of 1 serious disease, some of them in the mother pregnancy, Brain structure develop to abnormal, also caused certain effects on future personal emotions, such people are born with pessimism, a little uncomfortable but outside stimulation, they will not open, more easily than normal to form depression, emotional runaway or suicidal. Of course, there is also the generation of the acquired character, which is stimulated by intense emotional events.

For the onset of suicide or psychiatric cases, high risk group, behavioral phenomena and reasons I made the following summary:

The new join is not more than three months, usually at the junction of Winter and spring, March or April, and the fall, September or October, three or four hours in the midnight.

The proportion of first-line employees is higher than that of staff.

Often bow, not dare face people.

Often make mistakes, fear of failure.

Often write diaries, remember most of the sad things.

Poor sleep, frequent headaches.

Phantom hearing.

Parents divorced, from a lack of parental love or mother, from childhood they were forced to work to support the family, the whole year did not back to home.

Autistic, lonely, no Friends.

Suffered from emotional and physical injury.

Remember that it was a late night, three o'clock, I was awakened by the telephone Bell: " Someone jumped in XX dormitory!" People notified the ambulance pulled away, it was the first time to call the police, come on!" I rushed to the location of the accident and saw the blood on the ground. "They can't find the badge from female worker, this dormitory has eight floors, live in more than 800 employees, it was late at night we do not dare to alarm staff, afraid of affecting their emotions. "I listen to the report of the dormitory supervisor, worried, if we can't find the identity of employees in time, can't grasp the information, for future troubleshooting will be very difficult, but late at night to wake up all the staff must cause a wide range of emotional fluctuations, more impact will cause..., the working people began to rushes up, I became calm, from the blood to the ground with the same upper direction to look carefully to the outside of the floor, see the third floor of the fence left a more obvious mark, my heart tightened, ordered the dormitory supervisor on the corner of the third floor of the room gently to find, see if there are new discoveries? The result is immediately available. I ran to the woman's bed directly, the first see her badge put on the bed, next to a notebook, I did not think too much, opened her diary, the last one wrote her choice of death decision, let family do not grieve for her, the previous record can see out of mind confusion, There is no way to figure out her heart knot in a short time. At that time the police came, in order to protect the scene of all the witnesses and physical evidence are taken away. After we received the hospital formally notify the woman after rescue invalid death notice, we informed the family came to the factory understand what happened and went through controversy, stalemate for several days, family took a "compensation" to leave, the case calmed down.

Before this incident closed, one day ER team called me again: "XX production line sent a female worker to here, her behavior is very strange, speak not clear even gibberish, we let the plant doctor checked, the body is not sick, but completely lost the normal words and deeds, paralysis on the ground." "It was my first time to see this scene, it is difficult to describe the behavior of the female workers I saw, sleep is not paralyzed sleep, paralysis is not paralysis appearance, the way of action is like the gorilla in the zoo, more than the orangutan is worse, the consciousness can't control their behavior, there is no speech at all. I was only ordered ER team: immediately know where there is a mental hospital, immediately sent to there. Looking at the staff sent to the hospital, as I described at the beginning of this article: Several security guards caught her in the car, of course, did not use violence. After the employees have been living in a mental hospital, spending hundreds & thousands of the medical expenses like "burning the money", the family appeared slowly after our repeat calls, when we asked them if the employee had a medical history, the family hesitate to answer, the company should take care of the staff's medical expenses and the worker family member accommodation costs, three months, HR and Department colleagues tired, her family was also tired, her family actually left the staff regardless. I was so angry that I called her family and gave them a scolding, I asked her family, "Have you ever loved your loved one?" I asked them to come back immediately or the company would give up treatment! There is no way to do this: if your family doesn't care about the worker's illness, let the company take full responsibility? But from the bottom of my heart, I sympathize with the worker and her family because they are all victims. the burden was quite heavy, so I made the preparation to heal her sick and send her to home.

When the mental workers are still lying in the hospital, the condition has not any improvement, but also late at night, I received another factory call about a female worker jumped to suicide, people have confirmed death, hospital is not willing to pull away the corpse after the examination, we had to contact the funeral home late at night to pull away the body, looking at the bag which was carrying the corpse be put on the carriage truck, my heart is shaking, another poor life!

That day my ER team supervisor sobbed in front of me: "I don't think I've done a good job, we've had so many activities, we want all the employees to work together and play together, but no matter how hard we try, we can't attract the people who need us mostly. They feel lonely all day but do not want to go out of their own world, how can we help them, I feel that I did not get them out of the mood is my responsibility!" The head of ER team was the kind-hearted, naturally fill with loving person, I was worried that she could not withstand the pressure of the time choose to give up. So I enlightened her, the method is always more than the problem! We check the information, we consult experienced experts, always find a way to stop! we found out the expert!

Professor Li Deep-rooted academic, but also obsessed with practical problems of research and solution, the first time he went to our company:

First he understood the situation of our company: High-tech electronic products need labor-intensive people to complete the manufacturing process, the size of employees close to 20,000 people, not a high turnover rate, but each month to replenish the loss of 300 to 500 of the employees, there is a sharp low-season, the peak season desperately overtime trace for shipments, off-season worker to take vacation have home rest, employees from all corners, the cultural level is not high school graduation, biased towards women, aged between 16-35 years old marriage age.

Professor Li then advised us to immediately launch a psychological seminar for frontline managers, for frontline production worker, and for new employees.

Teach them about frontline execution:

1. Recognize personal emotion and manage it
2. How to make a difference in the personality of subordinate employees
3. How to manage subordinates and get along with subordinates of different personalities
4. How to react to an emotional reaction from an employee?
4. How to deal with the employee's excessive emotion?

Educate frontline production worker:

1. Recognize personal emotions and manage it
2. How do you react to other emotions?
3. How to help the company deal with the emotional problems of others
4. Employees are obligated to participate in this training

Teach new employees:

1. How to adapt to the new environment?
2. How to communicate with people? How to get acquainted with friends and men?
3. How to get along with your boss?

4. How to get along with your family?

5. This content is covered in the training of new employees.

He also coached our ER team members

How to answer the call of employee counseling?

How to resolve the stress of self-psychology

This is how he taught me:

Do not think you are the savior, all the emotional problems of the staff can resolved, even oneself also deep into the vortex of emotion, now many engaged in psychological counseling of psychological experts and scholars, talk about there are too many suffering too much tragedy in the world, falling in this vortex, oneself also suffering from depression, Even to suicide.

In the case of a mental illness that has been converted to morbid condition (as I mentioned earlier), do not stay in there and send to the hospital immediately, as staying in the company can cause great harm to both the patient and others.

He instructs us how to design the questionnaires to find out job-seekers' emotions problem, how to hide the key questions, and all the candidates who have an unusual answer to the key questions, and avoid the problem from the moment of the interview.

Finally, he taught us to conduct internal investigation, at risk level to make the intervention counseling of active psychological problems, or in the production off-season timely for the treatment of dismissal.

After the implementation of his series of guidance and measures, the effect is obvious, more than two years the company has not repeat any suicide and staff emotional cases, we established a deep friendship with Professor Li and frequent exchanges information.

After I left company V, I brought the method into company E and Company J. Company J in this regard to establish a more perfect system than Company V, originated in the United States companies are not acceptable to have such staff suicide occurred, but just before I entered the job, a staff drunk and with the security chase slip down to the ground, leading to a lifetime handicapped.

I was "fortunately" to take the difficult account left by the predecessor, on the one hand, the family of the employee claim compensation, on the other hand to deal with the emotional problems of employees, because the United States headquarters do not believe that employees will be chased into the room without any reason, from the second floor of the window fall down, they expect us to have "truth" investigation, timely handle the employees' pessimistic "sentiment. For the "truth" I have no time to detail check, but such a large company, I know that there is no effective way to manage employee sentiment, sooner or later there will be an accident, an early accident or a late accident will be. Taking advantage of this crisis, I can help the company build a complete system.

I contacted with Professor Li again and asked him to recommend his strong disciples: Zhimin.

Together we plan to build up the psychological counseling room, the beauty of its name as psychological station: Private space, warm furnishings (comfortable small sofa, soft pillows, oil painting of facing sea), warm wall color, young employees like it.

We started the literacy and sharing of psychological knowledge of employees, collected the sign design result of psychological counseling and organized other publicity activities.

For stress, interpersonal relationships, emotions, personal growth, neurological illnesses, employee interviews and telephone counseling, we summarize the results in categories:

For the telephone psychological consultation is further classified to deal with:

Pressure	Interpersonal relationship	Emotion	Personal growth	Neurological

26.32%	31.58%	15.79%	23.68%	2.63%
10	12	6	9	1

The results of the telephone interview are further classified to deal with:

Pressure	Interpersonal relationship	Emotion	Personal growth	Neurological
7.55%	37.73%	15.09%	33.96%	5.66%
4	20	8	18	3

We had 6PF, EPQ, SAS, SDS, SCL—90 psychological test of our employees.

We set up the staff Psychology Club and carried out a series of activities:

1. Team coaching: Small Team 10 to 15 people in the department coaching, large team building across departments
2. Outdoor Outreach
3. Interpersonal communication
4. Psychological decompression
5. Psychological cues
6. Open Harvard Happiness Course
7. Emotional management
8. How to face anger, sadness, jealousy, anxiety, fear, shame, guilt
9. How to change yourself and cherish yourself

This is our 2013-year Mental Club annual activity plan.

1. The opening of the counseling

    Objectives and content: Recruit new members, on-site consultation and on-site quiz

    Time: March 2013 (week)

2. The language of the Heart

Objective: To promote mental health knowledge

2.1. Mental Health Knowledge Contest

Time: May 2013 (1 week)

2.2. Mental Health Knowledge Propaganda

Mental Health Knowledge Contest

2.3. Specific arrangements: the update of mental health publicity column in the dormitory exhibition once per week, the holding of mental health knowledge contest, divided into mass quiz and team competition way.

2.4. Chinese Sinology Meditation Poetry Recitation Contest

Date: June 2013 (day)Specific arrangements: The organizing Committee to formulate the content of the poem, each employee can participate, read a complete verse can get a gift.

2.5. Separated one dormitory as a unit, can recite a full text of the provisions of the Organizing committee poetry content, the employee can get a beautiful gift.

3. The Dance of the Heart

Objective: To enrich the staff's leisure time, improve team cohesion and execution

3.1. "When everyone adds fuel, the flames rise high" team cohesion and execution improvement competition

Date: November 2013

Specific arrangements: The whole plant to w/c or departments for the unit registration, participate in the competition, the competition is divided into the preliminary (integration knockout) and the final.

4. The shadow of the Heart

Psychological film,

Time: March 2013--February 2014

Specific arrangements: The monthly playing of a film, before playing with PPT to ask questions, trigger thinking.

5. Mirror of the Heart

Goal: Annual psychological Club activities Review, recruit new members

Time: January 2013 (week)

Specific arrangements: show a year since the psychological club activities photos and milestones

You can see the activity of the staff counseling is one year to the late monthly theme never stop, employee relations group is often the busy group of human resources department, you ask me why do so many activities? I'm going to tell you how many times I'd rather have to do it than one time of Employee psychiatric or suicide incident handling, we are very busy at Company J, but we have not had a similar case in more than five years, it is really not easy in a company of 13,000 people.

14.We just follow someone to strike!

Here's a report of a thrilling through strike I've been at company E.
9.12 Strike Report
September 12, 2007 to the morning of September 14, some employees of the company dissatisfied with the company's pay adjustment and raised the strike, causing some production bog down, now report the whole incident process of the whole strike and related treatment as follows:
1. Review of the strike process:
September 12 evening around 8 o'clock, the company XX Department the 3rd floor night shift of block 15 worker began to refuse to follow the normal arrangements and began to strike. Some staff (nearly 200 people) rushed out of the floor, go to parade, gathered at the entrance of XX canteen. The reason for the strike is that the wages of the company's staff and indirect employees have been adjusted, while the company's hardest, lowest-paid direct employees have not been adjusted, they are required to adjust their wages in accordance with other nearby companies.
Around 9 o'clock in the 12th Night, the strike began to spread rapidly, the 3rd floor of block 15, the second and third floor in block 5 & 6 began to have strike, production ceased.
At about 12 o'clock in the evening, some employees refused to return to their production floors after supper, began to gather in front of block 15th lawn, headcount increasing, reaching nearly 3000 people at the most approximate number. Government departments are beginning to intervene.
Around 1:30 on 13th, the company announced the latest wage adjustment program (see attachment I), the basic salary of all staff adjusted to 750

yuan/month, and adjusted overtime pay, take effect from July 1, 2007.

In the morning at 2 o'clock on 13th some employees dissatisfied with the company announced the adjustment plan, rushed out of the factory, nearly 400 people tried to rush into XX bus station in front of the State road, but was forcibly blocked by the government departments.

13th 3:00, company's management tried to persuade and in cooperation with the public security departments forcibly dispersed, the workers who trying to bring impact to the National highway back to the factory lawn.

3:30 The lockout department began to call, the staff returned to the floor, the factory order began to return to normal, but back to the floor staff still refused to produce, even if agreed to start, production speed is very slow.

4:30 every floor order back to normal, night staff strike basically subsided.

After 7:00 13th, the block 15 and Block 16 workers learned that the strike had begun and went out of their production buildings to gather in the big lawn. The strike soon spread to block 5 and 6 XX departments.

On the 13th, around 9:30, the staff of the large lawn gathered nearly 3,000 people, the government departments intervened strongly, repeatedly blocked the staff rushed out of the factory's attempt, blocked the company's South Gate.

13th around 11 o'clock in the morning, the company convinced the strike workers return to work, announced the reward policy of work resumption, on 13th to resume (including on-the-job normal production) staff reward 50 yuan, 14th resumed reward 30 yuan, 15th reward 10 yuan, later than 15th still refused to return to work, in accordance with absenteeism policy for treatment.

12 O'clock Noon, the company announced the emergency announcement (see attachment III), with government dept request the workers return to work, gathered in the big lawn staff go back to their own floor dining.

2:00 onwards, the company began to organize the worker of the floor to sign the resumption agreement (see attachment IV). But there is widespread resistance among employees. The signing rate was not high all afternoon.

On the night of 14th, XXX Night staff still cannot work normally. Until 12 o'clock in the evening, the floors have returned to normal gradually.

On 15th, the departments were still on duty, monitoring the plant order and not finding anomalies, and the strikes were basically appeased.

The processing of the company solution and related treatment:

From the night of the September 12 strike, the Ministry of Personnel, the administration and the production department were all involved in the process of persuading the strike staff.

The company has introduced a new salary adjustment and return to work reward program.

During the strike, the company provided free 13th lunch, and supper.

During the strike, HR cooperated with the production department to convene several small-scale communication and coordination meetings with staff to understand the real thoughts and concerns of employees.

In the course of the strike, two employees who had taken the lead in the unrest were dismissed and forced to leave the factory immediately.

121 employees who resigned during the strike were immediately resigned and paid a total of $ xxx.

All the employees who resumed work signed the resumption agreement.

Involvement of government departments:

The 12 Night, XX Street Office, comprehensive Management Office, armed Forces, XX Labor station, xx Police station, XXX Labor Bureau Supervision Brigade and other government departments began to intervene, investigate the cause of the strike and coordinate it.

13th 2 o'clock in the morning, when some employees tried to block xxx National Road, the government department mobilized more than 300 police force, successfully intercepted the strike staff. Prevented the further deterioration of the situation.

In the morning of 13th, XX District government, labor unions, Public Security Bureau, Labor Bureau and XX town related departments are sent to the factory help to calm down employee.

In the afternoon of 13th, the Government's relevant units issued a joint announcement to indicate that the strike was illegal and that employees should resume work. They grouped into departments to convince the workers.

In the morning of 13th, the government departments dispatched riot police to block the company's doors until the afternoon of the factory order returned to normal.

Strike causes analysis:

XX Labor Bureau announced 2007 annual salary adjustment program, clearly stating 2007 XX city Minimum wage standards are not adjusted. But at the same time, it put forward the salary adjustment guide line. At the same time, Shanghai increase the minimum wage to 850 yuan/month, Dongguan also announced that the recent adjustment of the minimum wage, resulting in general staff pay higher expectations.

XXX Department of a small number of management personnel prior to the dissemination of the company in July 2007 may increase the basic salary to 830 yuan/month news, a few nearby companies recent increased wages, deepen the staff's expectations of pay-off.

Nearby company named XXX in last week had strike, the company raised wages, causing employees "The follow-up effect.

Frontline management personnel's fierce management method caused resentment, accumulated the dissatisfaction of the company.

The company has made adjustments to both the staff and the indirect staff, the direct worker feel that they have suffered unequal treatment for the direct labor. In the process of adjusting employees' wages, the real mentality of the direct employees is not fully investigated, the drastic reflection of the direct employees may be not taken into account.

On 12th, all employees of the company's wages paid into the account, some employees did the wage comparison. The fact that the salary of indirect staff raised but the direct employees were not added, each other expresses dissatisfaction eventually raised the strike.

The department's direct managers were unable to appear on the strike immediately and were unaware of the unrest diversion, leading to a deterioration of the situation.

Day shifts and night shift colleagues influence each other, leading to the spread of strikes. Problems exposed during the disposition of strikes:

1. The middle management of the company lacks the necessary understanding of the front-line staff mentality, can't reflect the employees ' real mentality to the decision-making, so that the policy distortion.

2. The company's overall policy focused on positive effects analysis, but did not carry out enough negative impact analysis, resulting in the policy of the relevant factors considered inadequate.

3. The management of the frontline management in the production sector is rough, sometimes even in the pursuit of production to abuse to the workers, the worker looks them as the company's representative, treat their behavior as corporate behavior, resulting in labor relations tensions.

4. The channel for staff to relieve pressure and tension is not smooth, staff resentment has not been able to be channeled, in the face of universal problems are prone to resonate, led to the scale of the suspension or strike.

5. In dealing with strikes and other emergencies, the company does not have a mature contingency plan, the Department of Cooperation between the lack of tacit understanding, only by the credentials of their own experience to take temporary response measures, can't form a division of responsibility for the

resultant force, on-site management is chaotic, the pace of the department is inconsistent, can't effectively stop the development, Led to the strike from the department to the whole plant, from the plant inside to outside. It is strongly recommended that the company set up contingency plans for emergencies, dividing the responsibilities of various departments in emergencies, the communication and coordination mechanism between departments.

Report Completed

The incident has been passed 10 years, when the strike occurred in September 12, 2007 night, I just flew to Shanghai branch for business, when the first time to receive an urgent report, the whole night has been contacted to understand the situation of the scene, gave guidance and ideas what to do next? The next morning rushed to the airport, asked all the airlines only the first flight is 10am in the day, which is the most "slow" flight of my life, I was worried, back to the company was 13th noon, looking at the staff twos and threes standing, squatting, sitting in the workshop and the square, I am quite sad, A founder of the industry for several decades developed the top of the evergreen enterprise, may have fallen, although I am only an employee, only the third hand of HR, but a strong sense of responsibility let me load heavy duty of calming the strike.

Looking at the tired, in a state of utter stupefaction my direct boss, I and the group CHO directly agreed and immediately announced the encouragement proposal encourage employees return to work. At the same time to draft a request for staff to return to work and the letter of commitment, but most of the staff is not willing to sign on it, I thought it isn't right, I directly asked workers, why did you strike? Don't you not cherish this hard-won job? They gave me the same reply: "We just follow someone to strike!"

Sounds like "herd effect" is serious, I have to find a way to circle this flock of sheep!

At this time, I and the GM of the administration, Mr. Ye found the Party Secretary of the city in the late night, I begged him on behalf of HR: "I hope the government can come forward help our enterprises, lobbying workers to return to work as soon as possible, only to return to work we have the basis for further consultation, the Government can speak out the key words at the key time" the Party secretary of the city nodded and immediately to hold a communication meeting with the workers' representatives, clear that the act of strike is illegal.

At the end of the meeting, employees remained reluctant to return to work. Time went by another night.

On the third day, the situation did not change, the staff saw the company's management and security went ahead try to communicate with them began to run away, run with security like playing "hide-and-seek" game, the scene is quite chaotic.

In this chaotic time, I did not hesitate to pick up the portable horn, to the workers to say something from my heart: Folks, when I picked up the microphone, I feel that my responsibility is very heavy, because I talk to you today about you and my work and livelihood, we have old ones and small ones in the home, We do not want to strike, we all need this job, only we work, then the company can complete the order, we can get wages, so I strongly appeal, you stop running, as soon as possible to resume production, I can promise you: HR will be in-depth investigation to employees feel dissatisfied with the place, the company will make improvements! "

The whole audience is quiet.

I started from the nearby production line, instructed the line workers return to the station, the person points to the first pull to start!

Then there's the second one.

Then there's the third one.

Immediately after all the production line to see the front three production lines resumed, have to return to their own position to start their own machine!

That night, all resumed.

I finally could lie down and rest after having 52 hours of sleepless days

I fulfilled my promise to collect the dissatisfaction feedback from employees without any delay, which accumulated the long-overdue problems, in order to protect privacy, I hide the sensitive part:

	Question
SALARY	Basic Salary and OT pay comply with the Labor Law.
	Basic Salary has increased to RMB750. The salary difference caused in July and August should be paid.
	Basic pay increases to RMB800 from 1st Jan 2008.
	Basic pay needs to be above RMB800, eg. RMB830 to RMB850.
	No seniority wages. No benefit different between long service and new employees.
BONUS	Living cost allowance is required. Suggestion is RMB50/ person. month.
	Full attendance bonus and year-end bonus are required.
	Appraisal bonus is necessary to differentiate good performance and bad performance.
	The night shift bonus is too low.
	The night shift bonus for extra line and the night shift bonus for assembly line are not same. Why?
ALLOWANCE	Multi skill allowance is too low. RMB100 per month is acceptable.
	No allowance after the 9 work procedures exam. Why must wait for so long?
	In epoxy stacking dept, the working condition is bad (epoxy powder and oil are corrosive which cause employees' hand rankled, very

	noise, high temperature). Why have not hardship allowance?
	It's suggested to give hardship allowance to tin collision because of smoke.
	Hardship allowance for chemistry related work procedures cannot wait for procedure check after 6 months.
	Health check for special procedure employees should be arranged by the company.
	Salary increment cannot combine meal allowance and monthly bonus.
	Why didn't assign us to join multi skill examination and enjoy the allowance if pass it.
ATTENDANCE	The unpaid leave cannot be replaced by OT hours or weekend working hours.
	The shift transition/material shortage/machine broken hours cannot be replaced by OT hours.
	OT hours should be lower than 120 hours.
	RMB10 cannot be deducted because of forgotten to punch the card.
	Shift changing is too frequently.
	Company should treat employee equally. Why IDL increase salary but DL do not?
	It's too early for morning shift.
WORKING	Employees must sit on the floor during the lunch break.
	It's hot in workroom due to switch off air conditioner or broken down.
	Hand out short sleeved uniform.
	Protective stuff is not enough
	Fixture runs fast, reduce the headcount but the output is same or higher.
	Do not reduce standard worker headcount.

	Due to the pollution and high cost of smoking apart machine, the company change new machine. The low-cost machine has more pollution.
	Line workers must be cleaners to clean the line.
WORKING REALATION	Management should care more about employees.
	Too much target. Workers feel heavy pressure.
	Difficult to take leave.
	Line leaders are fierce in controlling workers.
	It's no use to complain to line leaders, counselors, ER Team.
	Why does the employment contract print out beforehand without any negotiation?
	Standing to work is too tired.
	No rest for long working hours of afternoon shift and night shift.
DORMITORY	Poor condition in the dormitory. Too many people in 1 room.
	Water and electricity fees increase a lot from July, from RMB10 to RMB20 even to RMB40.
	It should be no charge for solar water heater.
	Too much cockroach in the dormitory. Pesticide spraying should be carried out once per week.
	It is noisy in dormitory zone. Night shift employee cannot have a good rest during daytime.
CANTEEN	Very poor food quality and high price (it's worse after inflation). No change or reaction after complaints. Hope company could solve it.
	Does the canteen food price increase also after we get the salary increase?
MED	Poor medical skill and low service standard in health center in Dormitory W Zone.

	Old edition medical insurance card cannot be used in Shajing hospital.
	Employee pays RMB4 per month for medical insurance without any receipt.
	How long have new employees wait to get the social security card?

I have the first time to understand the dissatisfaction of the staff to submit to the Senior HR and the company's boss, I believe they have never had so much attention to staff dissatisfaction.

I did not have a serious bias towards the staff but kept a cool head, and I immediately draft the following policy:

Contingency Plan for E Group

    1. The propose for Contingency Plan

    1.1. The establishment of a unified command, grading responsibility, clear responsibilities, cooperation, rapid response to the emergency treatment mechanism, effective disposal of emergency group incident, minimize the impact of the incident on the company's normal production order.

    1.2. Establish early warning mechanism to prevent and reduce the occurrence of emergency group incident.

2. Scope: Apply to all Chinese sites of the group

3. Contingency plan for strike-grading:

Category of Strike grading:

3.1. A grade of strike incident refers to the occurrence of a cross-plant, cross-departmental, cross-floor and other major strikes.

3.2. B grade strikes are strikes that take place within a department, across lines, shifts or employees of the same type.

3.3. C grade strikes in addition to minor strikes, other than grade A and grade B strikes.

3.4. Organization and command System

3.4.1. The Contingency management headquarters coordinates the work of the Contingency teams in order to handle the strikes, including the Human resources department and the Director of the Administration department as their fixed members. The strike involves the management of the Department as a temporary member (Grade A strikes are attended by SVP and Grade B strikes are attended by the general manager).

3.4.2. Where the members of the command are unable to take part in the processing of A and B strikes after they have occurred, the authorized officer shall be appointed in lieu of their participation in the headquarters work.

3.4.3. Contingency management headquarters under the contingency teams, designated by the Headquarters team leader, responsible for the implementation of the headquarters decisions.

3.5. Command team responsibility

3.5.1. Assess the grading of strikes according to the report of the production department.

3.5.2. Kick off the plan, form the contingency treatment team, appoint the head of the group.

3.5.3. Arrange the specific division of the contingency response teams.

Make a decision on the question of feedback during the strike.

The grading of strike and the degree of impact determine whether to take the appropriate access to the blockade.

Coordinate the coordination between the contingency teams.

Research, the development of information dissemination, public opinion guidance and other measures.

Resolve other important matters in the course of the disposition of the strike.

3.6. Responsibilities of Production Department

3.6.1. After the strike incident happened, the direct management personnel immediately report to production managers, HR manager.

3.6.2. The Department production manager should contact the administrative department immediately after receiving the report, request to arrange security maintenance in the production workshop in order.

3.6.3. Inform and arrange the management of the Department in the quickest time to the scene, isolate the strike crowd, stabilize the situation.

3.6.4. Identify the cause of the employee's strike and report to the command team.

3.6.5. Strengthen on-site management of other production units to prevent the spread of strikes.

3.6.6. Arrange for the frontline management to protect the power supply, fire protection, important facilities, critical channels, prevent damage, and request security assistance if necessary.

3.6.7. Arrange to take the register on the strikers.

3.6.8. Assess the exit impact of the strikers and arrange for a fill/resume program.

3.6.9. Complete other matters assigned by the Emergency Command Team.

3.7. Department Personnel responsibilities

3.7.1. The Department personnel manager should report the relevant situation to the HR manager immediately after receiving the reports.

3.7.2. Assist production Department to participate on-site maintains production.

3.7.3. Assist the production department to identify the cause of the strike and report it to human resources.

3.7.4. Extracts the personal data of the organization and employees who are actively involved in the strike and confirms the list of other participants.

Participate in HR Emergency team work and assist on-site processing.

After the strike subsided, the event analysis report was prepared for reference by the Human resources department.

Complete other tasks assigned by HR department's contingency response team.

3.8. Responsibilities of Human Resources department

3.8.1. Collect information about the exact number of people on strike, line, etc., and report to command team (for rating and response measures).

3.8.2. The consultation representatives who formed the company party began to consult with the strikers and collect the opinions and requests from the strikers.

3.8.3. Assist Production Department and administration department to isolate the strike crowd and prevent the strike from spreading.

3.8.4. Report on the strike situation to the Labor Department and ask for assistance in dealing with it.

3.8.5. Arrange ER team to go deep into the strikers, gather real information and appease the mood of the strike.

3.8.6. Arrange for labor union to assist the strikers in electing the negotiators.

3.8.7. Arrange legal staff to assess the opinions and requirements of the strikers and the company's response, seek the help of the outside legal counsel when necessary. Make sure the company acts legally.

3.8.8. Prepare the appropriate meal supply according to the command team's meal arrangement during the strike.

3.8.9. Arrange the dormitory management staff to take notice about the dormitory area, found that there are employees in series and other abnormal situation, immediately report to the headquarters.

3.8.10. Arrange the staff turnover procedures for the calculation and payment preparation of the departing staff, at any time according to the instructions to handle the separation of the staff.

3.8.11. Arrange the recruiting team to make the recruiting plan for the vacancy.

3.8.12. To deal with the organizers and active participants in the strike process.

3.8.13. Arrange for the person to collect the information during the strike process in case of any report.

3.8.14. Finish other work assigned by Headquarter.

3.9. Responsibilities of the Administration Department

3.9.1. According to the Production department report, the deployment of security quickly rushed to the scene, isolating the strike crowd.

3.9.2. To strengthen the control of key locations, key facilities and important access routes, in accordance with the arrangements of the Headquarters.

3.9.3. Designate security force support plan, provide security force at any time according to the command's request.

3.9.4. Make the personal security work for the important person of the company.

3.9.5. Arrange other daily security work to prevent other people from stealing or damaging company property.

3.9.6. Arrange external liaison staff to report to relevant government departments, request government intervention, support to solve the strike.

3.9.7. Arrange for the person to be responsible for the scene of the strike video recording, as the basis for processing.

3.9.8. Deploy transport forces to ensure 24-hour demand during the strike.

3.9.9. Responsible for the liaison between the headquarters and the contingency teams during the strike (intercom and loudspeaker are recommended).

3.9.10. Reception of government staff assisting the company in dealing with strikes and providing relevant information as required by government departments.

3.9.11. Finish other work assigned by Headquarter.

3.10. Responsibilities of accounting department

3.10.1. Cash is prepared according to the command team's requirements to ensure that the settlement and other cash requirements are met at any time during the strike.

3.10.2. Arrange manned duty and provide cash payment service.

3.10.3. Finish other work assigned by Headquarter.

3.11. Responsibilities of other departments

3.11.1. Pay close attention to the Department's staff mentality and emotions, immediately report to the headquarters.

3.11.2. To strengthen the management and control of key facilities and important channels in the sector.

3.11.3. Register the employee who is not in normal attendance in the department.

3.11.4. Arrange for the reception of important clients during the strike (try to avoid).

3.11.5. Inform the management of the Department to be on standby and provide support at any time according to command team orders.

3.11.6. The statistics report the frequency and the number of the Department to prepare for the logistical supply during the strike.

3.11.7. Finish other work assigned by Headquarter.

3.12. Cooperation and coordination of various emergency response teams

3.12.1. During the handling of the strike, all departments shall perform their respective duties in accordance with the unified dispatch of the headquarters.

3.12.2. In the course of the strike, if other contingency teams are found not to perform their duties according to the plan, or if there are problems in the process of implementation, they should report to the headquarters immediately and be ordered to correct by the command team.

3.12.3. If the relevant personnel are seriously irresponsible and affect the coordination of the work, the command shall decide whether to suspend the employee's duties and designate the replacement person.

3.13. Prohibited items

3.13.1. No person shall release any relevant information about the strike without the authority of the command team.

3.13.2. No person shall, without the authority of the command team, plan for the collective activities of the strikers in the factory premises, such as commuting, dining, etc.

3.13.3. No person shall make any substantive commitment to the strike personnel without the authority of the command team.

Then we immediately cooperated with the security department to organized a large-scale accident drills;

Purpose of the exercise

1. To protect the personal safety of all staff and the loss of company property, so that all staff workers have a safe and comfortable working environment;

2. Establish a strong security guard team, establish a set of perfect command system, do all kinds of safety prevention work.

3. Prepare and improve the technical prevention facilities, provide the hardware and software and the design and training plan, strengthen the preventive awareness.

4. From this activity to improve the overall staff of the crisis management awareness.

Not only have I experienced the strikes of tens of thousands of people and effectively calmed down, I have also experienced a provocative two employees supported by behind-the-scenes international organizations to call on employees to strike, finally by the company's internal justice-minded employees to take the initiative to stop the incident, the full report was as follows:

March 24, 2013 4:50, a woman named Lou XX (Joined on September 15, 2009), and a male worker named Chen xx (Joined on January 27, 2011), the body hung posters, holding leaflets in hand are constantly plugged it into the hands of employees, posters and leaflets mentioned:

Asked for increase basic salary to be RMB600

(Remark: Grade I employee salary RMB1350+Comprehensive allowance RMB230+Ave performance bonus RMB100=RMB1,680, higher than government min salary RMB1300)

Keep agent labor and contract labor income to be the same, when they have been worked for more than half year, must be transferred to contract labor.

(Remark: Agent labor Vs Temp worker ratio: 64%:36%) Stand to work

(Remark: We already started from the third quarter of 2011, one BU change stand work to sit down work)

Cancelled the time limitation go to washroom

(Remark: Start from Sept in last year we already cancelled the registration of going to WC, openly announce this to the employees, make the following survey after announcement) Develop Management

Reselect the labor union chairman

(Remark: Labor union is voted by public, approved by local government, there were more than 6,000 labor union members)

When the other two employees Chen XX and Quan xx saw their two call to strike immediately run forward to catch them, next to the colleagues at the same time swarmed and hold them down to the ground, at the first time to notify the security, after that resume all production, not impacted.

Afterwards, we immediately convened an emergency meeting:

1. All managers and staff communicate and understand the expectations of employees and let them know the truth and avoid misunderstanding.
2. Prepare emergency contact telephone number to ensure 24 hours of contact at any time of day to strengthen the night shift management.
3. We also print posters and leaflets that are distributed to employees let them know the facts.
4. Inform labor agent companies and security companies to ensure that they are paid on time without deduction.
5. Treat two people with aggressive strikes with humane treatment, provide food and necessary care, communicate directly with them about the information behind them, ask them why they want to do so, at the same time, thanks for stopping another two employees.
6. Inform police and district labor unions, let them conduct investigations and listen to their opinions on how to deal with them more appropriately.

7. The latest news will be the first-time report to the United States Group headquarters.

April 1, 2013, after the last two workers called the strike was immediately stopped by another two workers, we received a few rumors and the words of graffiti in the washroom suspected employees also planned a strike on April 1, we immediately start the following precautions:

We report the situation to the relevant local government departments: including the Enterprise Construction Bureau, the Public Security Bureau (by their further report to the NSA), of course, the first time also reported to the Labor bureau.

We traced what was true to the two employees who had the odd behavior: Eventually the NSA gave us feedback, in fact a total of three employees involved in the incident: two employees of Company J, one is the staff of the cleaning company. They were all instructed by "black-hearted lawyers" and the NSA was still investigating who was behind the scenes.

We immediately launch the internal special working group to train managers on how to communicate with employees, obtain first-hand information, how to respond to emergencies, attach training materials.

HR arranges the 1-and 2-level staff tea talk with the workcells that are strongly related to the incident, while the labor Union arranges for the staff Tea talk of each workcell, we use this communication channel to deliver positive information, while still responding to all the questions about the six points of the last call to the strike.

We restarted the "Monthly staff birthday Party", "45 Beer Festival" on April 1, which was stopped by the financial turmoil in 2008, but we need to recover as soon as possible at this critical moment.

At the same time, the production department in the night to adjust the production arrangements to change the night shift.

We emphasize the management of the Labor Agent company, because two workers came from Labor Agent companies.

Repeatedly review the labor agent company pay wages on time, buy insurance on time.

An anonymous employee questionnaire will be arranged and the results transferred to the Labor Agent company for improvement.

Establish a procurator mechanism to manage the quality of Labor Agent company they give to their employees.

Through the information platform to send more and more positive information, so that the new employees get the company first-hand good news and understand that the company has good benefits: "For example, business insurance and staff-level coverage, a variety of activities, dormitory facilities such as washing machines and air conditioning are also equipped.

The manager of the Office of the day and the functional department to ensure that they can concentrate on the emergency command office in 15-30 minutes. We also confirm with the government that they have enough manpower to maintain safety.

Liaise with vocational secondary schools and labor services companies to ensure that they are able to provide adequate human resources to replace staff when needed

April 5 Ching Ming Festival holiday passed, the company keep peacefully, the company headquarters SVP sent a thank you words: "Folks, see the company's management team set up by the emergency teams to get the results, this result also reflects your excellent emergency management and to take care of the people-oriented leadership awareness." Thank you for your excellent leadership! "

15.How to lay off employee? I experienced to be laid off

"' Hire people ' and ' Fire people ' is the basic skills of HR to be trained," Fire people is the most difficult psychological "Gate" you must pass through: Face the employees who will be dismissed, afraid of but can't afraid of, try to hide but can't hide, an important step you have to go forward. Many HR try to escape this, finally choose to give up, like HR rookie in the American famous film "In the Cloud", because she can't accept the reality of their own dismissal of the employee suicided finally choose to forgive HR career.

If you are determined to go into HR business, suggest you look at this movie, one of the sentences to the HR people are very enlightening: "Dismissal like Buddhism 'release souls from suffering'", if in this "fate" among the party did not fulfill the responsibility, one choose to give up, to both sides it is a difficult decision, HR is to help both parties to have a speedy end, support them to release the burden then go to another shore.

When taking dismissal, put yourself into the employees' shoes, keep empathy, if one day you were him/her, how do you face? I have personally experienced being "fried", to understand deep in the bottom of life, experiencing the life cycle of the feeling. At that moment is both angry and heartache to be, still have to fight for the short pay of compensation, I met the notorious boss in the industry, he is still blaming me for the final confrontation with him, but the only thing I admire in the process is one of my subordinates, she can quietly cross me directly complete the whole set document for dismissal, quietly to finish all formalities with me, this " **pay back in the same coin** " trick, a clear feeling of "slapped on my face" make me thoroughly awake, learned the most essence of "Fire people". **To dismiss, the first HR** need to control your **own emotion, not because of the dismissal of the staff's** intense emotional impact on your **own emotional also over** "keeled", the dismissed employees is your colleagues, this has not changed.

In the last month, a colleague in Hong Kong was cut by the company by paying 3 months' notice, she ask for 1.23 days of annual leave pay during notice period, in three days repeat called Hong Kong HR to consult, Hong Kong HR colleague lost the patience, only ask me for help, the voice of the dismissal of employees is full of anger, blame and distrust, exactly the same situation when I leave company W, as the HR intermediary and as the "executioner" feeling a bit bad. But this does not affect you to do a professional job, I calmly understand the appeal, carefully explained in accordance with the rules and regulations, tell the employees what is to be asked, what should not deserve to be asked, again and again to explain until she clear about it, when heard her deep frustration and disappointment, but have to agree with my explanation, peace and clam is restored.

You have to care about not only the employee's side, but also the boss's side. You have to learn to be the boss and the employee 's balance beam.

Just this month, I dismissed a project manager of Hong Kong computer department, as a project manager, he did not have a thorough understanding of the internal customer's needs and information about the background of the system supplier, chose the wrong system supplier and did not reflect and resolve the project problems when there were many, resulting in a project investment of over HK $1.2 million. It can't be used in the start. According to the terms of the project employment contract, the company gave three months' notice period, but he also repeatedly asked for the project bonus, my boss refused, because it is the employee's mistake caused the company 1.2 million HKD lost. Summarize the experience of failure: as the direct boss of project manager and the company's boss in choosing such an important supplier should "do it yourself", not every time to find a scapegoat, the Employees made mistakes often blame the boss why in the company to deal with employees like " Doing good deeds can't atone for a crime " "disowned" "not soft", in the outside instead donate this donate that to do the philanthropist? That's because the boss has to find a psychological balance. In the company if the boss is always compassionate, he is not running the company but the temple, company must for profit purposes, hire employees are also for benefit earn, not to help the boss to make a profit but doing the wrong thing desired more, whichever company can't accept this. But often the dismissal makes the boss uncomfortable, he is also aware of the dismissal will make the employees lose the job which for surviving, but only this job he can provide and stop at any time.

To safely dismiss employees, understand the background beforehand, "arming" is a key step:

If it is due to shrinking business, it is necessary to make a reduction, let employees know the truth, the company is cut by the reduction of business volume, starting from the top of the company, let employees have a better idea, avoid hasty action, rebound fierce.

Of course, we must pay attention to the impact on customers, to give customers "face" rather than "disgrace", timely report due to orders reduced, to compress the efficiency action plan, let them "regret" on this, together to prevent the excesses from the dismissed employees.

If it is because of the performance of the reasons, we should make good use of 360-degree assessment, issued an evaluation form to the surrounding colleagues to collect feedback, if it is not good where is not good? Let the dismissed employee understand that this is not the boss one-person comment but the surrounding colleagues on his/her presence is not satisfied. If the feedback is good where is good? When the feedback is good, why does the head of department have to dismiss the employee? As HR to understand the reason, do not only listen to department head, fire people can't settle all.

If it is because of the reasons for the violation, can give employees 15 days of investigation and cooling-off period, buy time to transfer staff out of the scene, on the other hand to give each other cool time, in the master of the full written, physical, data, and video recording and other evidence to submit all the evidence to the professional Is there a risk involved in evaluating the operation? On the notice of dismissal, according to which clause of the labor law or company regulations? Why did you dismiss him/her? Each project lists the losses suffered by the company in case the employees sue the company, the two sides well-reasoned to action.

If it is old courtiers or employees of advanced age, to the time of the dismissal, the best solution is " The Removal of Warlords by Drinking " let the boss himself to express enough respect and love to this kind of colleagues, better than HR "take the knife with a gun" in accordance with which section which sentence of the law to dismiss the employee.

Dismissal communication process look like to pronounce the sentence, the process is painful for the employee, so time should not last too long, control within 10 minutes, the words clearly.

It must be the department head to coordinate, fully explain the reasons, as the competent authority to recruit subordinates will have the courage to face him to dismiss him, do not blindly push HR to the cusp, 365 days a year there are 5/7 of the time they have been facing day and night, resulting in this "unbearable" result, a lot of time is the interaction between them, " A slap does not sound "even sometimes is because of the supervisor communication with subordinates in a wrong way, said the subordinate didn't follow his management direction so dismiss the subordinate, but no longer, because this boss communication is not smooth, work can't carry on, this boss was eventually called away by his boss, in dealing with this kind of" Negotiation dismissal "of the incident, usually is the boss and subordinates "Each says he is right".

In the process of communication, HR is responsible for interpreting the law and calculating compensation, withdraw the disputes between the supervisors and subordinates. Many companies have not done so to compensate for their legitimacy; After the company has done this, the upside-down the employees crave more, this is human nature, understand this will be better to deal with the psychology of HR. Like the project manager I mentioned earlier: Michael did a bad job, ask for the company compensate bonus to him. Even with the terms of the two sides verbally agreed to the clause still return to court. Some employees asked to resign, one heard the resignation has no financial compensation, its words said the company forced her to leave the job, similar to the its words of the case, I have seen accustomed not to blame, HR only can protect their own is: All the statements are false, leaving the evidence is the most true, ordinary heart treatment on the fault of the people, people live with their own fault.

Do not sprinkle salt on the wound of the employee who being dismissed! HR must remember this, no matter how shameful his/her behavior is, you must "leave scope"! Because you are likely to face who is a highly aggressive employee, under sudden pressure, will trigger an equally unpredictable rebound, I have personally dealt with an injection molding worker who has just been called into the office from the high-temperature workshop, where he was initially scolded by the slashing, when the supervisor finger point to the employee to say: " You made such a big mistake, I asked HR to fire you on today! " The words once said, the worker was forced to lose the rationale, conveniently picked up next chair with the Iron feet threw to the supervisor, an eyelid of the supervisor ripped off by chair foot, drawing the blood, employees see this situation immediately fled, but finally caught by the policemen, sentenced 13 years imprisoned, Because the head of the supervisor he hurt no longer be able to close his eyes, waiting for him may be one-eyed blindness, he and his subordinates paid a heavy price on the physical and mental.

In dealing with this kind of emotionally aggressive employees, I have deep experience, because I dismissed the employee who hold the gambling in the company, even at the working hours to track employees to collect gambling debts, employees reported this to the police station, police station timid local triad forces and pushed by using the evidence isn't solid and afraid to accept the case, I was instructed by David to expel the employee. I felt like the way Jesus felt at the last supper, knowing that he was being betrayed and being crucified, I still must proceed? The night before, I went home inform the family about the situation and the company decided to act, I told my family, if anything happens to me, you need to know why it caused. Husband comfort me, if he is the underworld boss, will he personally chase gambling debts? It's a little chieftain at best. God knows he is the first post of the underworld, but from the time I invited this company's true "Boss" and the security manager, as well as other department heads enter the conference room, the security manager was trembling with fear, I knew his "weight" then. At that moment I do not know where the courage and brave came to me, I let him sit next to me, not half a meter away, I took out all his work hours do not do work, go everywhere to chase gambling debt video and record time, take out the evidence about the debt to the staff to collect from gambling, ask him if you were the company's boss, Your employees do not make any sense when you go anywhere, so the company decides "there is no obligation to pay for his immediate dismissal." I was afraid he didn't hear clearly, so spoke out a word by a word till the whole sentence speak to him. After listening to my "sentencing" he stood up and rushed out of the office, then he summoned the triad of small gangs, smashed the company's security room, with steel ball ejection Company's external wall glass, so that ask the line people said to me to come to my home "revenge" ... even general manager David advised me to go home to have rest for a few days to avoid the limelight. Do you think I'm not afraid of? I was a human of flesh and blood, but I rejected David's so-called kindness because I knew that if the guy was going to do something, I can't escape, but if he had any personal injury to me, I would never forgive him. I've been through a couple of cases in a similar situation: The husband and wife have been fired at the same time because they use their positions to purchase the materials and the services to company in private channels, earning millions of benefits, I put the anonymous complaint to the group headquarters, assist the Internal audit department to find out the facts and inform them to leave, as the "Company's police" you still have to deal with, in the United States company, you as the HR head, you have to take the lead in dealing with "Felon"

In addition to "Felon", another class of the most difficult to deal with people who have sensitive information in hand, Conney is the Company J handle Customs affairs manager, Steven is CSR(Corporation Social Responsibility) Manager of M Company, they grasped the company sensitive information, for this kind of personnel to deal with rapidly, Leave enough sensibilities, early to move away all the information and make a backup, before announcing the dismissal to inform the computer department to stop mail and access right to the internal system, but the time to inform the computer department is also not too early to avoid the action plan exposed.

Do not expect too much of the job handover of the employee to be dismissed, but to prepare for the damage. Let employees leave as soon as possible rather than procrastinate.

Avoid union involvement, whether it's China or Cambodia I've never seen them offer any help, but in China it's a symbolic way of going through the motions and asking for the Union's approval when dismissing employees.

I've also fired two indirect bosses, Adam & LH inside Company J, why did I have to dismiss them directly? The main reason is that no one dares to touch them. Because they love to say love to write, in the Company J in a broad circle, from CEO down to the car driver, no one does not know, dismiss such key figures, should be called the third difficulty kind to deal with? Such people usually put their management ideas marvelous, as if they don't eat the human food. But they usually have a business without fear, there is nothing to publish a critique speech of the character offended a lot of people, many people is to see in the eyes and hate in the heart, they will not be the early step down but their character also created they will inevitably encounter the consequences of failure, both their boss are in foreign countries, words firmly inform me: "Dismissal, immediately execute!" In the face of money, the ordinary two people advocating the Chinese culture are all forgotten, demand more and more to bargain with me, regardless "face" problem. After the negotiation, we can still make up, call each other "friends", doing HR job like mastering a "magic mirror", can see everyone's real face clearly.

Handling dismissal, "holding the Regiment" is the most difficult situation, but due to time and cross-border communication constraints, forcing you to quickly to clean up, you have to face the transnational law, cross-border law, both sides are not stained, both sides are stained. How to put these twisted knots open is quite difficult and to master the skills, otherwise "Unable to sever when cut, more mess when sorted out, it is parting grief in my gut, A taste I cannot breathe out... I was just trying to figure out that the termination of the contractual relationship for more than 100 Chinese employees working in Cambodia was a full toss-up for months, but in the end I had to clearly point out the direction: regardless of the relationship of the employer and the employee to the contract, the world's disputes are for their own benefit, Dealing with disputes is the choice and balance of interests.

16.After Lay Off, what next?

I've been at a critical juncture in the survival of three companies, now helping Company M to get out of mid-term earnings crisis.

I was most impressed by the fact that I had been working in Company V, which was in 2001, experienced a 1998-year Asia financial storm without any negative impact on the contrary, the company's management, Portentously, ran to United States to acquire the American telecom giant company L, using more than $300 million in cash, lacked of experience in the acquisition and merger of the whole process of, did not consider the talent is the most important asset, did not settle the original company's experts and technical personnel issues, after confirming the acquisition, 300 professionals continued to submit the resignation letter, elite talent in any country including United States were hot, they slightly "show" the resume to other big companies, a lot of competitors immediately showed the olive branch, only three months, hundreds of experts resigned and only left 96 professionals, all the research and development projects and machines were withheld there, the lack of spare parts, resulting in the products can't be shipped out, the whole group of cash flow immediately caused direct impact, even 10 million of RMB wage was the problem and need to collect from here to there, at that time my first feeling was afraid, worried about such a good company would fell down.

At that time, HR must dismiss at least one hundred or two hundred employees per day, the department head even do not know how to explain with the staff about the dismiss reason, the treatment of the employees are dismissed like criminals, directly call the security lead people to the HR office directly, and take away the computer immediately, the employees were dismissed, feel helpless and anger, Only vent their dissatisfaction to HR, one day they do not want to leave the factory immediately, I run to negotiate with them, the leader of a staff pointed to my nose said: "You immediately compensate us N (One months of economic salary compensate each full service year) +1 (one month notice), Otherwise we will sue to the Labor bureau. "N+1? What do you call n+1? 20 years ago, HR was not aware of the compensation for the economic compensation, I just returned from Hong Kong to do HR job, you asked me Hong Kong's labor law I will be very familiar with, the domestic staff was always count to the final working day no more, when I was young and fledgling I answered them categorically: " If you're going to sue, let's company to the end." I said it too rash, afterwards I reviewed myself. Employees, by group appeals to the Arbitration office and the court, a few months in a row, the company can't stop dismiss and the employee keep to raise appeal, HR struggling to deal with the lawsuit, internally still can't stop the pace of dismissal, facing the double pressure, I have a "Everyday live in purgatory" feeling.

We can't patronize the people who were leaving, put emphasis on the impact on those who stay! HR organized a very timely communication and training to senior management:

First, we played a video about the chairman of the group spoke to employees around the world, informing employees

The latest changes in the company, summarizing the financial position of the past year and looking forward to the coming year, tell the whole group of major decisions to restructure.

Telling employees how to deal with the **setbacks of a natural part of life**, identifying the challenges we face, needs to be re-positioned:

For the consumer telephone business, the main measures are to improve the efficiency of operations and reduce unnecessary operating costs;

Consolidate and strengthen the operation of the American market;

Close production and repair lines in Mexico, relocate the production to mainland China-Dongguan plant;

To reduce and save costs from UK mobile Phone Development center;

Merge the Contract Production Service Department and the Multimedia Product Division;

Improves the efficiency of production lines in the Department of Electronic Education products in the mainland and Hong Kong, while also merging the operation of the European market.

The group's turnover increased to HK $1.3 billion by 27.6%, but the first loss to HK $200 million since the establishment of the company in 1976 was mainly due to the acquisition of company L and the lack of critical spare parts resulting in large orders being canceled or delayed.

The company's development relies on technology and innovation, the company still invests 5% of its profit margin for research and development.

Company's future direction and focus on the company's transition period how to increase profits;

Emphasizing that people are the most valuable resource of the company, the Chairman will keep a monthly report to the staff, hoping to hear all the valuable feedback from all employees, if necessary, they can send an email directly to the Chairman of the group.

Finally, they are welcomed to participate in this training & communication;

In the beginning we first asked the students, "there is one thing in the world that is immutable, what is it?" Is change, the constant change is the eternal unchanged."

As a result of the recent transformation of company V, the burden of the staff, the challenges and the instability and other factors, they need to play a new role, take on new responsibilities, can employees handle these?"

"Tell the staff that the typical response to this change is shock, self-protection, retreat, recognition. "Ask the staff to ask themselves how long they are staying at each stage."

To remind this change is inevitable, not a threat, it can be successfully reversed. It is important to have a positive attitude towards management change. We shared, "Who Moved My Cheese?" Fable story. This fable is a relaxed way of dealing with the crisis, perhaps the reader should be able to read the book in just 60 minutes, but its meaning can inspire the reader to face and deal with changes in life and work.

After listening to the story, ask the staff, how do you feel? "To abandon the old cheese and look for the new Cheese "We got the expected result: The managers at the scene agreed.

Then I and the manager repeated the moral of Aesop's fable and encouraged the managers to lead the change together.

-Facing challenges

-Re-change your attitude

-Arming themselves to face change

-Be proactive and take change as an opportunity

We want the staff to use a SWOT chart to analyze the company's current situation:

Strengths: The world's largest manufacturer of electronic education products, in electronic education products accounted for the leading position, cordless phone project has a great potential development capacity, high-tech flexible production manufacturing, pay attention to product development.

Weaknesses: Insufficient resources to reflect the market changes in a timely manner.

Opportunity: The market demand is very big, such as the cordless telephone market demand is big.

Threats: Fierce competition, weak U.S. markets, and Europe.

Through everyone's self-summary, understand that the company can't become "big but not strong", we should be changed from the "Titanic" into a "speedboat": Unified action to improve efficiency;

Appoint the head of the project;

To make a positive response to change in the market;

Identify the future direction of the group: rebuilding the group's values and restoring the likelihood of profitable growth.

Focus:

Focus on the core of business, focus on high-profit products, more attention to market sales.

To indicate a vision:

The future of the company is bright, beautiful, the first loss in 24 years can't represent the future of the Gray, for the company, business opportunities are many, resulting in a decline in profits is only a temporary factor, learn lessons, more focus on market trend.

More importantly, high-quality management and staff efforts, the company must be better than before, more brilliant.

Company V has gone through a painful process of cross-border litigation to recover the substantial loss of the acquirer due to the facts of the malicious concealment, to re-take the track of healthy development. Experienced in the "Ice & Fire two worlds" experience, just know that it is not easy, but also gather valuable experience of HR led the team go out of "purgatory".

Each can be bigger and stronger companies must have experienced a crisis, experienced a large dismissal process of staff, do not think that clear away the people will be the end of everything, dismissal is the final choice, often caused by the injury to the person who left, cause the person who stay empathy by seeing the sequela, if not timely mitigation, will directly affect productivity.

When I joined Company J, it was just slashing staff and reducing employee benefits: Because Company J 's biggest customer: Company N stopped their order overnight, their orders occupied for 60% of the company's total orders! Share price fell 90% from USD35 to less than USD3.

The former HR handled employees' dismissal case inappropriate, he was afraid of facing the employees, causing more than 60 maintenance workers blocked his office in order to claim back the compensation, the marketing department guys raised the complaint on today, on tomorrow hold a joint appeal, the day after, Scold with GM in the mail, if not enough then face to face to scold, still not enough then question me: Why our top 500 company A is doing so? Do you know company B doing this and doing that, why do we don't study, like a knowledgeable old professor in the challenge of the wisdom of pupils? The internal friction was extremely serious and nothing had been solved.

At that time seeing their mail in and out like "Challenge Contest" I claimed down, I even had a feeling of admiration, these BU guys each one is glib, English expression ability better than the foreigner, from a different point of view endless express their own point, each with high-strength and stand apart from each other! I kept silent, I was observing, I want all the wire puller to "jump" out, one does not stay. A full three days did not stop for a small but not too small problem-the company modified shuttle bus lines and prices. After three days I was so angry that came out a "frontal punch"-a short and precise mail to make the problem clear, which is called " Leverage competitor's strength to hit back" The whole company quiet down, GM no longer need to personally "scold" with BU guys, praised me can be "Nova", make me don't know of laughing or weeping.

I haven't "fight to the end" intention with BU guys, because I am such a newcomer, from HR department, which used to be "admit the wrong", they did not put me in the eye, and now incredibly positive response to their "authoritative view" they have always regarded, shocked and do not know how to respond.

Then I thought: It is really a waste of human resources not to use these BU guys, why do not make full use their "eloquence"? They are too leisured, must figure out one way: I suggested three bosses that our branch is now at the juncture of life and death, whether we should focus our energy on the same direction: we come out the idea of our future development strategy: we faced the biggest customer had quit, how to re-open the potential order? How do we filter different customers? How to expand the market to different regions?   This is exactly as one wishes or hopes for the bosses and BU guys, each one heartily poured out numbers of smart ideas, the meeting ended up by we designed one gesture that all our fingers pointing to the same direction implied concerted efforts, turn hostility into friendship, took a big photo. Wire puller are really more than martial arts and high-strength Salesmen, not a year, made Company J back to the original revenue, this is an HR war: to "recruit" enough staff, the previous redundancy on the operational Department like "cut all the trees and no one left" we have to hire back with a short period of three months! But I was happy to be, because I had easily weathered the "crisis" passed away.

Each company has the different crisis, has its reason, Rome isn't built in one day, we often see only the tip of the iceberg, the deeper reason still needs to capture. Company M is one of the most difficult employee relationships I've ever experienced: you ask any employee, would you like to leave the company by getting compensation, more than 90% of the employees will reply to you: I do! None of the top executives in the company has more than 2 years of seniority.

As described in the previous interim results have been red, there must be reason: Annual market shrinkage, product technology is not high, competitive, with twice " daring exploits "-dare to contact with the bank to borrow the first barrel of gold invested on the sweater industry, 17 years ago dared to make a strategic change: The company moved from China to Southeast Asia poor countries, In order to get the "savage growth" opportunity, but the poor countries in Southeast Asia also copied China's large increase in the minimum wage caused by three times the cost of manufacturing, wages rose uncontrolled, but customers stay in the situation of daily price reduction.

I had to go through the third adventure of my life-to help the company get out of trouble and lead the company:

Significantly reduce SG&A costs to be 10% of revenue;

Departments to review departmental budgets and costs, to strictly tighten unnecessary expenditure;

Reduction all employees of one of the final procedures of the Cambodian plant, and strive to minimize the low-season manpower and wages;

To consolidate departmental management, expand the scope of management and reduce the management staff;

Select the talent, released the poisonous talent, reorganized finance, HR, logistics and other key departments.

Adjust the internal work flow, compress the time of shipment, and deal with the inevitable trend of the market demand;

Re-straighten material, transportation, production, shipping process, save the transition time.

Inventory store take, clean inventory, revitalizing the capital funds and materials. Review ERP system on the situation, abandon the flashy suppliers, replaced ERP suppliers familiar with the industry's and mobilize the entire company to focus on the system installation and analysis of the use of functions.

Invest enough manpower and money to concentrate on the innovation of fashion design, process and material selection, focusing on the training and development of employees.

I am the whole project leader assigned by boss, I do not know if I can success or not? But I feel that the effect of the results come out sooner or later, I have confidence on myself

17.International expatriate staff 's caring: All-in-all, sickness and death

I had no time to go to the Singapore boss David's home to find out what 's going on? This remarked a black record in his heart & rankled in his mind. Later, I went to the backward countries to travel, living in the conditions of the company dormitory felt the different standard of accommodation between countries, felt uncomfortable, no door for complaints, because the management Department of expatriate staff accommodation Standard is HR, complaint to our self-department, they feel "You are finding our fault", Faced to the toilet full of stains, covered with dusty mirrors, riddled with window screens, covered with body smelly quilt, two consecutive nights can't fall in sleep, the day is still in the time lag to work. It is understandable that foreign colleagues are "demanding" about accommodation location and standards, so that each one can understand each other's position in the real situation.

HR spend more energy in this area, although the surface seems to be very small, I have to accompany the company GM Everywhere to find a room for more than two months, saw no less than 20 rooms for finally settled down, the company pay more than USD8k cost to let him temporary live in hotel apartment. When there were a large number of foreign colleagues like Company J has more than 100 heads, just concentration or separation of accommodation is a problem, which will lead to the following transportation problems, if foreign employees are allowed to separate accommodation, any dispute they had with individual landlords, HR also need to deal with, HR imitation property management company. I have suggested that companies consider cost-savings of using Asia-Pacific Training Center one four star hotel as accommodation, but the plan has not yet been formally proposed already be one vote rejected by the company's SVP, the company would preferred to spend more than USD34k per month let these employees has individual accommodation do not want concentrate their accommodation-American admired liberty.

Apply for a work visa, it is not simple "to apply": At first HR self-learn how to apply? What have procedures been passed? Which department? What do you apply from the employee's home country? What kind of Visa does the working country apply for? How long will it take? How to renew? The various information should be systematized.

It is necessary to fully reflect the need to recruit foreigners in China for the preparation of visa information for foreigners, because China itself is a large labor force, if it is a basic position, such as engineers and managers themselves in China is already a fairly ordinary position, immigration Management Center has the right to refuse. For applicants from relatively backward countries with border disputes, the Immigration Department can refuse without explanation, one of our Indian colleagues has been subjected to this treatment, the department is forced to consider recruiting other personnel or transferring R&D Dept to Singapore plant.

As such, HR needs to explain clearly to foreign colleagues, so I ask HR who handle foreigner colleagues' issue to conduct training on communication skills, I have experienced a complaint from a Malaysian colleague because she has to apply for a new job visa, the process last for 21 days has not been done, wrote a mail consulted with our colleague Edward, Edward begins with a simple reply to her question: "Did you ask me if the work visa was completed? It is proceeding." The Malaysian colleague immediately flew into a rage to send me a complaint email asked:" Do your subordinates often challenge IQ of internal customers"? I was also confused by her complaint, then looked at my subordinate e-mail at the same time, understood what happened: Edward has not the meaning to challenge the colleague IQ, but simple reading English mail, the colleague thought he is challenging her IQ. This is the misunderstanding caused by the different understanding of communication between people in different countries. In order to reduce misunderstandings, facilitate foreign colleagues to understand the process of processing and adapt to local work, we have specially produced a new guide for foreign colleagues in the manual, which even includes the introduction of local characteristics of the tourist spots.

It is closely related to how the company plans their future development and the company's development strategy to develop standard terms of employment contracts for foreign colleagues.

To use the template of Company J for the introduction of classification:

International Dispatch (IA) – An employee who is dispatched to another country within a fixed period and is willing to return to the place of dispatch at the end of the assignment. IA maintains an employment relationship with the place of dispatch during its residency. IA usually receives additional benefits and allowances during the residency period. English "Expat" (expatriate) is often used to describe IA.

Long-term international dispatch – the dispatch period is usually 1-3 years and is limited to 5 years. Strategic assignments for senior leaders/strategic assignments at the expert level.

Short-term international dispatch-90 days to 1 year for short-term skills transfer/development growth assignments.

Local plus– employees accept local terms and conditions of employment in another country, but additional benefits/allowances are received during the transitional period (typically two years) as part of the interim assistance.

Frequent travelers -employees travel to another country for more than 30 days, but less than 90 days.

International Transfer– permanently accepts the local conditions of employment in another country and will not return to the home country.

All the people who enjoy international dispatching treatment should be able to get performance score more than 3.5 points, the manager or expert level or above, approved by BU-VP and finance director.

Because of this, the group has set up a global talent mobility team to follow up on the contract formulation and management of remuneration and benefits for foreign colleagues.

Because the dispatched employees come from different countries and are dispatched to different countries, we must consider the labor law of the sending country and the working country, tax law, employment law, foreign Exchange Management law and other parties face the impact of the dispatch of staff treatment, drafting the template of employment letter:

Private and Confidential

Date:

Dear XXX,

We are pleased to offer you an assignment as XXX in XXX, China. The effective start date for this assignment will be XXX and is anticipated will last for a period no greater than XXX months. During this assignment you will report to _____, Title. On completion of your assignment COMPANY J will repatriate you from China to the United States.

This letter confirms the mutual understanding between you and COMPANY J regarding the terms of your relocation and foreign assignment in China. In addition, this letter outlines your compensation and benefits for the duration of your assignment.

TOTAL OVERSEAS COMPENSATION

- Base Salary. Your base salary will be the amount of $XXX,000.00 USD per annum payable bi-weekly. Your paychecks will be generated in the United States from a US payroll system for the duration of your assignment.
- Cost of Living Allowance. You will receive a cost of living allowance (COLA) to offset the expense of goods and services in China. The

monthly amount of $XXX.00 will be paid to you in quarterly installments of $XXX.00 at the beginning of the quarter, paid in equivalent local currency. This amount is intended to make up the difference in the cost of living from your home to host location. It is not intended to cover 100% of your host country costs. Your COLA will be reviewed on a quarterly basis and COMPANY J reserves the right to increase or decrease this amount based on the cost of living differentials and exchange rate fluctuations.

Bonus. You will be eligible to participate in the Bonus Plan applicable for your position.

- Tax Equalization Adjustment. COMPANY J shall ensure tax equalization between China and USA. A public accounting firm of COMPANY J's choice will perform tax equalization calculations annually for each calendar year. The resulting tax liability will be paid on your behalf and settled at the end of the tax year. These amounts will be classed as taxable income in the year of payment. COMPANY J will settle any remaining tax liability upon year of return to US.

  If questions, COMPANY J will arrange for you to have a confidential, pre-departure meeting with the public accounting firm, PWC, to discuss your individual tax issues.

- Termination. If your assignment is terminated for reasons other than cause, COMPANY J will cover the cost of airfare for you and your family and the cost to relocate your personal belongings. If you resign during your assignment COMPANY J will not provide repatriation airfare or household goods move back to US.

FOREIGN SERVICE ASSISTANCE PROGRAMS

- Currency Exchange. COMPANY J will cover the cost of bi-weekly currency exchanges. This should be submitted in your regular business expense reports.

- Relocation of Personal and Household Goods. COMPANY J will pay to move your belongings from Florida to Guangzhou. COMPANY J will pay for the reasonable and necessary costs of shipment of normal household goods, the reasonable and necessary costs of shipment of miscellaneous shop, hobby and sports equipment and the reasonable and necessary costs of shipment of books. All other costs shall be excluded those related to shipment of high value items requiring special handling such as boats, jet skis, RVs, rare paintings or rare art pieces. COMPANY J will pay for moving insurance at a rate of $XXX per pound up to $XXX coverage. Any additional insurance will be your responsibility.
- **Relocation.** COMPANY J will cover the cost of leasing some household goods or you may choose to receive a one-time allowance of $_____ net to assist with the purchase of household goods.
- Housing. COMPANY J will cover 100% of the housing costs in China including utilities. This will be arranged locally with HR Department. COMPANY J will not be responsible for any disposition, rental or management of the current home country housing.
- Host Country Transportation COMPANY J will provide transportation or a transportation allowance for the duration of your assignment. This will be arranged locally with the HR Department.
- Home Leave and Vacation. You will be entitled to vacation days in accordance with your home country policy for the duration of the assignment. If you are accompanied by your family COMPANY J will provide 1 home trip per year for you. If you are unaccompanied by your family COMPANY J will provide 1 home trip per quarter for the duration of your assignment. Travel should be planned as far in advance as possible in order to secure the lowest flight prices.

In lieu of home leave, you may choose a travel allowance equivalent to the cost of airfare for you and your family. This allowance will be paid on a monthly basis in your home location and represents a net payment. COMPANY J will gross up and address any respective tax liability due on this payment.

- Emergency Situations. Should an emergency arise while you are on assignment, you will be covered under COMPANY J's International SOS program. Should it become necessary for you to return to the United States due to an emergency COMPANY J will cover the cost of your airfare.
- Language Training. You will be provided with a short Chinese language course.

BENEFIT PROGRAMS

- Group Health and Dental. You and your eligible dependents will be covered under COMPANY J Global benefits for medical insurance while on assignment. For enrollment materials please contact XXX at XXX.
- Short- and long-term Disability. You will be eligible to participate in COMPANY J's Short Term and Long-Term Disability plans and any changes to these plans will be made fully available to you.
- Life and AD&D. You will be eligible to participate in COMPANY J's Life and XXX plans any changes to these plans will be made fully available to you.
- 401(k) and Employee Stock Purchase Plan. You will be eligible to participate in COMPANY J's 401(k) Retirement Savings Plan immediately. You will be eligible to participate in the Employee Stock Purchase Plan per the provisions outlined in your original offer letter.
- Profit Sharing. You will be eligible to participate in the Employee Stock Purchase Plan per the provisions outlined in your original offer letter.

Notwithstanding any other language in this letter, you remain employed by COMPANY J "at will", that is, you or COMPANY J can end your employment at any time for any reason.

After you have reviewed this agreement, please sign the enclosed copy(s) of this letter and return one to XXX and one to XXX. The other copy may be retained for your files.

Very Truly Yours,

XXX

Global Mobility Manager

Acknowledgement

I confirm my agreement to the terms and conditions of my assignment to COMPANY J.

Signed _____ XXX

Date _____

The contract format of each country is similar, making appropriate changes based on the unified version of the group. Of course, there are many details that cannot be counted in the contract, such as the arrangements for the education of the children of foreign colleagues, the company will grant different standards according to the level of subsidy, foreign colleagues to learn the local language subsidy, from the tropical countries sent to the cold or temperate countries of clothing allowance, etc. We refer to the Aon Professional Advisor report format to compare all the benefits in 100 sub-point operations worldwide, we plan for 95% unification, the remaining 5% items can have 80% flexibility of the free grasp, easy to deploy between any two countries, and the other branch exchange comparison.

The so-called 95% unification, the remaining 5% items can have 80% flexibility of the free grasp, for example, 2012 China Social Security Bureau issued a new regulation: Foreign employees also need to buy five (injury, medical, maternity, pension and unemployment), encountered the general objection of foreign employees, because foreign employees also need their own contributions, However, they do not plan to work in China until the age of retirement, so they prefer the company to abandon the implementation of the plan, but **Company J** has always been a law-abiding company, or decided to fully implement insurance for foreign employees, HR ready for a consistent communication plan, is to increase employee benefits at the same time ask employees to insure.

However, as a result of the five risk, 1 months after a Malaysian colleague died in a car accident, the company can help his family claim more than RMB900,000 reparations.

Believe that the handling of employee accidents is unavoidable for HR, but the handling of accidental deaths of foreign employees I believe that there is no one experienced, nobody is willing to experienced, once encounter, handled properly, let everyone know how to deal with it appropriately

It was April 10, 2012 noon, the Malaysian colleague go out to have dining, took unlicensed rental car at the intersection without traffic lights did not cross the road from the right side of another small ordinary bus, two cars collided, resulting in the car's Malaysian colleague special severe craniocerebral trauma, traumatic shock, chest, lungs, ribs, The clavicle was completely damaged, and another Chinese female colleague from the same car was hit by a broken rib, a hepatic fissure ... Two people were immediately sent to the nearest hospital, the hospital informed the company to immediately sign for emergency rescue. At that time, I sign on it with shivery hand, from the operating room to see the colleague's head has been held open in the operation, do not remember how many hours of waiting, see this colleague from the operating room was pushed out of innocence completely without consciousness, head swollen like a watermelon. The attending surgeon made it clear to me that the family had to come to the last of him within 24 hours, or he might not even see the last time. I heard this and immediately came back to the company, on the road received the company's SVP call, I asked him if I should tell his family the truth, because I have been contacted his wife the first time after the incident, poor family still think if it was a liar phone, when the person doing a job in foreigner country, It is unclear what happened for his family and where has he been working" The living is really harsh, "You should tell his family. " SVP immediately instructed. I put the former doctor's speech all recorded to his family heard, the other end of the phone raised the cry of the family members in pain ... The family promised to take the entry visa immediately and catch the fastest flight. We have informed the Malaysian Branch to provide comprehensive assistance.

More than 10 o' clock the next morning. I received his wife and sister at the airport with the director of operations in China, no other male family member was escorted, I reported the latest situation in the car, they told us another misfortune in their family, the colleague's brother was suffering from cancer and was being rescued in Malaysia, The Malaysian colleague himself took his brother's two children to himself so that they could take care of them to grow up, but what happened?! How can the suffering of the world happen at the same time in this family? My heart is sad for them, but only to do try my best to help them. I immediately called all the management and staff of the department to make donations, inform all the group's insured companies, as far as possible to take care of two injured colleagues, but also closely follow up the traffic police investigation results.

Time to the third day, early in the morning, the hospital informed by full rescue ineffective, employees died. I signed the death notice for my family while the poor brother didn't dare to sign it. After his family insisted that the corpse could not be cremated to be shipped back to Malaysia, we immediately assisted in contact with the hospital, the Malaysian Embassy, even the funeral parlor and the airport, the next day to complete all formalities, the staff members of the family on the third day to return home, before leaving they bowed to us with deep thanks, In their opinion, no one HR department has done as well as we do! Indeed, our entire HR department helped them pick up the footage from the company that was in the vicinity of the incident, we called for donations, the first time we helped them to complete all the insurance claims, so that their families were compensated for more than 3 million yuan in full.

We discharged our duty and hope this colleague can rest in heaven.

18.To protect integrity will be more difficulty than complying with integrity?

The following reports are published in Company J Asia Compliance Electronic Journal (2016, second edition)

Expense reimbursement fraud: Eric is Company J's client and he travels to Company J for a project investigation. During the weekend, Company J's staff, Wesley, took Eric and Eric's team to a local KTV entertainment. The reception is a total of six people and consumes about $4,600. Before Eric's trip ended, Wesley also bought a $750 gift to Eric.

Wesley bought the gift and did not take the invoice at the KTV, but received a $7,500 invoice from his friend. After that, Wesley gave the invoices to his subordinates, Lisa, for reimbursement. Lisa filled in the claims with these invoices which Wesley gave to her and is submitted to Wesley for approval. After receiving the reimbursement, Lisa handed over $7,500 in cash to Wesley.

This case involves bribery and expense reimbursement fraud and other acts.

-Conflict of Interest: Three employees (manager level) The partnership invested in the establishment of a company in which three employees each held 1/3 per cent of the company's shares. The company mainly provides the testing equipment and related services required by Company J. For the sake of hiding, the three men used their relatives ' names when they registered the company.

Since then, the three managers have used their powers to make their own company a successful supplier of Company J, have given large quantities of orders to the company without public bidding.

At the same time, the company purchased testing equipment and services, Company J pay more than the market price. Also, several Company J employees who worked under the three managers left their own companies and competed directly with Company J in certain areas of the business. These people use

Company J resources, including Internet, EMAIL, and telephone, to do their private businesses.

Conflicts of interest are the violations of Company J policies.

-Process and policy: a small factory affiliated to Company J expects its business to grow by 50% in the short term. In order to meet the needs of business growth, the company's management decided to expand its plant area within six months. At the same time, the Operation manager of the plant decided to personally take charge of the plant expansion and renovation project to ensure the project completed on time. However, the project didn't go through public tender process, the operations manager selected the supplier without consulting any of the relevant departments. And all communication between the Operation manager and the project supplier is based on mutual trust and verbal communication.

The plant's expansion and renovation project will be completed in about one month and ready to be put into production. However, the project has been exposed to a variety of safety hazards, such as cable connector exposure, safety equipment is missing or improper placement, production license and safety certificate missing. It is estimated that the project has a budget expenditure of about 30%. Due to the lack of project contracts and related supporting documents, the factory finance can't be paid to the project suppliers, resulting in economic disputes between the plant and the supplier.

Violations of Company J business processes and policies may result in loss of the company's business.

The above three cases were under high confidential and were jointly broken by the internal audit department.

In fact, Company J has the integrity policy, each person in the entry must sign:

Code of conduct

COMPANY J 's unique Company culture, centered on having the best people in the world and empowering them to excel, has made us a leader in the diversified manufacturing industry. We have nurtured this culture carefully over the years and I am deeply gratified by the way people from all over the world have readily accepted and worked hard to preserve the unique characteristics of COMPANY J's culture. I would like to remind everyone that an important part of our culture is to conduct our business with the highest regard for integrity and business ethics. As we have grown, we have formalized aspects of our Company culture in training through COMPANY J's Learning and Development Team and the "Rules of the Road". We believe it is equally important for us to formalize our expectations regarding business integrity and ethics and our "COMPANY J Code" will serve this purpose well.

We pride ourselves in being creative, flexible, open and empowering. Our day-to-day business interactions with each other are guided by the COMPANY J "Rules of the Road". You should look to this set of guidelines to have an appreciation for our unique and empowering Company culture. The "Cultural Creed" portion is particularly helpful in this regard. We believe that by minimizing bureaucracy and maximizing control of your own destiny, you will make the best decisions for the business.

In all cases, our business decisions must strive to be in accordance with the highest degree of professional business ethics. We have an obligation to our shareholders, to each other, to conduct business lawfully and with the utmost integrity. Look to COMPANY J Code for guidance in meeting this important obligation. The COMPANY J Code is not a list of "Don't do that." It is simply impossible to envisage all possible business scenarios that might be encountered when drafting a Code such as this, so we expect you to look to this Code as a beginning point for charting the right ethical course to follow. Where the COMPANY J Code is not explicit and you are in doubt, you only need to employ one essential principle: "Do the right thing".

Sincerely,

Mark T. Mondello
Chief Executive Officer

Goals & Expectations

The COMPANY J Code underscores our fundamental values and is intended to help us understand how to make proper and ethical day-to-day business decisions. For the purpose of this Code "employees" should be deemed to include all COMPANY J directors, officers and employees.

The goals of the Code include:

Informing employees of the cultural and behavioral expectations for engaging in proper and ethical business conduct.

Providing guidance for relevant regulations, laws and policies affecting our employee's day-to-day activities.

Facilitating a process for addressing issues and questions involving appropriate business conduct.

Identifying a confidential means for employees to report suspected violations of the law.

Key cultural expectations we hope this Code will facilitate:

Compliance with all applicable regulations, laws and policies governing our business conduct worldwide.

Being honest, fair and trustworthy in conducting all COMPANY J activities.

Being aware of and avoiding conflicts of interest between work and personal affairs.

Sustaining an atmosphere of fair employment practices extending to every member of the COMPANY J workforce.

Helping to ensure a safe workplace and protection of the environment.

Nurturing a culture where ethical conduct is recognized, valued and exemplified by all employees.

COMPANY J is ever-changing. We operate in a dynamic industry and, as a result, every ethical and legal issue simply cannot be anticipated and this Code cannot provide all the answers. It must operate as a guide to help you resolve ethical and legal questions. It should be read and interpreted in a manner consistent with the geographical locations in which we do business. It is our responsibility to use this Code and our common sense when we have questions regarding our behavior or that of others. When all else fails, we must ask for assistance when answering such questions. Most of all, we must always simply "do the right thing".

Business & Expectations

Integrity - A Cornerstone of Who We Are

A cornerstone of the way we do business is clearly our integrity. All interactions with customers, vendors, suppliers, shareholders and fellow employees are to be conducted with the utmost integrity, honesty and mutual respect.

Determination - Our Constant Drive for Excellence

We must continuously strive for excellence. We can never be satisfied with who we are today...even if we are number one. We can, and will, be even better tomorrow.

Empowerment - Our Employees Are Our Most Valued Asset

We will strive to build a team that is empowered, dedicated to self-improvement and professional growth and committed to winning. And we'll have fun while we are doing it. That means we do not tolerate any unnecessary bureaucratic or political behaviors. Simply put, we'll always try to "do the right thing" in how we interact with each other.

Respect - Our Business Partners

Our strategic business partnerships with customers, vendors and suppliers all produce shareholder value. We must nurture and grow these relationships by conducting our daily business in a respectful, honest and competitive manner.

Commitment - Our Shareholders

We are a publicly traded Company. We have a duty to our shareholders to increase the value of their investment and to vigorously safeguard it. We owe it to them to continuously "do the right thing" in each facet of our business. That means we must be at our best not only competitively but ethically as well. We will strive to increase shareholder value each day.

Records

Maintaining Accurate Records

All Company records must be accurate and complete. They are necessary for the proper management of the business, and the law specifically requires it. Records must be maintained with enough detail to accurately reflect the Company's transactions. Financial statements must always be prepared in accordance with generally accepted accounting principles and presented fairly, in all material respects, the financial condition and results of the Company.

Proper records management is an important matter for COMPANY J. The failure to manage records according to the COMPANY J

Records Management Policy and Schedule could have serious business and legal consequences for our Company. Use common sense and observe standards of good taste regarding content and language when creating business

records and other documents that may be retained by COMPANY J or other third parties. This includes e-mail communications. While they are a quick and easy method of communication, e-mails should always be utilized as an important business tool and a professional mode of communication.

The Senior code

An Additional COMPANY J Code for COMPANY J's Principal Executive Officers and Senior Financial Officers

Providing COMPANY J investors with accurate, dependable information is of critical importance to COMPANY J's management team and the COMPANY J

Board of Directors. Ethical practices anchor COMPANY J Management's philosophy for running our business and our Board of Directors is committed to holding itself up to the highest ethical standards. COMPANY J's Management and Board have proactively taken action to comply with Sarbanes-Oxley and NYSE corporate governance requirements including the adoption of an additional COMPANY J Code specific to our Principal Executive Officers and Senior Financial Officers.

Our employees

Equal Opportunity and Diversity

COMPANY J offers equal employment opportunity to qualified individuals without regard to their race, religion, color, national origin, age, gender, citizenship, marital status, disability, sexual orientation or other factors not related to their job performance. We believe the diversity in skills, abilities, experience and backgrounds of our employees is a strength and encourage it in all areas of the company. We encourage and support self-development through individual assistance and the opportunity for professional growth provided by COMPANY J's Learning and Development Team.

Our Work Environment

We encourage a work environment that is free from safety and health hazards, intimidation and harassment, or any other behavior not conducive to productive and excellent work. We must be aware of and abide by all health and safety rules applicable to our jobs.

Personal information of employees will be respected and safeguarded. Access to such records is restricted. COMPANY J will comply with all applicable laws regarding the disclosure of personal information about our employees.

Communicating with Each Other

Employees are encouraged to communicate respectfully, openly and honestly with one another including supervisors and management. COMPANY J respects, encourages and welcomes employee's opinions, attitudes and concerns in our continual effort to be simply the best.

COMPANY J Assets

We have a responsibility to properly use and protect the assets of the Company. Assets can be both tangible (such as buildings, furniture, computer systems and equipment, inventory, tools and funds) as well as intangible (such as trade secrets, work time, marketing and pricing strategies). All electronic information transmitted or contained in the Company's information systems is the property of the Company and should be properly safeguarded and used only for job-related purposes.

Personal Use of COMPANY J Assets

Employees are expected to use common sense when using Company assets to perform routine personal tasks during non-work time such as placing personal telephone calls, faxing, sending personal e-mails and briefly accessing legitimate commercial websites. Access to e-mail and the Internet may be monitored in accordance with applicable law and there is no assurance of privacy. Visiting websites that contain racist, pornographic, gambling or other inappropriate materials is prohibited. Other specific examples of inappropriate use of COMPANY J assets are the personal use of: Company vehicles for non-business reasons; Company tools or equipment; Company paid mail; Company supplies; Company assets for personal gain and long-distance services at Company expense. It is important for each of us to be familiar with, comply with COMPANY J's Information Security & Risk Management Policy as well as COMPANY J's Social Media Policy.

Taking Advantage of Corporate Opportunities

Employees should not take for themselves personally, opportunities that are discovered using COMPANY J property, information or position.

Insider trading

U.S. securities laws, and the laws of most countries in which COMPANY J does business, prohibit trading of any stock or other securities while in possession of inside material, nonpublic information regarding those securities. Insider trading, insider dealing and stock tipping are prohibited at COMPANY J. These are some important definitions that will assist you in understanding the types of activities that are proscribed.

Inside Material Nonpublic Information: any non-public information that a reasonable investor is likely to consider important in making investment decisions. This includes any non-public information that would influence your own decision to buy or sell a company's stock or other securities. Even the appearance of insider trading should be avoided.

Insider Trading or Insider Dealing: Personally, buying or selling stock or other securities of a company while in possession of inside material, nonpublic information about that company.

Stock Tipping: Disclosing inside material, nonpublic information about a company to allow a person to buy or sell stock or other securities of that company based on that information.

Observance of the following will help you to avoid an allegation of insider trading:

Do not buy or sell stock or other securities of a company while you have material, nonpublic information or inside information about that company.

Do not recommend or suggest that anyone else, buy, sell, or retain stock or other securities of any company while you have material, nonpublic information inside information about that company.

Do not disclose material, nonpublic information inside information to others unless they have legitimate business reason to know it and such disclosure is made in compliance with COMPANY J 's Regulation FD Policy.

If the inside information concerns COMPANY J, disclosure is only appropriate if it is necessary for COMPANY J to carry on its business properly, you have taken appropriate steps to prevent misuse of the information.

Consult with COMPANY J Legal if you have any questions.

Please follow this link to read and comply with COMPANY J 's policy on Insider Training.

Global Competition

COMPANY J engages in free and fair competition throughout the world. Most countries have laws ("antitrust" or "competition") that prohibit restraint of trade through such activities as price-fixing, allocating customers or territories and abusing a dominant market position. We must abide by these laws. These laws have been, and continue to be, an important contributor to the free markets in which we operate. Each employee should endeavor to deal fairly with COMPANY J 's customers, suppliers, competitors and other employees. None should take unfair advantage of anyone through manipulation, concealment, abuse of privileged information, misrepresentation of material facts, or any other unfair dealing practice.

Competitors' Information

Any information that COMPANY J distributes must be accurate and objective including information regarding our competitors. No employee should make false or misleading statements about competitors, their products or services. Obtaining information about the competition is an important and accepted practice provided it is accomplished in a proper, legal and ethical manner. There are limits on how such information may be collected, especially confidential information. We must be careful never to cross the line of impropriety when seeking competitor information. It is clearly improper to knowingly acquire confidential competitive information through misrepresentation, deceit or false pretense.

Conflict of interest

COMPANY J recognizes and respects that employees may take part in legitimate financial, business and other activities outside of their jobs. However, those activities must always be lawful and free of conflicts with respect to our responsibilities as COMPANY J employees. We must never misuse COMPANY J resources, influence and assets or otherwise discredit COMPANY J's good name and reputation. A "conflict of interest" occurs when an individual's private interest interferes in any way with the interest of COMPANY J.

Avoiding Conflict:

Disclose to your immediate supervisor any outside activities, financial interests or relationships that may present a conflict of interest or even appearance of a conflict. Exercise good judgment in all personal and business dealings.

Never misuse COMPANY J resources or assets by using them for other than a legitimate COMPANY J business purpose.

Obtain management approval before accepting any position as an officer, director, consultant or employee of any outside business concern.

Never compete with COMPANY J.

Red Flags Signaling Possible Conflicts of Interest

Holding a financial interest in a company that does business with or that could otherwise affect COMPANY J's business.

Taking a job that may interfere with your job at COMPANY J or tempt you to use COMPANY J working hours or equipment to carry out that job.

Misusing COMPANY J resources or influence to promote or assist an outside business.

Conducting business with, or employing, a spouse, relative, or close friend.

Gifts and Entertainment

In certain circumstances, the offer and receipt of gifts and entertainment are an accepted practice to establish and foster valuable business relationships. Gifts and entertainment are broadly defined to include physical things; such as events, trips, services, benefits and anything else of value. Inexpensive business gifts as well as routine entertainment functions and business meals will not generally violate this policy if they are appropriate for the circumstances and do not create an appearance of impropriety. We must always be vigilant to exercise good judgment in this practice. All gifts and entertainment must comply with COMPANY J's Foreign Corrupt Practices Act, UK Bribery Act and Anti-Corruption Policy and Global Travel & Entertainment Policy.

Intellectual property

One of COMPANY J's most valuable assets is our intellectual property. This includes our patents, trademarks, copyrights, trade secrets, and other confidential information. It is our legal and ethical duty to protect not only our intellectual property but the intellectual property of our customers, suppliers and other companies with whom we do business.

Safeguarding Intellectual Properties

Identify and distinguish between COMPANY J's intellectual property and that of others with whom we do business.

Protect it with appropriate documents such as nondisclosure and confidentiality agreements. When appropriate clearly mark items as proprietary and confidential.

Do not duplicate, install or use software in violation of COMPANY J policies, copyrights, trademarks or applicable license terms. This includes software installed on your computer or on network areas.

Do not allow outside parties to use the COMPANY J logo or trademarks unless authorized by COMPANY J Communications Department.

Do not improperly share any of COMPANY J's sensitive, confidential or proprietary information with others. Be aware of the appropriate scope of the information to be disclosed and protect it with an approved non-disclosure agreement and by marking it as confidential and proprietary. If you require assistance first contact your supervisor or COMPANY J Legal, if necessary.

International Business

COMPANY J conducts business in many different countries and is committed to following the laws and regulations in effect wherever we do business. All transactions must be conducted in accordance with applicable laws.

Such Anti-Corruption laws include the United States Foreign Corrupt Practices Act ("FCPA") and the UK Bribery Act ("Act"), which prohibit the payment or offering of anything of value to government officials for the purpose of securing or maintaining a business advantage. In addition, the Act makes it a crime to give or offer anything of value to any person (public or private) as well as to receive anything of value from such parties in order to secure or gain a business advantage. The FCPA and Act also require the Company to maintain accurate financial records and adequate internal financial controls. Each employee must be alert to the potential for improper payments, including inappropriate gifts. All gifts and entertainment must comply with COMPANY J's Foreign Corrupt Practices Act, UK Bribery Act and Anti-Corruption Policy for explanations, processes and examples of the applicability of these requirements with COMPANY J business activities.

COMPANY J will not participate in any boycott not sanctioned by the United States or the United Nations, nor provide information that could be construed to further unsanctioned boycotts.

Waives

Only the Board of Directors, or a designated committee of independent directors, may grant waivers from the provisions of this Code involving an executive officer, financial executive or director. Granting of any such waiver shall be promptly disclosed to shareholders and otherwise disclosed as required by law. Any other employee may request a Code waiver from his or her immediate supervisor, and such waivers shall only be acquired with the advance approval of COMPANY J's General Counsel. In general, the granting of waivers is discouraged.

Enforcement

Abiding by the COMPANY J Code

Our employees are not only encouraged, but have a responsibility, to bring violations or suspected violations of the COMPANY J Code to an appropriate party. You may report such violations to your supervisor, Human Resources, Internal Audit or COMPANY J Legal.

Suspected legal and other wrongdoing may also be reported via the COMPANY J Integrity Hotline. Visit the COMPANY J Integrity Hotline page for more information.

Employees who report wrongdoing in good faith will not suffer punishment or retaliation. However, any attempt to misuse the COMPANY J Integrity Hotline or the provisions of this Code to wrongfully and intentionally harm a person by making false accusations or engaging in other improper conduct will result in disciplinary action, including possible termination of employment.

Integrity hotline

Reporting Suspected Wrongdoing: The COMPANY J Integrity Hotline

COMPANY J does business honestly and with integrity. We need the help of all our employees to maintain the highest level of integrity. If you learn of any suspected wrongdoing, please report it to the Company, either by speaking to a supervisor or by using the COMPANY J Integrity Hotline.

Any COMPANY J employee may use the COMPANY J Integrity Hotline to anonymously report any suspected wrongdoing, including such things as:

Theft of COMPANY J assets

Unlawful or improper accounting practices

Unlawful or improper performance of a U.S. government contract

An operator, employed by a company other than COMPANY J, will answer your call, take the information you have to offer and forward a report for appropriate follow-up and investigation.

Any attempt to misuse the Ethics and Compliance Program to intentionally harm a person through false accusations or other wrongful conduct is prohibited.

However, honest reports made in good faith will be taken seriously and dealt with appropriately.

The following options are available for anonymously reporting any wrongdoings:

Telephone number within the U.S.:

1-877-217-6328

Outside the U.S., the telephone number is posted at your facility. Operators are available 24 hours per day, in any language.

You can also anonymously report your concerns using a web form: www.COMPANY JHotline.ethicspoint.com

Regulation FD

Fair Disclosure

COMPANY J is committed to the timely and fair disclosure of information about the Company without advantage to any analyst or investor, consistent with the U.S. Securities and Exchange Commission's Fair Disclosure Regulation (also known as "Regulation FD"). COMPANY J believes it is in the Company's best interest to maintain a current, active and open dialogue with investors regarding the Company's historical performance and prospects.

To help ensure we meet these objectives we have implemented a detailed policy specifying not only who may make such disclosures on behalf of the Company but also in what particular manner they shall be made. It is generally the Company's policy that only those specifically authorized Company officers trained in the details of this policy shall be permitted to release information about the Company to the public.

Please follow this link to read and comply with COMPANY J's Regulation FD Policy.

I, _____	(Employee printed

name), have read and understand the COMPANY J Code and further agree to follow the COMPANY J Code as spelled out in this Policy.

SIGNATURE AUTHORIZATION

Employee Printed Name:	
Employee Signature:	
	Date:

One of the cultural tenets of Company J: "We will not dismiss an employee for his unintentional mistakes, but we will relieve him of his employment when the employee conceals the error."

The company has policies to prevent nepotism:

Nepotism Guideline for Asia – MAY 2010

PURPOSE

To establish a guideline to promote objective judgement and a motivated workforce in the absence of conflict of interests and perceptions of favoritism in the workplace.

SCOPE

This procedure is applicable to all employees in Asia

APPROVAL

Changes or deviation of the procedure may be made upon prior approval from the Human Resources Director – Asia

DEFINITION

Nepotism - describes a work-related situation where there is a potential for favoritism granted to relatives, without regard to their merit.

Relative - includes spouse, children (natural, adopted or legal guardianship), parent, sibling, grandparent, aunt, uncle, corresponding 'in-law' and 'step' relation.

Chain of command – the formal line of authority, communication, and responsibility within an organization which identifies the superior and subordinate relationship.

REFERENCE

Not applicable

RESPONSIBILITY

It is the responsibility of all managers to ensure that their employees are aware and in compliance to this guideline.

PROCESS FLOW

Not applicable

. GUIDELINES

8.1 COMPANY J will always hire employees based on the employee's experience, skills and merit and will promote equal opportunity to all employees. However, there may be circumstances where business necessity may require certain actions to avoid business related conflicts of interest or a potential issue of favoritism.

8.2 The following guidelines will be observed in the event of employing or placement of relatives of current COMPANY J employees:

8.2.1 Relatives are permitted to work in the same department provided there is no direct reporting or no supervisor to subordinate relationship exists. There should be a gap of at least 2 levels of reporting in between the 2 relatives within the same chain of command. For example, Relative A reports to Supervisor 1 who reports to Supervisor 2 who reports to Relative A1.

8.2.2 Related employees shall have no influence over the wages, benefits, career progress and other terms and conditions of the other related staff members

8.2.3 Employee who marry while employed, or become part of the same household are treated in accordance with these guidelines. If in the opinion of the management, a conflict could arise as a result of the relationship, one of the employees may be transferred at the earliest practicable time.

8.2.4 In the event that the relative relationship is established, the Management reserves the right to make any transfer decision. Management will consult with the employees and the final decision made is the prerogative of the Management.

8.3 It is the responsibility of the employee to raise any potential issues due to changes in personal status, reassignment or hiring which conflicts with this guideline, to his/her immediate supervisor and HR Manager.

8.4 It is the responsibility of the HR Manager to investigate any reports of nepotism or areas of potential conflict and to take the appropriate actions.

8.5 Any exceptions to the guideline must be approved by the Regional HR Director and the Functional Vice President.

9.0: RECORD RETENTION

Not applicable

The company has the policy for Grievance handling.

Policy/Procedures			
Policy No. 11-HR10-0GEN-006-A	Rev:	Page: Page 1 of 3	Effective Date January 1, 2003
Subject: Grievance Procedure			Approved By
Issued by Michael NXXX			GXXX Ong

Policy Statement

Purpose

To resolve employee concerns fairly and efficiently, to enhance management-employee communication as well as to improve teamwork, cooperation, and relationship.

Scope

This Policy is applicable to COMPANY J

Approval

Revision to be made with prior approval from Human Resources Manager and final approval by Managing Director.

DEFINATIONS

Nil

REFERENCE

Nil

Responsibility

The Company expects that each employee shall be given fair and honest treatment in all aspects of his or her employment. Supervisors and managers shall treat each employee with respect, shall not demonstrate personal prejudice, or grant unfair advantage to one employee over another.

Each employee may express his/her views concerning Company policies and practices to management with grievance form (see attachment). Each employee is responsible, however, for expressing those views in a fair, honest and non-abusive manner. Every employee should be committed to make positive and constructive criticism.

Each employee is responsible for following Company rules of conduct, policies, and practices. Should an employee disagree with a Company policy or practice, the employee should express his or her disagreement through the Company's grievance procedure. However, an employee is expected to comply with the disputed policy or practice until the disagreement is resolved or the policy or practice is changed.

No employee shall be penalized, formally or informally, for voicing a disagreement with the company or using the grievance procedure.

Every complaint, question, problem or suggestion with grievance form (see attachment) shall be considered and answered as quickly as possible. The employee should be informed that the Company is dedicated to working with him/her to make a fair, honest, prompt, and objective determination regarding the problem, complaint, or suggestion. It is the employee's responsibility to give the Company's grievance procedure an opportunity to resolve the situation. HR department shall be available to advise the concerned employee about how the procedure works.

HR department shall advise Company management at each level regarding interpreting policies and procedures, preventing unnecessary delays, and opening avenues to resolve problems between the employee and management.

Attachment

Nil

Procedures

Each employee shall follow these steps to express and resolve problems, concerns, and disagreements:

Presentation to Immediate Supervisor: First, the employee should discuss the issue with the immediate supervisor. This should be done privately, or with a representative of the Human Resources Department present. The supervisor shall try to resolve the situation as quickly as possible. The supervisor shall decide based on the facts, Company policy and a discussion with the Human Resources Department. If the supervisor cannot resolve the problem to the employee's satisfaction, the supervisor should invite the employee to refer to the Functional Manager.

Presentation to Functional Manager/HR Manager. If the problem concerns the employee's immediate supervisor, the employee should go directly to the Functional Manager/HR Manager and meet privately. The Functional Manager/HR Manager shall investigate the employee's problem, gather all relevant facts and opinions, and respond within a time frame. If additional time is required, the employee shall be notified of the delay and be given an accurate indication of when an answer will be forthcoming.

Presentation to Managing Director. If an employee is not satisfied with the Functional Manager/HR Manager's response, the employee may discuss the problem with Managing Director. The Managing Director will help the employee present the problem to the Functional Manager and the Managing Director shall discuss Company policy and practice, any legal aspects of the employee's concern with the HR Manager. Together, they will determine an appropriate and final response to the employee's problem.

Attachment

Grievance form

The company has 24 hours of integrity hotline, usually received complaints will be sent to HR for the first time to do investigation and response, HR department must complete the preliminary investigation and report the results within one months. The group records the complaints and cases of the factories through the system.

The company regularly organizes "anti-corruption prevention and bribery training", the headquarters of the legal department organize the training, managers or above must attend and take the registration.

However, "The upper beam is not right, the next beam crooked, these malpractice, corruption bribery cases, in fact, the upper layer of greed than the lower level much more.

I often deal with the behavior of staff violations, repeat reinforced the department head:

HR do not want the employee to make mistakes, we do not want to dig a "pit" for staff drilling!

诚信热线

▢ 诚信经营。我们需要所有员工通力协作，才能维持最高水准的诚信。如果您知悉任何涉嫌不法行为，请直接通过主管或通过▢诚信热线向公司进行举报。

▢员工及他人均可通过▢诚信热线匿名举报以下问题：

- 偷盗捷普财产
- 回扣和贿赂
- 非法或不当会计行为
- 违法或不当履行政府合同

届时会有一位外部公司 (EthicsPoint) 聘请的调查员接听您的电话、记录您所提供的信息并转发举报内容以进行适当的跟进和调查。▢严禁主管或员工对通过此流程举报信息者采取打击报复行为；当然，您也可以匿名举报。

举报热线：4▢
每日 24 小时接线员恭候
提供翻译服务

您还可以通过 以下网址举报问题：
www.▢.ethicspoint.com

12/2013

WHERE PASSION MEETS PERFORMANCE

Don't think HR departments have much pleasure in taking these "good and evil" actions. HR to take the investigate is often taking a risk of life. We are the company police, but not armed, relying on the company's manuals and systems, silver tongue and "fair to everyone" mentality.

Department head should fully cooperate with HR to carry out work, "Is that is, not is not", can't be biased to help and the idea of shielding, this is actually not easy, I have been tangled in whether to dismiss a subordinate, because she made a false claim for more than 900 yuan of job allowance, I found out, she confessed, return money back to the company, When the group's HR SVP talked to me about whether give her a demerit or to dismiss sentencing, he asked me, "If you can lenient to the HR guys, how do you make other irregularities?" "I had no words at the time.

Afterwards, I open to communicate with the subordinate: "I feel that I am going to fire you now, just like I am taking the blame, I am willing to help you find the next job, but I hope you learn from this painful lesson, do not let the next person disappointed." She left peacefully, though it was her first job after graduating from college and had hard work for six years.

HR in dealing with these cases but look down by the management level, some even think is this the management problem of HR?

When the employee has the behavior violation, has the department management layer jumps out to question; Why don't your HR stand up and deal with these actions?" At this moment, I would not hesitate to refute: "What is your department's supervisor doing?" I learned this from Mr. Sheetoh, he once listened to my report on staff disciplinary irregularities, he is not to question why a worker can play video games and sleep on the line, but turned around to ask the production manager, how much has the average OT for workers? The department manager replied, he told him that you would start to lower the worker's overtime limit by 10 hours next month, because the employees are using working hours playing the game, and your supervisor did not arrange the work, the next punishment was the department head.

It is the iron law that catches and rings.

Because of connivance, the employee cheat OT situation more and more fierce in Company J, because employees regard OT as their earned income, when seeing the others took more overtime, they can't take less, even if not work but to cheat overtime to get a little money.

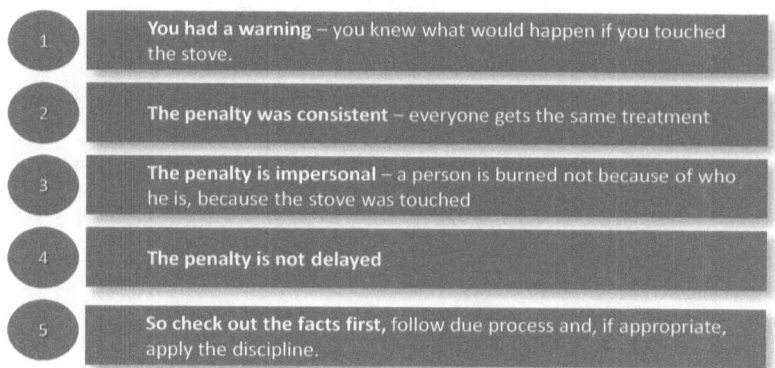

EICC audit will not pass and the labor costs will be uncontrolled, so the boss personally instructed: "For nothing, cheat overtime equivalent to stealing, the company has not used your labor, you have to cheat money, form with theft, must be dismissed, no excuse."

After this, according to my preliminary statistics, the dismissal of more than 50 employees are due to cheat overtime, but employees are still cheating, HR is still speculation, the most heinous is that we received a complaint all the way to the production manager one couple heads, in the possession of sufficient evidence after the same dismissal not excuse, and their list in the system is All Black, Can never re-enter the factory, I received a number of non-compliance staff sent a letter to my WeChat, said pitiful, even sent to me about his 80-year-old parents and three-year-old daughter photos, I express sympathy but resolutely rebuffed. Later developed into an investigation into the equation, a complaint security group on the joint Attendance Unit, the Legal group to check attendance and video, never miss. Even the customs connections in our company, the same was expelled, the other side relied on a strong background, the company sued the court, indeed to uphold the integrity "than" Keep good faith "is still difficult, but the law is still to maintain equality for all, we won the final.

Including myself is quite difficult to refuse this kind of interest temptation, because I am also a person, I received a variety of gifts, I all rejected, the group has been on the use of labor agent and headhunting company has been repeatedly reviewed, I mostly welcome, because The wise man knows he knows nothing, the fool thinks he knows all, I always been a blank, no stain.

I do not accept, also deal with other people to return the bribery, one of the cases let me open my eyes: The company's senior material manager responsible for the company's procurement, logistics, warehousing, and customs clearance management, a considerable number of services are used outsourcing, once he and the supplier went out to eat a potluck, parting, the supplier gave him two cans , the manager repeatedly declined but the supplier insisted on the small gift to his child, so he took it, after return to the home to open the milk jar, only to find that the full hidden RMB150,001 stacks of RMB! This senior manager was panic, first, he was unwilling to go to jail for bribery; Second, he did not want to offend the supplier, because their background are strong; So he found the boss at the first time, I would "take the risk to save the other", I accompanied the manager and the boss met the supplier, told him: "We are doing business in the local, won't be violated the company rules." Then RMB150,000 is wrapped and returned intact.

Finally, I would like to say: if I can choose, I really do not want to deal with these "broken things", I have to face open gambling and the underworld boss and clean him out of the factory because he went to the factory to open a gambling debt, I have to run to the police station to face hands and feet to wear the chain of subordinates, his wife kneeling on the ground to plead and create the dilemma scene to me, I used to released hundreds of illegal employees to clean up factory, broken their rice bowl, all and all, experienced life and death, spirit and desire of the fight, mental and energy expenditure, Is it hard to keep integrity or to maintain integrity?

19.Did provide the old bed with the worm to employees to sleep?

"Did we provide the old bed with worm to the employees to sleep?" This is the question I asked the boss, the problem was a bit direct and embarrassing, until now I keep the photos, these photos I directly sent to the company vice president, let her knew how did her subordinates manage the dormitory? How did they treat the employees?

I lived in 10 squares room putting 3 bunk bed slept 6 persons, when have been working in the Hong Kong company, live in rent dormitory limited space, in two years, a 90 square meters room lives in 12 colleague, The difficulty is for eating and drinking you can imagine, among them have the reason to have the dispute, but also has the joy in this six peoples' room, I was the last to join, looking at the hatred in the eyes in a house, hug myself finally can work in Hong Kong in the early 90s, the excitement to learn advanced management methods and work way was dismissed totally, I lower my head without a word go to the bedside lying down, For three consecutive nights I couldn't sleep at all, the crowd in the room and the transportation noise outside the window, I asked myself why I had to come to Hong Kong from my comfort home? To the fourth night I was tired, a sleep until dawn, people are the survival of the fittest.

There is no table in the room and there is no place to eat, we will use big paper box put luggage bags into it, do not worry about where did put the box. No shelves to put books and sundry on our own hands at the end of the bed set up a wooden shelf. Roommates are good comrades love to learn, each ear stuffed with headphones to listen to the English and Cantonese anyway, who can't quarrel with anyone ...., in order to release mom and dad worrying, I asked the roommate took one photo for me and said I lived very well, but my sister knew what I said wasn't true: because the photo focal length is too close to, the room area must be poor, how to compare the house with more than 100 square meters in the home only live in three people? If you know what I said isn't true, tell my family it's time for growing!

Inspected the dormitory just been to Company J, it is the most annoyed that nearly half of 2000 rooms are leaking, called the house keeper to understand the situation, they show me the plastic pipe on the wall, it can be broken lightly, I try by myself: Oh my god! Even if my woman's hand can easily crush it, such a Jerry-Built Project, how can't leak?!

Seeing employees sleeping under a wall dripping with water, I was sad want to cry, because my family was poor in my childhood, no money to repair the house, a rainy day, under the rain outside the room, under the rain inside the room also, in the house we had to use plastic bags to pull up the tent, only place to sleep is under the plastic bags, the whole night listen to the "tick" of the leaky rain, that feeling unbearable ... The time passed 40 years, in this big multinational company, with all day shouting "People-oriented", do we really care about employees? Do you have a look at how well the employees live in? Why are we making this kind of Jerry-Built Project when we are shouting "Quality is the first" for the whole day?

I felt it is unfair, looking for the Facility Department Jimmy, asked him claim back the company lost from the builders, he played the trick to me, advertised in the year by using 18 months built up these 7-storey dormitory, quality problems are unavoidable. I could not help but take advantage of Senior Vice President 's visit time to raise the problem, the company must grant USD190k to fully renovate all leaky rooms.

At that time, I received the Japanese branch HR manager visiting, he told me that the Chinese factory dormitory was look like Japanese factory 60s' living standard, a full lag of half a century! Hear this statement, national sense is coming from the bottom of my heart, No! I want to do a good job in China, compete with the Japanese "Radish" Factory!

This is more than 2000 rooms, more than 9,000 people "home", I request to convene a monthly dormitory communication conference, set goals: "Staff can tell the problem, we can solve it!" "I asked the dorm supervisor to go to the dormitory to live with the workers and the general staff, so he knew how to improve it.

Dormitory experienced 10 years of wind and frost, "the exterior wall looks like the old newspaper", we want each house to re-trap and paint, the cost for each house is USD30k to USD40k, we budget it then one floor by one floor to do renovation.

Each floor of the aisle wall paint into a different color, seven floors just like the seven colors of the rainbow.

We are on the first floor of the dormitory painting, each department has its own unique location, has its own theme, the company unified to the exterior wall paint, all departments of staff all "bouncing off" "to dictate" how to paint on the wall, that kind of enthusiasm and "rejuvenation" you can't imagine, and then by the staff vote for the winner, Bonuses are not much, but the dorm is decorated with colorful, lively.

Later this activity extends to each floor set a theme, employees take the elevator to each floor, elevator door open, see the walls are full of pleasing theme painting and encouragement of famous sayings, every day employees see these, to keep comfortable & happy feeling.

A big garden with green grass but no flowers "one day a subordinate of mine walked through the garden with me and said, I thought, how didn't I notice? We immediately instructed to plant the colorful flowers, varieties of flowers we took from the mountain seed harvest back, do not spend a penny.

We also put a part of the garden private plots, contracted to all departments to grow fruits and vegetables, each department also give their own private plots renamed, what " Emulating Da zhai for Agriculture " "QA experimental plot" "Two acres of land" and interesting names broke out. In order to facilitate staff fitness at the same time and save costs, from the outside auction back to the closed fitness center equipment, low-cost in the dormitory to establish a high standard of fitness center.

There is library, video game Center, audio-visual room and training center in the Wellness Centre. It's right next to the dorm.

The development zone Government also built a community center in the dormitory to organize counseling and training activities.

In the dormitory, there is a gazebo with the barbecue yard.

Indoor 16 World-class badminton courts.

Outdoor provided basketball court, volleyball court, outdoor fitness center, every month there are different theme competitions.

Do our endeavor to design signs, lamps and lights of Dormitory, colorful lamp hanging in mango tree planted in the dormitory, feel charming.

The company organizes Mango Festival every year, in the ripe of mango, all departments use all the equipment what can be used, lift the bridge, looks like the monkey to take the moon from the water, vow to take the mango off from the whole plant 156 mango trees.

The dormitory installs the radio station, the daily broadcast the factory news, the staff song program, let the staff live in the melodious music.

Staff counseling room, infirmary, supermarket, bank, post office, etc. everything. Below the dorm is the garage where employees can apply for free parking by priority.

Staff Dormitory close to the highway noisy night can't sleep, we put on soundproof glass

To the dormitory equipped with washing machines, dryers, the company is responsible for cleaning. Each floor of the TV room and the soup room hang the staff's photographic work, decorated beautifully.

Raw termites, a lot of room bathroom wooden door wooden closet was rotten, we are looking for a variety of durable and easy to clean alternative products in the market, first test then replace by batch.

There's a contradiction between roommates. We will immediately arrange to transfer, often organize networking activities to integrate the relationship between employees.

In order to facilitate the movement between the plant and the plant, to avoid accidents, the company provided transportation support, and repeatedly consult with government to build bridges between the factory and the plant.

Because the local hotel accommodation is expensive, so the company vacated the room allow staff family to use during the visiting, 3 stars grade decoration standards, a 15-day period of use, the double charge of expiration.

The health and energy use ratings are assessed on a quarterly basis, and prizes are awarded for each floor.

Dormitory 5S Improvement Column: Publication of monthly dormitory renovation records: How much is the wall painted? How much has the leaky room been renovated? How many doors have you painted? How much is the hand-washing tray and toilet squat replaced?

You might think it would be nice to see this, the company is willing to spend money, but what do we spend more on the basic accommodation needs? We are more focused on facility management and update protection and more on feedback from our employees, but there are two items that we always insist on:

Insist on energy saving

Specify for each room and even each person's specific daily water consumption, the best and worst monthly use record of the room, for the worst to be done beyond the cordon of the staff issued a written warning, and by the direct department head personally issued. A reminder that if this occurs for the second month in a row, all usage charges will be charged at cost price.

The collaboration with Facility department installed solar water heaters on the roofs of all dormitories, and the project saved electricity costs in just two years to recoup all the investment. After that, the heating electricity is free. The scheme has been extended to other branches in China.

1.3. The collaboration with Facility dept in the plant-wide developed energy monitoring, at any time from the computer screen to find out which area of the water consumption of the point of loss control problems, because we find out water watering more than two times, to find out which floor water pipe leakage take immediate repair. The scientific monitoring system was also written to their CSR annual report by Customer HP promotion.

We always adhere to the employees clean up their room, employees of private space and privacy can't be violated.

In the Company V administrative department clean up the dormitory room, the dorm keeper followed the employee and sweep the seeds who ate melon spit seeds on the group. But in the Company J will not, the team leader set an example in the dormitory to do 5S: fold quilt, divided into the season color hanging clothes, toothpaste toothbrush put the position, the direction of shoes, all made planning, filming video, wrote quarters 5S song, share with staff to see, the team leader personally bring employees visit their dormitory and share 5S experience. The housekeeper has the key to the public space, but does not have the key of the staff room, to repair and to do the hygiene, the door must be knocked out before entering the room. This should be unacceptable in other companies.

The last place to test Dormitory management skill: early planning, reasonable arrangements for bed resources.

Manufacturing orders are often up and down, no people? Can hire back, but the dormitory is not commanded then build it up immediately, no dorm? Can search from everywhere, expensive? Cheap facilities shabby, in foreign market customer audit accommodation standards with reference national standards, auditors take the ruler to measure the size of the room and bed sizes. The amount of orders came down, more people? Can be immediately streamlined, but the dormitory is fixed assets can't move.

Another problem is that the proportion of male and female employees is asymmetrical and recruitment cannot be gender-discriminatory, but dorms are divided between men and women. So it adds a lot of difficulty to the split floor. The dorm space is not enough, the company will give subsidies to encourage employees to go out to stay, put too much to take back is a painful thing, in Company E monthly subsidy is nearly 800,000 yuan, the financial turmoil needs to be recovered overnight, employees were dissatisfied. Summing up the experience, allow outside accommodation according to the occupancy rate of over 80%, in the decline occupancy rate encouraged return to dorm, allow the welfare of the outside to play the role of the reservoir.

The system of dormitory housing is made by HR, which is the operation of most companies. In order to save resources for scientific allocation, we have used a disabled staff dedicated to the dormitory to write a set of IT program for dormitory room assignment, the same difficult like hotel assignment, may be more complex than the hotel room, because the hotel does not have the taboo of male and female partition.

Large Dormitory management we want to borrow the idea of property management and hotel administration, so I asked the dormitory supervisor to learn the theory of the two management methods, after that the company take over four-star hotel management in the economic development zone, although they are just a group of ordinary dorm keepers.

20. The headache canteen management can be HR awarded score

Canteen business must introduce competition mechanism, tens of thousands of companies only allow exclusive canteen in operation, sooner or later there will be problems. In Company E and Hong Kong's famous xxx fast food company, put millions of yuan to purchase dishwasher washing machine, invited German experts to develop a complete set of food safety monitoring system, the end of the staff did not enjoy the real benefits: meat per meal not more than 10G (two tablets), so that the whole plant nearly 20,000 employees complained loudly, Finally two parties made a huff.

So in Company J, lesson learn before, although the canteen's space is limited, we still insist on the introduction of two food companies to operate the food factory, the effect appeared, the food must be renewed often, divided into four seasons to change, each meal must provide at least 56 dishes, we nicknamed 56 races 56 kinds of taste, Because the suppliers on both sides have 28 dishes, total is 56 even more. Have self-choice, meal set, dishful rice, noodles, spicy soup, hamburger Western food, big bowl dish, hotpot, stew, steaming, pastry bread, porridge powder fritters ... The price from half a dollar RMB3.14 to **high classic or economical up to your choice.**

The company randomly invites employees to conduct a monthly satisfaction survey on the recent improvement, environment, variety, taste, price, sales speed, service attitude, health, nine questions on a comprehensive score, published monthly satisfaction survey results, It is gratifying that the most headache of the canteen management can become the human resources and Administrative Department of the additional sub-item: Because the monthly opinion survey score is always more than 80 points. My One-third boss Dave joked with me that he had not seen a mass complaint about the canteen for a long time. Hear the voice of appreciation, but I constantly in the spur oneself can't let the complaint occurred; to continue manage the canteen, this situation, like the CCTV Spring Festival Gala, constantly innovate to meet the tastes of the audience is actually very difficult thing.

The public Canteen weekly newspaper (publicly issued in the company network/company public number), announced the most popular dishes, per meal consumption, weighing the number of standards, fire training (by EHS Department guidance), canteen 5S clean situation.

Implementation of the "One day one fruit, doctor away from Me" welfare, we subsidize RMB0.5 yuan/person. Day, to spend RMB150k per month, but GM Sheetoh told the Asia-Pacific VP, he believes that employees have a grateful heart, the company's input will reap the employees' hard work, the company was worth to invest, by the end of the year the company business immediately turn around.

Implementation of the employees ' food-saving Incentive scheme' "Don't leave foods in the plate" action, the staff demanded and all ate up can get a bottle of canned drink, in fact, drinks are free of charge provided by the drinking supplier, we installed container-type sold drinks in the canteen.

We saved the food, compared to the same period last year, the saved amount all donated to orphanages and the elder homes, when the staff were hand carrying their donate food go into these needy groups, from their heart accepted a double-meaning education: There are many people in the world to be rescued, we have no reason to waste. On the other hand, " It is Better to Give Than to Receive ", allowing them to feel their own little giving can help others and gain the respect from others.

The responsibility of the management canteen is me, so I am very worried about food safety, in addition to our **own departmental management to** conduct **rigorous training, but also to** conduct **systematic training** to the supplier canteen

Part I Canteen Management Organization structure

Daily work schedule of canteen employee, stipulate hourly work content.

Part II Food safety and health management system

The ISO file containing tableware disinfection, which specifies the disinfection time and temperature;

Food sample retention system, sample retention time, temperature, take photo on each meal, records retained for 30 days;

Part III Food Quality Assurance Control system

Food blending Oil Quarterly inspection, Food Inspection Bureau report

Part IV Safety regulations and special case handling

A rehearsal for a food poisoning event is explained on the spot

Part V Kitchen Safety Management

Part VI Equipment Operating Procedures

Part VII Reward and Punishment system

Part VIII Restaurant Facilities Management

The canteen I managed had a small fire, although in time to extinguish at that time by the security, the impact of a breakfast meal, this incident gave me a good lesson on the ground, finally understand the whole set of canteen cooking equipment structure, principle, and how to maintain, how to troubleshoot the source of staff restaurant hazards thoroughly after the fire.

A modern large-scale kitchen contains a hookah hood in addition to the lampblack system, electrostatic degreasing machine, smoke exhaust fan, smoke exhaust duct, air blower, fresh air duct, lighting fixtures, distribution box (including lines), high and low temperature cold storage, natural gas pipelines, water supply system, kitchen fire extinguishing system. Need to regularly clean the oil, to avoid the furnace head part prone to fire directly into the entire pipeline, in order not to affect the food for the staff, we stipulate that every long holiday to do maintenance.

In addition to fire-fighting facilities, we must also pay attention to the kitchen waste garbage removal treatment, the treatment of oil residue, so as not to deal with the long-term sewage caused by blockage. We have received complaints from suppliers of our diesel oil for the re-refining of gutter oils, making it necessary for us to pursue our own case, as the US company stipulates that suppliers who dispose of our waste must be professionally qualified and must abide by a socially responsible system of integrity.

Canteen supplier selection has the secret, at the beginning time promised very good afterwards is not the case at all, the transfer of the right of management is even more a problem.

We take the form of open tender, 5S members participate in the voting screening, without notice to participate in the bidder's customer site for 5S standard inspection, on-site interview staff feedback and record on-site recording, to the bidders to view the whole process of food procurement transport cleaning and cooking.

Then the Department of Marketing, operations, accounting, the composition of the assessment team, on meat feeding, food prices, food procurement, hygiene, disinfection, customer satisfaction, new food plan, variety quantity, taste, staffing, management level, training system ten indicators to make an assessment.

Attached the bidding proposal for your reference:

Canteen supplier on-site evaluation score, assessment score, Q&A score in three parts. These three parts according to 40%, 30%, 30% of the proportion of the summary, the highest score of the bid; In the case of the same maximum score, the bidder will decide the final winner by negotiation.

Supplier on-site evaluation score: Canteen Committee audit the canteen supplier site scores. This score has been evaluated and is provided by MRO.

The original supplier canteen scores can be evaluated by the canteen Committee on-site. The final is divided into: Each canteen rating score *100%*40%.

Bid proposal score: Supplier pull in raw material score + operating plan score. Material evaluation According to the meal (5-yuan, 3.14-yuan package) accounted for the meat amount: Now 3.14-yuan package cooked the meat amount is 65g, 5-yuan package cooked the meat amount is 100G. After opening the bid according to the supplier's meat quantity standard to give the score: Pull in raw material score = new Supplier total meat amount/ Total Existing standard meat amount*100%*15%

If the amount of meat given by the supplier is far exceeding the value of the meal mark, it can be regarded as dishonest and can be calculated according to 0 points. The operating plan score is the evaluation score for the Supplier Management Program: The variety of rice & oil, the highlights of the operation and the benefits to the staff of the party. Operation Plan score = The raw material pulls in score *15%+ Scheme score *15%.

We have established a clear and award-winning system, clearly stated in the supplier contract: If the employee's support rate is less than 60%, and the contract is terminated immediately."

Suppliers have disciplinary violations, the tender contract also set out the penalty ordinance, once found, immediately issued a fine notice, the fine is all for the staff holiday snacks. Holiday add foods, budget fees, employees vote to decide what to eat, the company never interfere.

Regular inspection of supplier power consumption, water consumption and natural gas volume, the company bear a fixed amount of RMB 0.4/person, overspending responsible by the supplier.

Average daily operating income, safety and health, energy-saving aspects (electricity), employee feedback, product innovation Performance Excellence in the Monthly can get 3,000 Yuan.

But the management of the factory canteen is difficult, because from the rental plant is the government's own institutions to operate, we can't teach and can't scold, in fact, the number of employees has reached nearly 3,000 people, through the communication we hope to make improvements in specific aspects, once invited them to visit the plant to exchange, they shouted to increase the price, Three Canteen is not two kilometers away from the cafeteria, this canteen charge extra High: a dollar per meal, less meat, less choice, food is not fresh, so toward a vicious circle, employees in the plant to simply go back to the factory to eat, the supplier often put forward the application for price increases, we have a reasonable section to reply whether it is feasible. We try to follow the manufacturers (also government-owned institutions contracted canteen) to negotiate together with the canteen suppliers, to "fired" the government-run canteen supplier, but the government units is not willing to give up, rather to "loss" do not fancy the interests", but we concern about the staff's feelings and reflection, We even pay all decoration, even self-designed modified electric meal ladder, I hope to be able to upgrade the service of the sub-factory canteen. "The emperor did not hurry but the eunuch hurries it".

Three canteens originally planned 5,000 to 6,000 people dining reached 20,000 passengers/day, even plan to increase to 2,000 or more, the usual canteen equipment regular use 7-8 hours actually were using 16 hours, even customer hospitality, we use the staff canteen to arrange meals, customers like our honesty.

21.In three months went to five provinces only for hiring 100 staffs

It was in the company E, I was hired and went in as HR project Manager, it was 10 years ago, in HR seldom heard of such a sinecure, thinking, "Where there is a need where to go for the motherland."

At that time, HR could be the department of the full recruitment, there were 190 vacancies in the hand! Excluded the department manager did not issue a headcount demand requisition but already orally required to find, six recruitment commissioners were struggling to cope, all day stall in each talent market, each department director did not know what to do? Use all the time desperately urge, even sat into my immediate supervisor HRD 's office, would not get people would not leave, my immediate supervisor felt frustrated, sent me to support the recruitment team, to solve the long-awaited problem of the department.

Just as the hiring manager sat next to me, her eight-degree "Soprano" often haunted my ears, called directly to rival companies to scold each other about why they were digging talent from company E. A while unhappily came from HRD office, a while with this one of HR peers gossip complained about hiring, a while oneself run to sympathy with the staff, a while to open the computer like having the revenge banging with the keyboard desperately, I "distressed" for her fingers and keyboard. But I seldom saw her in the interview.

The spectators also anxious, no way, what 's the internal recruitment, what 's the buddy program all announced. But the man who should go still to be dug away, the person who should come in still not come in.

Plant had more than 2000 indirect staff, more than 5,000 indirect workers, in each month, 2% to 3% turnover rate, it is necessary to find back hundreds of people to fill in.

Just take over this "hot sweet potato", I did not plunge into, but first participate

in their daily journey:
1. Talent market is not effective, 100 to 200 candidates stepped in, recruitment units to add up equal with the job seekers, even more than candidates, the level of job seekers only meet the grass-roots position requirement.
2. Senior Talent Job Fair, same as the above situation, Shenzhen has accommodated a lot of manufacturing and large companies, the company desperately in the hunting of talent, Company E propaganda were quite common, there weren't outstanding personality and company strengths.
3. Recruitment website wasn't effective, just publish ordinary recruitment ads and download resumes, a huge number of vacancies, a huge amount of job seekers, the vast sea of people couldn't find a few suitable talents.
4. The recruitment of fresh graduates in other provinces were out of the business, recruiters and department heads would not be responsible for the results of the recruitment look recruitment as a travel benefit.
5. Use headhunters, even headhunters were questioning: Why your company lack so many people could maintain normal operation? This was also implicated in the end of the needs of personnel who would made the decision? How many candidates did the department need to be screened? But in contact with headhunters, one headhunter suggested me: Why don't you use the company open day to solve the recruitment problem by once? Open day, what was open day?
6. Internal recommendations were not effective, even with our long-term project co-operation of Harbin Institute of Technology professors, but also with us lamented that the university were taking a lot of defense development projects, good students they needed also.

Company E is a leader in the development and manufacture of motor, rank the first or two in the world, each year with Japan's largest competitor in the race which is the world's top one, only research and development to win in the market, the company's big Boss Patrick Wang in the truth, so he would like to look for the talent making and researching on motor, Even the machinery and tools for making motors are talented, because there is no stronger motor industry in China. So we are looking for the vast majority of electrical machinery research and development engineers, such talent only Harbin University of Technology and Zhejiang University has a special department to train talent.

I gave six recruiters a rough account, every vacancy, an average of six candidates for interviews, from the search resumes to the first round of the phone interview to arrange the first round of interviews, after many rounds of interviews, 190 vacancies will find 1140 job seekers, arrange for half an hour of each interview time, Each of you will have to work 16 hours a day on average for 18 days without eating or drinking. What the Pity the recruiters are. Every day, struggling to deal with the recruitment but also facing department director of "Persistently Urge" phones, do a series of complex and non-resistant data statistics report. It seems like these department heads are looking at what the past data can dig out some marvelousness.

To change such a decline, I shout:

1. Ask the hiring manager to give us the time allow us to do things better than desperately urge us.
2. One by one work with the hiring managers in key departments to study the needs of key talents, in the process I found that the recruitment of those positions, repeated to recruit.
3. **Re-packaging company promotional materials, highlighting the industry leaders, the market size, the strength of research and development, the strong customer base, as well as** the welfare of **employees, unified color uniform font, and the ads made into small sheets, large sheets, banners and other forms, convenient distribution and posting, even if the interview can't success but also building up employer brand.**

4. Every job fair and talent market booth, should take the best position, no good position not to participate in, request the organizer put our advertises in the first three, otherwise do not participate. Focus on the Monday talent market once a week.
5. Every time the advertise take the first page of the ads, in addition to the cost of publishing, the most influential companies must establish a broad network of contacts, until today, more than 10 years later, I am still in close contact with 51job, JobsDB, ChinaHR friends, close relations in business.

10 days after the three northeastern provinces job fair, three months went to five provinces only for hiring back 100 staffs, in the cold winter ride over the body sat hard, with a sentence " **For you I am pining myself away without regret.** " to describe our desire for talent is the most correct, I still remembered that I was taunted by the hiring manager "Ran three provinces only recruited back 100 engineers?!" I was silent, not fought with her. Because everyone has eyes to see who was really doing things. Sooner the hiring manager discreetly left the job.

However, the burden of recruitment fell on me, just at the same time I got pregnancy, because it was elderly primipara, the family was too nervous let me give up work to take rest in home, I did not listen, I love my career, I also love my family, I enjoy love both at the same time, also the Feeling love by the two, Thank my husband he knows me very well, he once joked with me: "You can be a special housewife if you stand that loneliness." Of course, I could not withstand this loneliness, pregnant 5 months continued to fly around for the recruitment, until the aviation restrictions after 5 months the pregnant woman could not get on the plane again.

The recruitment of the outer provinces is always "Distant water can't quench a present thirst", we often go to the outer provinces, slowly their talents go to the developed regions to find better opportunities for development, and the mainland's economy has also developed rapidly, such as Chongqing, Wuhan and so on, Shenzhen's non-restrict zone are not comparable to these key developed western cities.

I must develop more and more effective recruitment channels, open the door Welcome to the company Open Day, is the most effective one. Can you imagine that the company in one day to attract more than 600 suitable interviewers to the company interview Hall, at the same time to arrange for the whole plant tour, categorized to complete the written test, interview, on the spot to talk about the salary and make the job offer, is it what a vast project? As I mentioned earlier, the headhunting company gave us an idea, because of the budget problem, we finally did not cooperate with the headhunting company, but swam by ourselves, see how far it could be.

1. It took less than two weeks to search for suitable interviewers in triangle zone, through their network, to greet more job seekers, to send a uniform invitation letter and replied letter to the job seeker;
2. In the major recruitment sites, the recruitment of newspapers posted on the company's open-day advertising, so that they sent their resumes in advance, we were in bulk pushed to the hiring manager to read beforehand.
3. The day in Shenzhen, Dongguan and Guangzhou, the major recruitment market, the bus outlook and the front put the large advertising, the spot suitable for picking up the candidates to the company interview hall.
4. Let the job seekers and department managers had the repeat interview opportunities, because the different business unites' positions had a very high similarity, so each interviewer we provided at least twice interview opportunities, encouraged the department managers to recommend each other, if the interview of their own department of the position was not suitable, the initiative to recommend candidates to the next department.
5. In the process, we arranged for the waiting candidates to watch the group's presentations and videos, visited the company's work and living

environment, provided the company's working meals, let them personally understood the future work environment and the company's humanistic culture.

6. The most important step is to make a quick offer, we put C&B compensation and welfare team and BP all mobilized to do the job on the spot, this is the experience and the way to accumulate, according to the candidate's experience, education, skills, and level, with the Recruitment department Manager to discuss, Prepared the salary and structure information of the original department staff in advance to make a decision about 3 to 5 minutes.

The first company open Day, we once successfully recruited 122 candidates, filled 82% vacancies, the recruitment team played a turnaround, after a long time, we no longer need to run to the provinces to recruit, I just used this time to take the longest holiday in my life: three months of maternity leave, During the period also remote command recruitment team renovated a large-scale centralized all recruitment functions as one of the recruitment center, in order to face the rapid change of company developed to 35000 headcount size at that time.

Cooperation with headhunters-a story behind each position.

Now there are a few headhunting companies, as HR, may see this market good to do, we all come to share bar, so skim over WeChat, you will see eyeful headhunting micro-letter ads are, just curious that no one fit for me?

I also thought about doing **headhunter** job, **for a while free time**, not more than **one month, I** was hunted by **Company E.**

In the Company E we recruited faster than headhunting, so headhunters couldn't build a successful case, the final choice was give up. These headhunting friends all grind their teeth said to me: should you at least give me a meal to eat?!

The real start of using large-scale of headhunt Services is in Company J, former Chinese boss looked at who wasn't pleasing to the eye: "Cut all the trees in the forest ", when implementing an important project found that the key talents were insufficient, all the function managers 24 hours a day to operate, made a mess, new hired talent did not stayed for one month then submitted resignation letter at once, because couldn't cope with such high-intensity work, mobile phone camera industry talent is quite unpopular, how easy to find a job, why come to EMS company facing a customer relentless accusations? At that time, GM Sheetoh under the serious pressure both from upper and lower, there was no way only told to me solemnly: "You have to give me total 21 people in one months in all the functional departments to fulfill shortage of serving customer A, I do not care what the new method you will use, the past approach does not work!" I knew he was right, because in the market the candidates who understand optical photography, micro-electronic technology is rare, usually working in mobile phone or camera development department of famous world brand companies, who will consider to leave easily? Their resumes were not found on the site, and it was impossible to take the initiative to find a job. The last straw was only to find a headhunt company.

I think a few companies use headhunting like "blanket research", but I use headhunter like blanket researching, because many headhunters are very enthusiastic at the beginning, all said that they are personnel familiar with the industry's high-end technical, but when you share all the vacancies to them, really can understand the requirements of the position of technology, and the corresponding recommendation of not a few people, the last can become more than a few; Another kind of headhunting, regardless of what is what, first to throw a batch of related and unrelated people to you, see if you can pick several, in fact, it is wasting the recruitment time.

I have the patience to tell each headhunter the specific needs of each job, the patience of the search for each of their resumes, arrange an interview, ask my subordinates to do the same, my subordinates complained to me: there was a headhunt company had pushed 50 job seekers, we have arranged interviews, but the other party seems to always can't catch the characteristics of the person we want , do we have to abandon him? I asked her: "What is the attitude of this headhunter?" was he going to push it with his heart?" The subordinate replied: "He has been still pushing with heart." I told my subordinates, "Keep him." 51 job Seeker's push was successful, and it got out of hand! The reason is very simple, the headhunter found a key talent we want, he helped us to find a series of related talent, that year, he earned Company J one million headhunting Fee, we became good friends, because he helped me in one month almost offered what we needed.

" Different in profession makes one feel worlds apart; different trades are separated as by mountains " Put this sentence in the headhunting industry is more appropriate, if the headhunter began to contact you to boast about all industry can recommend the candidate that you can't consider cooperating with him.

1. You should visit these headhunting companies, personally talk to each other, you will have a deeper feeling.
2. How many vacancies do they have, what 's the customer do they have? How many similarities do these customers have with your company and what positions are they entrusting? If the future cooperation is not successful, this headhunting company will not turn against each other, to dig away the elite from your company?
3. How do they proceed the researching? It is also a factor to consider if the process is too long. More listening to the Headhunting is also for the future of our own reference.
4. At the beginning, do not entrust headhunters for too many vacancies, they will not be able to do so, you can entrust them 1 to 2 vacancies, observe their performance, without successful cases within three months, they will choose to give up also.

Now company M main product is sweater, some time ago we wanted to recruit

Chinese and English Japanese marketing manager who understand the sweater design, the beginning also could **not make head or tail of something**, finally we found a special do sweater industry headhunting Company, soon found the right talent.

But headhunters are not to be abused because they are expensive.

Linkedin has 300 million users, will you use it well?

The British headhunting company in Linkedin to browse my resume actively contact me, I talk to my colleagues, when you design a job advertisement, you have to fall into it, you have to ask yourself, if you are a job seeker, will you consider such a company? I often deal with the marketing manager of various websites, make clear the function and layout of the website, make use of these functions, I also sell myself in the company promotion, want to know how to recruit must know how to sell oneself, your future relies on your own design.

"EGE employee get Employee " internal referral fee rose from $1000 to $5000 to $20000, only for crazy recruitment.

This was Company J to centralized the recruitment from the factory, by the factory Chase, there was no way but to use the internal channel calls for more talent to join, the effect was not as fast as the incentive bonus amount rise.

To centralize the recruitment of dozens of factories in the Asia-Pacific region into a talent recruitment center, the middle of the needs of the people and interview arrangements to spend more time and resources, so that the basic problem was not in the door to shoot the head of the group's decision-makers to predict, the result was doomed to failure, After running 1.5 year, the talent hunting Center announced return to under the plant management.

22. Close to year end, I want to target DL candidates by using "Machine Gun"

Close to the year end, as a child I was looking forward to the new year coming because there will be new clothes to change and chicken legs to eat, now being tens of thousands employees multinational enterprise HR head, I am mostly afraid of the Chinese New Year, because at the end of the year there will be a large number of peasant worker shortage, I often kidding with the Department head who urged manpower: I want to target DL candidates by using "machine guns"!

This is one report public posted by Mercer consultant company in 2012.

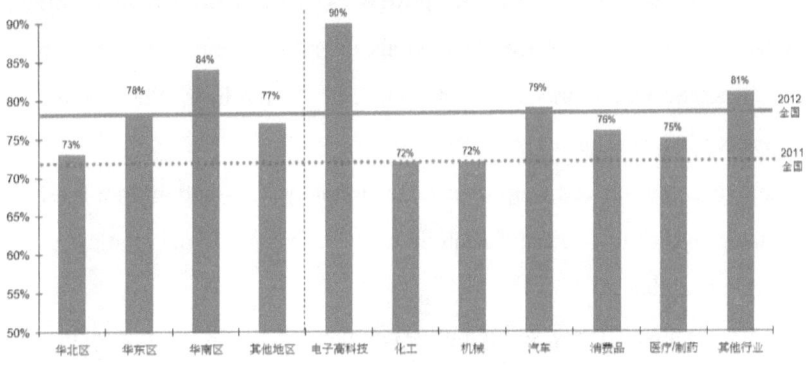

What's the problem?

There were a large employees quit before CNY (Chinese New Year holiday), they don't come back after CNY, Company J has statistics show that 2-3 months before and after the Spring Festival of the year, the turnover rate jump to the highest peak in a year, more than 10%/month, need to hire a large number of workers.

Problems caused?

Labor shortages, high hiring costs, and a chaotic production plan before and after CNY. According to our statistics around the company's results: caused 39.3% of companies delay in the delivery, 14.3% of companies existing problems, in order to avoid delivery delay, such as by air, the resulting aircraft costs may be a shortfall in profits.

At the end of the year, in China will perform "Rob people War" among employer companies, dispatching companies and migrant workers, the intensity of the level can compare with the three kingdoms' war: In the end who is the winner?

1. From the company's point of view, at all costs only for the timely delivery of the security of customers. Manufacturing is non-explosive industry, the cost of employment increases one time, how much profit will be offset? It is Obvious.

2. Labor Dispatch Company: The high price does not equal to the higher profit, in the information developed era, the Labor dispatch companies having the price war. Service value does not dominate. It also bears the risk of a difference in quantity.

3. Employees: high-priced wages make the company's low-and middle-level management and white-collar unceasingly envy. It seems that the employee is the last winner, is that true?

The company is not a charity, so high price companies are only temporary hired workers for top order last for 2-3 months. After the order has been finished, I am sorry you should return whence they came, the staff must re-find jobs, change jobs to re-adapt to the environment. What if it is inappropriate to change?

Let's go home early for a year. There are parents or children in the family. They earned 5 months ' wages from September to Spring Festival. One month earned

RMB4,000 that is a total of RMB20,000, you earn two months high salary RMB6,000/mouth, 2 months RMB12,000.

It seems that there is no winner in this high-priced war ...

In the long run, the company should develop core suppliers (dispatch companies, schools), in the market shortage, the core suppliers solve manpower shortage problem, each other become a community of destiny, to be the long-term partnership resist to risk. It is not the problem of the wages, but the company's large demand must rely on the support of the core suppliers. Establish long-term, mutual benefit, win-win partnership with the dispatch company.

1. The establishment of a specific assessment system, publish the recruitment result openly, so that manpower suppliers rely on "true ability" to earn a living, in each year, dig out unqualified suppliers from the list, and constantly introduce a competitive core supplier.
2. The number of labor agent companies can't be maintained too much and it is inconvenient to manage them. To make the dispatch company work efficiently.
3. Share real-time production recruitment plans with labor agent companies, pre-set incentives for year-end hiring, share with them, even reserve the necessary manpower in advance, "store up grain against famine"
4. To prevent them from playing the trick among customers, to analysis the turnover rate between the dispatching companies, to communicate with the direct staff to understand the quality of their service to the staff.
5. Coordinate with the schools need to involve the labor agent company, because the secondary and technical schools are "Good Catch", even if we direct "bargaining" "Grant the plaque" "talk about sponsorship tuition" and so on, can knock on the few "interns". Looking at the "internship" of college students or secondary school student sitting in the car went thousands of miles, went through the hardship of selling here and there, you can

understand China's education failure place: On the one hand, the cultivation of the students have too much repetition mismatch market actual demand, on the other hand, The school is charged by the hour for the internship introduction fee, squeeze profits from the students.

Would you rather pay a high-priced agent fee to bring in temporary replacements for hourly workers and student workers to get through the "annual labor shortage" or do you have a lot of money to keep employees? Company J is full of puzzle for years, we continue to compare the methods and costs of the surrounding companies, in China each branch of the continuous comparison, learn from each other, but throughout the year, we are still very "struggling."

If pay agent fees recruit temporary workers to replace non-key positions, the quality problem happened in May, the product is sold to the customers you know how bad the quality of the product produced during the Spring Festival!

If spend a lot of money to retain the internal staff, we calculated the cost of RMB1,000 per person, 10,000 people will pay the cost of 10 million, manufacturing profits have been thin like blades, 90% employees have no intention to leave, we have to fight for the loss of 10%, no matter how many times to do the survey, each time get a different result, Because many workers really do not know what they want, more closer to the Spring Festival, the results closer to the fact, so we have to do three times survey, including asking employees:

When will you go home?

Will you quit and go home?

Reason?

Will you join again?

Do you need ticket booking?

What are your suggestions to the company?

At last, we direct asked: When do you go home?

We tried to get RMB1,000 per person to pay retention awards, with a focus on low-level employees, two consecutive years of trial, the results of 2% to 3% loss rate decline, the third year we decided to revert to the original method, average RMB300 /person, because we compare the average 2.5% The improvement rate is equal to RMB250 of 10,000 people, we spend a high price of RMB1,000/person "buy people", about RMB250,000, this calculation is too easy to clarify.

We are forced to do something desperate, systematically drive retention:

1. Thousand people's dumplings feast activities, the company inside three days hold 100 banquets, from the 27th to 29th, even open lunch banquet, in order to make staff stay in factory not to return home, in those days, I tried to eat dumplings, because every meal to accompany staff to eat dumpling.
2. The lucky draw amount from the first year RMB5,000, increase RMB1,000 if each year, has been increased to RMB8,000, later changed to have the lucky draw RMB10,000 in the production line.
3. Considered at the end of the year the workers return home to have Blind Date, to organize the Spring Festival dating and hold collective wedding activities, so that employees in the factory form the marriage.
4. Send the blessing to the hometown: Employees can't return home, we call on the staff to design their own New Year greeting cards, awarding prizes, so that the staff selected the most intimate favorite words and composition to print out, distributed to the staff who want to speak with the family, cover the company's postmark, affixed the company's stamps, sent back to families thousands miles away.

    At the same time we also design the blessing of the New Year WeChat.
5. Guessing Lantern Festival
6. Let 's look at Spring Festival Party, the company arranged open big screen TV in the canteen, let staff watch the Spring Festival Gala, the leader

personally sent candy to staff.
7. The same treatment for having leave, if the staff are willing to work overtime during the new year, so that employees get overtime pay and leave.
8. Provide the visiting room
9. Send spring Festival couplets
10. Send gift
11. To ensure the return rate of the employees, the return ticket is booked for the employees.

By the survey 100% employees know the company's N gifts, also recognized N gifts has a positive impact on production, in the first year of the implementation Company J turnover rate dropped down 6%, the effect is significant, after that the effect decreased year by year, so the annual new program, other people celebrate the festive time is HR showing super ability time, we need to contact the Labor agent desperately hire worker, engage in activities to retain staff, but also to face the boss of various departments to report progress, the most headache problem was: At this moment brother company also sent a letter to ask for a rescue, asked to support more people to Tianjin factory, because they received a brand new phone model orders, start life and death competition with the world's largest rival company F, but it is reported that company F has placed the recruitment booth to the station's exit, so that the first time to "Rob" the Workers! In the face of such a tough situation, the group instructed to transfer the certain number of workers to Tianjin branch.

My first reflection: "Why?!" We don't make money than them? We're not bigger than them?

However, I can't have negative feelings, this is my boss gave me the "assessment & feedback", I would like to express our branch of "Generosity", our branch of "Strong Ability".

I must conduct another survey among the staff, who came from Tianjin? Who would like to go to Tianjin factory to feel the local customs of Tianjin? Learn about the operating model of a brother company? A northern Spring festival? Make a long trip? There are so many good words to use. If the employees are willing, all the necessities should be taken care of. There is only one purpose: to complete the recruitment tasks assigned by the group as soon as possible.

Finally put more than 100 "treasures (People)" to make up enough, but also "Grab" high-speed rail tickets, but also buy cloth and carrying, but also reminding, Sheetoh GM always love staff, check every detail, every detail can't have problems.

At least we sent the staff to Tianjin factory, from then on, my phone did not stop: a moment asked How so bad the Tianjin factory accommodation was, even the daily bath hot water couldn't be ensured? Why can't I bathe in every day? Not enough lockers to hold the phone? A supervisor often has scold? I don't know which one can be follow up? Security issues, communication issues, accommodation issues ...

The supervisor also has the supervisor's complaint: Your staff was very delicate, not obeyed the arrangement, even did not work but to receive the salary,

The two sides to go back and forth, we only can try to appease as far as possible, always we are not at the scene, employees are our assets we still want to protect. After two months the last support staff returned, it is already the spring season, we have a difficulty year, no need to use machine guns, the people still be hired back, the people left later on, but also "successfully" to provide the support task to the brother factory.

23.Is the labor agent extort the hard-earned money from dispatching worker?

Should HR folks still remember "Labor dispatch management regulations"? At that time, the policy was issued two years before effective date of the actual implementation date: Require company can't use dispatching workers exceed the number of employees 10%, the term can't exceed 2 years, the dispatch worker insurance contribution location is the employment location, dispatch worker only work in temporary, alternative positions, Support for three types of jobs, in contravention of the law ordered to rectify. Now it looks like this is the two session of the Government. Whether the transition to the implementation of the previous government brought down the legal issues, the original ordinance publishing was "seriously", many companies spent a lot of time to study how to deal with, because they used dispatching workers to reduce the monthly payment of social insurance and Housing Provident Fund, As well as the burden of paying high compensation in accordance with the law when dismissing employees, but also to solve the problem of finding out the shortage of sources of work when recruiting by self. Instead, the government agencies and institutions cost too much for the future to bear the social security, so that the implementation of the regulations can only be "lightly put down", become dead letter. But because of this ordinance, the problem of these "alternative" Labor management has aroused the deep problem of whether the "Labor agent company" behind the scenes is extorting the hard-earned money of the dispatching workers?

The so-called alternative includes student workers, dispatched hourly workers, processes outsourcing, dispatch workers four ways. Labor agent companies are often used in four ways, which way can make money will go which way.

That was after the financial crisis, a substantial recovery for Company J orders. In order to ensure that the recruitment at the end of the year is not a problem, HR quickly organized the school-enterprise cooperation, the Labor agent company with the long-term cooperation were invited to participate in the meeting of cooperation with secondary schools and technical schools, 34 schools accept the invitation:

1. We take the initiative to grant these institutions to send the students to the company for long-term;

2. In the meeting, we take the initiative to open up our company's pay and benefits compare with our competitor: Two F Companies;

Inviting these school representatives to visit the company's working and living environment, we even send their students to speak in the meeting and lead the tour, let the school representatives and teachers to catch up, this is the most contagious;

Any questions raised in the meeting, three parties to discuss the solution together; Because we want these teachers and school representatives really help their graduates to find good employer company. At the same time, we also accept their delivery of interns, to be helpers during the new year, or 3-6 months internship, the department will not consider accepting interns normally, because the internship time is short, lost soon after training, but considered the difficulties of recruitment in the year end we only have to accept.

What government organized "Spring Breeze Plan" for campus recruitment tour just like a formality, ineffective.

The use of hourly workers is very common, Base on time pay, count social insurance, welfare and so on into the hourly wage, so that the hourly workers can get cash at the first time, they do not need to pay social insurance. As for the labor agent companies to get labor agent fees, some more than half, the less ones with 1/3 of labor costs.

Compare with the other employment relationship, labor agencies and hourly workers can get more, so they are more willing to do hourly work, the source is quite adequate, once order place, hundreds of hourly workers immediately run to your door get ready to the job. Because of this speed, I made a big mistake: at the end of one year, the production department was demanding 300 people, even if the hour workers they could acceptable, Due to the urgent situation I had to worked with labor agent company, considering Mr. Guo could sent the workers to us in the most difficult time, I asked him at first, He responded: "No problem, Not only said 300 people, even 900 people they had. I overjoyed when listening to this, urged them to send the workers to us, add more headcount for better selection. Unexpectedly they put 900 people into one coach after one coach send over, this time production department supervisors are "choosers" over there, we do not know the regulations of using these hourly worker: "To come together, to go together", because they are gathered from the surrounding villages, many are a family work together, If you hire a person do not hire another person, they will choose to give up, waste a lot of time to pack up but they do not come, more than 900 people make uproar, finally really pick by the company no more than 100 people.

At this time we asked Mr. Guo to pull away the rest candidates, do not stay in the company, however he called the candidates to leave but the candidates doesn't want to leave, Don't know what did he committed to these hourly workers, we do not know and do not want to intervene. These workers were living at the foot of society ladder, finally sat in the scene of recruitment one night did not go, made me this "initiator" hard to explain what happened, but also need to negotiate all night with the head of the Labor agent, let him pull people away, deadlocked all night, last to the noon of the next day, they were willing to leave.

Since then, I am cautious about the recruitment of hourly workers, until the new plant go into production, product is quite strong seasonality, Urgently in one month to recruit 3000 short-term workers last half a year, but only used six months, it is depends on Labor agent to negotiated with workers about accommodation and social security arrangement, we do not want the labor topic to mess up, finally we decided with top management, signed off long term contract with labor agents for the long-term cooperation, daily supply manpower on demand.

The real dispatch of "False" outsourcing in the name of the use of piecework of wages settlement, actual use the time to settle wages, is "playing the trick" alternative employment mode, the Chinese law apply to "No prohibition in law can be done", so a lot of companies in drilling this loop hole. In today China's manufacturing profits just like paper-thin, to use what can be used to make them survived.

Labor dispatch is the most used model of Company J, more than half workers in the Labor dispatch management regulations have been gradually turn the labor force into a formal staff, resulting manufacturing costs continue to increase, finally the United States headquarters compare China's labor costs with Malaysian Penang Three factories parity, Chinese factory all be defeated, Not to mention the comparison with the Indian factory and Vietnam factory, finally look at the new law implementation closely, seeing other companies are all wait and see but not action taken, we also do not want to be the first person to try the crab, freeze our action, recover to half proportion workers are dispatching workers.

Half number of people close to 7000, need to use 8 labor agent companies, too much labor companies difficult to control, basically they are finding "fish" inside to a "pool"-looking for workers in the surrounding, can't find much fish, if their own "fish" is not much, "fish" will be "pumped away" in the recruitment season, This is what we are worried about, because our company paid to Labor agency company Labor management fee is only 60 yuan/person, below the market price of 80 to 100 yuan. But our demands on labor companies are no more than other companies.

In the beginning we visit the Labor agent, look at their size and management level, then decide whether long-term cooperation, regular annual elimination of two companies, in fact, from the process of the visit you have strong feeling, those are intentions in business, even being labor agent to standardize management rather than halfway "Black" labor agent.

HR invite multiple departments to make assessments, using the company's existing set of vendor qualification review to decide whether to use:

1. Company Registered Capital
2. Management level
3. Machine Equipment
4. Technical capabilities
5. Service capability
6. Amount of Labor
7. Adaptability and ability to complete recruitment tasks on time
8. Quality Assurance System
9. Labor price
10. Terms of trade conditions of payment
11. Corrective actions
12. Continuous improvement

There are good labor agents, they will send the right-hand assistant to the long-term factory, responsible for the daily recruitment of worker and handle the payment of social security, to deal with serious incidents such as illness or violation, with the management standard of Labor agent company to deal with, they are relatively sophisticated and smooth, but also need to constantly monitor and follow up, even not to mention the bad management.

What happens to employees, the first time to find the using labor company, in their concept: Big Eat big, find the most powerful. For example, the salary pay on time, Company J has always been on time to pay, even pay early, once the labor company received Company J salary transferring, took the money and run away, the workers are chase Company J, learn the lessons, Company J simply take over all the work of payroll from Labor agent company, It is stipulated in the contract that the labor agent company must pay the salary to the employee's account first, can be reimbursed from Company J to the corresponding wage later on.

In the process of labor companies also have sly time, such as the theft of staff's social security fees, this is really a "technical job" when HR began to think that wages are calculated by us, the wages of social security fees have been deducted, the payroll print out by us, labor companies and monthly withholding details submitted to us to review, How can be a problem of withholding social security fees?!

In the beginning, we received complaints from employees and immediately transferred to the Labor agent company to deal with, when slowly found that the situation has been repeated then we began to alert, by contacting the Social Security Bureau, from the Social Security Bureau extract to check the actual payment of labor agent company records, only to find that these labor companies are not to buy social security in the one month of new join and in the month of leaving, but the information they send us uses a false copy to muddle through! Poor labor and poor our employer, accumulated a short year there are more than 3 million! These Labor companies each one kept silent, summed up a sentence: the employer with the dispatch unit relationship is like the relationship between cat and mouse, always catch the sore always can't be finished.

The existence value of the Labor agent company is also to conceal the problem that the employing unit treats the dispatch workers ' unfair treatment, for example, at the beginning of Company J, we use the name of the comprehensive work system, The treatment of all dispatch workers over the weekend is counted as 1.5 times, resulting in unequal pay for the work of the phenomenon, this time out as a shield or Labor agent company, but instead we see the labor turnover rate is too high, finally actively amend the weekend overtime formula.

Company J use Labor agent company's biggest effect, or to explore the source of the labor, that is one thousand or two thousand of the manpower need to operate a recruitment center, to raise nearly 10 or 8 recruitment professionals, but also can't ensure that in the quiet of the development zone how much workers can find out, finally we decided to let HR do higher value-added HR work, as for recruitment should be assigned to the labor agent company.

Attach labor agent daily management regulation for reference:

1.0. PURPOSE

This policy was issued to ensure our company can recruit qualified operators and conduct the daily management to ensure regular production.

2.0. SCOPE

This policy is applicable to labor recruitment and the daily management of our company.

3.0. DEFINITION

    3.1. The labor agency daily management policy includes:

    3.2. The responsibility of the labor recruitment team

    3.3. The responsibility of the labor salary of C&B team

    3.4. The responsibility of labor company

    3.5. The responsibility of audit team

    The management of labor agency include: the evaluation of the new labor company\ the probation of the new labor agency \the performance management and order assignment management of labor agency\the survey of the labor fees\the wage issuing to labors\the social-insurance contribution.

4.1. The o-chart of the labor agency daily management:

4.1.1. Labor recruitment team

4.1.1.1. labor agency

4.1.1.2. Recruitment team

-Recruitment team of the labor recruitment

4.1.1.3. C&B

-Responsibility of payoff the salary of labor

4.1.1.4. In audit team

(HR, MFG, Fin, Pur)

4.2. The responsibility of the labor recruitment team:
- 4.2.1. Know the requirement of the manpower
- 4.2.2. Strict follow the policy to issue Recruitment notices, test, interview and check the certificates
- 4.2.3. Cooperate with training\C&B\MFG\labor company
- 4.2.4. Prepare for the report forms of labor recruitment
- 4.2.5. Contact with the labor company
- 4.2.6. Check up the name list of entrants

4.3. Labor company:

4.3.1. Base on the vacancy of the company to issue the recruitment advertisement and organized personnel to sign up;

4.3.2. Strict to check up the qualification of the candidates;

4.3.3. Daily arrangement of the labor (accident\ payoff\ social-security)

4.4. The responsibility of C&B in charge of payoff the salary of labor
- 4.4.1. Responsible for making monthly wage report of labor
- 4.4.2. Responsible for accepting and checking the monthly documents proving by labor agency.

4.5. The responsibility of the audit team

4.5.1. Responsible for the evaluation on the labor company

5.0 The Evaluation of the new labor company

5.1. Our company take important in every company which have intention for recruitment services suppliers, before the service for our company, we will assess with them. Base on the requirement of the application form. Our company will base on the company actuality decide if we will expand cooperate with the labor companies and to organize the assessment, the assessment standard will base on the application form.

5.2. The probation of the labor company

The new cooperation of the company is looking for a four – month probation, in this period, the disqualified company will be terminated the cooperation.

5.3. The performance management of labor company

Our company will evaluate the agent performance every month. This evaluation will be the confirmation of offering business on peak season.

If the performance evaluation on the labor agency failed, our company will require the company set a corrective action plan. Monthly performance evaluation results will be the gist for the following time order assignment. Details about the performance appraisal procedure can refer to the attachment. According to the respective agency supply ability, the highest score is A, analogy grade B\C… The standard for assigning order in midseason is as belong:

The order assignment grade of next month	Totally requirement							
3 services company	Performance grade	A	B	C				
	Percentage of assign order	40%	35%	25%				
5 services company	Performance top grade	A	B	C	D	E		
	Percentage of assign order	30%	26%	20%	15%	9%		
6 services company	Performance top grade	A	B	C	D	E	F	
	Percentage of assign order	29%	25%	18%	12%	9%	7%	
8 services company	Performance top grade	A	B	C	D	E	F	G	H

	Percentage of assign order	26 %	23 %	15 %	11 %	10 %	6 %	5 %	4 %
Rank	H I J P Q......	K	L	M	N	O			

To better meet the needs for production and new operators in the tracking, our company will choose the number of labor agency according to the number of recruitments as below.

The number of people be recruited	The number of the companies had been attended the recruitment
Less than 60 people(content 60 people)	3 services company
60 to 150 people (content 150 people)	5 services company
151 to 200 people (content 200people)	6 services company
More than 200 people	8 services company

The company which the performance was worst in two continuous seasons, our company will stop the cooperation with it.

Labor agencies are forbidden to ask for any referral fee from applicants. All related referral fee claimed by cooperated job agency must comply with government's law & regulation. To ensure the supplier can abide by related regulation's requirement, our company request new employee to fill up "new hire referral fee survey form" for audit purpose, those agencies which were demonstrated incompliance would be given punishment or service termination.

5.4. Contract labor receiving salary

5.4.1. C&B team will send mail to MFG clerk to check if operators' salary of each month has been received.

5.4.2. MFG clerk will check with operators if they received the salary then feedback to C&B team.

5.4.3. C&B team will give mail to finance to inform money transfer after confirmation.

5.5. Contract labor social insurance contribution

5.5.1. Labor agency need to give the Monthly Social Insurance Changed Name List with the seal of social insurance bureau both the original and the copy to C&B team on every 19th. C&B team will check them both and return the original to labor agency.

5.5.2. Labor agency needs to give the Monthly Social Insurance Overall Name List with the seal of respective company to C&B team on every 19th.

5.5.3. C&B team will ask labor agency to send the name list by email on 21st after checking all the information.

5.5.4. If labor agency didn't provide the name list on time, our company will not pay back any fees.

5.6. Daily communication

    5.7.1. Can use email communicate simple concerning.

    5.7.2. Must use official letter with company seal concerning finance; must attach governmental document if concerning government.

24.Both recruiters & managers need to be trained：How to hire the right people?

Both Recruiters & Managers Need To be Trained: How to hire the right people? Absolutely!

A statistic shows that average success to hire an employee needs 24 job seekers, the efficiency of recruiting is important! To attract job seekers, the recruitment specialist will

1. Ensure that the hiring manager is fully aware of the need time to fill in vacancies
2. After the labor market analysis to provide the hiring manager the most appropriate candidates to meet his expectations, salary level match job seekers' market price.
3. Build up excellent talent supply pipe line, don't forget to track these outstanding talents.
4. Recruitment ads keep concise and complete, it is best not to exceed 20 words.
5. Report the size and quality of job seekers to the hiring manager and adjust ads as needed
6. Appropriately calculate the effect of different channels base on the recruiting site.

In the stage of decision-making

7. Respect the interviewer and save the interviewer's time during the interview process.
8. In the interview process to maintain the sincere commitment of both sides.

In the beginning:

9. Provide more information about the business, such as the preparation of Buddy partners, the participation of corporate community activities, and the

sharing of policy systems.

10. Work with the hiring manager to ensure successful onboarding

11. Make sure the onboarding process is smooth and give a good impression to the employees in the job

12. Before entry into the background of the investigation, especially for managers or above, finance, HR, custom, procurement department and other sensitive positions should pay attention to the former employer company review collection.

Attached Training Summary page

We want to give the recruitment specialist and department manager specialized training "Behavior interview rule", because the department manager including myself always thought "can do" is "Can do", as long as grasping the technology, doing the work, after the theory of training and research, after a certain period of time, then deep understand the logic.

In fact, the behavior of the interview is not a profound truth, it follows the theory is: "Past behavior is the best proof of future performance" It can use "Star" to replace the four key factors of the interview:

S=Situation

T=Task

A=Action /activity

R=result

Before the interview

View application Information

View the concept of the dimension and the key behavior

1. Start: 2 minutes

2. Key background view: 6 minutes

3. Planned questions about behavior: 6 minutes per time for a single degree of control

How Well Do You Manage Candidate Touch Points?

Companies should examine the effectiveness of candidate interactions

	Touch Points—Attraction Phase			Touch Points—Recruiting Phase			
Touch Point Experience (Percentage of Candidates Using)	Professional/ Social Networking Web Sites (34%)	Third-Party Online Job Boards (41%)	Company's Corporate and Career Web Sites (31%)	Interaction with Recruiters/ Headhunters (56%)	Interaction with the Hiring Manager (28%)	Interaction with Current Employees (28%)	On-Site Interview Process (N/A)
Candidate Activities	• Develop initial perception of company's employment brand through Internet word of mouth.	• Read and compare job descriptions. • Apply to positions.	• Browse corporate and career information. • Form impression of the employment brand from visual/multimedia communications.	• Campus recruiting and job fairs. • Targeted recruiting outreach (headhunters). • Initial interview	• Campus recruitment events • Job interview	• On-Site job interview • Job referral • Internship	• Interview scheduling • Site arrival • Receiving offer or rejection letter
Questions to Test Your Touch Point Effectiveness	• Do we actively monitor networking Web sites to understand and manage our image in the labor market? • Do we have strategies to repair the dissatisfaction expressed by candidates or employees on these Web sites?	• Do the company overview and job posting include key EVP/employment branding themes? • Does the job posting include a link to our corporate and career Web sites?	• Are our corporate and career Web sites easy to find, user friendly, and well publicized? • Does our career Web site include employee stories or testimonials?	• Do recruiters and headhunters understand the key elements of our employment brand and communicate them effectively? • Are recruiters and headhunters equipped to tailor the brand message to different talent segments?	• Do managers understand the key elements of our employment brand and communicate them effectively? • Do managers set the correct career expectations for candidates?	• Do we know who our employee advocates are, and involve them in recruiting efforts? • Do employees exhibit behaviors that exemplify our brand values?	• Do we provide a realistic preview of workplace culture while candidates are on-site? • Do we treat candidates with respect and care regardless of interview outcome?

Overarching Question: Are we proactively aligning candidate experience with our employment brand at every touch point?

4. Time to complete: 10 minutes

To design a tracking problem for the job seeker's experience

Evaluate the time for each part of the question and answer

Time hints (estimated time)

During the interview process:

Use the tracking questions until you've completed the questions on each of the key issues in stars, clarifying the questions and answers to the bottom.

After the interview is complete

Evaluate the data.

Think about the questions asks and the answers he gets when the interview is complete.

Classification according to the unique degree

Score the answer for each request (valid +) (invalid-)

Weigh each of these weights:

Similarity-How close is the situation to the target work at that time?

Impact degree-how important is the situation and outcome at that time?

Time-the time of the action, the interview should focus on the interviewer's past two years rather than the long story.

To do

Get ready: Read the results of your CV and psychological test and prepare to ask questions.

Control time: Get the job seeker to the subject

Stay neutral: Avoid short talk and agree to the answer.

Take notes: To evoke memories and facilitate analysis

Unification: The question of unifying the same position

What you need: Ask yourself what is necessary and what is the best skill

To avoid:

Jump to a conclusion: the first impression is about

Say too much: listen 80% speak 20%

Avoid prejudice: age, background, marital status should not affect your decision

Being a glib person: the principle of star should be tightly fastened, specific, Task, Action, Result

Over-commitment: Be careful not to overdo the challenges and benefits you face

Combining behavioral interviewing training with training on competency Model courses:

Competency models (competence model) are a combination of competency structures for specific job performance requirements and are an important basis for a range of human resources management and development practices (e.g. job analysis, recruitment, selection, training and development, performance management, etc.). Founder McClelland that competency models are "a set of related knowledge, attitudes and skills that affect the main parts of a person's work, relate to job performance, be able to measure with reliable standards, improve through training and development". Guildford argues that "competency models depict motivations, traits, skills, and competencies that identify the best performers and performers, as well as a set of behavioral traits required by a particular job or hierarchy."

Internationally-accepted 67 competencies, 9 performance dimensions, and 19 obstacles and stop factors

At Company J, the Asia Pacific Senior President, together with various branches GM, first defining all manager-level competency models, thus to ask what question positioning each job seeker, estimate what level of answer to get.

Company J Manager level competency Model:

1. The ability to collect, analyze, and organize information
2. Communicate ideas and information
3. Planning and organizing activities
4. Ability to work with other people or teams

5. Solving problems with research data and technical methods

6. Solve the problem

7. Using new technologies

Understand the company culture

Let's take about the "Problem solving" test of the general competency model decomposition:

1. The ability to solve problems is clearly defined. That is, combining the company's vision, strategy and post functions to explain what is the ability to solve problems. This is defined as the ability of company employees to analyze and propose solutions to the problems using concepts, rules, and work procedure methods.

2. The ability to solve problems through data collection, investigation, interviews and expert analysis and assessment to obtain the critical behavior of problem-solving ability. Through these processes we set up the following behavioral groups that obtain problem-solving abilities.

2.1. Objectively look at things and be able to define problems broadly;

2.2. Can systematically analyze complex problems and be able to make inferences and observations to determine the relevance and causal relationship of the problem;

2.3. Be able to pre-analyze the company's resource environment before formulating the solution;

2.4. According to the company's rules, procedures and methods, as well as personal experience, professional knowledge and other proposed solutions;

2.5. Can advise company leaders to make decisions in an appropriate way.

3. Design an interview questionnaire outline based on the key behavior of problem-solving ability. Through the analysis of key behavioral groups, the interview questionnaire be set up as follows:

3.1. Do you think you're good at analyzing problems? Can you list two examples of your previous work to prove your analytical skills?

3.2. Please tell us about a difficult problem you have analyzed and the advice you have given.

3.3. Please tell us what is your usual way of dealing with complex problems? Can you give me an example?

3.4. What are the steps you usually take when you analyze complex problems?

3.5. If you are divided into 10 standards, how do you play a part in your ability? Why?

3.6. Do you have any experience in analyzing your own mistakes and how do you remedy?

4. Supplement to the revision of the problem outline

By answering the above questions, we can reveal the information about the behavior of the candidate, which can be used to evaluate the candidate's ability to cooperate. However, in the specific interview process, how can we judge the authenticity of the applicant's narrative? This is to fill in the details of the above questionnaire outline-that is, 5W tools to enrich the above questionnaire, to grasp the details, you can help us to explore the following questions about behavioral information.

4.1. How did you deal with it?

4.2. Have you succeeded? Why?

4.3. What happened later?

4.4. What was the dilemma you were facing? How did you deal with it?

4.5. What aspects or how did you succeed? Please have a talk.

4.6. In what ways or how did you fail? Please have a talk.

4.7. What did you learn from it? Wait a minute.

Design Interview questions scoring table

According to the candidate's answer to the interview questionnaire, in the interview is mainly based on the experience of the candidate, task and performance results, such as the score.

Question Number		Interviewer	
Duty	Action	Result	
□1 □2 □3 □4 □5	□1 □2 □3 □4 □5	□1 □2 □3 □4 □5	
1. Indicates that the candidates had duty in the past is not difficult; 2. Indicates that the candidate had duty a slightly difficult task in the past; 3. Indicates that the candidate had duty difficulties in the past; 4. Indicates that the candidate had duty in the past is very difficult; 5. Indicates that the candidate had the task is extremely difficult;	1, Indicates that the applicant's past actions do not have difficulties; 2. Indicate that the applicant has had a slight difficulty in acting in the past; 3. Indicates that the applicant's past actions are difficult; 4. It is very difficult for the applicant to act in the past. 5. Indicates that the candidate's actions in the past have been extremely difficult;	1, Indicates that the applicant has achieved the results of the past is not difficult; 2, Indicates that the candidate has achieved a slightly difficult result; 3, Indicates that the candidate has reached the results of a difficult degree; 4, Indicates that the candidate has achieved a very difficult result; 5, Indicates that the applicant has reached the results of extremely difficult;	

PI Training

At Company E and Company J, we arrange PI on-line test for manager or above interview. In the Company E when only puzzled to read the report, as if not to say who can't be recruited, so as the reference effect isn't big.

Later, Company J, invited descendants of the family of PI system founder come to China from the United States to teach in person.

We transfer the lessons we learned into internal training, not to train up each manager or interviewer become a PI expert, but to know how to choose, motivate and retain key talent. Is it suitable for post and team, Boss?

PI: Predictive index Chinese translation as a forecast index.

PI is a tool for talent selection, encouragement and retention behavior analysis. It uses a set of on-line analysis system to analyze the behavior of specific personnel and the motivation that employees should have.

PI used as

1. Understand and predict how people respond to the environment and people they face.

2. Connect individuals and their performance to specific business objectives.

3. Understanding the individual's specific motivations

4. Refining efficient leaders and leading teams

5. Enhance staff cohesion

PI included ABCD four indexes

A represent : Dominance

B represent : Extroversion

C represent : Patience.

D represent : Formality

The online system uses a series of words in the form of questionnaires to ask the person being tested to choose the words that best reflect their characteristics.

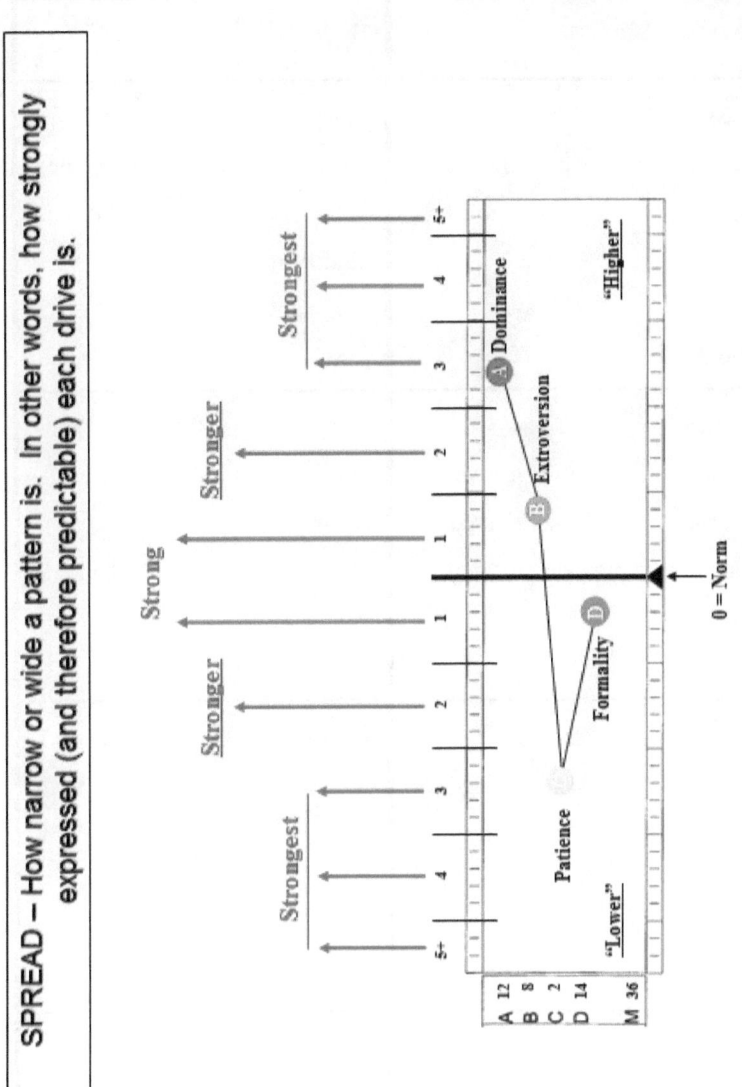

Note: This illustration indicates that the farther away the indicator is from the center axis, the greater and stronger the measure.

PI	Low		High	
A	Agreeable Accepting of company policies Seeks harmony	Cooperative Accommodating Comfortable with what is Risk averse	Independent Assertive Self-confident Self-starter	Challenging Venturesome Individualistic Competitive
B	Analytical Imaginative Reflective Reserved	Serious Introspective Task oriented Matter of fact	Outgoing Optimistic Selling Delegates Authority	Meets new people easily Enthusiastic Empathetic Socially poised
C	Tense Restless Driving Impatient	Intense Sense of urgency Fast-paced No need to finish	Patient Stable Calm Deliberate	Consistent Seeks to create a family-like atmosphere Steady
D	Casual Views details as less important than results Undaunted by	Informal Risk Tolerant Comfortable with risk Freely delegates details	Self-disciplined to the standards Cautious Conservative Conscientious	Diligent Attentive to details Precise Organized

	criticism or rejection	Non-conforming by nature	

Note: PI does not tell us what the person being tested will do, and he will tell us why the person being tested wants to do it.

When the work we provide coincides with what the person in the test wants to do, the person who is being tested will be more motivated to do the work which will be more satisfying and efficient. If the behavior required by the job is not what the employee wants or likes to do, the data shows that he needs more training and persuasion to improve his ability to meet the requirements.

PI	Low	High
A	Encouragement, Reassurance Harmony (rather than friction) Understanding supervision	Independence Recognition for own ideas Control of own activities/work
B	Opportunity for introspection Recognition for technical & intellectual accomplishments Freedom from office politics	Social interaction Social acceptance/recognition Symbols of prestige, status
C	Variety Change of pace Mobility	Long-term affiliation Stable work environment Familiar surroundings, people & work
D	Freedom from rigid rules & tight controls	Certainty – know exactly what the rules are

Freedom of expression	Specific knowledge of job
Opportunity to delegate details	Freedom from risk of error

Note:

Dynamic

The PI file of an employee reflects the specific motives of the employee.

Leaders can then speculate that their subordinates are motivated or not.

Management is a one-to-one activity. A leader, when fully aware of his/her motives, can fully combine the requirements of a job with the needs of an employee to truly motivate others.

In order to give all managers a hands-on experience, we give all managers to do a round of PI test, the results of each report as a model to open the explanation, the most peculiar point, GM Sheetoh & me PI file model is exactly the same, so we finally understand why I work with him so in tune with.

25.The recruitment of fresh graduates-Fight repeatedly after suffering repeated defeats

About 10 years ago, when I talked to the HR circle about whether I should recruit fresh graduates, they shook their heads and said to me, "How could you keep fresh graduate?" The company spends a lot of effort in vain, all work for others without getting any benefit for the company".

10 years passed, the companies in China facing the problems is not only the question of whether to choose fresh graduates, but also to choose the elite University or the second-tier college "cheap labor"-shift to the frontline management of worker? Expanded recruitment for many years, repeated the " Manufacturing in a rough way and massive production " of the university education, the annual supply of millions of fresh graduates, so that the company only can recruit students by following market trend to lower labor price, I have record Company J from 2007 to recruit fresh raw salary of 2300 yuan, the annual increase of 100 to 200 yuan in base salary, By the time of 2017, the jump in ten years: the final income compare with the line workers left several hundred yuan difference. On the other side, the company is going to spend all the attention on the lack of professional knowledge of college education to the graduates, to the knowledge and experience needed to make up for the students, smart students can immediately "be sold" to other companies. So, this is the company's human resources reservoir to approach "blood" or "bleeding"? Let fresh graduates unify ability and interest? Is it the value orientation of the enterprise and the real match of the Graduate's career development? Now the recruitment of enterprises already be post 90' graduates, how to take care of their own characteristics is also a learning.

The design and manufacturing motor talent is difficult to find, we need to hire mechanical graduates but to retrain the principle of motor. Company E develop plans starting from 2003 to recruit fresh graduates, calculate the cost, the first year put into training fees and wages, HR is Project Commander, organize the campus recruitment, then arrange self-training by departments, three months' probation, fresh graduates regularly submit reports to the Supervisor and Department manager, Department supervisors and Managers assess the performance of their work in a timely manner to give feedback, supervisors monthly evaluations, and managers quarterly make assessments. Report to HR in time. In addition to this fresh graduate to pass six months, a year of assessment, graduates must ensure that their annual assessment score, pass the assessment then graduation certification can be granted. Annual salary adjustment should also be made into the fresh graduate recruitment program and budget, for later checking.

At that time in order to reduce difficulty of running among many schools and organizations to interview, we decided to go through the Western cities: 10 days to visit Jiangxi University, Wuhan University, and Xi' an electronic science and technology campus to recruit.

Immediately re-design the budget, posters, campus presentations, interview topics, the list of travel and so on, why? Because the previous HR only rely on campus and organizers help with job ads for the booth, HR and department head look at the campus recruitment as a "welfare" to the outer provinces, they are not responsible for the recruitment result.

To design campus recruitment ads as sales ads, to have the beauty of PPT. It's not just cold numbers and statement. Display the best strength of our own to the job seekers, I offered the recruitment ads to professional advertising company to design, the effect can convince ourselves.

The campus presentation is designed address to the three major issues that graduates are most concerned with: vacancy, payroll, requirements, openly publish:

1. Shenzhen hukou

Company for qualified employees to handle Shenzhen hukou and related file transferring.

2. Working hours

8 hours 5 days a week work, 10 days annual statutory holiday, and enjoy 5-14 days paid annual leave.

3. Social Security

According to government regulations to contribute social insurance for each employee.

4. Living conditions

The company provides free dormitory; Employees are encouraged to rent outside house and the company provide housing allowances accordingly.

5. Company Bus

A round trip shuttle bus is available for employees who live in Shen Zhen and Bao An.

6. Entertainment Facilities

The company has a gym, basketball courts, tennis courts, ice hockey courts, internet cafes, karaoke, libraries, for employees to use.

7. Purchase House Subsidy scheme

Company to provide housing financial support for qualified employees in Bao An, Shenzhen.

8. Career development

Achieve personal development through internal job posting and provide career planning for employees.

9. The university offers a variety of knowledge and skills training to its employees and is associated with many well-known universities in the country, offering a wide range of university education programs to its employees and providing master/doctoral scholarships to some of its best employees.

Salary Level:

Very competitive, based on the principle of high-paying talent wage level in the same industry;

According to the specific performance, the year-end performance award can be awarded up to 1.5 times of the monthly salary.

Written examination designed by the technical departments, in the beginning the department head were happy that "Bowl out" graduates, I remind them that the problem can't be too difficult and can't be too easy, all use choice questions, spend 45-60 minutes to complete, convenient for HR read and give the mark on examination papers .

We contacted the graduates ' teachers in advance to find out all the details of the recruitment arrangements, including the location of the interview as far away from the test venue. We invited the president of the students ' union, because they are familiar with the campus situation, the students have the absolute appeal, they have all the graduates communication information, the relevant department of the teachers and directors of the department, we will knock on the door to visit these teachers, the teacher began to work, publicity company's strong background, "Call" their students to participate in our graduate briefing.

Campus recruitment is very successful, at least more than 800 graduates participate in each campus, department head interview from the morning to late night, each one dry but continue: "All are very good students, it reminded me that I can't join so the good universities in my school days"

In the following three northeastern provinces recruitment tour is also a victory, we can use the "Pick one from hundred" proportions to find the most suitable for the best students: engineering background, growth in China's long history of industrial development city, income level staying in the middle and low, more eager to the South economy zone to develop, temperate places better for long-term development, They have excellent academic performance, good English skills, dare to face foreign customers. Of course, the company has a variety of technical projects to be developed waiting for these top-notch students to break: We focus on the introduction of the establishment of the company's post-doctoral workstation: In the name of a postdoctoral workstation to recruit doctors, annual salary commitment is not less than 80,000 above the market price. Attract people with lofty ideals by settling accounts, lodging and providing a beautiful office environment. The company has been studying but long-term attack not broken project as the focus of post-doctoral research, the implementation of dual-tutor system, from Harbin University of Technology to provide academic mentors, help students open questions and responsible for the interim, and outbound assessment reports, the company is responsible for providing guidance and feedback in the work of the technical tutor to the Doctor, Doctor go to the company for the development and research work, to participate in academic exchange activities, the company bear all the cost. Base on the investigations and tutor recommendation, we recruited two doctors into the station in that year, they later developed into the company's technical backbone, to help customers solve one after another technical difficulties.

The same set of campus propaganda materials and arrangements, HR team of Hong Kong head office moved to Tsinghua University graduates of the special Job fair, finally only to greet the admission of no more than 15 graduates, success ratio of "0", no targeted recruitment market no strategy adjustment, the result is doomed to failure.

I was just joined Company J, 25 graduates of the Chinese factory and the Malaysian Penang factory with the same number of interchange training for six months of the project kicked off, the graduates during the internship period of the total income can reach RMB7,300 yuan at the same time accumulated in foreign work experience, but the project apply for a work visa because the Malaysian government rejected.

In fact, from the perspective of Graduates Company J has a complete set of corporate training, in the Chinese factory and in the factory in Penang received the same training is not very different, so recruited people in six months, adapted into all the process and work environment, even the graduates are automatically abandoned to be Penang internship.

In the first-tier city recruitment is different from other cities, Company J Positioning Guangzhou Top universities: South China University of Technology, Guangzhou Foreign Language University, Guangdong Industrial University. There are many opportunities for graduates enrolled in these institutions.

The headcount of graduates needs to be budgeted in each year, the headcount of employees estimates to lose in the next year or two and the amount of manpower required to expand the business will be approved by HR and general Manager.

In addition to the recruitment strategies mentioned above, our key questionnaire survey of those who are still in office from these three universities to understand what is the most important skill to help new graduates survive in Company J? What is the most improvement in recent graduate recruitment? And so on, combined with their feedback, we have targeted the redesign of the content and process of the presentation, the subject of the test and the list of benefits that the company provides.

Promote the company's brand and recruiting information by sponsoring the most popular basketball games on campus.

There were many video edit by group, but no one introduction on the whole group, consulted with the group's public relations, they couldn't shoot out for a short time, then shoot by ourselves, we can design how to shoot, let each branch shoot their most beautiful scene and combine together, momentum naturally came out, The video is shared among the branches of the Chinese region.

At the prestigious universities in Guangzhou, we invited more students than any other companies: More than 1,000 people per campus speech, even the channels and windows of the lecture room stood full of people!

At the beginning of the presentation, we did not want to show the company's information in a hurry, but asked the students in the field what the image of the best employer in your mind would look like. Please draw on the white paper in one minute. The atmosphere of the scene was suddenly mobilized, at that time each classmate enthusiastically spoke, in the end what picture they use to describe the best employer's image I have not remember, but Company J over the years by the major media selected as the best employer, has been rooted in the hearts of graduates.

The most persuasive of the graduates are the introductions from their Brother & sister, we arrange their brother walk out amongst them, let him leisurely go to the stage in the middle, told to the younger brothers and sisters, he join four years five times to the United States plant to move the project to the Chinese factory..., of course, this is the scenery, but also tell the people in the present , not every graduate has the opportunity, the price may be four years to work around the night: Midnight conference call, overnight to solve the problem ..., "No Pay no game" applicable to any country.

Turn to the most eloquent training mentor David, he did not introduce the group's background, but asked the audience in the presence of what 's the major products for Company J? There are a few can provide the right answer, this is not surprising, Company J has never had its own brand of products, David made a joke to take out a bag of apples, tell everyone these are apples five yuan of a kilo, just bought from the company door, then slowly take out of the pocket of an Apple iPhone, To show you this is the latest Apple third-generation mobile phone: manufactured by the company. The scene atmosphere was immediately pulled to the climax, even me who has been sitting behind and the designer of this game also felt a shock, be proud of our own company.

I never waste any company resources, even the marketing department most often sell companies and products, the usual favorite internal support Department of David and Steven was also used to answer the graduates a lot of sharp questions, they are battle-hardened, For graduates most like to mention but the least easy to reply in public, the question: How much will the company's salary to be? David, who was also the high-flyer from Zhongshan university, volunteered to share with you: "You don't have to ask the company what 's the price to hire you, you should ask yourself, how much can I value in this market?" spoke with forked tongue, meaning profound.

To the end of the presentation, we arranged for a memory contest-to learn about the information the graduates have heard about the company.

After the presentation, followed by a written test, we designed the topic to include:

1.1 General Knowledge: English test 1.5*30 = 45 points, 40 minutes

1.2 Career trends: 20 minutes or 5 minutes

1.3 Case study: 20 minutes

2.1 Professional basis: noun translation 5 mins

2.2 Professional quiz: Q&A 15 minutes

Examination questions must be completed within the specified time and published results on the spot. The demonstration and written examinations of the entire campus are once complete within 2.5 hours, the next step is to invite the qualified graduates visit to the company and conduct a second round of interview. Our interview approach also takes a unique approach: No leadership discussion, 56 minutes to complete the three-stage test: self-selected products and marketing, the group discussed and agreed to, presentation and defense. All the interviewers silently observe the pitch, support, teamwork, the communication and influence that the graduates demonstrate in the process, which they must survive in Company J in the future.

Pay, benefits, and training are often the most tangled places for graduates.

As David said in his speech: "You don't have to ask the company what the price to offer, you should ask yourself, how much can I value in this market?" We put the salary of fresh graduates to the market salary 1/4 quartile, three years 1/2, five-year 3/4 quartile position. But later found that the speed of the company to the fresh graduates to make special treatment, can't catch up with the rapid changes in the market, so in second year we have four times adjustment to fresh graduates, Compared to the company 1.5 times to the annual increment, one-time bonuses, individual excellent special adjustment, a variety of methods have been used, but frequent changes resulted in the company and graduates are not at a loss, not necessarily effective. The excessive personal verbal commitment of the head of department lead to high expectation of graduates. Always consider the inter-factory transferring, to unify the factory between the remuneration package. The new bring the impact to old graduates in the same factory, as well as the fair treatment between the campus recruitment graduates and individuals walk in different from the society the experienced talent.

Having finished the red tape of the Chinese government, after processing the follow-up registration and transfer resident permit procedures, the graduates began a three-month company training, including new induction training, process testing/equipment Introduction, business group concept, corporate training and business group model commissioning, cross-departmental concept, on-the-job training, examination/certification, Here I take the most common training course for production line supervisors as an example:

EIT training for production line supervisor

Item	
1	Basic knowledge

1.1	Understand WC products process
2	Professional knowledge
2.1	Good arrangement for production resource (HC, Test, tools etc)
2.2	Build plan achievement
2.3	Team coaching and team work
2.4	Provide manufacturing data
2.5	Lean Concept
2.6	Manufacturing budget and control
2.7	Feedback and solve problems
2.8	English skills
3	System & Procedure
3.1	Be familiar with all procedure related to manufacturing
3.2	Be familiar with Manufacturing production system (including E-Pull, SFM, E-MSD, SPC, MES, SAP)
4	Management performance and requirements
4.1	OLE\OEE goals and achievement
4.2	DL Cost goals and achievement
4.3	FPY goals and achievement
4.4	DPM goals and achievement
4.5	5S and discipline control 5S
5	Management knowledge

5.1	5S Management	
5.2	Communication Skills	
5.3	Time Management	
5.4	Planning and execution	
5.5	Team Building	
5.6	Escalation	
5.7	Presentation skill	
6	Employee Relationship	
6.1	Regular Meeting with Production DL	
6.2	Regular Meeting with new DL	
6.3	Face to face communicate with resign DL	
6.4	Meeting With line leader and floater	
6.5	Organization team building	

Different departments and positions by the Training department and each department manager to develop specific training programs and content, regular assessment.

In fact, too early to help recent graduates tailor-made long-term training programs do not have much practical significance, but let them operate as early as practicable, the actual participation in daily operations and projects have practical significance. They need mentors in their daily work and not trainers in the classroom.

In order to encourage fresh graduates to "action learning", we use the originator of Action Learning, to share with graduates the example of inspiring others' success in life. To encourage graduates to study different issues and projects, cross-section of the establishment of the team, the company provide mentors, by their own theme, slogans, limited time to complete, finally in the six months after the internship to show what they found, what improvements have been made, what achievements have been learned.

Half-yearly training internship has passed, HR arrangement Questionnaire survey, the graduates' feedback on their training and Buddy, the relationship between the departments to deal with, also let them reflect on their own shortcomings, for their own specific development and improve the goal.

In order to keep this millstone for their whole life, we encourage they draw one picture on the wall of Asia training center, record they made a progress together with the company.

26.Training essence, can you make it clear?

If possible, I would like to share all the training courses we have designed with everyone!

As HR head I often struggle with the role of HR in training, if HR department own a professional trainer team, or take the role of "organize and promote training coordinator" will be better?

I have made two efforts, finally found that HR has more to do is clear understanding of the company's strategy, clearly understand how to build a training system to speed up the development of the company's strategy, but also conducive to the development of human resources management strategy. To build a training system, creating a culture of learning, helping departments to clear their key skills and competency models, searching within and outside the company for technical experts with corresponding key skills and the ability to win, train these technical specialists to become trainers, effectively training and maintaining accurate training classes and training courses for employees.

What is the company's strategy?

What is the system of training?

How to promote the culture of learning?

How to build a key skill and a competency model?

How do I find a technical expert?

How to train technical experts?

How to make trainer have substance in speech, say with certainly?

This is the way many companies training leaders don't know how to explain, how to execute.

What 's company strategy?

It is the direction of the company's efforts and the results hope to get. An interesting example, GM Steven just arrived, formulated the company's strategy: to build a "SMART" factory, strong push industrial 4.0 and EMS2.0, he began to ask department heads what is industrialization 4.0? Everybody dumbfounded, no one can answer, Steven "ridicule" our ignorance, let everyone learn what is called Industrialization 4.0, gave a hint: Siemens company pushes Industrialization 4.0 most successful. These managers are "blind busy" every day, who knows industry 3.0 or 4.0, none put anything in their heart. But HR head must be conscious, even the strategic direction of the boss did not understand, how can be HR head?

I do not want to be the next "be ridiculed" target, find Siemens's HR counterparts, verbally heard their interpretation, also personally visit, led by German experts, the understanding of the industrialization 4.0 originator of the company how to build machine automation, what's data intelligence. Thinking is not enough, search the relevant information on the Internet, the more confused, ran to Guangzhou library to borrow a limited number of books, because at that time at home very few people are talking about this topic. Books always give you the best summaries, especially those written by national experts:

Germany Industry 4.0-Germany use the information technical system to make production equipment intelligent, so that the factory becomes a self-disciplined decentralized system of intelligent factory. By then, cloud computing is only one object of use in manufacturing, not a hub for manufacturing.

American industrial 4.0-GE, Cisco, IBM, AT&T, and Intel have set up an industrial Internet consortium that is redefining the future of manufacturing.

Japanese Industry 4.0-Energy re-creation, the robot is solving Japan's disadvantage.

China Industry 4.0-the most complete supply chain, the most industry-wide category, we are missing: Technology and innovation!

I really became the next "target" of the boss, because he wants to use the power of HR, let each employee understand what is called Industrialization 4.0. Listening I'm an HR guy, Well versed in" industrialization 4.0, Steven overjoyed, instructed HR organize "literacy" training, so that all employees understand the industrialization of 4.0, we immediately take action. After a round of literacy, Steven find this department manager to ask what is called Industrialization 4.0? Then ask that Department director did you think of how to do industrialization 4.0 in your own department? Aroused everyone's psychological curiosity, until later everyone understood what is called Industrialization 4.0? Everyone is talking about industrialization 4.0. Everyone is thinking of industrialization 4.0. We organized a professional technical training: Learn how to make industrial robots, how to explain the principle of complex robot production, how to use the motor, bearings, synchronous belt, control machine, hardware and software control to implement the prescriptive operation.

The goal is to accelerate the company's strategic implementation: the manufacturing of industrial robots to replace 24-hour repetitive work: such as loud noise, pollution, labor intensity, handling, assembly, welding and other work.

We have an industrial robot expert of a brother company to be a mentor, he has too many successful examples to share, he designed the industrial robot, can "singing and dancing." at the annual party.

As a result, we ended up rolling up our own sleeves for Industry 4.0! Make our own SMART factory!

Lead by GM, the departments can imagine and list out their own department of intelligent factory projects, submitted to the department manager to discuss the sort of implementation, GM personally led the key projects. When the project was successful, he celebrated and was complacent while watching the new projects implemented.

The evolution from "0" to a successful project, you will see the commitment by leaders, leading learning and participation in research and development, departmental managers participating in learning, sharing ideas, systematic thinking, employees being constantly encouraged to improve their skills and performance, and creating an open attitude to learn from each other. Employees pay attention to the application of market automation technology, and continuously evaluate the feasibility of internal references. This is the true embodiment of the company's learning culture.

Our company was interviewed and published by the American Times Magazine because of its excellent performance in driving industrial automation at a low cost.

Different organizational structures determine different training models: centralized, federalism, and free-mix. We have integrated the centralized system and the free combination system.

The most obvious centralized training mode is the company-based training, led by the group sub-functional departments, set up the necessary training content by the level of the development, join, promote, transfer and separation should be re-training the content of the corresponding post, to ensure pass the examination. Take my own corporatization training as a good example:

All employees have a clear understanding of the content and the standards they want to train, learn how to use the computer system, to submit work reports and specific work content by daily, weekly, monthly;

Each department manager is responsible for collating the key contents of the respective departments, such as internal HR has a whole, separate different functional groups specific training content.

Cindy's JABILIZATION AGENDA

Stage	Item	Topics	Owner
Part I	1	Conduct the routine on-board procedure	Cassie
	2	Meet CM and FM	Peggy
	3	Brief introduction to HUA HR Team & Section Officer	Peggy
	4	Introduce Huangpu O-Chart & HR O-Chart	Peggy
	5	Overall HR Function & Practice Briefing	Peggy & Mounter
	6	Recruitment Section Briefing	Cassie
	7	ER Section Briefing	Cassie
	8	C&B Section Briefing	Nicole
	9	Training Section Briefing	Ling He
	10	Entertainment & Activities	Jumbal
	11	Administration Section Briefing	Stone
	12	E&E HR	Maple Huang
	13	Security Section Briefing	RX Chen
Part II		Jabil China HR Operation Practice Sharing	May Wu
		(May's input)	
Part III		**Huangpu HR Job Handover**	**Peggy**
		On-Going Project	
	1	Offsite Meeting - Meeting Minutes & Action Plan	done
	2	Identify Compentency to be A-Grade Team	done
	3	Employee Opinion Survey- Result & Action	done
	4	ER Candidate	done
	5	SER/EICC audit	done
		Outstanding /Follow- up Issue	
	1	Derek Giam - to be follow up with Green Point	Nicole
	2	Radford Compensation Survey - Global	done
	4	Offsite Strategy Meeting - BU at Crown Plaza on Dec. 17	
	5	Long Service Award - Dec. 14th by TP Yuan	
Part IV		**Huangpu HR Job Handover**	**Mounter**
		On-Going Project	
	1	CNY Project	
		-Contract DL Service Bonus	
		-Contract DL Recruitment Fee During 25-Nov-2009 to 31-Jan-2010	
		-School Cooperation Event	
	2	-Review Guideline	
	3	HP HER Project	
	4	W/C IL Survey	
		Outstanding /Follow- up Issue	
	1	Y2009 Handicapped Audit	
	2	Y2009 Non-exempt IL Focal Review	
	4	Jumping Stair Case Follow Up	
	5	Booking train ticket & bus transportation arrangment study	

The following is the Corporatization training I done for my subordinates.

The corporatization training is ranked after the induction training, that how do we arrange induction training?

The content of induction training is quite rich:

At first, the company cultural translation on FCD (Focus on employees, Commit to customers, Deliver the quality), the indoctrination start from the first day.

Core Value

Delivers quality results

Achieves customer satisfaction

Seeks continuous improvement

Effectively solves problems

Exhibits flexibility

Effectively collaborates

Many people will ask: do we need to recite these things? We never force employees to do these rote, unpopular things, the company is everyone's, the company's culture is everyone's habit, the company's core values are employees enter the company's "entry voucher. " unconsciously influenced by constantly hears or sees, step by step, what need to recite?

1. let employees devour EICC, electrostatic protection, ISO9000, ISO14000 and OHSAS18000, TS16949, and so on a set of theory, in fact, is a difficult thing, but the customer's requirements must be met, so we put the theory of safety, The indoctrination and production process of the fire concept evolved into video, making it easy for all workers to understand. After that, we will distribute the handbook to employees so that they can remember.

2. In order to instill the lean concept into our employees on the first day, we put "analog" production in a new classroom, giving it a sense of how to continuously refine the production line and reduce waste.

3. In order to save time and manpower cost, we also carry on the lean improvement to the induction training, emphasis the key points, the whole

journey from three days change to three hours, the results of the exam is similar. All staff are taught the rule of role, to clarify their roles, conduct and decision-making scope. The company hangs out a code of conduct in each manager's room and each conference room, so that every employee can see it.

Since May 2013, the company unified a global version, each department head introduces their own department functions to the new staff, each time I introduce HR and system to the staff by using one hour, I think still did not talk about the focus.

By operation, market and accounting the three-pack decision-making, the matrix company's structure is Company J 's unique and successful management model, this chapter is also the focus of the induction training, so that the business group managers and account managers know what should be done and how to do? Define the functions, objectives, budgets, statements, necessary meetings, Profit and Loss calculation of each department and other specific work contents.

In the United States, corporate copyright and intellectual property protection training is especially focused on the staff level, and the code of purpose is known because it is communicated with too much code.

Lean training, no best only better

Training and certification of lean production to each manager, each manager must learn 15 series of lean theory, and personally lead subordinates to complete the required number of Lean project promotion and implementation, in order to pass the bronze and silver certification.

To carry out the corresponding study for each level, no bronze certification not eligible for promotion.

The training cited a large number of videos and examples, from the success story of the Toyota family, we followed the trainer to play games, training quoted a large number of various large companies how to do lean success case video, we saw how the Boeing Company made the machine, We saw how the Toyota company made vehicles, even in person Toyota and Honda Company manufacturing vehicles, we also saw how the shell-type shopping malls in and out of the goods, how to manage logistics? Even families in the United States have introduced the concept of 5S management: How to place clothes and footwear, how to place tools, such a shallow case proves that lean production exists in every detail of our lives.

For each course theme the managers need to go to the designated production line to identify problems and implement solutions based on knowledge learn from training. in a class two managers had the quarrel even to fight, each other did not realize the point of lean production in the discovery and point out the problem, is it allow? Of course, in the United States company everyone is fair, each has the right to express their own views, the group's CEO Tim inconsistent with the views of subordinates, two people to fight up in the company's back stairs, the next day two people still work together, with bruises, Tim didn't mean to "kill" the employee, and the employee didn't even consider resigning, would a Chinese company allow such situation exist?

In order let the trainees understand it, we take the detection into video & photo, so that different countries, different factories, different department managers work together to do lean projects, understand the fact, solve problems together.

Along with the lean production, the company set to have Gemba Walk in every week, GM lead the managers for:

Engineering
• Poor layout design
• Poor grasp of production/flow principles
• Inappropriate equipment/tools

Quality

- Lack of FMEA before production

Materials/Purchasing
- Poor grasp of direct inventory levels
- Poor control of indirect materials

Production
- Workplace organization and discipline
- Insufficient detailed analysis of rejects
- Lack of feedback
- Management of Incoming Materials

Program/Business
- Poor grasp of inventory levels
- Communications and plan changes
- Poor grasp of 5S principles
- Manpower planning and retention

Together to find a common solution to the problem, will not forgive any one production line any one department. Public posted the results of the improvement of reducing how many costs, accept everyone audit.

Similar training also has JOS Rapid Response to the quality control system, in the U.S. company "Meeting time", "Discussion topic", "How to control the result" have been standardized.

QRQC Meetings

Line QRQC
- Real-time line problem solving
- QRAP
- 5 Whys
- CA & PA
- QRQC LPA
- Unsolved issues escalate to Zone or CAC
- Line Leaders, Technicians, Supervisors

Meeting Leader: Supervisor

Zone QRQC (option)
- Complex multi-bays/areas
- Prelude to CAC
- Unsolved issues escalate to CAC
- Line Supervisors, Line Managers, Shift Engineers, WC Support staff.

Meeting Leader: Supervisor/Line Mgr

CAC
- Daily Mfg metrics review
- QRQC Opens
- FPV
- DPM
- WIP
- OTD
- LPA
- etc
- Engineers, Support Staff, Line Managers, WCM

Meeting Leader: Line Manager

Workcell JOS Meetings

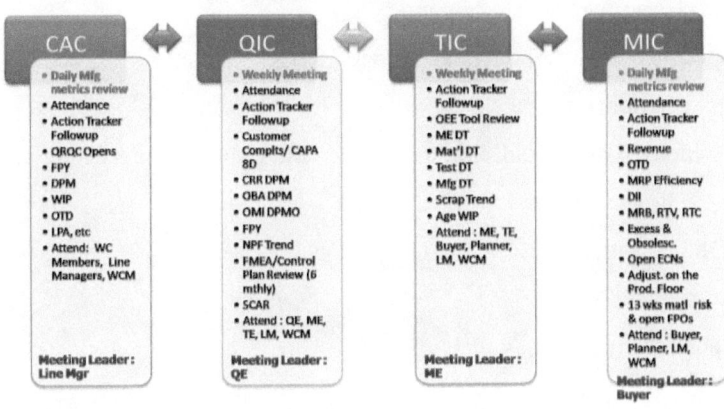

CAC
- Daily Mfg metrics review
- Attendance
- Action Tracker Followup
- QRQC Opens
- FPY
- DPM
- WIP
- OTD
- LPA, etc
- Attend: WC Members, Line Managers, WCM

Meeting Leader: Line Mgr

QIC
- Weekly Meeting
- Attendance
- Action Tracker Followup
- Customer Complts/ CAPA 8D
- CRR DPM
- OBA DPM
- OMI DPMO
- FPY
- NPF Trend
- FMEA/Control Plan Review (6 mthly)
- SCAR
- Attend : QE, ME, TE, LM, WCM

Meeting Leader: QE

TIC
- Weekly Meeting
- Action Tracker Followup
- OEE Tool Review
- ME DT
- Mat'l DT
- Test DT
- Mfg DT
- Scrap Trend
- Age WIP
- Attend : ME, TE, Buyer, Planner, LM, WCM

Meeting Leader: ME

MIC
- Daily Mfg metrics review
- Attendance
- Action Tracker Followup
- Revenue
- OTD
- MRP Efficiency
- DII
- MRB, RTV, RTC
- Excess & Obsolesc.
- Open ECNs
- Adjust. on the Prod. Floor
- 13 wks matl risk & open FPOs
- Attend : Buyer, Planner, LM, WCM

Meeting Leader: Buyer

JOS FM Staff Meetings

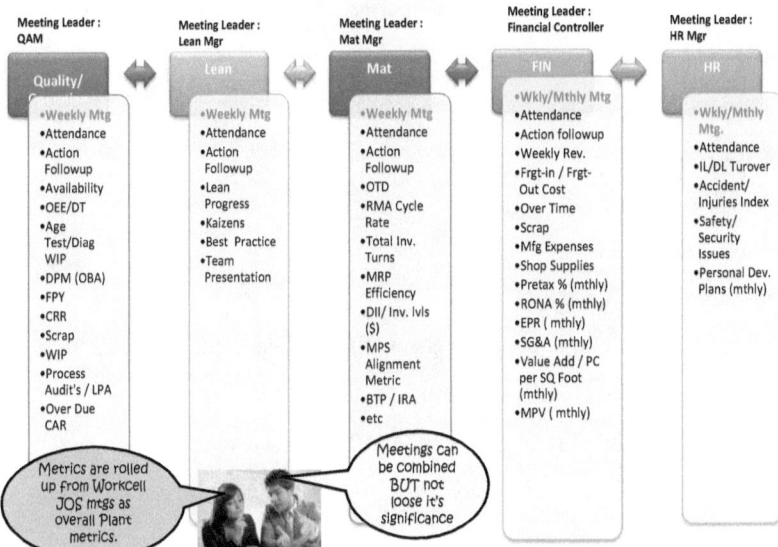

Meeting Leader: QAM

Quality/
- Weekly Mtg
- Attendance
- Action Followup
- Availability
- OEE/DT
- Age Test/Diag WIP
- DPM (OBA)
- FPY
- CRR
- Scrap
- WIP
- Process Audit's / LPA
- Over Due CAR

Meeting Leader: Lean Mgr

Lean
- Weekly Mtg
- Attendance
- Action Followup
- Lean Progress
- Kaizens
- Best Practice
- Team Presentation

Meeting Leader: Mat Mgr

Mat
- Weekly Mtg
- Attendance
- Action Followup
- OTD
- RMA Cycle Rate
- Total Inv. Turns
- MRP Efficiency
- DII/ Inv. lvls ($)
- MPS Alignment Metric
- BTP / IRA
- etc

Meeting Leader: Financial Controller

FIN
- Wkly/Mthly Mtg
- Attendance
- Action followup
- Weekly Rev.
- Frgt-in / Frgt-Out Cost
- Over Time
- Scrap
- Mfg Expenses
- Shop Supplies
- Pretax % (mthly)
- RONA % (mthly)
- EPR (mthly)
- SG&A (mthly)
- Value Add / PC per SQ Foot (mthly)
- MPV (mthly)

Meeting Leader: HR Mgr

HR
- Wkly/Mthly Mtg.
- Attendance
- IL/DL Turover
- Accident/ Injuries Index
- Safety/ Security Issues
- Personal Dev. Plans (mthly)

Metrics are rolled up from Workcell JOS mtgs as overall Plant metrics.

Meetings can be combined BUT not loose it's significance

FEMA Learning: Courses are not for Quality Department but for each dept

What is FMEA?

A method to identify potential failure modes.

Identify potential effects of the failure modes.

Generate a risk priority number.

Identify actions which could eliminate/reduce the chance of the failure from occurring. Continually improving the process.

Documenting the process.

The benefits of an FMEA

Identify potential risk areas & their effects

Lower yields & efficiencies;

Downtime;

Loss productivity;

Defect, customer returns, safety and reliability issues etc.

An organized and disciplined method for eliminating potential failure causes.

Provide a continuous improvement cycle for an overall process.

When to use FMEA

New Product Launches.

Design Reviews.

Process or Product Changes.

Preventive Maintenance.

Ongoing Continual Reviews.

Create an FMEA – S, O, D Score，S-severity, O-Occurrence, D-Detection

Training for employees' work and interest needs

The company's training funding up to RMB10,000 yuan/year, the company only asked to sign a one-year service contract, 10,000 signed six months, 20,000 to 40,000, signed 1.5 years, 40,000 above, only 2 years, the company has never limited application, but the real applicant is not many. The reasons are external and internal: the external curriculum is duplicated, there is no novelty, employees want to use limited time for online learning and textbook reading.

Company E-learning System has thousands of online courses, can learn at any time, have a dedicated colleague monitoring, Success factor personnel system to track the situation of each person completed. Global talent stock takes on the key skills, technical talent are ready.

We introduce champ education system to train employees' speech skills, because the staff basically must give speeches, especially in the face of clients, the high management came from Corp, English, PPT, Excel, and speech skills are indispensable.

Bella and me participated into group's the best practice competition, to learn the presentation skills. Employees involved into with great attention, because the learning skills can be used in the work, quite seriously. Toastmaster education system 80% is to improve public speaking skill. 60% Exercise organization's planning ability. The support staff organizes spontaneously, this training system provides the basic guidance, lets the staff each other to discover the speech question, reminds each other, make the progress together.

The company introduced the "Master degree on Global English Learning" global training system, to find a teacher from the market specializing in English language training, from the pronunciation began to correct a bunch of "good speaking" English managers.

As for the effectiveness of training we use the four major indicators to measure the training satisfaction, test pass ratio, the headcount who receive training, as well as the technical certification ratio.

We hold training activity month:

1. Establish a public WeChat learning platform to encourage all employees to join.

2. The English corner has been established for many years, regularly held parties,

so that employees feel that learning English is a very relaxed and happy thing.

3. English speech and recitation contest, to improve the English learning and presentation skills.

4. Hold a variety of skills competitions & Team challenge match.

27. We train up hundreds & thousands of engineers by TR & MER trainings

TR is "Technician Ready" Training.

MER is "Material Expert Ready" Training.

Planner, buyer, Technician are the root of Company J, they occupy over 50% of the IL headcount and have the biggest impact on our customers satisfaction and direct bring value to operation efficiency! What kind of challenges are they facing?

In Guangzhou site, there are more than 7,000 product models running in our site and every month, we receive more than 680 engineering change notification. That means our products are changeable in every minute, which require our people capability upgrade against the time! But our internal customers said that your trainings are not good enough, your training content out of date! We are not happy about that!

We went to Wuxi and Shanghai site, we consult the regional team, they also face the similar challenges, but struggle on the solution.

To solve the problem, we develop Excellent Ready program, the program has 4 key points:

1. Get to know the RIGHT skillset requirement for each position
2. Train up Planner, Buyer, Technician- Fundamental (Execution level) Ils talent to be The Best
3. Develop Update training materials
4. Get to know the training effectiveness.

For project scope, the program focuses on the fundamental?? Ils and focus on functional technical knowledge!

For finance impact. Some trainees get promoted to the next level after the training, we only need to recruit fundamental people instead of senior people, so we save the labor cost. We use the Company J internal resources to develop the

program, compared with the external resources, we avoid the extra training cost, which is USD100K

Additional benefit: when people's capability improved, they perform well in their job and they will feel self-fulfilling. For sure, they will stay in Company J longer.

From this chart, you can see the timeline for DMAIC of our project.

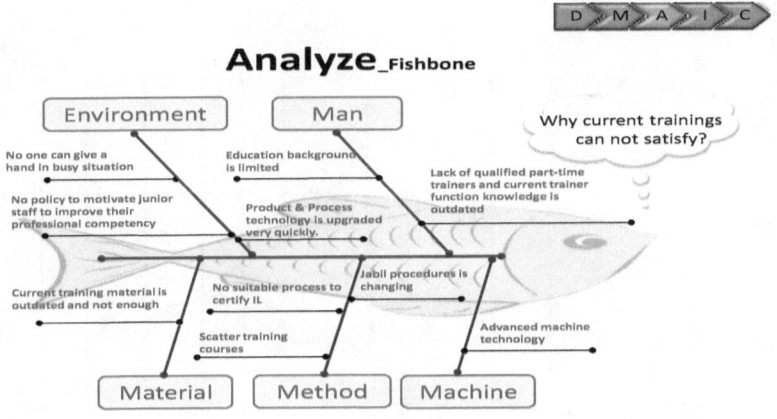

An effective training process has 5 steps. We want to know which steps have the problems, we have done a survey and the shareholders dissatisfy three steps.

We continue to conduct the second level study. For the analyze step, only 29% of the function have the clear and complete analysis on functional technical skillset requirement. For the develop step, both the trainer number and training courses number do not change much in the past 2 years. For the evaluation, only 20% of the training courses have the training effectiveness assessment.

We use the fishbone diagram and C&E matrix to analyze the defined problem? We focus on the top 4 causes.

We continue to use 5 why to find the improvement action. We get 4 actions: the first action is "Establish complete functional technical skillset ", the second action is to build up delicate trainers' team; The third action is to invite competent resources to train up trainers. The last one is to set up standardized training effectiveness evaluation process.

Our final solution is to work with Company J internal resources COMPANY J ASIA TRAINING CENTER instead of external consultancies, since

COMPANY J ASIA TRAINING CENTER are more familiar with Company J procedure and cheaper.

Analyze_Causes & Effects Scores

Category	Rating of Importance		Why current training can not satisfy	Total Scores
	X	Y	9	
Material	Current training material is outdated and not enough		9	81
Man	Lack of qualified part-time trainers and current trainer function knowledge is outdated		9	81
	Education background is limited		1	9
Method	No suitable process to certify IL		9	81
	Scatter training courses		9	81
	Jabil procedures is changing		3	27
Environment	No one can give a hand in busy situation		3	27
	No policy to motivate junior staff to improve their professional competency		3	27
	Product & Process technology is upgraded very quickly.		3	27
Machine	New technology requirement of machine		3	27

Analyze_5 why

Root	Why	1 Why	2 Why	Required Improvement
Non standardized training with low competency level	Scatter training courses	Training by requested	No competency framework	Establish functional competency framework
	Current training material is outdated and not enough	No one to handle training material	There is no dedicate team	Build up dedicate team to update training material
	Insufficient and unqualified part-time trainers		There is not competency resource to train up professional trainers	Invite competency resource to train up professional function trainer team
	No suitable process to certify IL		No standardized procedure to define the certification method	Build up Jabil standardized procedure

Our program mainly consists of 5 steps.

1. Step one base on the new job description and new business requirement, we redefine l technical skillset for each function. Base on it, we get to know how many courses we need. Based on the courses list and trainees' amount, we know how many trainers we need.

2. HR modify trainers allowance policy to motivate more people to join the trainers' team. The Function recommend the people with good function technical knowledge to be the trainers. After that HR and COMPANY J ASIA TRAINING CENTER interview them to see if they have the willing and right personality to be the trainers.

3. COMPANY J ASIA TRAINING CENTER train the trainer candidates how to be a good trainer. Teach them the concepts of teaching and the methods of course design, improve the efficiency of the solution, the technical basis, self-recognition, and the solution of the map and other teaching knowledge.

They give the next level of staff a list of courses, write textbooks, try lectures, improve teaching materials, and customize the learning Framework.

4. 80% is functional knowledge, 20% soft skill

Measurement	Assessment
Technical foundation	35%
Hands-on (Practical)	35%
Technical Solution	15%
Case Study (Project)	15%

5. The manager of the functional department monitors the accuracy and timeliness of their textbooks and certified amateur Trainers. Then they are formally given the next level technician training, exams and Certifications. Because they are personally led by the engineers, they fully understand the difficulties of the next level, so through the training of professional teaching skills, improve the skills of the whole department of basic staff at a very fast pace. The training exam is very rigorous, but through the rate of 89.6%, passing the exam is each level to upgrade to the next level of ladder, if not pass the exam, can't be promoted, the purpose is to standardize each level of skills and competencies, in order to improve the product quality in one Step.

Finally, the functional department manager, the BUM assesses the performance improvement Situation.

We have skillset, trainers, training materials, but how to make sure this program can run non-stop? How to make sure that the knowledge from trainers and training material are up to date? We set up the program procedure which is in the process of DCC. This procedure tells us when to do, what to do, how to do. Training effectiveness evaluation process is just one part of it.

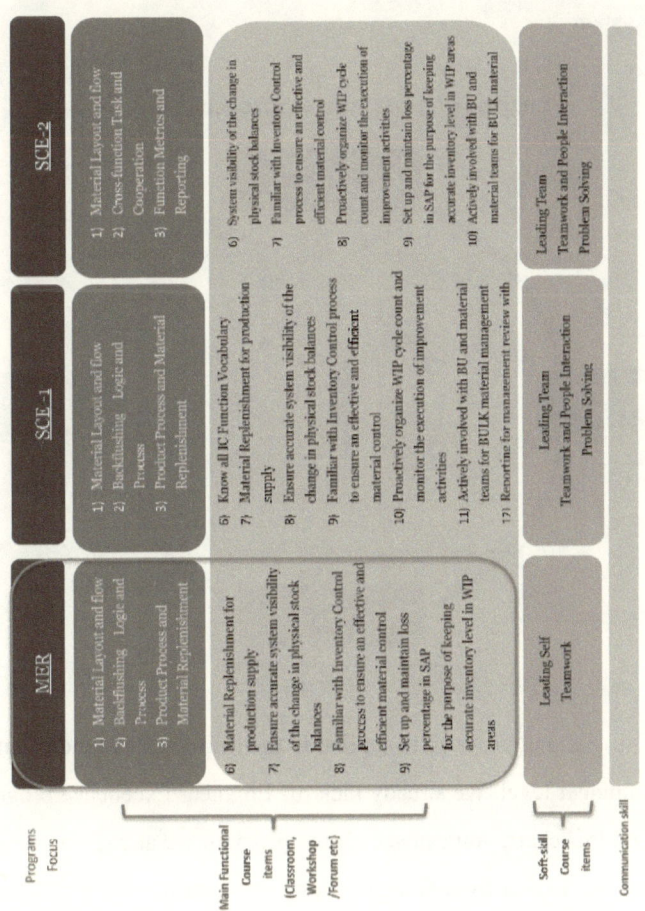

After we finish the first round of training program, we redo the survey and satisfaction rate from internal customers improve a lot!

We use to have a lot of individual trainings, which make us confused. But for our training program, everyone gets to know what is the capability requirement at the very beginning, then join the classroom training which is based on the capability requirement, get certified. improve capability, finally get promoted. Apart from All this, we have established or update the proper procedure and policy to make it work smoothly. That is why we call it fundamental Ils

replication system

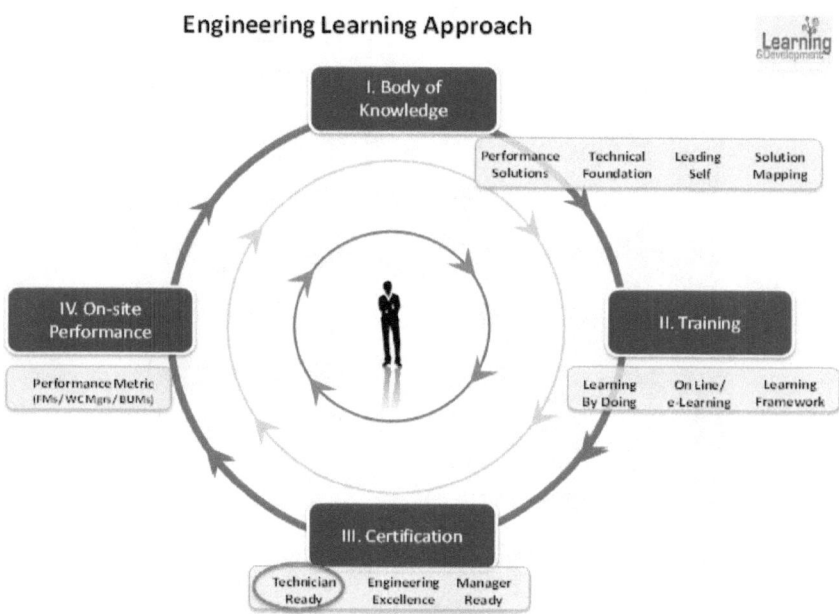

The systematic training program is applied to the next level of fundamental Ils. Let us say Engineer level. We already kick off Engineer Excellence program in the June. from this chart, you can see all the program we already do or plan to do. What you can expect from Guangzhou site is that different level of people will have different systematic training programs.

Here is the achievement of the program, we set up complete function technical skillset, Train up 108 trainers and develop 201 courses, finally we set up the program procedure.

We totally certify 723 people and 150 of them get promotion, the labor cost we have saved per original planning. Moreover, we are happy to see that the turnover rate of these trainees dropped down 45% from 2% to 1.1%, which is much lower than the total IL turnover rate.

After 24 weeks (six months) of training, the course achieves its intended purpose:

trained up 100 amateur trainers, 800 engineers, and reducing training costs by more than USD60k per year. Reduce the manpower need for 7 people, get internal customer departments accordant appreciation, the development of the most valuable training materials, the same course also copied to other factories, we get benefit together.

NPI Course assists in the introduction of new products.

The introduction of general new products Exists:

1. Excessive recruitment or lack of manpower; The turnover rate is large, support and resources are insufficient.

2. No project leader.

3. Lack of competency: inefficient communication; Insufficient for the analysis of new products, insufficient control of the process, insufficient knowledge of the information before the introduction of new products, and lack of ability to remedy the deficiencies of the product design; Not according to the requirements of the customer each link requirements for adequate training ... Lead to a serious lag in execution force.

In the EMS industry, customers trust you, will place the new product orders to you, if the introduction of new products existing problems, orders immediately suspended, will cause the impact for the Company's reputation, will be "notorious".

Together with the department, we study the key factors for the successful introduction of the new NPI project:

Each department has the new project

NPI Success Factors

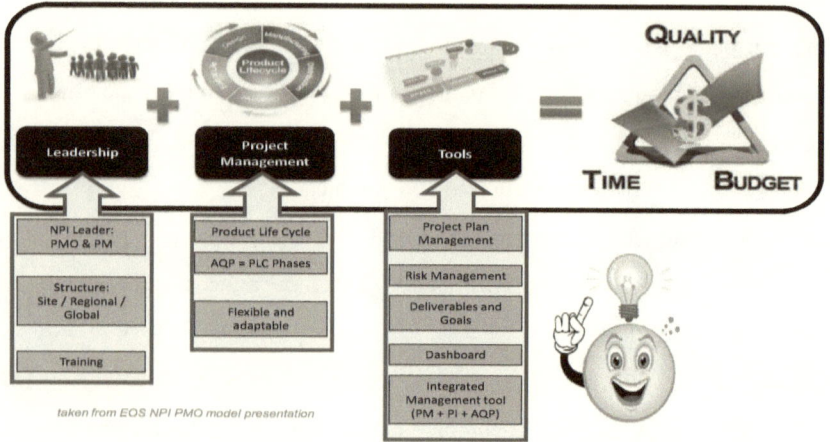

leader, define the responsibility. Responsible for follow up the new project introduction training;

Training team Train up DL product knowledge, quality, system, Anti-Static and a series of systems, processes; 50% Classroom study, 50% internship, let the old one lead the new one, arrange "buddy" help each Other.

Established Tiger Team assist DL Basic Worker Training - Basic level training, OJT and certification training, on-the-job training and certification training, they are grade three or above (7 Levels) employees with two or more skills, Can complete the whole production assembly process independently. Responsible for the introduction of new Products.

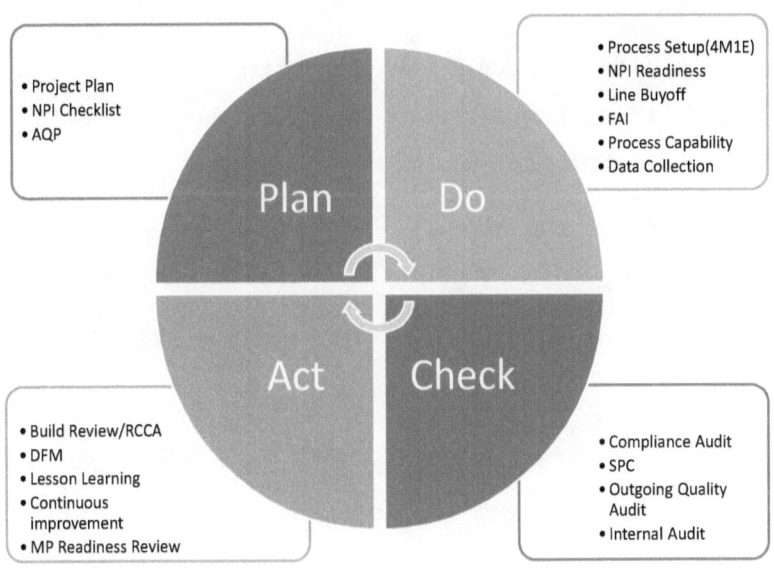

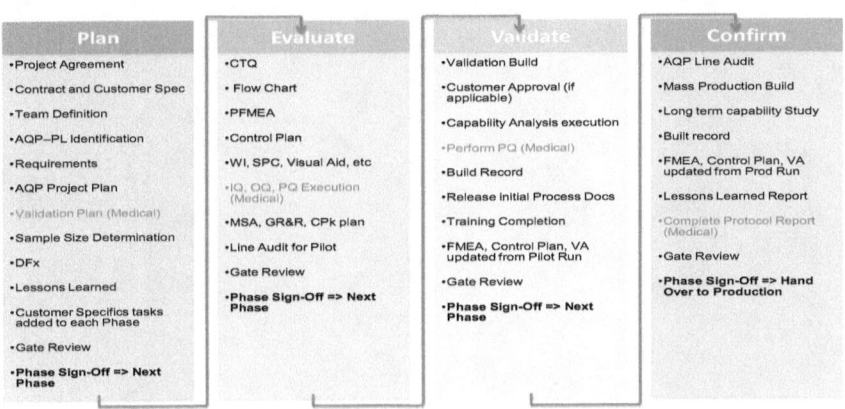

IL training is the whole process management and control, to achieve customer expectation, included product life circle understanding, how to catch the key point of every process, management and settle customer demand, purchasing, root material and process quality control, package etc. We should focus on key process training.

How to identify the new production line checking list.

We organized Cross function training, the different dept cross dept to hold training, learn together, understand and support each other.

28. DL also needs training and career development

PWT is a training program dedicated to DL career development, followed by a training program for D2I (direct to Indirect employee), T2E (technician to engineer).

Few companies will consider Worker-grading career development, and no one cares about them other than "managing" Them. We design this approach as a system for employees to achieve self-improvement skills. The attrition rate, absenteeism rate, and accident rate were reduced. Build up career ladder, provides career development and promotion channel.

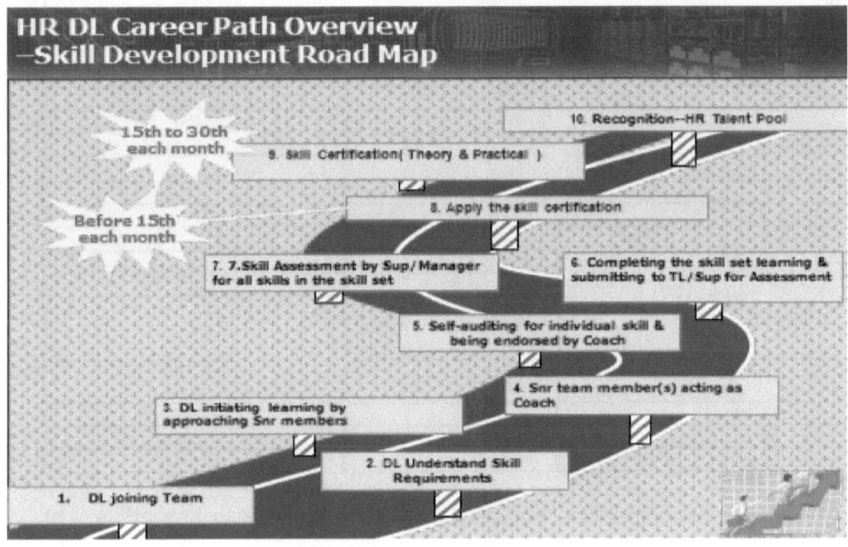

The skill requirements of all levels of the positions are summed up as cultural examination questions and On-line questions, with mentoring method, so that each level of the last level of training to explain to the next level of specific requirements, the next level of put the efforts to understand, to meet the requirements in the corresponding service time, with the recommendation by the line leaders, in 15th of each monthly public examination computer system immediately rank by score, the quota eliminated unqualified person, then the system automatically generates and publishes the examination pass list, the staff obtains the promotion next Month.

With training PCBA station training subjects and accumulated basic credit, credit accumulated to the total number of points required to obtain the exam qualification:

工位（PCBA）		基本学分
Normal		0
Test (ICT—FVT)		1
PROGRAMMING		1
Solder		1
AI		1
MPM		1
DEK		1
HSP		1
GSM		1
NXT		2
BONDING		1
QC		2
REWORK		2
Board Clear（清洗摄像头）		1
无尘室		2
助理选拔通过者		3
技能大赛优胜者（只包括QC, Rework, NXT），每半年举行一次	前5名	4
	6至15名	3
	16至40名	2
	41至后面（取决于当期报名人数及考试成绩而定）	1
有重大贡献者（需获得WCM&FM或以上人认可）		2
年度优秀员工		3
月度优秀员工		1
部门以上团队活动优胜者		1

Organically combine training, career development and compensation and benefit structures

Regularly according to the proportion of each level of the number of people quota, the required seniority of the promotion, the required training, open different levels of the package information to the public, can judge the skills of the "star" on the uniform of the workers.

按标准百分比 Mainplant

级别	生产部 (MFG-IAE)	生产部 (MFG-HY)	生产部 (MFG)	品质保证部 (QA)	采购部 (PUR)	生产计划部 (Planning)	库存分析员 (IA)	货仓 (Warehouse)	IQC	分厂物流报关 (Ship&Cus)	人力资源 (Opts)
1级											
2级	50%	50%	50%	0%	0%	0%	0%	0%	0%	0%	0%
3级	30%	30%	30%	30%	0%	0%	0%	0%	0%	0%	0%
4级	8%	8%	8%	25%	10%	10%	10%	10%	10%	10%	10%
5级	7%	7%	7%	20%	30%	30%	30%	30%	30%	30%	30%
6级	3%	3%	3%	15%	40%	40%	40%	40%	40%	40%	40%
7级	2%	2%	2%	10%	20%	20%	20%	20%	20%	20%	20%

现有人数 (截止到2016-11-23)

Grade	生产部 (MFG-IAE)	生产部 (MFG-HY)	生产部 (MFG)	DL QA(2211140)	PUR	Planning	IA	Warehouse	IQC	Logistics	HR Opts
1	527	714	1241								
2	1108	1652	2760								
3	1019	1194	2213	160			1	3			1
4	295	525	820	88			1	12	6	1	34
5	113	154	267	19	2		14	33	10	8	35
6	83	89	172	41	8	7	21	38	5	10	38
7	59	68	127	32	7	6	8	24	2	2	29
Total	3204	4396	7600	340	17	13	45	110	23	21	137

按比例计算各级别人数

Grade	生产部 (MFG-IAE)	生产部 (MFG-HY)	生产部 (MFG)	DL QA(2211140)	PUR	Planning	IA	Warehouse	IQC	Logistics	HR Opts
1											
2	1602	2198	3800	0	0	0	0	0	0	0	0
3	961	1319	2280	102	0	0	0	0	0	0	0
4	256	352	608	85	2	1	5	11	2	2	14
5	224	308	532	68	5	4	14	33	7	6	41
6	96	132	228	51	7	5	18	44	9	8	55
7	64	88	152	34	3	3	9	22	5	4	27
Total	3203	4397	7600	340	17	13	46	110	23	20	137

职位空缺 (正数为有职位空缺)

Grade	生产部 (MFG-IAE)	生产部 (MFG-HY)	生产部 (MFG)	DL QA(2211140)	PUR	Planning	IA	Warehouse	IQC	Logistics	HR Opts
1											
2	-33	-168	-201	0	0	0	0	0	0	0	0
3	-58	125	67	-58	0	0	-1	-3	0	0	-1
4	-39	-173	-212	-3	2	1	4	-1	-4	1	-20
5	111	154	265	49	3	4	0	0	-3	-2	6
6	13	43	56	10	-1	-2	-3	6	4	-2	17
7	5	20	25	2	-4	-3	1	-2	3	2	-2

We pay attention to the positive guidance and encouragement to People. By mobilizing the enthusiasm and sense of responsibility of frontline staff, we can reduce errors and waste in the process of production and service. It is also based on such a concept, only against the fault and make people have a sense of fear as a means of performance appraisal.

Each level of the design of the test is focus on 5M1E concept, by the department responsible for quarterly Updates.

Individual Recognition

★	1 Star – Skill Level 1	初级生产操作员
★ ★	2 Star – Skill Level 2	1级操作员（通过2级技能审核）+2级操作员（尚未通过3级技能审核）
★ ★ ★	3 Star – Skill Level 3	2级操作员（通过3级技能审核）+3级操作员（尚未通过4级技能审核）
★ ★ ★ ★	4 Star – Skill Level 4	3级操作员（通过4级技能审核）+4级操作员（尚未通过5级技能审核）
★ ★ ★ ★ ★	5 Star – Skill Level 5	4级操作员（通过5级技能审核）+5级操作员（尚未通过6级技能审核）
★ ★ ★ ★ ★ ★	6 Star – Skill Level 6	5级操作员（通过6级技能审核）+6级操作员（尚未通过7级技能审核）
★ ★ ★ ★ ★ ★ ★	7 Star – Skill Level 7	6级操作员（通过7级技能审核）+7级操作员

- Skill Level Shown on Uniform

完美工作组架构图

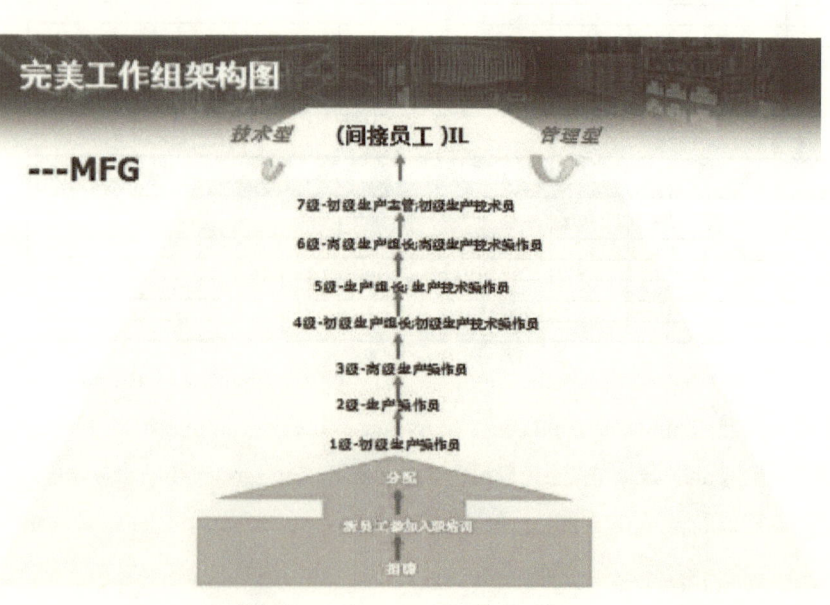

HR also developed a computer test system and set up a test center, we reuse production line computers, write test program, put more than 2000 test questions into the system for random selection, employees You do your test, I do mine, understanding is understanding, not understanding is not understanding. There is not the situation who cheats who defends, and the answer to the exam can immediately saw. The exam also contains the part of the machine; we cooperate with the Department of the Executive to design the practical questions to check employee operational skill.

Regular review of PWT exams and promotions:
1. Where is our distance?
2. How to improve?
3. Schedule of training?
4. How to improve the enthusiasm of employees?

The Monthly HR report also shows how many skills the employee has acquired through the PWT exam, and we set the goal: to ensure that 40% of employees have one or more skills.

On the basis of PWT system, we further developed a set of PWG system with the production department, which matched the skills required by the workers to operate the station and the skills of the actual employees, verified by the computer system to ensure that the staff had the skills required by the work Station.

D2I and T2E training, are we in destructive enthusiasm?

D2I (direct Labor to Indirect Labor) refers to the promotion training of directly train up workers promote to indirect staff, while T2E (technician to Engineer) refers to the train up technicians for the promotion to Engineers.

Before we started this project, we had quite struggling, is it a bit destructive enthusiasm to use a closed education for just six months to train a bunch of direct frontline workers into indirect workers with technical and frontline management?

A group can train up 30 people, need so much? The head of department questioned the viability of the project, and I was playing drums because I knew that the experience and skills behind the promotion at every level would take time to Accumulate. Since the Asia-pacific training Center has been opened up, we always try to give opportunities to employees, to develop the company, I have convinced the heads of departments to recommend the excellent DLs, as listed in the following table, these selected students did go through a layer of screening, can be said to be cream, stricter than the college entrance examination. Each trainee is awarded a seed program contract for a one-year service Period.

DL2IL Program – Selection Process

Selection Criteria:
- ✓ Grade 5 or above
- ✓ More than 1 year service in Jabil
- ✓ B performer or above in the last performance review
- ✓ High School or above or equivalent
- ✓ English basics
- ✓ Willingness

Step 1:	Nomination as per selection criteria
Step 2:	Paper Test on Functional Jabilization
Step 3:	Paper Test on English basics
Step 4:	Interview by committee
Step 5:	Simulation & Group Interview - LGD
Step 6:	Confirm candidates
Step 7:	Sign training bond and Kick-off

JABIL

The content of the training is very rich, focusing on language, functional skills upgrading and preliminary management Skills. At graduation, held a report of the performance of the ceremony, the students speak English quite frequently, it sounds very good.

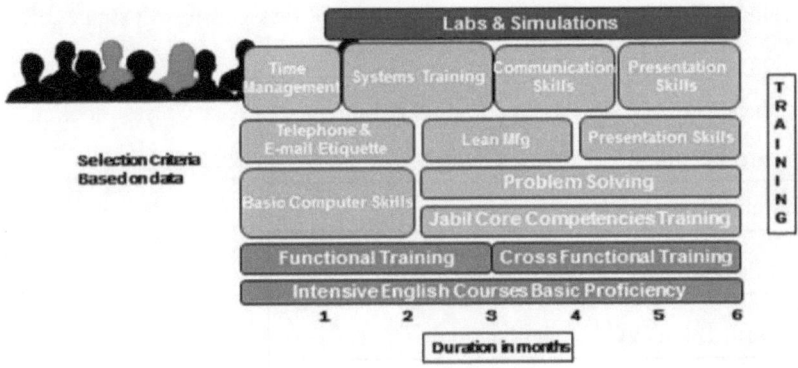

Arrange employee Feedback survey, 60% said they learned a lot, 50% excited that they can enter a "new" environment, need to lead the team, need to use English to report, read the mail, need to deal with difficult issues, need independent thinking to promote lean improvement, to share the results with Peers.

In the following year, the attrition rate for the trainees was "0".

But when the second batch of recommendations was launched, the head of department was reluctant to respond to me in private, the trainees were enthusiastic about their work, and they were eager to learn, but probably more suited to the production department and the warehouse, to the extent that they needed professional skills and fluency in English, they were not equal to a level of trained indirect employees, In particular, the decision-making aspect is not clear on the Priorities. So, the training program slowed down, it was only provided to production and warehouse staff.

29.MIT training is not a training program in MIT

MIT training is not a training program in the Massachusetts Institute of Technology, USA

This is an introduction to this course by the training supervisor, please look at the topic of this training course:

No.	Training Topics
1	Lean overall & Lean tools
2	Department or WC Standardization
3	Manager role and responsibility
4	Strategy making
5	Brown certificate and VSM practice
6	NPI Management and Qualification
7	Management History and Masters
8	Achievement management
9	Project Management
10	Problem Solving & Trouble Shooting
11	WC Statement and P&L
12	Culture & propaganda
13	Customer Service Training
14	Influence

15	Training/Coach
16	Retention management
17	0 defect approach
18	Presentation skill
19	Transforming Talent into Strategic impact
20	Hiring
21	Supply Chain Overall

GM Steven is talking about management theory, management Master, and sharing the key points of the theoretical analysis of the various school of thought. How do professors become professional managers?

He asked each deputy general manager and senior manager to be responsible for the relevant topics, I had two topics closely related to HR:

1. High Potential talent-the secret to leading the Strategy's continued success
2. Training/coach

Good guy, I did more than 20 years of HR, It seems this time I have to " To Borrow Arrows with Thatched boat ", I immediately consulted with Steven, what did he wants me to tell the contents?! He instructed me to see the book "talent war" and come to discuss with him afterward, I take action immediately, found out at least three books for this "name", When I finished reading the book and discussed it with Steven, I was confused because I really didn't see what I could learn from three books. At that time, he shared with me the course of the lectures, it was totally unrelated with the "Talent war"! The original name of the book, "the differentiated workforce" translated as " High potential talent-the secret to lead the continued success of the strategy"

The summary for key points:

Strategic positions feature a high degree of variability in performance, even if there is only one incumbent in the role

Strategic positions often require a high level of expertise

Strategic positions aren't defined by how hard they are to fill, workforce scarcity doesn't equate workforce value

Not all positions in a job category must be considered strategic for some of the positions in a job category to be considered strategic

Strategy positions typically represent less than 15 percent of the workforce.

We finished 21 systematic teachings for all managers, but Steven asked for more, his requirements: All managers must review the content of each course, the key points to remember, after the completion of the course, each manager of the lottery to answer three questions, if three are not answered must retake, re-take still failed, immediately stop salary increment, if still failed, automatically disappear by self! Managers listen to this, scared, listen to take notes with all the effort, this is a few years have not seen the same situation, haha!

After MIT and Engineer Ready training programs organization, we developed "MR-Manager Ready" Course together with Asia-pacific Training Center is an analysis of the leadership of the Vice-manager and project manager of the marketing department, followed by a series of training and coaching, in order to clarify the details, I share all the documents that I have included in the Process:

First, we conducted a two-hour closed online test of 10 trainees on the three themes of nine leadership, resulting in specific results:

Thereafter, a further analysis of each competency is reported:

At the same time, comparing the results of all the participants, the results show that their leadership is generally at a moderate level and not ideal:

In order to learn how to give feedback to 10 participants, get them to know a "real self", HR and trainee supervisors also specifically have learned how to give positive feedback to the Trainees:

Make a person feel at ease and let them know how you will walk through the feedback process.

Manager Ready Leadership Talent Audit Report

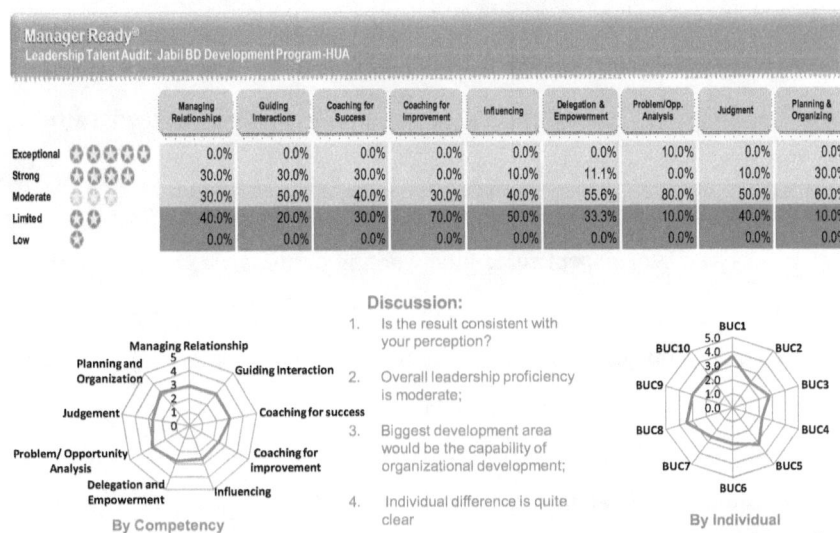

Give some background info to them, Human Development, certifications, and other details that can help them understand themselves. (Establish credibility?)

Ask the participant how they feel they did, where do they think they did well or have opportunities? (Show them a list of competencies measured)

Optional: could ask them how they feel they are able to demonstrate these strengths on a day to day basis on the job. If not, how could they, and what support would they need from their leaders and team?

What did you think of the experience? Check their level of anxiety of receiving feedback.

Discuss next steps they can take in terms of sharing their feedback and creating their development plan.

Feedback is for development purpose ONLY so you can gain clear insights and focus on your specific areas of strength and growth areas....

Review the format of the feedback report the rating scale around degree of proficiency. Indicate that you will navigate them thru the report and how to review the information while highlighting key strengths and development themes.

Discuss blind spots if any and key areas of opportunities. Ask them to think about how these areas could strengthen their leadership and what challenges or barriers they have when facing the improvement.

Ask if the information is consistent with feedback received from others.

Ask if they've already spent some time working on these areas and what they have done.

Share DDI development plan template they can use and to go back and read the report more thoroughly to determine their own areas of focus and priorities.

Encourage them to share the results with their immediate leader in a summary (or you can choose to share the actual report) and enlist their support in their areas of development along with additional feedback and input.

The following is the report that gives feedback to the staff, department heads and trainees to see, understand and communicate together:

DEVELOPMENT CENTER SUMMARY REPORT

Candidate Name: XXX	Date: May 15, 2014

STRENGTHS AND GROWTH AREAS

Overall STRENGTHS demonstrated across simulations:

1. Building & Managing Relationships	2. Coaching for improvement/success
Clarifying the situation by seeking and sharing relevant information that helps to identify issues, concerns and solutions; Acknowledging others' feeling and responding with empathy; Develop ideas and solutions based on others' suggestion; Asking for help and leverage others' skill and gain support.	Building on others' ideas or solution to come up with a plan; Gathering information about the situation and the individual's feeling and concerns and analyze the causes of the behavior; Describing behavior problems by sharing facts and others' viewpoints; Checking for individual's actual understanding about the problems.

GROWTH areas:

1. Influencing	2. Problem/Opportunity Analysis
Achieving agreement to plans or idea through appropriate influencing strategies; Involve others in defining the situation and reaching a solution to gain acceptance of ideas; Acknowledge others' concerns by responding to their feelings	Interpreting information to identify cause-effect relationships; Identifying potential problems or trends that affect work outcome; Seeking information from all relevant sources; Focusing analysis on the most likely causes.

and facts surrounding the situation; Stress the importance of serving the larger organization; Agree on specific actions, contingency plans, and measures of progress by confirming agreement and agreeing on next steps.	

People Management/ Developing Today's Talent & Getting Results through others:

•Identifies required capabilities, strengths and skill gaps of individual and team performance.
•Actively listens and provides feedback; develops and coaches others.
•Skillfully communicates the information people need to be productive.
•Knows how to make things happen; actions are focused and intentional.

XXX's behaviors that demonstrate a moderate degree of proficiency include: identify required capabilities, strengths and skill gaps of individuals; seek and build on others' ideas or solutions to come up with a plan; gather information about the situation and individual 's feelings and concerns, encourage people to develop.

Behaviors that would help XXX become more effective in this competency include: offer adequate support in terms of time, resources and guidance as direct reports engage in their assignment and development; discuss how the behavior change would generate positive impact and develop follow-up action plan to ensure behavior change;

establish a plan to monitor and measure progress and celebrate success; promoting empowerment based on team members' current skills and capabilities.

Problem Solving/Decision Quality:

• Able to synthesize a large amount of complex data to identify critical information or decide;
• Considers broader implications when making decisions
• Advances problems towards a resolution despite ambiguity or uncertainty

XXX demonstrates a moderate degree of proficiency in behaviors that include: recognizing the need to gather additional information to understand the issue more accurately; creating complete and relevant alternatives for addressing problems; considering all possible positive and negative outcomes before making decision.

Behaviors that would help XXX become more effective in this competency include: develop unbiased understanding of the issues by gathering information from all relevant sources; identifying the cause-effect relationship; spend time on defining the decision-making criteria carefully to ensure all other stakeholders' buy-in; selecting the most appropriate solution and approach solve a problem; taking promote, definitive action to build work groups' confidence and commitment by using appropriate influencing strategies.

Communication/Motivates others:

• Skillfully communicates the information people need to be productive.

XXX demonstrates a moderate degree of proficiency in behaviors that include: Good listener, to concerns of others' and acts; convey message clearly and expresses self in a concise manner; demonstrates a calm and rationale demeanor; precisely understand other's message and emotion as well as the meaning behind.

Behaviors that would help XXX become more effective in this competency include: when interacting with others, ensure to generate value by confirming agreement or creating follow-up plan; demonstrating effective tone and skillfully communicate messages with a stronger presence as appropriate for a group discussion environment; check for understanding to ensure messages are well understood; calm demeanor sometimes can be perceived as a lack of urgency or interest.

Accountability:
- Establish clear accountabilities
- Delegates and empowers others to act.
- Creates relationships of trust

XXX demonstrates a moderate degree of proficiency in behaviors that include: great sense of urgency; confident and commitment to get things done; tend to look for fastest and simplest approach to get somewhere; get support from senior leaders.

Behaviors that would help XXX become more effective in this competency include: sharing appropriate responsibilities with peers and team members through setting up clear accountabilities; using time management skill to ensure tasks done in the required quality and deadline; constantly check if any additional resources, equipment, budget and personal time is needed in order to carry out the tasks more efficiently

and effectively.

Learning Agility:
•Learns quickly when given new tasks •Energetically seeks information and new ideas from a variety of sources •Able and willing to learn from experience and apply it to new conditions
XXX demonstrates a moderate degree of proficiency in behaviors that include: identifying the learning needs based on job requirements; quickly find the learning resource and start to learn; embrace change and open to new and different things; lean from peers and superiors. Behaviors that would help XXX become more effective in this competency include: frequent reflection to learn from experience and apply it to new assignments; transform experience into more systematical knowledge through coaching; solid learning plan based on personal development plan.

Participants hear reports and supervisors' feedback and set their own specific improvement plans for implementation step by step:

By following up we organized a series of training activities, such as: redesign of the customer visit corridor, re-organizing the presentation to the Customer's company, how to deal with difficult customer complaints and so on. Training and activities throughout the year, a monthly Arrangement.

Each time we follow "Grow" format, summarize the knowledge points they have learned from the activity and use them effectively.

We put the heads of department and Students together to develop a year-round promotion plan, quite clearly telling everyone that the two of 10 outstanding trainees will be promoted, and the end of the two trainees are terminated. To the results show as we expected, the end of the row of two trainees automatically disappeared, two of the performance of bright-eyed trainees were immediately promoted to the company as marketing manager, independent face the customer, open new Markets.

30.EAP project support hundreds of employees getting educational degrees

When applying subsidy for supporting staff to improve their educational degree program in every year, I always face three bosses challenge: "Do we need so much masters?" However, in every year I always get their approval, they would question but they were very clear, to help employees accept the University's Orthodox education, obtain academic qualifications. We help the employees to success, change their fate, even change the fate of their whole family, their knowledge will sooner or later return to the company, even if they left the job, a grateful heart to the original employer company, although the annual cost is enormous, 2016 reimbursement is RMB738,000, in that year the company supported 30 college students, 30 undergraduates, 5 masters. Company J has been launched the program for nine Years.

Since the company spends a lot of money in every year and hope that employees get the benefit from it, for each screening and adoption of the details, HR well control it. For example, the selection of graduate student funding is the most intense, the elimination rate is 29:5, because the applicants are excellent employees, many of them have passed the entrance examination in the reading, they are engineers or other positions, even to the Company's deputy general manager, obviously you can see their thirst for knowledge.

HR arranges interviews to check how they are going to show the actual work plan to demonstrate for the Company after receiving a degree. We design an important proposition topic for company need to make change and make decision, let 29 selected colleagues to discuss with Non-leadership group, the results of their discussions to demonstrate, in the process, the judge observed the team the key factors included spirit of each applicant, communicate the persuasion ability, How to influence others, presentation skills, Decision-making quality, We want to choose elite among elites, open internal selection, result will open to all, no one has Complaints.

For the support of college and undergraduate education, we use the National standard Entrance Examination, the staff meet the requirements of service term and performance can participate in the examination, according to the overall ranking to obtain admission Qualifications. In order to save resources and let the staff have to choose their favorite subjects, we have tried online education, but the quality of network education can't compare with face-to-face teaching, it is too flexible, so we stopped in the second year, we choose the courses related to the Company's business, such as electronic, testing and IT, insisted on university teachers to teach in Person by weekly.

As for the funding methods and the terms of the contract, I believe this is what many peers want to know:

Agreement for Education Subsidy Program

Our joint conducting with South China University of Science and Technology aims to improve the comprehensive qualification of our employees, and provide a platform for learning and academic upgrading. This project will involve the payment of tuition fees by our staff and the company to provide subsidy for employees, in order to ensure that the employees participating in the project are aware of their own payment projects and the Company's funding Program. The signing of this agreement makes it clear to all employees of the relevant Requirements.

Student Pay the Bill Plan

The student who participates in this project should pay the studying cost: the credit fee (120 yuan per credit, Total 85 credits), The teacher is paid for the lesson (150 yuan per hour, a total of 177 hours. The trainees share the Burden, teachers' travel expenses ($ 115 each, Total 187 Times.)The trainees share the Burden.)

The student credit fee will be charged to the University. Teachers' pay and travel pay is charged by the Instructor.

The amount of each semester will be charged according to the course arrangement of this semester. Before the start of each semester, it is all handed in to the South China University of Science and Technology and related Instructors.

Corporate Funding Solutions

In order to encourage employees to participate in the project, the company proposed a subsidy scheme. The funding ratio is: 30% compensation of the First-year trainees passed the examination, the second year of the trainees passed the examination compensate 30%, The third-year students pass through, 40% compensation. Must be reimbursed by invoice or Receipt.

Funding Methods: after the completion of the academic year, the company will be based on the feedback of the students in the university, the students have qualified to pass the subject examination, in August each year to reimburse the funding cost. If the students fail to pass the subject examination, they will be reimbursed in the next year after passing the examination. If the student has a subject at the completion of the pass is still not passed, the cost will not be reimbursed by the Company.

3. Special case Processing

3.1. If a student resigns during his or her studies or is dismissed for violating the Company's rules and regulations, The Student's study will be completed at other locations designated by the college. The company shall not be liable for any costs and liabilities during this period.

3.2. If the student labor contract expires, the company will not renew its contract. Then this participant will be able to continue to participate in this Project. However, the company will no longer grant funding for its academic year and subsequent Fees.

3.3. If the remainder of this class is less, the remaining students cannot afford the teacher's instruction and travel Expenses. With the students, companies, colleges and universities agreement to stop the teacher oral training courses.

3.4. The company reserves the right to the final interpretation of this agreement, and in the case of change, the company will change the terms of this agreement in a coordinated and consistent condition.

3.5. This agreement is in two copies and each party holds one copy. Have the same legal effect.

The staff confirm   The company confirm
Signature：   Signature：
The employee ID number：
Date:

JEDII

JEDII Asia-pacific Training Center facing the difficult in the establishment and management

ASIA-PACIFIC Training Center Hardware investment is huge: four-star hotel specifications, the former development zone of foreign investment activities center, using the government recommended decoration Company. Plant HR role in the project: From the initial training team management structure needs to be aligned, hotel catering, housing and entertainment department, 100 People Management team, to make Hotel decoration, monthly hotel operation cost of the budget, with the team's efforts, a cost of tens of millions of projects finally Complete.

The building is easy to build, but the instructor is not easy to find", to have trainer also have students, people to be trained up, need time, to practice, to recognize. The original orientation of the organization was China training center, but move to a super-luxury place, the University's Independent management did not upgrade to be a true corporate university, the independent and profitable university became the Company's heavy burden of "cost" center. Many colleagues are questioning: the content of training center in Asia-pacific is not different from the factory Department's own training?! The training resources at the Asia-pacific Training center and in different factory plants began competing against each other, and at some time, the management of the group and the management of the plant began to question: do we need to afford this expensive four-star hotel standard in the empty Asia-pacific training center?

Under the pressure of cost control, many projects have become destructive Enthusiasm. But the head of the department cannot easily promise to accommodate all of the trainees ' post-graduation. In front of us is to give up or continue to hard run? But we have invested a lot of money, we always must use it to drive D2I, T2E, TR, and MER projects, our training team in the plant and trainers and consultants in the Asia-pacific Training center are leveraging each Other's strengths.

If I had to start over: I would suggest that the company should have a clear idea of the position of the university, is this a business or do you want to make it an ideal state? In other words, if I ran the business by myself, how would I run? Do you have a mentor? Change the circle of view? Is this the mentor for the Department's training? Do you have any trainees? Are these students willing to pay the training fee continuously? How do you organize them into training? If restart, I would have been more inclined to hire a mentor with experience in Learning. In addition, the training time is also very important for the allocation of trainees, learning always understand the practice of the process, destructive enthusiasm only in self-deception, not enough time training is better than not training. Travel costs for trainees and trainers in other parts of the country are considered, when the employee is trained, the employee chooses to leave, the company is saddened to get back the compensation from the trainees. All these negative factors must be considered earlier, not only enthusiasm and waste, the Company's large investment does not actually spend on the employees.

31.Boss said why is my company losing the money?!

As of today, I have joined company M for another 19 days, joined the company, and I have created a record: the company spent nine months convincing me to join, but I spent a short year to complete my historical mission, help the company: to clean up the bruising, had life and death battle, move Forward difficultly.

Company M is a family-style enterprise, has been opening a factory for 38 years, "starting from 30 years ago to live to the present: you can see the place that other people can't see, do what others can't do, define others can't define, if you can do these three you can succeed, my personal view for the future is always firm." This is my boss Mr. Liang taught me the heartfelt words.

A "airborne" enter into the new company, the most common practice is to try to obtain performance as soon as possible, in order to get the big Boss Affirmation. Each company has its inherent corporate culture, not a day or two days to form, defects are inevitable, enter the work state, then slowly change the status or which you think it is not standardized.

Understand the needs first, look for deficiencies and defects, and then choose to stand. I let myself adapt into the culture as soon as possible and get the recognition and the support of colleagues more important. Never forget that "HR" is a service department, to survive in this business, you must let people feel that you are supporting, serve their person/department. therefore, after obtaining the necessary information, in the work, do not blindly stand in the Department of the point of view to carry out the work, but the combination of the need to choose a gradual and orderly. Remember, not to deny what the predecessor did, more encouraging, then modify it.

Understand the character of each person, especially the boss, the boss can be the boss, many of his views naturally lofty, sometimes we only see the problem point, do not see the complex background of the problem, but the background is very important.

1. The first stage of mastery of the above to collate and classify diagnostic analysis.
2. Assess the problems and deficiencies in each module, each link (analysis of the root causes of the problem and the specific situation of deficiencies).
3. Identify key "constraints" that need to be improved to communicate with the parties, solicit opinions from others and formulate "improvement of the implementation plan" in conjunction with their own views.
4. "Program implementation": have meeting to determine the responsible person, time period, required support resources → implementation → check → improve → feedback.

Note: Flexibility as a sublime virtue, all rivers run into sea, humane care and other life philosophy.

1. The second phase of the work seeks to solve the problem, gaps and reach a rapid improvement breakthrough.
2. Formulate rectification, improvement measures and implementation Plan.
3. Translate measures and program into executable, easy-to-implement, concrete work Plans.
4. Planning the functions of the department, the division of labor, staffing, and re-unification the work of the Department, execute the work plan.
5. Follow up and supervise the implementation progress and accuracy of each work (implement 4R execution System mode).

Phase IV curing work methods and techniques, continuous PDCA improvement (long-term Persistence)

1. Personnel and personnel, work after the first person

2. To reach a certain height and depth, we should use the idea of world view and methodology to guide the problem solving.

3. Working mode curing down, lead the team to pay attention to:

3.1. Problem Solving ability, balance is the level

3.2. Coaching ability, to develop subordinates to help subordinates grow up

After walking through the two stages of "understanding" and "diagnosis", Eugenia, the company general manager who hired me in, finally chose to leave the Company sadly. The main reason: The choice of the Company's strategic issues, the old and new management style conflict: First to do bigger business then become profitable, or first do profitable business then become bigger? His daughter could not change Mr. Liang Family Management mindset at last, when all the reliable people of family members who can rely on are exhausted, there is not successor to take the lead.

There was no time to allow me to do more scrutiny and assumptions, I will carry the heavy burden to reduce 60% labor cost, especially the support departments occupied 9% of total gross profit, if still maintain 16%, 13.5% Gross profit has been taken up by the logistic support department and the loss is maintained.

After discussions with the Company's boss Mr. Liang, we set a clear target for 2018:

1. Ensure annual revenue exceeds US $80 million;

2. Control support and administrative costs only account for 10% of the total cost of sales;

3. The average gross margin is guaranteed to be above 13.6%;

Then I put forward 10 projects to streamline manpower, integrate departments, reduce intermediate process and resource waste in the four parts of the Company's business, materials, operations and logistic support, and finally adopted the most critical solution through in-depth discussion: first cut from the most loss-making Cambodian PP factory. Other factories and logistics departments also must "make a decision" to streamline 20% staff. This company has never faced such a difficulty environment, as HR head wait for the boss and various departments of the high-level to "Assign the task", I have not "hesitated" to take on the responsibility, although I know the Difficulties.

To face and deal with the headaches of structural reorganization every day, I felt more difficult than I had imagined:

First we must consider our customers ' reaction to this streamlined action, so I drafted an unsolicited notification letter on behalf of the President of the company:

Respective XXX customer

In order to improve organizational efficiency, productivity and the competitiveness of our MXX company, we decided to streamline our PP organization structure by combining two finishing working process teams into one. From this positive changing, we can eliminate the waste of idle manpower while entering low production season. Change never be easy: we must settle employment relationship with 800 workers by fully compensating the workers with Cambodian labor law requirement.

For making this change to be most effective, management already communicate openly and honestly with our employees regarding the reason for the change and the whole plan, managers also listen to the employees and provide support when necessary in order to keep the morale high among the employees. At the same time, our management team take steps to prepare the workforce in advance of the change. Proper planning includes production line relay out, reduced unnecessary working process, combined tasks among the stay employees so that each worker responsibility enlarge but remain the same work loading.

With the intimacy communication, we report this change plan with your respective customer and looking forward to your strong support and instruction to us!

Tks & rgds

XXX

CEO of MXX

The customer received with a calm reaction and immediately instructed their Company's responsible colleagues in Cambodia to assist us in the implementation of the streamlining of operations.

To have a good plan to action, I run to production to count headcount, I communicate with the factory director in order to persuade them to take action, drop down the labor cost.

Labor contracts existing a lot of disputes, the Chinese staff, foreign workers, local formal workers, contract workers, temporary workers, according to Chinese law to deal with Chinese employees or according to the employment of Cambodian local law calculation? Staying in Cambodia for many years, the supervisors of China is uncertain, see is there a good chance to change the job, but concern about their seniority, they are unwilling to leave the job do not take the compensation.

Cambodian labor law separates the employment methods of the long-term contract, fixed contract contractor, use 25 days as a unit of time limit, hourly count of four ways, employees always want to start from their own, take which is the advantage of their own, vise verse the company is also thinking about how much can save.

There were 200 employees at the minimum wage in PP site because they do not have the minimum output requirements of production, the actual situation is a year worse than another year, there is no minimum production requirements for 7 months, the production has not been accelerated for many years, the management of the company did not take timely clearance action, Postpone and postpone the problem and expand Again. There are no effective channels and effects to communicate with employees and trade union Presidents.

Administrative expenses are huge, for example, a medium-sized factory of less than 3000 people with eight cars and nine drivers, most of them for internal personnel usage.

Even the workers are asking, "even if we can figure it out, it's impossible for the company to make money if it keeps up this status, but our boss can't see it." "

I am quite clear that the only increase cost will be maintaining the Company's losses, if the reduction action can be carried out one day earlier, the company will save a day of cost, to cut staff start from the last work process, Cambodia's reduction not like china, according to law to compensate is not so easy, must inform the labor union, union representatives and the numbers of unions representatives, they will put forward a lot of unreasonable reasons, if the company simply refused, the situation will be frozen, they can notify the workers stop the job, both sides immediately stalemated into a state of confrontation, the workers do not work and leave, how can you lay off me? My priority is to clean up all the union representatives at first! I asked the factory manager and supervisor to give me the list of all the trade union representatives they knew, I broke it down one by one by sending profit, they promised to help the company to complete the streamlined actions then left, so that through their mouths to tell the workers that the company has been handled by law, they should signed off the final payment. But consciously or unintentionally, the worker is unwilling to sign the compensation scheme, and finally we use the Cambodian Ministry of Labor to come forward and issue a formal approval, agree to the Company's streamlining actions to prove that the deal is Legitimate. For nearly one months, we have completed 1,100 staff streamlining in batches, without a Riot.

When I woke up late at night, I often asked myself if I had broken a lot of People's Rice bowls (Jobs). But the next day, I still must "Clean up my mind, sharpen the lip, keep a clear mind and bargain with the employees, maintain the compassion and empathy to persuade and settle the dismissal problem."

While streamlining the Cambodian PP plant, I need to streamline non perform KP plant staff at the same time, with the extra employees of the sales and support departments in Zhuhai, china, the staff of Macao served for many years, among them, the old courtiers who have "worked" with the bosses for more than 30 years, and the staff of the Hong Kong head office, Including the project manager responsible for ERP system development-Michael, this guy used nearly two years developed ERP system to use false data, resulting in the system will not be able to use the system normally, internal customer complained, The company boss Mr. Liang personally, finally made a difficult decision: "if the introduction of the system did not bring good results to the company, why did we continue to use it?" The project was suspended, before that invested more than 1.6 million Hong Kong dollars in investment were "burned up in the fire", under such circumstances, Michael was still as bold as brass to ask the company to issue a project management bonus to him.

Thanks to him, for more than 25 years of HR, never need to run to the Hong Kong Labor tribunal sit in the dock, in order to deal with the case of Michael, I added a reluctant personal experience, although the company was awarded win the lawsuit, but the feelings of both employment sides all lost: an hour before the trial, I was sitting on a bench outside the courthouse alone, I was torturing myself. what happened to company M? How could my predecessor hire a mediocre who is so incompetent that he spends his mind on the wrong place? What are the management of company M doing?! What are the staffs of company M doing?!

I can't understand is that the Cambodian staff request company to dismiss themselves, all stop didn't work, incredibly excuse because of fear of the company escape that they can't get compensation! Facing such a situation you will have a serious reversal of the feeling of thinking! When I was in the middle of the night plane rushed to the Cambodian factory, went into the screaming employees, I felt my whole body was empty, I was on the phone with the company boss Mr. Liang report the situation of development, I exclaimed over: "Mr. liang, If I was you, I might have given up 10 times, this PP factory, from top to bottom , from the bottom to the top are rotten to the bones of the Surface. " Mr. Liang listened to me, immediately made an important decision: "if I did not find the right person to manage the factory, why I maintain it?" instructed me to conduct a plant-wide shut down at Once.

At this time, I drafted the second letter to the client:

Thanks for your kind attention, below is our update to you.

By serious considering the heavy cost pressure of Phnom Penh area, our top management made the final decision that we will release all Linking and Finishing workers by fully compensate apply to Cambodian labor law, and we will not continue high cost run in PP anymore.

Meanwhile we will enhance the below operation:

1) We will move the machines to KP to increase the production capacity to ensure there is no impact to the business after shutting down PP;

2) We will upgrade (at least) 20% more production capacity in KP to keep the whole capacity as a Group before.

3) We will focus on CSR/Sustainability performance on KP to ensure the continuous improvement from now on.

This is the very difficult decision made from our top management, in order to sustain MXXX Group business growth and find out the other potential development opportunity from other location, we must take this challenge. As always, your support would be highly appreciated.

Please let us know if you have any questions.

Tks & rgds

XXX

CEO of MXX

Employment relations reach to the freezing point, employees are affected by each other: Your company ask me to leave? I must make a little gesture to vent, to cheat, to fight back, to sue the company, I feel the staff have the strong resistance with the boss.

Even the normal colleague Kylie told Me: "It's been a hell of a year for me working here in the Finance Dept." 。Because the boss is questioning the finance department all day Why is it a difficult account?

With Cambodia's 5-year minimum wage of nearly 3 Times-fold growth ($ 61 in 2012 to $170 in 2018), a series of social security and welfare policies have been enacted, resulting in more than 80% per cent of SME profits moved from China to Cambodia like paper-thin, running against the government's minimum wage, But the Cambodian Hun Sen government has pledged to raise the minimum wage to $250 by Year 2023 to win the election, which is unsustainable for the remaining 20% of the textile industry.

Many enterprises, in order to control Labor costs, have used the "wherever there is the policy there will be countermeasures", the use of satellite plants, the use of external processing, the use of temporary workers, to balance the minimum wage and the increasing cost of the increasingly harsh Labor legislation, as well as fear of the World's non-disorderly labor unions for the cost of the company add on heavy pressure.

Every annual review and individual adjustment like a battle with the Boss.

Even if the former general manager of the company made a commitment of performance bonus, Mr. Liang, will be stretched old face questioned: "The Employee's performance is not his personal made out, why should I pay him a Person's performance bonus?"

Cambodians love to play and have no discipline. It is your excellency's business that I get off my job while close time.

The headcount of overseas staff is too high to localize. It's not cheap for living index. But the goods couldn't ship out without them.

Employees work 5 days a week, in China and Hong Kong have used to be, but the boss felt it wrong, now Cambodia is still on the 6-day work shift, so he wants to "correct" it: In China to implement 5.5 Days/week working System.

One order clothes mixed the color, resulting in costs more than RMB200,000, tracing three working positions: PMC, Machine adjustment, and QA, each have their own explanations, it is the responsibility of others not mine, so the company is still forced to take clearance action ...

A large number of vacant factories, warehouses piled up several years of high-priced wool inside, a cashmere clothing in the market can be sold more than RMB2,000 per pound, incredibly there are more than 8000 pounds can be spread in the warehouse for more than 10 years for the worm-eaten, used machines and defective-shirts put there who know how to deal with?

The calculation of capacity is Wavering. Must be boss Mr. Liang make the decision to pick up or not...

From the boss, you see his helplessness and struggling, give up or insist? Strict control or runaway?

He said to Me: "if This company is on my own to run to make money, then I am a failure, I brought you back to tell me what to do?" What do you do?" But in many cases, it's up to him to decide for himself.

If we maintain such a situation, we will certainly lose, whether we admit it or not.

Mr. Liang quite clear in the heart, he told Me: "business is not to learn, is to practice." Before you start a business you should define what's the business not to do?

He told me the following 4 kinds of business do not do:

1. High standard of quality, rubbish price;

2. The delivery of a very urgent business;

3. Low profit, manual and miscellaneous;

4. The model is much more, by more batches;

At first, I heard his request I feel unreasonable, business placed over there and see if we do the business or not, still pick and choose, spent here and there, is it the boss worry about it? He used the data to do the analysis for me:

High standards of quality, fine work will cost more hours, even more QA and QC we need;

The delivery of a very urgent business, to be equipped with a larger number of workers, also spend more OT to ensure shipments, the profits are not enough to pay Overtime.

Manual miscellaneous will need more labor, three pieces has been made for the simple manual, which section should you choose to do?

The sample made too more, the cost of each piece is RMB385, if the number of items ordered less, the company Loss. Many batches, subcontracting more, ship to more countries more transportation and customs formalities cumbersome, will also lead to the loss of the Company. The sweater industry is quite flexible, can't be successful that you can see the secret that other people can't see, do what others can't do, define others can't define

All mistakes are caused by people, all the hope is to make it come true, Mr. Liang very clear about this, we have to restructure the management team, this is more important than shut down the factory and streamline the Company's staff, so he did not hesitate to, including:

General Manager-His daughter

Finance director

Supply chain director

HR director-my former

Three senior sales managers

Sample room general Sifu

The manager for electrical machine

The General Manager for Cambodian

The administration and ER director

CSR manager

Quality manager

Finance manager

Hired:

1. Experienced, Serious working attitude of the new customer development manager;

2. Experts in product development and production process improvement;

3. Has many years of experience in sweater manufacturing industry, financial controller;

4. A wealth of long-standing overseas factories to supervise the actual operation of QA and CSR merger experience of the manager;

5. HR Manager of long-staying in Cambodia;

Promoted:

1. Shipping manager for shipping, customs, transport all-inclusive manager;

2. The marketing manager of the biggest customer;

3. The factory manager of the biggest production plant to the factory manager of the whole plant in Cambodia (Total eight factories);

4. Production planning manager for China production plant manager;

In hiring five key positions of talent, we should hire some people, I talk with the boss Mr. Liang the most, he told me: "It is very difficult to recruit the right talent, the bad one I don't need, the good one often forgive to come, stay not long, I tried a lot, but most of them are failure, they made the mistakes, But it is me to bear the consequences, I was afraid. "

To support the boss, not fear any more, to interview and pick the right candidate, I have an agreement with him on what is a key talent:

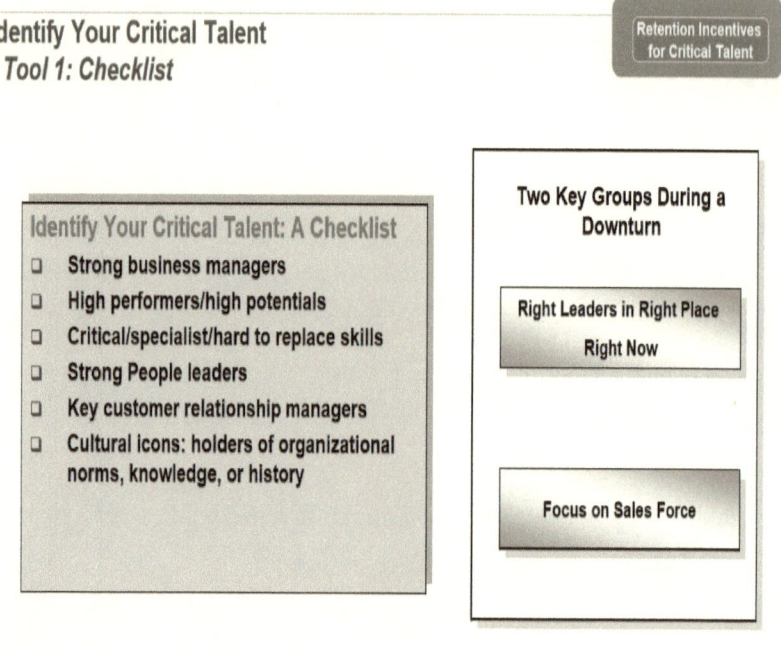

I have been interviewing more than 60 candidates in order to select a suitable financial controller, the last candidate chosen, Mr. Liang met three times with the candidate from Bangladesh, and finally determine this Candidate.

In my first anniversary, a new management set, experienced the company ups and downs, still stay with the company does not abandon the company, held a management meeting, we speak freely, to formulate the company's future management direction:

To maintain 80% of the existing customers, 20% to develop new customers;

Focus on high-priced customers;

Focus on product design.

Sample department to see how to improve the manufacturing process so that upgrade the quality of products;

Analysis and study why can other competitors sell the high price products?

Modified production line specifically to make high-priced goods;

Training new workers makes them Seiko and multi-skilled.

Break down the cost of each process, cost center, to make sure that every step is profitable, and that each cost center has a surplus.

No guarantee from the Company's management that the boss will be able to make money in the future, but I gave up the previous well-paid, comfortable and happy multinational company, plunged into this company described as "hell" by the staff, in the past six months focused on only one thing: restructuring, compression of 1/3 of the staff, the total of more than 2600 people, so that the company's labor costs reduce by more than 1/3, just this one, sustain the company improve of 9%.

32.Annual reviews and annual adjustment: One story in one year

Performance management, starting from the management of Labor cost, it is no sense to leave the cost alone talk about how to recognize value of talent! Without estimate the manpower cost, is more like "Nerd said crazy, said dream in the Dream".

The first thing to budget is to design the structure and control the headcount. It is not good to have less people, but it is a bad thing to be many. Company J 's Business volume grew three times bigger, but headcount has not increased twice, the headcount control is quite effective. How to do that?

The group requires each branch put all together to see the trend of each indicator of transformation cost (i.e., cost conversion: transfer of inputs into the output of the transport, material scrap, customs clearance, operation, Sales and overall administrative costs) included into the material, manufacturing, the cost ratio of support Department, DL&IL, machine depreciation, Construction Depreciation, fixed costs and other key factors, according to the results of the indicators to assess the performance of each branch, the distribution of quarterly Bonuses.

The quarterly budget system automatically provides historical data for the past 4 quarters for reference, requiring departmental managers to plan for the next 8 quarters of the budget, one of which they have to input their departmental staffing and payroll budgets into the budget system, the system automatically converted into hours of labor costs, staff salary based on the average amount for the same position. Each department manager quarterly show budget in the launch meeting, to make the best adjustments to meet the requirements of various departments, finally three pack audit from a different perspective, The department operate according to this budget.

In the quarterly budget start-up meeting, HR department should also publicly inform the managers of the department: what are the factors that will affect the rise or fall in wage costs: what are the effects of the national policies on the Company's labor costs in the quarter? Such as the plan to retain staff at the end of the year, etc. must be carefully informed. How much adjustment should be made for the hourly wages? How to explain the details to the customer? Because EMS is a labor-intensive industry, customers is abnormal sensitivity on the hourly price increase or decrease.

HR and other supporting departments to control the cost of the department, spend more than the Company's total business share to maintain a balance or lower budget. Quarterly HR need to prepare budget: their own departments lock in the proportion of indirect personnel and direct personnel. Department heads to explain, bosses more concerned about whether your total cost ratio is declining or not. HR should plan every benefit and activity throughout the year, each with a clear list of costs, each subject was reviewed by bosses.

The control of the headcount of IL is exceptionally strict, the monthly headcount report will be shared. According to high, middle and low three levels to see the average price of each level, to hire a "high price" people less headcount, to maintain the effective control of the overall labor costs, before the budget lock the departments clearly explain why need so many staff, locked after the increase in the need to explain the Reduction. Minimize the headcount of people who are unable to generate added value in supporting Departments.

At the end of each quarter, if there is more than 5% of the difference between the budget and the actual cost must made reasonable explanation, why existing the difference? What causes it? What actions will be taken to improve in the future?

At the end of each year, the annual salary review + special adjustment proportion of the budget is DONE.

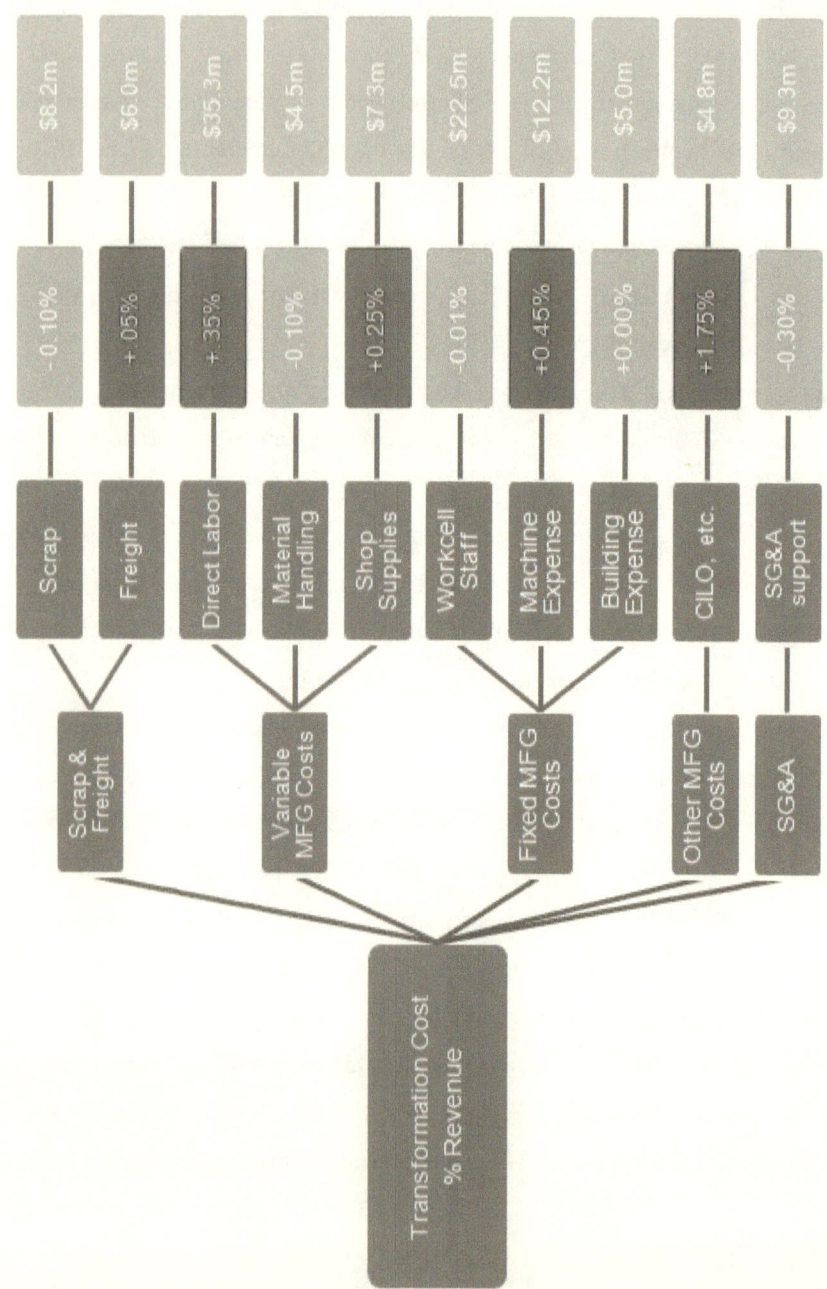

Data has been collected from market before starting the Salary Increase:

	DL	IL
Annual Review Date	Depend on government announce min salary effective date	Jan 1st
Consideration Index	CPI/GDP	Corp guideline for total salary review budget
	Collect nearby company salary adjustment information	Consultant provide market trend on increment percentage
	Our competitor salary adjustment information	Our competitor salary adjustment information
	Review different pay item reasonableness or incentives	Review different pay item reasonableness or incentives
	Review different grading differential	Align with Regional salary structure
	Social insurance impact by Base Salary adjustment	Social insurance impact by Average Salary adjustment
	Working hour cost impact	GPMP performance result
	New labor law requirement	New labor law requirement
	Cash Vs Non Cash benefit	Cash Vs Non Cash benefit
	Total labor cost control	Total labor cost control

Each salary increase will provide 3 options for three pack (operation, marketing and Finance) to choose.

Recall the past 7 years Company J Annual review, one year has a story:

Y2017

GM Steven looked at the Department's labor costs accounted for the revenue ratio, if there was a decline then give special adjustment, because EMS industry margin are limited: only maintain at 2%/year low profit level. Quarterly departments are required to report the special adjustment details, the Department labor costs are reduced then to be approved.

Y2016

Performance assessment scoring level standard

Annual salary review	Continue exceed standard	Exceed the standard	Meet the standard	Partially meet the standard	Failed the standard
Performance Grading	A	B	C	D	E
Score Distribution	5%	20%	60%	10%	5%
Performance Score	4.5 - 5	3.5 – 4.4	2.5 – 3.4	1.5 - 2.4	0 - 1.4
Salary adjustment	Follow dept salary range to make adjustment.			Not entitled salary review	

Relevant salary range statement

Salary Range: According to the influence of each position in the Organization's scope, responsibility size, work intensity, work difficulty, job conditions, job conditions and other characteristics of evaluation, to determine the relative value of the position in the organization, according to its value and combined with the market in the same industry wage level to determine the salary range of each position. Each year, the company participates in the market salary survey and decides whether to adjust the salary range of each position according to the market wage level. For this reason, each position has a relative value in the organization, which determines the maximum wage limit for each position.

Salary Level: The position of the Employee's salary in the salary range of the job. If the Employee's salary has reached the salary limit of the position, the Employee's basic salary will not be adjusted if there is no promotion or the salary range of the position is not raised.

For employees with a base salary that has reached their position salary limitation, the company grants a one-year monthly salary subsidy (lump-sum), without adjusting the basic salary of the employee, to recognize the Employee's hard work over the past year, the monthly salary subsidy refers to the average annual review percentage for the current year.

From the analysis results show that: there are more than 215 technicians/Line leaders/engineers, etc. distributed in various departments of various business groups, wages over the upper limit, such as a senior test engineer, wages can reach RMB17,871 (USD2,845/months), equivalent to twice more than the market price, Because they enjoy the Company's average annual review for many years, it is sure to cause great pressure on the Company's Cost. In the past, C&B colleagues have never proposed to freeze their wage increases, and now they have to freeze their salaries and even cut pay, only to get a monthly salary subsidy (Lump Sum pay), to take the higher average increment of 2015, replaced by 2016 average monthly salary subsidy (Lump Sum pay), they felt that the company was playing the trick with an employee with long service and excellent performance. the rumors raised, employees directly ran to my office, because in the United States companies who has dissatisfaction can escalate, not to speak I am HR head?!

Although the full communication has been with the Department head in advance, however under the situation of "The department head timid to say", only HR facing the Difficulty.

First, we share the current tough economic situation and the overall development of the company.

After that, we respond to questions raised by our employees publicly:

1. Why should set salary ceiling for the technician/line leader?

"Any position has ceiling, it is impossible to maintain the continuous growth, the ceiling point can be re-adjusted in accordance with the annual work performance, "pay as a result" rather than always sitting on the high salary position to enjoy higher growth." This is a unified system of remuneration system for the entire company, with a ceiling for all positions, applicable to the WORLD.

Why is there a lump sum (monthly salary subsidy), which is lower than the previous year, and is there any suspicion of a pay cut? "Pay by performance "means that the salary is to be graded with the performance of the individual and the overall increase has risen and dropped." The same practice apply to Shanghai branch, The Penang branch is also take effect earlier than CHINA.

After all the Department's employees have completed the performance evaluation, the proportion of each wage is calculated according to the performance level (total of 100%) and the total wage of the employee

(for Example) the level of performance of employees in different departments and the distribution of wages is not the same, the corresponding total wages in the proportion of the department's total wages will be different.

Performance grading	Under the low limitation	1st quartile	2nd quartile	3rd Quartile	4th quartile	Exceed the upper limitation
A	0.0%	3.0%	0.7%	0.6%	0.0%	0.0%
B	5.3%	6.7%	7.9%	1.4%	0.0%	0.0%
C	23.4%	6.9%	22.2%	3.8%	2.3%	0.0%
D	2.6%	2.6%	2.3%	0.6%	0.0%	0.0%
E	6.1%	0.0%	1.6%	0.0%	0.0%	0.0%

Base on above presentation under dept total budget (3%) condition we count out the salary adjustment matrix (For example) in the same dept, the employee performance grading is different with salary range, finally the employees entitled adjustment as below:

Performance Grading	Below Lower Limit	1st quartile	2nd quartile	3rd quartile	4th quartile	Exceed the upper limit
A	5.60%	4.90%	4.20%	3.50%	2.80%	2.10%
B	4.90%	4.20%	3.50%	2.80%	2.10%	1.58%
C	4.20%	3.50%	2.80%	2.10%	1.40%	1.05%
D	0.00%	0.00%	0.00%	0.00%	0.00%	0.00%
E	0.00%	0.00%	0.00%	0.00%	0.00%	0.00%

Confirm employee adjustment percentage

Two considerations for annual review percentage:

The employee stay in the existing quartile personal salary

The personal performance grading

For example: The adjustment status in dept A & B

Dept A adjustment matrix

Performance grading	Below the lower limit	1st quartile	2nd quartile	3rd quartile	4th quartile	Exceed upper limit
A	5.60%	4.90%	4.20%	3.50%	2.80%	2.10%
B	4.90%	4.20%	3.50%	2.80%	2.10%	1.58%
C	4.20%	3.50%	2.80%	2.10%	1.40%	1.05%
D	0.00%	0.00%	0.00%	0.00%	0.00%	0.00%
E	0.00%	0.00%	0.00%	0.00%	0.00%	0.00%

3 employees salary adjustment percentage in dept A

Employees	Position	Base salary	4th quartile	Performance Grading	Adjustment percentage
Zhang San	Technician	2500	No.2	C	2.80%
Li Si	Technician	3000	No.4	C	1.40%
Chen Wu	Engineer	4000	No.2	B	3.50%

Dept B adjustment matrix

Performance Grading	Below salary lower limit	1st quartile	2nd quartile	3rd quartile	4th quartile	Exceed upper limit
A	4.67%	4.08%	3.50%	2.92%	2.33%	1.75%
B	4.08%	3.50%	2.92%	2.33%	1.75%	1.31%
C	3.50%	2.92%	2.33%	1.75%	1.17%	0.88%
D	0.00%	0.00%	0.00%	0.00%	0.00%	0.00%
E	0.00%	0.00%	0.00%	0.00%	0.00%	0.00%

Dept B 3 employees adjustment status

Employee	Position	Base Salary	Quartile	Performance Grading	Adjustment percentage

Zhang Yi	Technician	2500	The second	C	2.33%
Li Er	Technician	3000	The fourth	C	1.17%
Chen San	Engineer	4000	The second	B	2.92%

Base on this adjustment percentage, everyone clears about "Force Ranking" force distribution and "The Last One Out" system.

Finally, we actively invite the Asia Pacific Compensation and Benefit team to intervene, to re-compare and evaluate the relevant positions and remuneration ranges from a third-party perspective, provide a direct explanation to the senior management and staff of the company, and work with the affected Employees.

Year 2015

The strike in China has a net increase of nearly one-third a year: pressure from wage collective bargaining is growing. The data showed that 23% of the respondents said they had formal wage negotiations with staff representatives in the 6 months 2015 years ago, with a ratio of 24% in 2014, 19% in 2013, and 9% in 2012, and 14% said they must pay collective bargaining at some Point.

Local governments are more stringent on the payment of social security funds continue to increase the cost burden of manufacturing enterprises. 71% of the respondents said social security payments were enforced more rigorously. If Strictly implemented, the enterprise for the staff to pay the "five social insurances one fund" (medical, pension, work injury, unemployment, Maternity and housing Provident Fund) accounted for 40-50% of wages, greatly increased heavy cost burden, especially the average proportion of the total cost of the surveyed enterprises has reached 22% of the Level.

The control of the use ratio of labor force in the interim provisions on Labor dispatch issued in 2014 also directly caused the continuous increase of labor cost. Each month this can lead to USD3.69/people monthly cost increment. Hourly wages can rise from USD3.69 to USD4.15. However, from 2007 to 2014, the minimum wage has risen by 224%, the rate of increase of 16% minimum wage per worker, has also led to increased overtime, the government has changed to allow employees and companies to pay more social security and housing provident fund, and eventually lead to the employee applied companies do not buy insurance for them, because they cannot afford it. This can also be the reason for the strike, which makes the foreign bosses felt incredible.

However, the labor market price is still rising, you can pay a high price, the same price the other factory can offer, at the end of the year, workers want to leave still leave, because more opportunities are waiting! Production department only know how to complaint, very little reflect how to retain employee in the front line.

We invited IMPACTT consultants to launch a survey of the Workers ' living index, which found that we were higher 49% than the average wage for the entire region (RMB2,333 Vs RMB2,976) and that 87% of the employees ' income was sent back to their hometown, poor Chinese migrant workers, the distance from home is for the life of the family needs. But even if the average wage in Asia is such a big one, the average wage for workers is still RMB80 from the level of basic local life, and the expectations of employees are still 20%, RMB585. the bonuses are not encouraging enough.

The restrictions on compliance cannot schedule excessive overtime. Therefore, the investigation agency proposed to eliminate the unequal treatment between the dispatching staff and the formal staff, let the staff know their career development prospects, tracking staff absenteeism and the reasons for the loss, in order to give management decision-making reference.

We accepted the advice of the consultants, and made a difficult decision at that Time: two times OT payment if all employees were treated temp worker or formal worker without difference. "To manage one company, Inequality rather than want is the cause of trouble ".

Y2014

Chinese enterprises in the trouble of the growth: demographic dividend reduction, the two taxes combined, the renminbi appreciation, domestic demand, weak exports, trade protectionism, the United States and Japan to promote employment, European debt crisis, Southeast Asia's advantages triggered foreign capital withdrawal, ASEAN with 20 years' natural competitive advantage ...

In view of rising labor costs and supply shortages in China, ASEAN will benefit from the outflow of foreign investment in China, with most ASEAN economies (except Singapore and Malaysia) paying significantly lower wages than China. Although wages in some parts of the country are still competitive, especially in the West, the shrinking labor force means that wages in these areas will soon catch up with the eastern sector. ASEAN's demographic advantages are also more pronounced. As of 2013, the median age of ASEAN population was about 27 years, and the median age of Chinese was significantly younger than that of 32 years. The size of the ASEAN workforce will also continue to grow in the coming decades, according to UN data, and 2010-2030 ASEAN workforce will increase by 70 million. By contrast, the size of China's labor force is expected to fall by about 70 million during the same period.

Company J is in the development zone strikes constantly: 39 companies continue to strike.

Countries in the intensive collection of processing trade in the current employment situation data, the initiative to propose the following areas need to improve:

Settle resident problem
Provide the low rental apartment
Provide basic medical protection
Settle children educational problem
Provide the employment insurance
Increase the position training allowance in the company
Reduce social insurance contribution rate
Create more continue educational opportunity
Speed up peasant worker urbanization
Keep currency stable

The internal environment of the company: the turnover rate has been rising by years and the shortage of skilled workers, the problem of worker's loss seriously affects the problem of quality stability, Scrap rate, rework rate, and the number of QA quality management staff, pull the long retraining, these are the costs of the company. HR has repeatedly made analysis to the senior level, but the response is limited and has not been adjusted for 19 months. The CPI with 3% speed in inflation. At this time, the group's senior SVP Bill flight to the factory for routine inspection, he always appeared at the company most need time, the last time is our branch encountered an NGO negative report, I caught this opportunity, when he asked me the staff turnover rate and overtime hours, I said: "High turnover rate, more overtime, overall income is lagging far behind our competitors." He knew the problem as soon as he heard it, because he started from the frontline test engineer and knew the employee's life was not easy. I told the truth, he asked David and his boss HH politely, "Are you comparing our workers ' treatment with those our peers who lag behind?" Do you consider working overtime to increase the total income of workers?" Two bosses keep silence, afterwards HH joked with me, if there was a gap in the ground, he would jump in immediately. Really difficulty situation for two bosses to handle, but no matter how hard, need to be fair to the workers: the company immediately raise base salary after the due date.

Year 2012

41% The company's management forecasts the business to shrink from 2011. The extent and manner in which the annual salary increases were promoted by the collective bargaining of trade unions was heavily publicized by the government.

The group announced the full-year staff-level Annual Review budget is 7.1%+ special increase of 1%, that is, the whole year 8.1% is still trembling to announce and explain, because in the past each year to maintain at least 8% growth rate.

The adjustment of the worker's minimum wage has determined the Annual Review. The sharp rise in the number of consecutive years of minimum wages, leading to technician at the highest level of direct labor salary increased higher than the Assistant engineer, above assistant engineer continue to bring the impact to the upper level, in order to balance, the company was forced to make corresponding adjustments to the Assistant engineer, which is forced to the level of each to be accompanied by a buffer-type adjustment.

China's VP require Shanghai, Wuxi and Guangzhou 3 branches' salary system unification, in order to do this, he called me went to the Shanghai factory, let me propose the unification, I first put the three branches pay cost to compare with our competitors: Showed two competitive companies' employees pay figures with GMs to review, In the end it is the bosses feel that their branch of the pay structure is better, do not want to accommodate each other to make the big change, there is no need to pull together, anyway, finally let 's see who can turn over more profits for the group.

Y2011

According to the Mercer Consulting report:

The global economy has experienced a steady growth in the trough of the 2009-year financial turmoil's frozen pay. The BRICS economies are growing rapidly. But prices kept low. China become the world's second-largest economy.

That year, 1.46 million people in the National Civil Service examination, scale comparable to the ancient gold nomination, to join civil servants = hand holding iron rice bowl.

China in the labor shortage:

The 23 provinces adjusted the minimum wage in the first half of the year, but the turnover rate of employees has reached 10.3% in half a year, and the labor market, which is larger than the supply, has forced many companies to move inland, and the country's policy of encouraging agricultural development has diverted a significant portion of the source of work.

The company began to compare the minimum wage cost of the 27 plants across Asia, we used labor companies to provide a real-time comparison of wage levels for other companies in the region, fearing that workers ' salaries would deviate from the market. "Workers, technical engineers and development engineers are the three most difficult jobs to retain in all manufacturing industries. In view of this phenomenon of turnover rate, we give professional-level total remuneration compared to other staff and management level of Annual Review, reflect on the special adjustment.

On June 1, 2010, after a succession of frozen pay surges and strikes in 2009, Foxconn abruptly announced a pay increase of more than 60% to $2000; Before May 31, in the South China Honda company suddenly announced a pay increase of 24% to 1910 yuan. However, Guangzhou area staff average salary is 1285 yuan (the government minimum wage is only 1100 yuan), the entire Pearl River delta manufacturing companies confused, do not know how to deal with.

More than half of the enterprises have a shortage of labor, Labor is not unlimited supply, the overall national unemployment rate is only 4.3%, intensive research focused on strikes and pay rise incident: Staff's demand is clear: Money! Gen Y's new generation of employees is hard to manage, with more than half of companies already planning a raise. Improve the working environment, strengthen psychological counseling, reduce overtime but at the same time increase employee income is the most common method. Many companies are planning to move factories: The movement from China to the low-cost countries in Southeast Asia, they handful seek help from the local government, but we use this trick. Let the government come in to help advertise and engage in activities, directing employees' attention to the positive side.

When I first entered Company J, all day struggling in the questions of the bosses "chicken and egg" which one should put forward question, while facing all day torture from different department set performance indicators? Why has the hourly wages multiplied in the past two years? How did the results improve? How much can you make sure that the turnover rate is lowered by the company's high-level consent? On the other side, the manager of the department, told me that the staff turnover rate was too high, and even if themselves had to go, the pressure was too heavy. In fact, who knows my pressure? Who knows what did HR do in the past two years?

Staff income is low, rely on 80 hours overtime to balance, in addition, the employees' living quarters to be deducted 80 yuan, the total income is lower than the competitor's close to 30%, so the turnover rate is particularly high. We made twice emergency adjustments within one year:

Stop the dormitory fee of 80 yuan/month deduction.

During the first half of the adjustment, the allowance was partially allocated to the basic salary to increase the base salary and overtime pay.

The reinstatement of the original allowance in the second half of the latter adjustment, with an additional level of $100 to the base salary.

Additional performance award for PWT workers: Selection of lean improvement, 5S, employee turnover rate, discipline, quality five indicators to assess, monthly performance results issued.

Staff level adjustment only for the low pay and the best performance 20% of the groups, for expatriate colleagues, we will follow the staff's home country annual review rules. Because it was just out of 2009 economic crisis, staff expressed understanding and acceptance of the company's arrangements.

In that year, I did more "build the foundation" job: to guide C&B team follow the group Unified Standards: Base on the position, the level of communication, innovation requirements, knowledge mastery, and the position of the risk of five indicators, the job to match all the positions, C&B team colleagues kidding they did not do a job matching before.

The company turned out to be different national salary adjustment time is different, the same country the same branch office salary adjustment time are also different, the special adjustment each month can carry on. Salary adjustment is a long and heavy thing, but repeatedly again and again in a year for the separation of workers: Ordinary staff, senior staff different levels numerous and varied, finally we decided that our branch standardize Annual Review time, even the special adjustment also concentrated to the 1st of 1,4,7,10, Simplify the process from unnecessary repetition. Of course, resistance is certainly, depends on how you communicate and resolve.

Recalling the past 7 years of Annual Review, the whole wave of China's ups and downs, the future of C&B structure of the manufacturing industry need to be deep plowing, store up grain against famine, so how to balance the impetuous between the company and the staff, cultivate mutual understanding and communication, it is not easy to reach "Win-win" situation.

33. Talking about performance before payment

C&B, the general understanding is the work of salary calculation, but the deeper understanding should be a few senior HR can be recognized, in fact, C&B management includes the performance, compensation and organization of the three major systems:

The performance system includes performance assessment, feedback coaching, performance evaluation, performance planning and performance culture.

The compensation system includes compensation management, compensation structure, internal level, external level and pay orientation.

The organizational system includes organizational climate, organizational skills, position management and departmental structure.

Human resources management, to learn from the marketing department of customer-oriented, business-oriented, through the data to measure the results, so that the performance of the culture deeply rooted; Learn human capital Management from the Finance Department, measure the value of human capital by Data report, and become the talent engine of enterprise development; Learn from the research and development department to predict the human resources requirements of business development through analysis of facts and data.

Take a 2015-year performance evaluation guide explaining how we do the annual assessment:

Performance management encompasses what effective actions we take to ensure that our goals are met, including goal setting, mid-and year-end assessments, and future behavior specifications.

The goal is to require peer and subordinate links.

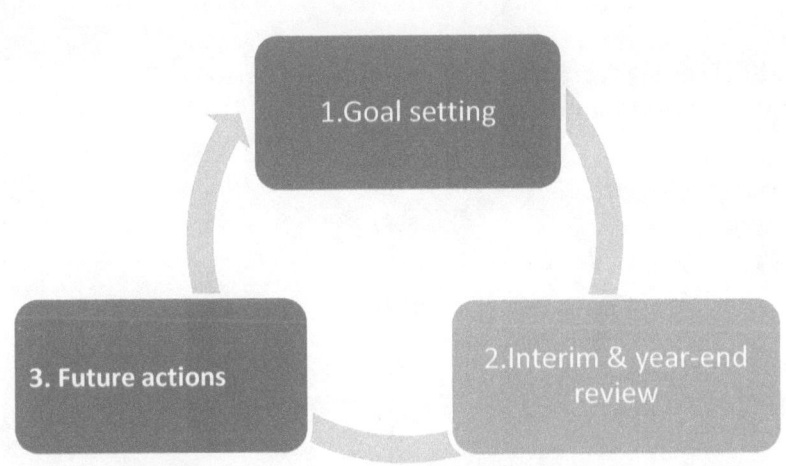

1. Goal setting: Vertically & horizontally aligned goals

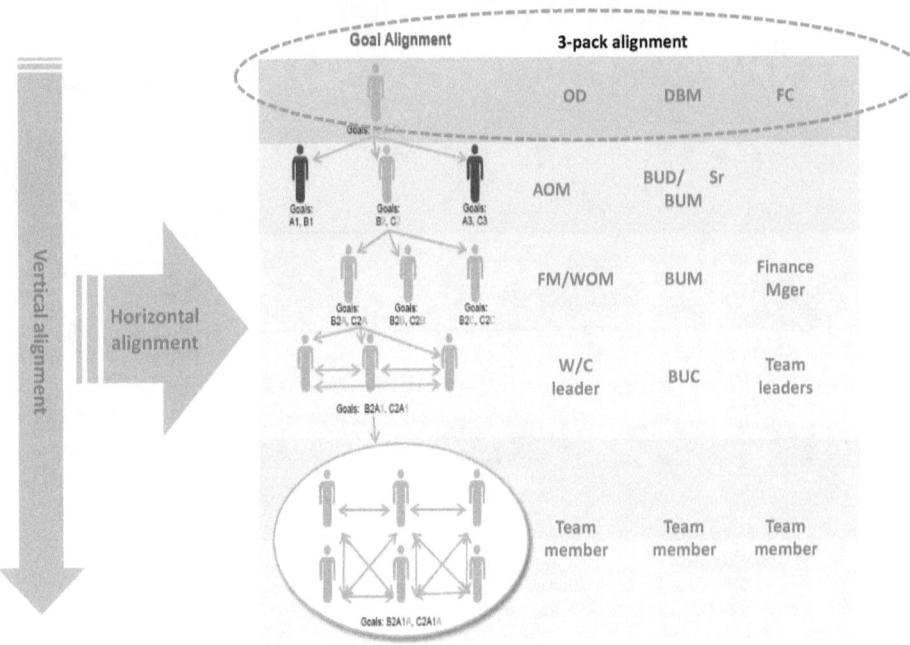

1. Goal setting: Vertically and horizontally aligned goals (Ops. as example)

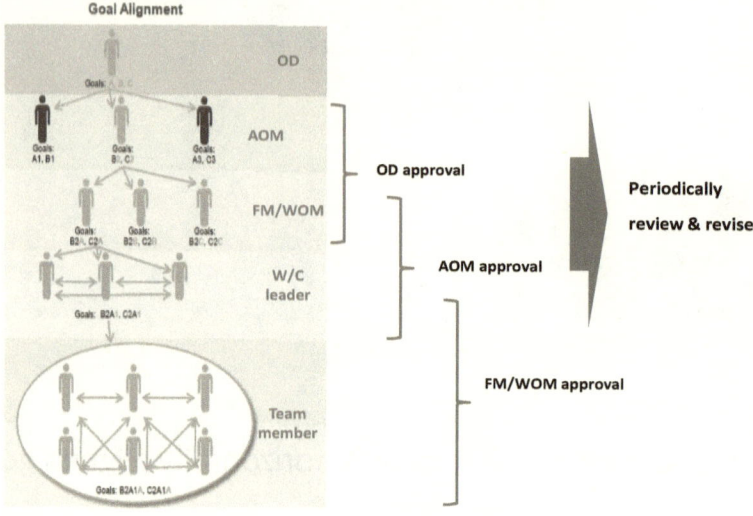

2. Goal setting: Tool-Value tree (Ops. as example)

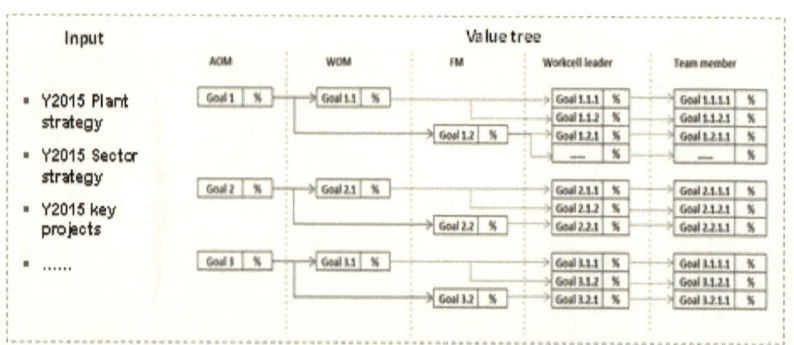

- **General rules:**
    - Balance Score Card: Strategic, Financial, Customer Service, Leadership
    - SMART: Specific, Measurable, Actionable, Realistic and Time bound
  - 80/20 rule
  - Total goals: 3-7 goals

The company base on the overall strategic objectives of the "value tree" concept for layer decomposition: the use of the Balanced scorecard four key factors, according to 20% factors lead to 80% of the results of the rule, require each employee set 4-7 goals, target requirements: measurable, concrete, can be put into action, achievable, with a specific timetable.

The company selects the success factor system to track employee goal setting and feedback, to record the progress of target completion and action tracking in real time, feedback from different supervisors, even the boss can ask the department to provide feedback on the performance and goal of the staff at any time:

Review and communicate in a phased manner.

3. Goal setting: Tool-Success Factor System

Please input the goals into Success Factor System for review and follow up

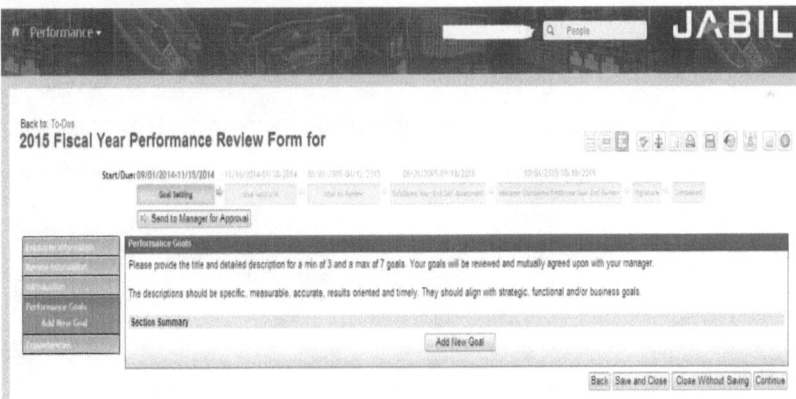

From the previous year of September to the November of this year, the process of performance evaluation runs through:

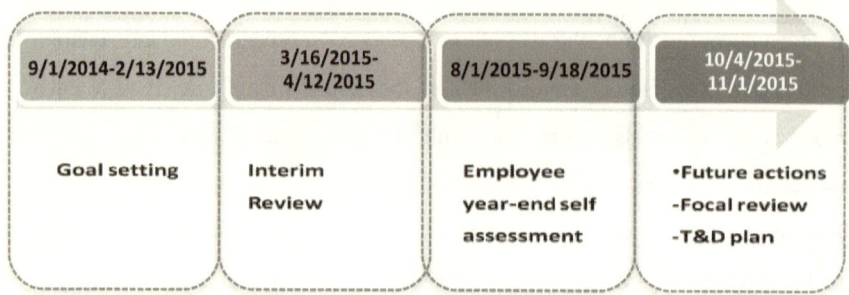

Employees with good performance are entitled to pay increase. Training and development ...

The company use a 360-degree assessment system for employee promotions:

Leadership 360° Assessment

1.0   360° Assessment Purpose
Thank you for participating in 360° Leadership feedback process. Feedback is a valuable part of our process because it shows our leaders how their actions are interpreted by a variety of people with differing points of view. It also helps our leaders identify their strengths and those areas that require improvement. Your feedback will be presented anonymously and in combination with other feedback providers, we encourage you to be as candid and specific as possible. Feedback is only valuable if it is timely, truthful and actionable. Thank you in advance for your candid feedback.
2.0   Providing Meaningful Feedback

Your role as a feedback provider is to:

• Be objective and honest. Provide both positive and negative feedback.

• Base your feedback on your observations over a period of time, rather than focusing solely on recent situations.

• Support your numerical ratings by providing examples and comments. Our leaders find the comments to be the most meaningful part of this process.

• Connect your examples and comments to the competency statement you are evaluating in each section.

Please avoid:

• Giving someone a higher rating because you've worked with them for a long time.

• Giving someone a lower rating based on the comments or opinions of others.

• Using shortcuts when providing examples, such as "same as previous comment".

3.0 360° Assessment Form

You can use< 360°Assessment Form>, we provide 2 versions of Chinese & English, you can choose one version which easy to be understood by you.

• Fill the score to the blank based on your observations & views, the scoring methods as below

Views	Does Not Meet Standards	Partially Meets Standards	Meets Standards	High Standards	Consistently Exceeds Standards
Score	0	4	6	8	10

Leadership 360° Assessment	Employee Name:		
	Employee SAP#:		
	Dept/WC:		
	Job Title:		
	Assessment Result		
	I	Builds Organizational Talent	0%
	II	Gains Commitment	0%
	III	Drives for Result	0%
	IV	Acts with Integrity	0%
	Total		0%

Assessment Items						
Please fill the score number to below blanks→	0	4	6	8	10	
Builds Organizational Talent						
1.1	Recruits and Develops Talent: Recruits competent people who fit with the values and principles for success in COMPANY J and builds effective teams					

	with complementary strengths.					
1.2	Provides Accurate and Timely Feedback: Creates a culture of open feedback to increase confidence and motivation and leads by example by giving specific and meaningful performance feedback. Ensures feedback is timely and constructive. Takes corrective action with employees where appropriate.					
1.3	Establishes Development Plans: Collaboratively works with employees to enable development goals to be met by identifying developmental opportunities that ensure employees realize their highest potential.					
Please provide examples in support of your rating.						
II. Gains Commitment						
2.1	Empowers Employees: Communicates clear expectations and pushes decision making authority to the most appropriate level.					

2.2	Encourages Open Door Policy: Is approachable and accessible, listens and responds to employee suggestions, ideas and concerns. Follows up with employees to ensure all issues are closed.					
2.3	Collaboration: Engages in constructive cooperation and supports overall team values and direction. Is constructively disruptive versus destructively disruptive. Works well with others and carries oneself with professional demeanor.					
2.4	Effectively Manages Conflict: Manages and resolves conflict in a positive and constructive way leading by example, escalating issues with a sense of urgency, and helping the team to release root cause barriers to success.					
Please provide examples in support of your rating.						
						|//
III. Drives for Results						

3.1	Manages Time: Uses structured techniques to plan activities and monitors progress against plans, conveying clear expectations for tasks and assignments.				
3.2	Identifies and Manages Resources: Prioritizes and utilizes available resources and negotiates for and accesses additional resources (including those outside of domain control) when necessary for critical tasks. Does not allow the team to overstaff in order to compensate for poor performance.				
3.3	Results Focused: Works tenaciously toward goals and sets high standards for individuals and team performance, with a sharp focus on the task and drives others to do the same.				
Please provide examples in support of your rating.					
IV. Acts with Integrity					

4.1	Demonstrates Honesty: is honest and open representing information accurately and completely avoiding distortion or embellishment of the facts.					
4.2	Keeps Commitments and Behaves Consistently: Maintains social, ethical and organizational norms firmly adhering to codes of conduct and ethical principles, ensures that words and actions are consistent.					
4.3	Personal Values: treats others with dignity, respect and fairness giving recognition to the right ideas of others even when challenged or resisted and is prepared to stand up for justifiable causes, defending and supporting to ensure the right outcome for COMPANY J。					
Please provide examples in support of your rating.						

The company has developed measures and plans for colleagues who need to improve their performance:

Performance Improvement Process (PIP)

Purpose

Performance Improvement Process (PIP) provides a guide to be used to raise unsatisfactory work performance to an acceptable level in order to reach the requirement of the position within 2 months.

Eligibility

The employee who is at the unsatisfactory work performance level in the annual performance appraisal, that is, cannot reach the requirement of the position.

PIP can be utilized at any time throughout the whole year.

Employees who accept PIP must obey assignment from the company and are not eligible to internal job application, salary increase and other awards.

PROCESS

The supervisor identifies candidate, initiates PIP and makes objectives and duration by filling out Performance Improvement Program. The objectives should be consistent with those of other employees in similar assignments.

The next level supervisor reviews PIP and supporting documents, makes appropriate amendments and signs off the form. The two supervisors work out a plan to hold a meeting with the employee.

The two supervisors hold a meeting with the employee. While supervisors try to create a climate of trust and participation, key messages of this Guide/Form should be conveyed to employees.

The supervisor makes overall amendments, if any, based on employee's written inputs.

The employee has the right to either accept or refuse participating with PIP. The signature on PIP indicates the employee accept PIP and should accomplish new assignments and performance appraisals according to the content of PIP. Refusal to sign PIP or refusal to accomplish the assignments after signature on PIO can include the termination of labor contract with notice period of 30 days according to Labor Law.

The supervisor, including next level supervisor if necessary, provides ongoing feedback and coaching, collects performance result, and conducts performance review.

By the end of the PIP, the supervisor decides on employee's Successful Completion or Unsuccessful Completion. The decision should be supported by next level supervisor. Successful Completion indicates that the employee can reach the requirement of the position and keep working, while Unsuccessful Completion indicates that the employee cannot be competent for the job after training or adjust the position, we will terminate the employment with 30 days' notice period according to Labor Law.

The supervisor provides the original Performance Improvement Form to HR and keeps copy.

Supervisors are encouraged to consult HR in each phase of the PIP process.

Attachment

Performance Improvement Program

PINPOINT/RECORD

PERFORMANCE IMPROVEMENT PLAN

Basic information：

SAP NO.:	Chinese & English Name:		Position:
Department:	Workcell:		Supervisor:
Plan Begin Date:		Plan End Date:	

Description of position related information: job description, Job requirement and goal setting

Job description	
Job requirement	
Goal setting	

Justification for Placement Under the Performance Improvement Plan (PIP)
Include summary of behaviors and/or performance in need of improvement. Summarize prior performance discussions regarding areas in need of improvement, including dates of discussions, expectations that were set and documented, and specific examples of work performance issues.

Areas for Improvement

Area(s) Requiring Improvement	Current Status	Specific Actions/Expectations	Measurement Date
Examples: Technical Skills Leadership Accountability Dependability Communication Collaboration	-	Identify specific actions or behavioral expectations that will demonstrate the required improvement in performance.	Identify dates for completion of specific actions as appropriate. (Some actions will be ongoing and not have a specific completion date.)

INVOLVEMENT

Supervisor/Employee Commitment– What commitments will the supervisor and employee make to improve performance:

Include designated intervals for regularly scheduled review and feedback of performance to specific actions/expectations, schedule of follow-up meetings (daily, weekly, bi-weekly), specific training, coaching, mentoring, key work partners, and available resources e.g. reports, customer feedback, emails.

My signature below indicates that this Performance Improvement Plan has been presented to me, and that its contents have been explained to me. I clearly understand that my failure to satisfy the specific actions and expectations contained in this document, or failure to maintain a satisfactory level of performance may result in termination of my employment. I understand that if I think the decision to place me on a Performance Improvement Plan is in error, I may appeal the decision but the Plan will remain in effect until and unless the decision is reversed or modified by management, as appropriate.

_____   _____
Employee Signature/date   Supervisor Signature/date

_____   _____
FM/Dept Head Signature/date   HR Signature/date

COACH/EVALUATE

Coach/ evaluate date: _____

Follow-up – Weekly/ Biweekly/ Monthly. Circle the appropriate on.

Summary of performance to date (What has taken place since last discussion):

No	Specific Actions/Expectations	Progress	Status
	Identify the specific actions	Enter the appropriate	(Red/Yellow/

or behavioral expectations you are reviewing at this checkpoint.	status of each action/expectation.	Green)

Green- What worked well & results achieved.

Yellow- What has reasonably improved but to meet expectations.

Red - What remained unchanged or deteriorated further.

Next actions to be taken & timeline:

The current overall status of this plan is ___On Plan ___Behind Plan ___Ahead of Plan

_____
Supervisor Signature/date

_____
Employee Signature/date

_____
HR Signature/date

COACH/EVALUATE

SAP NO.	Chinese & English Name	Position
Department	Workcell	Supervisor
Plan Begin Date		Plan End Date

Final Evaluation (Monthly / Quarterly)

Final Review and Recommendation:

Has employee successfully completed performance improvement plan and demonstrated the ability to sustain continued acceptable performance?

Please tick:

___ Sustained Acceptable Performance, qualified for this position

___ Occasionally Meets Expectation, not qualified for this position

___ Not Meeting Expectation, not qualified for this position

Supervisor Final Summary and Recommendation:

| |
| |

Employee Comments:

| |
| |

Next Action to be Taken:

___ Relieved From PIP

___ Track for another month (document/counseling required)

___ Track for another month (warning letter required)

Employee Signature/date　　　　　　　　Supervisor Signature/date

FM/Dept Head Signature/date　　　　　　HR Signature/date

First, the performance system management methods and steps, look down on how we set compensation management, compensation structure, internal level, external level and pay-oriented.

Building the Framework of Base Pay Management

A global grade structure provides an organized framework for making fair market driven pay decisions at COMPANY J. A series of steps establishes a progression in grades that reflect increases in scope and accountability for each job.

Internal Equity is defined through the Job Evaluation process.

Job Evaluations is a method of consistently comparing the contributions of a job to other jobs in the company. Several tools are used to conduct a Job Evaluation including: organization charts, interviews, and Job Descriptions.

Job Descriptions are documents defining the details of a job. They are used to compare similarly situated jobs in the company, to conduct market analysis of similar jobs in the market place to determine the appropriate pay rate for a job. The document consists of:

Summary – a 2 - 3 sentence overview defining the reason for the job in the company. It may be used to prepare internal and/or external job postings.

Essential Duties and Responsibilities – a listing of 5 - 7 primary functions of the job.

Skill, Experience and Education – the competencies, skill, and minimum education and experience required to enter and perform the job successfully.

Work Demands and Physical Environment – a list of physical skills, time spent performing physical activities, work conditions and environment, and/or any special requirements for the job.

External Competitiveness is established through jobs that are readily found in the market to benchmark salaries and create the foundation for ranges within the global grade structure.

Market Pricing aligns Internal Equity with External Competitiveness through analysis of local Cost-of-Labor rates. The data is obtained from international surveys including identified competitors. Market Pricing focuses on establishing fair wages to ensure the organization does not underpay (leading to high turnover), or overpay (leading to unnecessary production costs) for work performed.

The company hierarchy and compensation architecture are tightly linked:
Global Grade Structure
COMPANY J's Global Grade Structure groups jobs into three main categories: Support, Professional and Management. Jobs are differentiated in level based on progression in accountability, problem solving, and know-how.
Each level within the job structure is assigned a unique global grade, each with a pay range established through the local Market Pricing.
Management (M01 – M07)   Professional (P01 – P06)   Support (S01 – S07)

	MANAGEMENT		PROFESSIONAL		SUPPORT
GLOBAL GRADE	Manages activities of people. Typically, goal achievement is accomplished through performance of others. May be responsible for a functional area without direct reports.	GLOBAL GRADE	Creative, innovative work. Generally, requires university degree or equivalent in education and experience. Correlates to "Exempt" classification of US labor regulations	GLOBAL GRADE	Performance of assigned tasks. Generally vocational training is required. Correlates to "Nonexempt" classification of US labor regulations

M07	Senior Director				
M06	Director				
M05	Senior Manager	P06	Principal		
M04	Manager (Regional, Mega site)	P05	Expert		
M03	Manager (Site, smaller scope)	P04	Advanced		
M02	Supervisor	P03	Career		
M01	Supervisor	P02	Developing		
		P01	Entry	S07	Expert Technician
				S06	Expert General Admin / Senior Technician

					S05	Production Lead / Sr. Gen Admin / Intermediate Technician
					S04	Expert Labor & Production / Intermediate Clerical / Entry Tech
					S03	Sr. Labor & Production / Entry Clerical & General Admin
					S02	Intermediate Labor & Production
					S01	Entry Labor & Production

For a detailed summary of each grade level, please reference Global Grade Career Level Definitions.doc, available through your HR department.

Base Pay Administration at COMPANY J

The primary objective of Base Pay Administration is to ensure that an employee moves through the pay range at a rate and regularity that recognizes his or her level of performance and contribution to COMPANY J. The spread or width of our pay ranges allows enough room for managers to make pay distinctions between employees based on individual performance and contribution.

Each grade is assigned a pay range which represents the range of base pay opportunity available to an employee in that grade. All pay ranges include the prevailing market rates for all jobs in that grade.

Pay ranges have three important components: Minimum, Midpoint and Maximum.

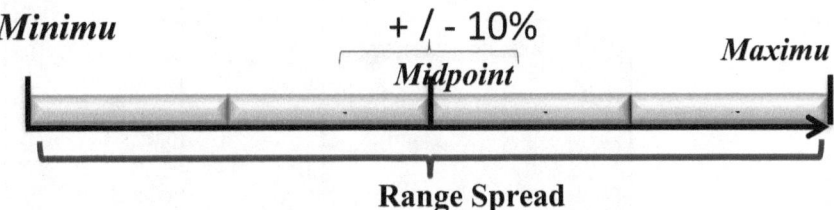

Minimum – the minimum pay rate the company will typically pay an employee in a designated pay grade. The minimum pay rate is typically awarded to employees who are new to the level of work and possess the minimum requirements for the job.

Midpoint – the middle of the range typically is achieved or awarded to employees who have been in the pay grade for a few years, possess full knowledge of the job, and individual performance is at or above expected levels. Individuals with pay rates that are +/- 10% of the midpoint are considered competitively positioned compared to the market.

Maximum – the maximum pay rate the company will typically pay an employee in a designated pay grade. Employees who reach the maximum of a pay range typically have been in the assigned grade for many years and may have reached the plateau for their given job role. Future increases to base pay will be frozen until the range is adjusted up or the employee progresses to a higher-grade level. Managers have several forms of Base Pay Management that enable them to make pay distinctions between employees in the same grade based on individual qualifications, performance, and contributions.

Forms of Base Pay Management	Purpose	Timing	Typical Percent Range
New Hire	Recruit qualified talent in the Labor Market.	Time of Hire.	Minimum to Midpoint
Promotion	An increase to Base Pay to recognizes an employee's progression from a lower grade to a higher grade.	Flexible	5 - 7%; or amount to bring to Minimum
Pay Adjustment (Lateral/Same-Grade)	Increase to Base Pay, e.g., career development, increase responsibilities/skills, transfer.	Flexible	3 – 5%
Merit	Increase to base pay to reward employee for performance.	Annual Focal periods vary	Varies based on country and budget

Merit Lump Sum	Rewards employee for performance without increasing Base Pay. May be used when employee is at Maximum.	Annual Focal periods vary	Varies based on country and budget
Market / Equity Adjustment	Increase to Base Pay for a fully performing tenured employee whose Base Pay is more than 10% below Market.	Periodic. May be multiple increases over 18 – 24 %.	Varies; Should be in combination with Merit Increases

When formulating pay rates for new hires or promoted employees, careful consideration must be given to the following:

Existing employee's pay, qualifications, experience and performance (Internal Equity)

Market conditions, including supply and demand (External Competitiveness)

Budget established for a job at onset of recruiting (Cost Consciousness)

Candidate's pay history, qualifications and experience (Pay-for-Performance)

Under most circumstances, it is appropriate to assign a pay rate between Minimum and Midpoint of the pay range. Note: an employee's pay rate should never be assigned below Minimum, or above Maximum of the pay range.

Policies and Practices

General

The defined base pay ranges for each country provides the framework for Base Pay Management at COMPANY J.

Typically, base pay recommendations should be targeted to fall within the minimum to midpoint of the grade pay range.

Base pay offers must be no lower than the minimum salary or hourly rate as defined for the assigned grade pay range.

Each grade pay range includes the prevailing wage rates for many benchmark jobs in the marketplace. When making base pay recommendations, keep in mind COMPANY J is a performance-driven organization in a reasonably volatile industry, therefore we target base pay that is competitive, but not overly so – base pay constitutes a fixed cost for the company and limits our flexibility to respond to market movement.

Base pay recommendations should always take into consideration the base pay of all incumbents currently performing the same job in the location (maintaining internal equity for similar jobs).

Internal Promotions

Promotional increases are expected to be in a range of 4-7% of base pay. Proposed promotional increases exceeding 15% of the employee's current base pay will require a review by a Regional Compensation team member and may require final authorization by the Vice President or SVP.

Offers of Employment

Base pay recommendations should follow the guidance previously outlined. Base pay recommendations exceeding 10% above midpoint will require a review of total compensation by a Regional Compensation team member prior to proceeding with recruitment or an offer of employment to ensure Internal Equity is considered & pay reflects the prevailing market rate.

Salary Review Policy

DEFINITION

SuccessFactors system

SuccessFactors is the Global Performance Management Process. The process uses a web-based tool to provide an online process for employees and managers to input, review, rate and digitally sign annual performance appraisals; to provide a traceable workflow tool to facilitate communication between the employee, his or her manager, HR manager and third-party reviewers.

IL (Indirect Labor)

DL (Direct Labor)

IL with flexible working hour (Based on the labor contract or agreement)

Departments of Operation include but not limited to: Planning, Purchasing, Supplier Quality Engineering, Inventory Control, Warehouse, Logistics, Customs, Human Resources, Quality Assurance, Facilities, Manufacturing, Manufacturing Engineering, Test Engineering, Industrial Engineering, IT, Operations.

Transfer--Moving an active employee to a new position, department, or location at the same level within the Organization.

Promotion - Moving an active employee to a new position, department, or location at a higher level within the Organization.

Job title adjustment - Moving an active employee to a new position, department, or location at a lower level within the Organization.

REFERENCE

N/A

RESPONSIBILITY

Departmental managers are responsible for identifying all the staffing needs of their department except for sector manager, the qualifications for each position within their department and their department employees' application of salary adjustment.

Assistant Operation Managers are responsible for identifying the staffing needs, the qualifications and the application of salary adjustment for the position of sector manager, workcell manager, and other direct reports of Assistant Operation Manager.

Company decides salary adjustment or increment percentage base on external market salary movements, cost of living, and the company's financial performance, affordability.

ATTACHMENT

4.1. Personnel Status Change Form

4.2. Performance Appraisal Form

4.3. Leadership 360° Assessment

4.4. Performance Improvement Program

4.5. Level of Average Rating

Grade of Appraisal					
Ranking	Unsatisfactory	Marginal	Creditable	Very Good	Outstanding
	E	D	C	B	A
Score	0 - 1.4	1.5 - 2.4	2.5 – 3.4	3.5 – 4.4	4.5 - 5
Description	Performance does not meet standards required. Requires significant improvement. Performance to be reviewed in 3	Performance occasionally meets agreed standards. other skill needs to be further improvement. Performance to be	Performance meets standards on a consistent basis. Demonstrates know-how.	Performance is frequently above standards. Demonstrates strong expertise and knowledge.	Performance is consistently above standard. Remarkable achievement & exceptional performance.

	months.	reviewed in 6 months		

PROCEDURES

Promotion

Promotion demand

Departmental managers are accountable for evaluating organization and employee development demand and identifying the employee promotion needs of their department and the qualifications for each position within their department.

Promotion criteria

Have the relative position vacancy in organization chart.

Employee finishes the training required for current position and meets the qualifications of new position.

Have been in their current position at least 12 months.

Have no current Performance Improvement notifications.

Have no salary review in the recent six months.

Have received at least a Creditable rating on the latest two annual performance appraisals.

Have completed according performance steps in Success Factor system

Have been an employee of the Organization for at least one year.

No effective written warning letter discipline records.

IL with flexible working hour in Departments of Operation and Finance, should pass Lean Bronze Certificate

Promotion process

If there is vacancy and the suitable candidate who meets the job requirements, the direct supervisor whom the open position reports fill up "Performance Appraisal Form" and get the approval departmental manager. If the candidate is a workcell member, PA form should get the approval of departmental manager and workcell manager.

Department Manager should submit the promotion name list to Human Resources Department on 15th of second month in each quarter, which is Jan 15th, Apr 15th, Jul 15th and Oct 15th, before the effective date of the promotion. Otherwise the promotion will be delayed to next quarter. Department submit the organization chart and Job Description for the new open position with employee signature to Human Resources Department at the same time.

Department provides Human Resources Department 360-degree assessment on the promotion to assistant manager level or above.

Human Resources Department review if the application confirms to the promotion criteria and return the non-conformed application to department. Meanwhile, Human Resources Department send out all the qualified promotion name list to Department Manager / Workcell Manager / Business Unit Manager / Assistant Operations Manager to review.

Department Manager / Workcell Manager / Business Unit Manager / Assistant Operations Manager review and promotion name list, and feedback to Department Manager in a prompt manner. Department Manager shall confirm the final name list to Human Resources by 30th of the month, and at the mean time submit the application to IL Salary Review & Promotion System.

The salary increment percentage will be proposed by Human Resources Department according to market and internal salary level and be approved by HRM, FM and Operation Manager or Finance Controller or Director Business Management. The salary must be in line with the pay scale and deviation requires Operation Manager special approval for Operation, DBM for BU, and Finance Controller for Finance.

In the third month of the quarter and before the effective date, Human Resources shall publish the final promotion name list to Department Manager / Workcell

Manager / Business Unit Manager / Assistant Operations Manager, who shall make a final feedback to Department Manager if any. Department Manager shall update Human Resources any changes. Finally, Human Resources submit the final promotion name list to Operation Manager (Director) for approval.

3-pack's approval is a must for the promotion to level of Business Unit Manager, Functional manager and Assistant Operation Manager or above.

Effective date

Promotion will be processed quarterly and the effective date is Feb 24th, May 24th, Aug 24th and Oct 24th.

Special salary review

Special salary review demand

Departmental managers are accountable for identifying the employee special salary review needs of their department.

Special salary review criteria

Have been in their current position in COMPANY J for at least six months.

Have no current Performance Improvement notifications.

Have no salary review in the recent six months.

Have received at least a Creditable rating on the latest two annual performance appraisals.

Have completed according performance steps in Success Factor system

No effective written warning letter discipline records.

If the employee is nominated for promotion, he will not entitle to the special salary review

IL with flexible working hour in Departments of Operation and Finance, should pass Lean Bronze Certificate

Special salary review process

If departments recognize special performance of employees or employees' professional skills are upgraded enabling them to perform at higher level, the direct supervisor whom the employee reports fill up "Performance Appraisal Form" and get the approval departmental manager. If the candidate is a workcell member, PA form should get the approval of departmental manager and workcell manager.

Department Manager should submit the special salary review name list to Human Resources Department on 15th of second month in each quarter, which is Jan 15th, Apr 15th, Jul 15th and Oct 15th before the effective date of the special review. Otherwise the special review will be delayed to next quarter.

Human Resources Department review if the application conforms to the special salary review criteria and return the non-conformed application to department. Meanwhile, Human Resources Department sends out the qualified special salary review name list to Department Manager / Workcell Manager / Business Unit Manager / Assistant Operations Manager to review.

Department Manager / Workcell Manager / Business Unit Manager / Assistant Operations Manager review and promotion name list, and feedback to Department Manager in a prompt manner. Department Manager shall confirm the final name list to Human Resources by 30th of the month, and at the mean time submit the application to IL Salary Review & Promotion System.

The salary increment percentage will be proposed by Human Resources Department according to market and internal salary level and be approved by HRM, FM and Operation Manager or Finance Controller or Director Business Management. The salary must be in line with the pay scale and deviation requires Operation Manager special approval for Operation, DBM for BU, and Finance Controller for Finance.

In the third month of the quarter and before the effective date, Human Resources shall publish the final special salary review name list to Department Manager / Workcell Manager / Business Unit Manager / Assistant Operations Manager, who shall make a final feedback to Department Manager if any. Department

Manager shall update Human Resources any changes. Finally, Human Resources submit the final special salary review name list to Operation Manager (Director) for approval.

Effective date

Special salary review will be processed quarterly and the effective date is Jan 24th, April 24th, July 24th and Oct 24th.

Transfer

The transfer procedure refers to the policy "Internal Opportunity Program"

There is no salary review for the inter-departmental transfer at the same level.

The transfer will be processed according to department request. Effective date will be 24th every month.

Job title adjustment

Job title adjustment demand

Departmental managers are accountable for evaluating employee's performance and identifying job title adjustment needs of their department.

Job title adjustment basic criteria

The direct supervisor whom the employee reports can apply job title adjustment and get the approval of departmental manager while the employee meets anyone of the below criteria:

Have received at least an unsatisfactory or marginal rating on the performance appraisal

Being in the period of Performance Improvement Program

Job title adjustment process

Departments recognize performance of employees or employees' professional skills cannot meet the requirement at the current position and make orally agreement by employee on job title adjustment and salary adjustment, the direct supervisor whom the employee reports fill up "Performance Appraisal Form" and get the approval departmental manager. If the candidate is a workcell member, PA form should get the approval of departmental manager and workcell manager.

The direct supervisor whom the employee reports fill up "Personnel Status Change Form" and get the approval of departmental manager and submit approved "Personnel Status Change Form" and "Performance Appraisal Form" to Human Resources Department.

Human Resources Department will review if the application is reasonable or evidence doc is enough and return the unreasonable and not-enough-evidence application to department.

The salary for new position will be reasonably proposed by Human Resources Department according to market and internal salary level and be approved by HRM, FM and Operation Manager or Finance Controller or Director Business Management.

Human Resources Department will sign "Labor Contract Change Agreement" with the employee with the assistance of department.

Effective date

The job title adjustment will be processed according to department request. Effective date will be 24th every month.

Focal review

Focal review budget

The Focal Review Matrix on salary increment percentage vs HC distribution percentage base on level of average rating (refer to 7.0) will be proposed by Human Resources Department according to market and internal salary level and be approved by OM, Finance Controller and DBM(3-packs) every year

Focal review criteria

Employee will be entitled to participate in focal review on the condition that he or she joins COMPANY J on/before May 24th.

Employees must finish SUCCESSFACTORS process at assigned date.

Focal review process

Department submit Human Resources Department the estimated annual performance average ratings in soft copy for all staffs in their department, which conform to the headcount forced distribution in focal review matrix approved by 3-packs.

Human Resources Department reviews if the estimated annual performance average ratings conform to the headcount forced distribution in focal review matrix and returns the non-conformed ratings to department.

Employee, manager and manager conduct annual performance appraisal through SuccessFactors. The appraisal cycle is Sep 1st of last year to Aug 31st, employees must follow timetable and finish SuccessFactors process at assigned date, otherwise focal review effective date will be delayed to the start date of next payroll cycle after the SUCCESSFACTORS whole process finish.

Human Resources Department review if SuccessFactors average rating conforms to the estimated average rating by department for each employee and route back the task of redoing appraisal to direct supervisor for those non-conformances.

Human Resources Department executes salary adjustment according to SuccessFactors average rating, salary percentile for each employee.

Salary increment rule for new hire, newly promoted IL

New hires in the year:

New normal work hour salary=Current normal work hour salary*increment%*service days/365.

IL promoted from non-grade-7 DL:

New normal work hour salary=Current normal work hour salary*increment%*service days starting from IL effective date/365.

Focal review effective date

Focal review is once per year and effective date is Nov 1st every year.

OTHER

Probation confirmation

There is no salary review.

Labor contract renewal confirmation

There is no salary review.

34.Oh, My God-The Manager pay will be cut 20%?

This is the project I don't want to do as HR head of Company J, not because how bad job I done, From the bottom of my heart this is the worst decision of the group, let HR to lead it, even I have to sign unfavorable "Unfair Treatment", personal felt seriously unbalanced, but still urged others to sign off "Accept to cut pay" commitment and return, this feeling like force myself to suicide.

From another point of view: To encourage changes in the program go through such a large range of so-called short-and long-term performance bonuses, like experienced a baptism of life, in the baptism you get more skills and patience, lifelong embrace.

It was one day in September 2017, I received a call from the new Asia Pacific Senior Human Resources director, YH, who vaguely said to me: "The group is considering revising all quarterly performance bonuses, which may be reduced by half, global unification is only issued once a year based on group performance." As soon as I heard, I knew the problem was big, and replied: "Why did the group do such a thing when the business grew smoothly?" The global unified group performance standards, our branch annual performance is the top of the queue, is the most efforts of a group, is it the biggest shock to them? Wouldn't it charged to be the Chinese government big pot system? The managers do not have timely encouragement only once payment a year, it will dampen their enthusiasm, are these problem Corp management did not realize? Why don't they ask the people for advice? The implementation of this will happen "earthquake", pls repeat think about the bad impact."

Looks helpless that company decision has been made, YH call is an early notice, just see my feedback, however I still said the most honest words.

The biggest change of the time:

1. The world's deputy general manager and the following level of 3,900

managers or more, unified quarterly bonuses per quarter according to their departments and positions to reduce the proportion of the maximum to 30%, I am in a gear from 40% to 20%;

2. The frequency of issuance is changed from quarterly to yearly and is issued once per year as a transitional period of two times in the first year;

3. The entire group must achieve the overall business objectives, or the total amount of personal bonus may be zero; Belong to the group headquarters position, according to 35% group Performance +65% individual performance decision distribution ratio, the rest of 25% group performance +75% individual performance decided to pay proportion, the group performance index can be adjusted within the 0 to 150% range, the personal performance index is controlled in 0 to 100%:

2017 Weighting of Performance Components

Goal-Based Plans		Metric-Based Plans (BD, Sales, OIP, SCDM)	
Corp/Div Performance Component Weight	Individual MBO Component Weight	Corp/Div Performance Component Weight	Performance Metric Component Weight
35%	65%	25%	75%

Up to 50% of the Individual MBO Component may be paid mid-year for FY17 only.

Weighting of components will be adjusted in FY18 to reflect potential impact on the business. Those in higher salary grades will generally have a larger portion of their total incentive based upon Corp/Div results.

Up to 50% of the Performance Metric Component may be paid mid-year for FY17 only.

For all:

Corp/Divisional Performance Component available Q1

Personal goals established Q1

Why was my reaction so big? This bonus has a long history, ten years ago, that is, Company J began to invest in China to build a factory, promised to all management a welfare, encourage everyone get more pay, as long as the whole branch to reach the target, branch reward, according to the specific performance of each business group, by the Accounting department in accordance with the financial data clearly calculated results, This is the policy released in 2007:

QUARTERLY PROFIT-SHARING PLAN – ASIA EDITION

The COMPANY J culture promotes ownership and accountability of all employees. In order to reward eligible employees for their efforts toward profitability, COMPANY J has established a Quarterly Profit-Sharing Plan.

1.0 WHO IS ELIGIBLE ?

An individual must be a **permanent** employee of COMPANY J. or a designated subsidiary with ONE year of service completed and a minimum of 250 hours of service during the respective fiscal quarter. Employee must be <u>physically present</u> at work for the stated minimum hours and this would exclude ALL paid and unpaid leave days.

2.0 WHEN AM I ELIGIBLE

After meeting eligibility requirements, participation will commence on the first day of the fiscal quarter following the ONE year of service – Sept 1, Dec 1, Mar 1 and June 1.

3.0 WHAT AM I ELIGIBLE FOR

If a profit share award is approved, a company contribution will be made payable to eligible employees for each Fiscal Quarter. The amount of the profit share will be based upon an amount deemed appropriate by the Board of Directors of COMPANY J Circuit Inc.

Profit share is based on financial performance of the plant and its ability to meet projected financial goals. Profit share percentage will differ from plant to plant. The Company does have the right to withhold any payments or portion of a payment to satisfy the participating employee's tax liability.

4.0 HOW DOES THIS WORK

Approximately six weeks following the end of the fiscal quarter, employees will be provided the profit share percentage that will be payable, if any. The Payroll Department of each plant will be responsible for the distribution of the profit share monies to the participants.

5.0 AM I STILL ELIGIBLE FOR PAYMENT IF I RESIGN

If an eligible employee tenders his/her resignation, the employee will still be eligible for the profit-sharing payment if he/she has **completed the fiscal quarter AND** is **still physically** working in the company **at the time of payment**. Both conditions must be fulfilled for payment.

6.0 EMPLOYEE TRANSFER

Should a situation arise where an eligible employee takes up an inter plant / inter group transfer where the profit sharing % differs, the payment of profit sharing will be based on the duration of service of employee. The employee will enjoy the profit sharing % of the group/plant in which he/she spends the most time (workdays) within the quarter. The HR Manager of the Receiving site will be responsible to administer this with the Finance Dept.

7.0 COMPUTATION

The base for profit sharing computation shall be as follows:

7.1 FORMULA

7.1.1 Profit Sharing Computation = Total Earnings per Quarter x Profit Sharing % per Quarter

Total Earnings is defined as all the payment that the employee earned during the quarter. Items excluded from total earnings are:

All allowances

13th month payment & Variable Bonus

Profit share amount from previous quarter

All reimbursements ie travel, medical etc

For India, total earning is defined as "Employee's Mutually Agreed Compensation Package" and includes retirement benefits if the same forms a part of employee's package (CTC) and overtime. It excludes payment for other benefits or welfare initiatives like insurance policy, subsidized transportation, subsidized canteen and/or anything in a similar content.

For Japan, total earning will include "Seasonal Adjustment" which is one of the components for salary.

Payment will be made base upon compliance to Clause 1.0, 2.0 and 5.0 if applicable.

8. SITE AND CORPORATE PAYOUT

8.1 An employee is only eligible to enjoy either a site profit share or corporate profit share.

8.2 Site Profit Share % - Applicable to employee who meets the 3 criteria as mentioned below:

(i) All Ops/Business/Finance/IT employees of a site AND

(ii) Supporting site activities only AND

(iii) The headcount will roll up under the SITE Ops/ Business/Finance/IT group

8.3 Corporate Profit Share % -Applicable to all Regional / Corporate / Global groups including
BUDs even where they have single site responsibility.

8.4 Any deviations to the above category of payout must be approved by the EMS CEO, EMS CFO and HR Director.

Effective Date: Sept 1, 2007

Internal Equity – fair and equitable administration of compensation across the company
ensuring practices are locally relevant.

External Competitiveness – total compensation opportunities reflect local and market relevant practices of world-class companies and selected COMPANY J competitors.

Pay-for-Performance – recognizes and rewards employees for their individual accomplishments and contributions.

Cost Conscious – rewards are designed to optimize shareholder value in relation to the cost involved.

Category	Title	Bonus Name	Bonus Mechanism	Approved by
Ops	OM, AOM	OIP	1)Quarterly Bonus; 2)Bonus=Quarterly Total Basic* N%. N% is bonus rate, max rate=40%	VP or OM
	Function Head			OM
	Workcell Head			OM
	Exempt IL(Sr. Staff)	Profit Sharing	1)Quarterly Bonus; 2)Bonus=(Quarterly Total Basic + Quarterly OT Payment)*N%; N% is bonus rate, it is decided by Corporate based on each site's performance	Corporate
	Non-Exempt IL			
	COMPANY J DL			
	Contract DL			
BD	Sr. BUD; BUD	BU Incentive Bonus	1) Quarterly Bonus; 2) Bonus=N. N is bonus amount, N<=RMB100,000	VP or Plant Level Sr. BUD
	Sr BUM		1)Quarterly Bonus; 2) Bonus=N. N is bonus amount, N<=RMB87,500	Plant Level Sr. BUD
	BUM		1)Quarterly Bonus; 2) Bonus=N.	

372

			N is bonus amount, N<=RMB57,500	
	BUC		1) Quarterly Bonus; 2) Bonus=N. N is bonus amount, N<=RMB22,500	
	Project Manager		1)Quarterly Bonus; 2) Bonus=N. N is bonus amount, N<=RMB15,000	
	CSS	Profit Sharing	1) Quarterly Bonus; 2)Bonus=(Quarterly Total Basic + Quarterly OT Payment)*N%; N% is bonus rate, it is decided by Corporate based on each site's performance	Plant Level Sr. BUD
Fin	Sr. Controller & Controller	FIN Incentive Bonus	1)Quarterly Bonus; 2) Bonus=Quarterly Total Basic* N%. N% is bonus rate, max rate=40%	Regional Controller
	Asst Controller		1)Quarterly Bonus; 2) Bonus=Quarterly Total Basic* N%. N% is bonus rate, max rate=20%	Plant Controller
	Sr Manager	FIN Incentive Bonus (Max		
	Manager			

		20%		

In the course of implementation, a document was re-issued in 2013 in order to clarify the methods for calculating the indicators:

Eligibility: Full-time employees performing site operational leadership or functional management job roles are eligible to participate in this variable incentive plan. Eligible job roles usually include the following types of titles: *Operations Manager; Facilities Manager; HR Manager; Inventory Control Manager; Planning Manager; Purchasing Manager; Site Quality Manager; Test Engineering Manager; Workcell Manager, etc.* For a full list of eligible job titles, please consult Global_Compensation@Jabil.com.

Performance Periods and Payouts: Incentive payouts will continue to be paid quarterly, against fiscal-quarterly goals. Final payout amounts will be reviewed by management and are subject to adjustment at management's discretion.

Maximum Variable Opportunity: The amount an individual can earn under the plan is called the Maximum Variable Opportunity and will be expressed as a percentage of annual base salary. The Maximum Variable Opportunity under the Plan is 40% of the quarterly base salary in effect the last day of the respective quarter, or actual quarterly bonus-eligible earnings as determined by local practice or statutory requirements.

Performance Metric Weighting: Payout of the Maximum Variable Opportunity is calculated based on up to 5 different performance metrics depending on job role, weighted as follows:

PERFORMANCE METRIC	METRIC WEIGHTING	
	Senior Director Operations	Site Operations Manager; Functional Management
Customer Satisfaction	25%	20%
Days in Inventory [1]	25%	20%
Scrap	25%	20%
Transformation Cost as % of Material Margin	25%	20%
Supplemental Measure [2]	N/A [3]	20%
Total Maximum Variable Opportunity	100%	100%

Goals for each metric will be set and approved by the respective VP Operations each quarter. Site-specific approved quarterly goals will be communicated to participants by Regional/Site Leadership. Workcell Managers will be measured against the respective Workcell results. All other OIP plan participants shall be measured against the respective Site results.

Each indicator one by one is normalized, here is an example:

Transformation Cost as % of Material Margin	Transformation Costs represent all costs making up Plant Contribution, excluding the Material content of the Workcell Profit & Loss (P&L) Statement. • Transformation costs: Scrap, Freight and Duty + Manufacturing Costs + Sales & General Administrative (SG&A) Expenses • Material Margin: The difference between total revenue and the sum of all costs related to Materials, Scrap and Freight is referred to as Material Margin • Actual Transformation Cost % should be lower than the TC % in the Lock, unless another target is agreed, and will be paid out according to this schedule: | Transformation Cost Payout Schedule			
% of Goal	=< 100%	>100 - 105%	> 105%
% Payout	100%	50%	0%	
---	---

This policy is very challenging and encouraging, managers have developed a habit, must do the best, not to drag everyone back, if achieved 35% or above we will applaud for celebration, a toast to the party, if not, we all want to save the day and night to achieve results.

From offering, Each manager's package has already regarded this benefit as part of the employee remuneration, divides their salary in the original company to divide into the fixed and the change performance bonus two parts, now take away the change part, the distribution frequency also adjusts for one year, if the staff really wants to contend with the company, The company is taking a lot of risk, but the top management of the group is really a kind of gambling mentality, bet to win the cost of recovering this, but they did not see the hidden behind this part of the company's high-level dissatisfaction, directly affect the future performance of the company. The group's only remedy: to filter out managers with a lower salary than the market line to make a special adjustment, but this creates a later problem, the manager who gets a special adjustment feels that his previous salary is lower. The manager who didn't get a special adjustment thought why not me?

This series of problems can be heart burning & brain burning to make a reply, to make a plan how to deal with, so we have a branch of the HR Heads, were concentrated together first "brainwashed".

The first is to give the project a tone, so that deliver what we want:

Key Challenges and Changes Needed in our Compensation Program

From our review, it is clear that we need to do the following to better support the business and improve alignment to our compensation philosophy and best practices:

- Better align with market and competitive practices
- Build a common incentive framework for our business groups and jobs
- Create stronger tie to overall business performance
- Better differentiate in a pay-for-performance environment
- Ensure we have the compensation budget to appropriately reward success

After that, the brain, from the interests of employees, is starting from their own, to imagine any possible problems, unified communication answer:

Conducting STI and LTI Conversations with Employees

As a COMPANY J leader, you play a critical role during times of change. Your mission is to help team members embrace changes and lead the way forward to achieve high levels of individual, team, and organizational performance. Your leadership and support will promote a smoother transition and a quicker recovery for team members. Start by reviewing the STI Frequently Asked Questions document. If you have concerns about information provided in that document, discuss with your leader to ensure understanding or to explore options for effectively communicating details to your team. As you prepare to communicate, use the following strategies to ease conversations with individual employees.

1. Keep a constructive mindset If you're gearing up for a conversation you've labeled "difficult," you're more likely to feel nervous and upset about it beforehand. Instead, try framing it in an objective way. For instance, you're not

delivering bad news about compensation; you're presenting an incentive plan that provides attractive opportunities for eligible employees who help COMPANY J meet annual performance goals. Conversations about sensitive topics tend to go best when you think about them as just a normal conversation.

2. Carefully rehearse your opening statement to provide employees with proper context. When employees are disappointed, it's often because they lack information. We recommend using the following opening statement to help employees understand the reasons for the changes and the benefits that will result. COMPANY J is making a few important changes to our short-term and long-term incentive plans. These changes apply to all incentive-eligible employees. They will enable COMPANY J to:

Better align with market and competitive practices. Build a common incentive framework for our business groups and jobs. Create a stronger link to overall business performance. Effectively differentiate rewards in a pay-for-performance environment. Ensure we have the compensation budget to appropriately reward employees for achieving results I would like to explain the changes in more detail. (Proceed to explain the plan and percentage changes that apply to the employee.)

3. Gauge the other person's reaction; listen and respond with empathy take time to process the other person's words and tone. Active listening is extremely important. If you really listen to what the other person is saying, you're more likely to address the right issues. Be prepared with responses to possible questions, comments, and concerns. Keep your language simple, clear, direct, and neutral. If the other person remains quiet or difficult to read, it's appropriate to ask how they are feeling. Asking shows that you care. Make sure your actions reinforce your words. For example, saying "I hear that you're concerned by these changes" lacks sincerity if you're scrolling through your smart phone at the same time. Allow freedom for the other person to openly discuss concerns, but do not

over-sympathize or allow venting to become counterproductive. Keep your own emotions under control. For example, don't say things like, "I feel so bad about saying this," or "This is really hard for me to do."

Close on a positive note Closing on a positive note could be as simple as letting employees know how much you appreciate their contribution to the team, or their positive attitude during times of change. If employees are ready to focus on the future, you might transition into a conversation about setting individual performance goals that align with business objectives. If a valued employee openly protests or shows signs of withdrawing, seek to clarify the employee's point of view. Listen carefully and make sure you understand all concerns. If appropriate, consider scheduling a follow-up conversation designed to generate ideas or identify opportunities that would re-engage the employee and deliver value to COMPANY J.

Just rely on HR to push all the management to implement, quite difficulty, so we asked SVP cascade down, if there will be any resistance, SVP to deal with, HR prepared the manager communicate content of all with a unified PPT version ready to let them know how to proceed.

Manager's toolkit: Anticipated Questions and Answers

This is a reference to help you respond to questions and concerns you may hear from employees, with consistent messaging from managers and leaders. Remember, if you don't know the answer to a question, let the employee know you'll get back to them; check with HR; and be sure to follow-up.

Overall Change

Q: This seems like a take-away. How is it "better" for me?

We recognize the immediate impact of these changes may be a challenge. But change always means opportunity—and we believe that in the long run, there are positive outcomes for all of us.

One of those positives is that our pay will be fairer and more equitable for everyone across job levels within a region—since we'll have consistency in targets and the weighting of business and individual components.

We will also have a clear picture of what the business goals are that we need to achieve (through the corporate/divisional metric)—which will tell us where to focus our efforts to drive the business. And better business outcomes benefit all of us.

Since it's a true incentive—earned based on performance and aligned to business goals and outcomes—we'll have a greater sense of connection to the business.

You'll have the opportunity for above-target payout when we overachieve on company (corporate/divisional) goals.

There'll be more differentiation in rewards based on performance. The corporate/divisional reward each year will depend on performance of the business you directly support. And we'll work to better differentiate rewards for individual performance, using the full range of potential payout (0% to 100%)—so that those who perform at the highest levels will be rewarded accordingly.

Overall the changes add up to a more strategic, responsible use of our compensation dollars. This supports the company's bottom line, which we all have a vested interest in.

That said, we recognize that these changes do affect you. We know that the payout timing, the change away from strictly individual performance-based payouts and the change in target percentages for some employees will take time to get accustomed to.

Q: We're all very high-performing at COMPANY J. Shouldn't our pay be above market?

Aligning target award opportunities to the competitive market is the most responsible method of administering compensation.

Actual pay earned each year is based upon the performance of the Company and each individual.

We have talented employees who are capable of driving outstanding results—and therefore earning above-target rewards based on the upside potential with our revised STI plans.

Q: It sounds like I'll be paid less to do the same work. How do you justify that?

We regularly benchmark total compensation opportunities (base salary plus target STI and LTI) with the practices of companies similar to us in industry and size. The reality is that in many cases, COMPANY J's incentive targets have been above market practices.

It's important that our incentive targets are competitive with the external market. At the same time, we're building in an upside potential on the corporate/divisional component—so payouts could be above target when performance exceeds expectations.

Incentives are meant to be variable based on performance that year, and not necessarily provide you the same amount every year. Over time we'll all acclimate to a stronger pay-for-performance culture, and realize the advantages of that.

Q: If our incentives are inconsistent, why didn't we do this before now?

Our business has continued to evolve over time, with accelerated change recently that has prompted us to evolve our strategy, and brought on new business challenges (to improve margins, expand reach, align costs, maintain financial strength and liquidity).

Our compensation programs and philosophy must evolve to support our strategy, culture and long-term sustainability. We need a plan that allows us to be nimble and proactive in how we engage, incent and reward our people.

Now is the right time to eliminate inefficiencies, provide consistency, and update and right-size our incentive plans to help drive the business and move us toward a stronger pay-for-performance culture.

Q: I don't understand how we just reported a strong year for our division and sector and you are taking away my equity awards and reducing my STI target award opportunity.

I understand your thoughts on it appearing you are being penalized; However, that is not the intention at all. It is our goal to align pay with market practices. Long-term incentives have always been discretionary, and approved by our shareholders and Board of Directors. Over the past several years, our annual share usage (total number of shares granted) has been significantly higher than industry practices. Management and the Board are taking the appropriate steps to align our grant practices with companies like ours.

Regarding annual incentives, our plan was not in line with prevailing market practices, nor has it been equitably administered. Our intention is to align the plan with market and allow our people to be compensated. Aligned with our pay-for-performance philosophy, our employees will continue to have the opportunity to achieve above market compensation for superior performance.

Q: Is our business in trouble?

No—however, we're all aware of our challenges, that we operate on very thin margins, and that our overall performance was below expectations during FY16. It's important that our incentive pay is reflective of our business performance. It doesn't make sense to always pay the same "bonus" dollars when our business performance fluctuates.

Q: What about base pay? Are we changing that too?

We're not freezing or making reductions to base pay.
We continually monitor base pay to be sure it's competitive with the market.
Targets

Q: Are our current targets really above-market? How do we know?
[Manager, note: Some employees might even bring in online pay survey info]
In determining competitive pay levels, we reference highly reliable data from

multiple independent survey sources that gather accurate pay information from companies like ours (similar in size and industry). The data allows us to pay by actual job duties as well as function and level. Data from online pay surveys are not scientific or reliable.

Q: Why did my target go down?

Aligning our targets to the external market is an important part of the direction we needed to go in.

Our short-term incentives need to be competitive, consistent across pay grades, and support our business.

I know it doesn't feel good; but this brings your target in line with what's prevalent for positions like yours among companies we compare to.

This is not a change that's directed at you individually or personally, but one that was made globally and consistently across the business.

Q: If my target is decreasing by so much, there's no way my pay won't go down. How is this fair?

We recognize this is a big change. In fact, it's a change that many people in all of our STI plans will be experiencing.

Simply put, our STI targets were inconsistent across jobs and pay grades and they were above market competitive levels in many cases.   We can't afford, as a company, to continue to pay above market levels without above market performance

We need to ensure that our STI plan is competitive and aligned with the market in our various geographic regions. And we needed to make sure it is equitably applied within our company across pay grades. It isn't appropriate that people in similar roles at the same level had different STI targets.

Q: This is all theoretical. How will I know my actual target and the weightings across the two components that applies to me?

I will be reviewing with each of you a personalized STI plan opportunity statement that shows your specific target and the weighting of the two components.

Q: Will I be paid less?

Not necessarily.

Depending on your new target, and with the potential for above-target payouts when performance exceeds goals, your incentive payout could actually be higher than in the past.

You can see your potential total opportunity for fiscal year 2017 on your STI Opportunity Statement.

Q: Why do we have to go to annual vs. quarterly payouts?

It is very uncommon to pay professional-level employees a quarterly "bonus". Best practice is to pay bonuses annually to allow for an annual assessment of business and individual performance.

Within COMPANY J right now, some organizations pay on an annual basis and some pay quarterly. This makes mobility between organizations very difficult. One consistent approach for COMPANY J will eliminate the issue.

And, we'll be better able to set meaningful and appropriate goals, and to measure how we perform against those goals. Three months doesn't give us a good picture of how we're performing (and could be partly why we haven't differentiated rewards too well in the past).

Q: I count on my quarterly incentive payouts. This will be a real challenge for me in terms of my cash flow.

It's a transition for many, and it's a necessary change for all the reasons we've outlined, both in terms of addressing an inefficient business burden and aligning with commonly accepted market practice We informed participants in September of the change to allow time to plan accordingly. Based upon feedback from employees however, we have determined that we will have a transition year in FY2017. The individual component of the STI will be paid semi-annually.

Over time you'll come to better understand how you and the company are performing for a year, and have an idea of what to expect for your incentive payout accordingly.

It's an important part of the shift—understanding that incentives are meant to reward performance; better goals are set when looked at over a year and performance and results are more effectively assessed on an annual basis; and payouts can vary from year to year.

Q: I already have plans for my bonus. Depending on my payout, this will create a real hardship for me.

We realize that may be the case for people.

This highlights why we need to make a change ... it's clear that our current incentives are more like deferred salary, and are considered a "given". That's not the purpose of incentives; they're meant to motivate us to achieve specific goals that drive the business, and reward us based on business and individual results. A true incentive is variable based on performance.

Q: What if individual my goals change during the year—will I not get a bonus?

If your individual goals change, there's good reason for it. And if there is a needed shift in priorities, you will have the ability to revise your goals during the year.

We'll be putting more rigor on setting relevant goals that support the business. Together we'll set your goals, and ensure they're based on what you can be reasonably expected to achieve. We can adjust your goals if there is a business reason for where we want you focusing your efforts and contributions.

We'll assess your performance against your goals for the year, and consider any changes in goals that occurred. You wouldn't be penalized for not achieving a goal that was dropped.

This also highlights the advantage of an annual incentive payout: we can better measure your performance against goals for a year.

Q: What if I change jobs—either to a new level, unit or region? How will it affect my payout?

As before, your STI payout will be prorated based on the number of days you were in each role, in that unit or under each different STI plan.

The only thing of note is that the target award opportunity and the weighting between corporate/divisional and individual components of your final role at the end of the fiscal year will be applied to the entire payout.

Corporate/Divisional Component and Threshold

Q: Why should part of my incentive be based on business performance? If I'm performing well doesn't that tell you I'm contributing to the business?

All of us can work hard and make strong contributions. But if the business performance is below expectations, it tells us we have room to improve on what we're doing or how.

Tying part of our short-term incentive payouts to achievement of specific business goals will help ensure we're all on the same "track" in terms of where we need to focus our efforts and what we're trying to accomplish.

Our shareholders expect (and demand) a certain level of financial performance. If we fail to deliver on reasonable financial expectations, it is unfair to our shareholders to pay bonuses at 100% of target.

Q: [From a corporate employee perspective ...] If one unit affects the overall corporate results dramatically, why should I receive no payout on that component?

As corporate employees, we support all areas of the business, so our rewards need to be based on the performance overall.

We're one company, and everyone's efforts intertwine. We'll all have more clarity on our business goals; and since they'll affect our incentive pay, greater motivation to achieve them.

Accordingly, we'll all share in the rewards when performance exceeds expectations, and likewise when it comes up short.

The Corporate component will be comprised of three independent pieces – EMS, DMS and overall Corporate performance. Each of these will be independent and it will be possible to earn an award for one or two components, even if one business performs below expectations.

Q: **[From a divisional employee perspective ...] How can I be held responsible for the performance of my entire division?**

The divisional metrics will be set at a level that gives you clear "line of sight" to what you can impact.

We'll all have more clarity on our business goals, and motivation to achieve them. We all must work together towards achieving the goals; and we'll all share in the rewards when performance exceeds expectations, and likewise when it comes up short.

Q: **What about the new Company threshold. Is this a way of COMPANY J being able to justify not paying out bonuses?**

No—that's not the intent.

It's part of ensuring our incentives are tied to our business results and drive a "pay for performance" culture; as well as being consistent with prevalent practice in the external market.

We don't anticipate this threshold being triggered.

It's truly a fail-safe measure that would only be used if the Company couldn't and shouldn't pay out incentives in the case of major crisis.

The threshold Company CANCOI requirement for FY17 is $300 million. For reference, we made more than $600 million in CANCOI in FY16.

If we are all working together towards our corporate/divisional metrics, we should have no problem meeting this threshold metric.

We will also discuss the issue of amending the legitimacy of the policy and finding the right answer together.

Everything is ready, Group CHO issued a unified notice to 3,900 management staffs:

In recent weeks you've heard how COMPANY J is taking important steps to strengthen our business for today and the future. Our organizational transformation—which includes rethinking how we work, making the most of our resources, and strengthening our pay for performance—is a key enabler to transforming the business.

We will be making some changes to our bonus plans, starting with fiscal year 2017, which begins on September 1, 2016. Noted below is important information so you can begin the year informed, focused, and ready to make the most of your COMPANY J Short Term Incentive (STI).

Why are we making changes?

Short-term incentives will help us focus everyone on common goals and what's most important to achieve, thereby driving the business; and providing rewards for results.

To meet these goals, it's important our STI plan is in line with market practices; is easy to understand; and creates a strong tie to the business.

What are the key changes?

We are:

Tying a portion of payouts to achievement of key financial goals by including an overall Company or Divisional performance component in everyone's STI awards

Revising the timing of incentive payouts for all employees to be annual rather than quarterly—based on your measurable annual performance vs. goals

Bonus awards for Fiscal 2017 will be paid in October of 2017. Note – this does not impact the timing of payment for any bonuses earned for FY 2016

Many of our employees already receive bonuses annually – this change will ensure consistency across the Company

This is in line with market practices – more than 95% of companies pay bonuses annually versus quarterly or semi-annually

Evaluating total compensation to be more consistent with competitive market and country-specific practices.

For some individuals whose incentive award is currently above market practice, this may result in a decrease in your target incentive opportunity in 2017

The large majority of employees' incentive target will not change, as they are currently aligned with market

Introducing "upside" (above-target) payout potential when company and/or division financial performance exceeds goals

For many employees, this will provide an opportunity to earn annual incentives above targeted levels – an opportunity that has not existed in the past for many participants

What should you do next?

We want you to be well-prepared to start fiscal 2017 with an understanding of what you can do and how you'll be rewarded. You will hear more details later this month and in October about how your STI will work going forward, and what it will mean for you. Your leader will meet with you individually to go over how these changes may impact you personally. You'll have plenty of opportunity during these events to get information, and get answers to all the questions we know you'll have.

We recognize these changes are significant and that pay is a topic of great personal importance, but firmly believe the decisions and actions we are taking are consistent with our values, market best practices, and our objective to strengthen our business today and for the future.

At the same time, specific to the personal change program (see the following attachment) to the person, HR and supervisor preliminary and staff communication to explain the key points. Observing their reactions, reported to Corp HR there will be any unusual cases.

Your FY 2017 COMPANY J Short-Term Incentive Opportunity

Employee: XXX   **Date: XXX**

Here is a personalized look at how your current incentive amount and new STI opportunity add up for FY 2017 in local currency. **Effective January 1, 2017 your annual salary includes a market adjustment of 9%.**

	FY 2016	FY2017
12 month base salary	339,336.00	369,876.24
Incentive percent	40% (at Max)	20% (at Target)
Incentive amount	**135,734.40**	**73,975.25**
	35%	65%
	Corporate/Divisional target amount (weight times target incentive amount) 25,891.34	Individual target amount (weight times target incentive amount) 48,083.91
	Possible payout, from 0% to 150% (Based on CANCOI results) 0 to 38,837.01	Possible payout, from 0% to 100% (Based on performance against your goals) 0 to 48,083.91

Your Total Maximum Incentive Opportunity

Assuming 150% corporate/divisional component payout and 100% individual component payout,

your total award for the year could add up to:

> **86,920.92**

Payout Timing

Annually, after the close of the fiscal year approximately October of each year. If your 2016 plan was paid quarterly, you will receive a one-time transitional payout of up to 50% of your Individual Component made approximately in March, 2017.

Note:

If our corporate business results do not meet a pre-determined minimum threshold, there will be no payouts on either component for all incentive plans.

You must be an eligible and active COMPANY J employee at the end of the fiscal year to be eligible for a Short-Term Incentive payout.

All of COMPANY J's incentive plan designs, performance goals, and provisions are reviewed on an ongoing basis. Therefore, COMPANY J reserves full rights to modify or terminate this or any incentive plan.

After the communication, the managers on the surface are calmly accepted, the next is the most critical step: Ask staff to sign off, return the document back to HR, this process as I said before: Just like I forced myself to "suicide", this is my second time in life, the previous time in the company E, the financial turmoil occurred.

Document all sign back, the first year implement special arrangements for a half-yearly bonus finally scheduled to release, under I repeat urge.

This time, also should be I left Company J, the time for retire at the height of one's official career, back to river and lake.

35.Stock grant- God glory ?

It was about 10 years ago I first touch the equity incentive scheme, I was looking at my boss: HR general manager of China granted two master degree employees in value to RMB 18,000 shares, they have served the company for more than 10 years, I saw the "great sense of honor" from their face, I was questioning in my heart: only the value of 18,000 yuan shares, is it worth so serious to grand it? I have not experienced the high-tech industry like Alibaba or Tencent uses equity incentives scheme to "Throw the money", I am still me, focus on manufacturing, the company a penny by a penny to earn profit, what spend on staff are true.

In the Company J, foreign employees basically have 85% discount to buy the company's share, the lower limit USD25k per year, the annual USD3,750 discount is the employee benefit, employees can choose the maximum limit of 10% wages to buy the company shares, in fact, this is shared risk of win or lost, When I joined, the company's stock dropped from USD30 down to the bottom of USD3. If the employee bought in by USD30 price, that is really a lost, at that moment the employees did not give up the company, until I left company, the stock price back to USD30, I am a Chinese employee cannot buy it but I can enjoy the company's annual share granting, got a small fortune from the company, which is obtained through the long-term service. According to the rules of three years binding, the first year to receive 30% shares, the second year to obtain 30%, complete the third year of service in order to obtain the last remaining 40%.

After numbers of years listing and the specific operation of the internal purchasing and share granting have been quite mature, to manage this plan is not difficulty, each step has been seriously considered, share with you for reference:

JXXX
2011 EMPLOYEE STOCK PURCHASE PLAN

The following constitute the provisions of the 2011 Employee Stock Purchase Plan of Company J Circuit, Inc. (the "Company").

Purpose. The purpose of the Plan is to provide employees of the Company and its Designated Subsidiaries with an opportunity to purchase Common Stock of the Company through accumulated payroll deductions. It is the intention of the Company to have the Plan qualify as an "Employee Stock Purchase Plan" under Section 423 of the Internal Revenue Code of 1986, as amended.

Definitions.

"Board" shall mean the Board of Directors of the Company.

"Code" shall mean the Internal Revenue Code of 1986, as amended.

"Common Stock" shall mean the Common Stock, .001 par value, of the Company.

"Company" shall mean Company J Circuit, Inc., a Delaware corporation.

"Compensation" shall mean all base straight time gross earnings including payments for shift premium, commissions and overtime, incentive compensation, incentive payments, regular bonuses and other compensation.

"Designated Subsidiaries" shall mean the Subsidiaries that have been designated by the Board from time to time in its sole discretion as eligible to participate in the Plan.

"Employee" shall mean any individual who is an employee of the Company or any Designated Subsidiary for purposes of tax withholding under the Code and whose customary employment with the Company or any Designated Subsidiary is at least twenty (20) hours per week and more than five (5) months in any calendar year. For purposes of the Plan, the employment relationship shall be treated as continuing intact while the individual is on sick leave or other leave of absence approved by the Board, an Officer, or a person designated in writing by the Board or an Officer as authorized to approval a leave of absence. Where the period of leave exceeds 90 days and the individual's right to reemployment is not guaranteed either by statute or by contract, the employment relationship will be deemed to have terminated on the 91st day of such leave.

"Enrollment Date" shall mean the first day of each Offering Period.

"Exercise Date" shall mean the last day of each Offering Period.

"Fair Market Value" shall mean the value of Common Stock determined as follows:

If the Common Stock is listed on any established stock exchange, the Fair Market Value of a Share of Common Stock shall be the closing sales price for such stock (or the closing bid, if no sales were reported) as quoted on such exchange (or the exchange with the greatest volume of trading in Common Stock) on the day of determination, as reported in The Wall Street Journal or such other source as the Board deems reliable;

In the absence of an established market for the Common Stock, the Board shall determine Fair Market Value on a reasonable basis.

"Offering Period" shall mean a period of approximately six months, commencing on the first Trading Day on or after January 1 and terminating on the last Trading Day occurring in the period ending the following June 30, or commencing on the first Trading Day on or after July 1 and terminating on the last Trading Day occurring in the period ending the following December 31, except that the first Offering Period shall commence on the first Trading Day on or after July 1, 2011, and end on the last Trading Day occurring in the period ending December 31, 2011. The duration of Offering Periods may be changed pursuant to Section 4 of this Plan.

"Officer" shall mean a person who is an officer of the Company within the meaning of Section 16 of the Exchange Act and the rules and regulations promulgated thereunder.

"Plan" shall mean this 2011 Employee Stock Purchase Plan.

"Purchase Price" shall mean an amount equal to 85 percent of the Fair Market

Value of a share of Common Stock on the Enrollment Date or on the Exercise Date, whichever is lower.

"Reserves" shall mean the number of shares of Common Stock covered by each option under the Plan which have not yet been exercised and the number of shares of Common Stock which have been authorized for issuance under the Plan but not yet placed under option.

"Subsidiary" shall mean a corporation, domestic or foreign, of which not less than 50 percent of the voting shares are held by the Company or a Subsidiary, whether such corporation now exists or is hereafter organized or acquired by the Company or a Subsidiary.

"Trading Day" shall mean a day on which United States national stock exchanges and the National Association of Securities Dealers Automated Quotation (NASDAQ) System are open for trading.

Eligibility.

Any person who is an Employee, as defined in Section 2(g), who has been continuously employed by the Company or a Designated Subsidiary for at least 90 days (taking into account all of the Employee's periods of employment) and who shall be employed by the Company or a Designated Subsidiary on a given Enrollment Date shall be eligible to participate in the Plan.

Any provisions of the Plan to the contrary notwithstanding, no Employee shall be granted an option under the Plan (i) if, immediately after the grant, such Employee (or any other person whose stock would be attributed to such Employee pursuant to Section 424(d) of the Code) would own stock and/or hold outstanding options to purchase stock possessing five percent or more of the total combined voting power or value of all classes of stock of the Company or of any subsidiary of the Company, or (ii) which permits his or her rights to purchase stock under all employee stock purchase plans of the Company and its subsidiaries to accrue at a rate which exceeds 25,000 dollars' worth of stock (determined at the fair market value of the shares at the time such option is granted) for each calendar year in which such option is outstanding at any time. All Employees who participate in the Plan shall have the same rights and privileges under the Plan, except for differences that may be mandated by local law and that are consistent with Code section 423(b)(5); provided, however, that Employees participating in a sub-plan adopted pursuant to Section 13(c) that is not designated to qualify under Section 423 of the Code need not have the same rights and privileges as Employees participating in the Code Section 423 Plan. In addition, the Board may impose restrictions on eligibility and participation of Employees who are officers and directors to facilitate compliance with federal or State securities laws or foreign laws.

Offering Periods. The Plan shall be implemented by consecutive Offering Periods until the Plan is terminated in accordance with Section 19 hereof. Subject to the requirements of Section 19, the Board shall have the power to change the duration of Offering Periods with respect to future offerings without stockholder approval if such change is announced at 15 days prior to the scheduled beginning of the first Offering Period to be affected.

Participation.

An eligible Employee may become a participant in the Plan by completing a subscription agreement authorizing payroll deductions in the form (including by electronic communication) provided by the Company and filing it with the Company's payroll office in accordance with procedures established by the Company at least five business days prior to the applicable Enrollment Date, unless a later time for filing the subscription agreement is set by the Board for all eligible Employees with respect to a given Offering Period.

Payroll deductions for a participant shall commence on the first payroll following the Enrollment Date and shall end on the last payroll in the Offering Period to which such authorization is applicable, unless sooner terminated by the participant as provided in Section 10.

Payroll Deductions.

At the time a participant files his or her subscription agreement, he or she shall elect to have payroll deductions made on each pay day during the Offering Period in an amount not exceeding 10 percent of the Compensation which he or she receives on each pay day during the Offering Period, and the aggregate of such payroll deductions during the Offering Period shall not exceed 10 percent of the participant's Compensation during said Offering Period.

All payroll deductions made for a participant shall be credited to his or her account under the Plan and will be withheld in whole percentages only. A participant may not make any additional payments into such account.

A participant may discontinue his or her payroll deductions during the Offering Period as provided in Section 10 hereof, or may increase or decrease the rate of his or her payroll deductions during an Offering Period by completing and filing (including by electronic communication) with the Company in accordance with procedures established by the Company a new subscription agreement authorizing a change in payroll reduction rate; provided, however that a participant may not change his or her rate of payroll deductions more than once in a given Offering Period. The change in rate shall be effective with the first full payroll period following five business days after the Company's receipt of the new subscription agreement unless the Company elects to process a given change in participation more quickly. A participant's subscription agreement shall remain in effect for successive Offering Periods unless terminated as provided in Section 10.

Notwithstanding the foregoing, to the extent necessary to comply with Section 423(b)(8) of the Code and Section 3(b) herein, a participant's payroll deductions may be decreased to zero percent at such time during any Offering Period which is scheduled to end during the current calendar year (the "Current Offering Period") that the aggregate of all payroll deductions which were previously used to purchase stock under the Plan in a prior Offering Period which ended during that calendar year plus all payroll deductions accumulated with respect to the Current Offering Period equal $25,000. Payroll deductions shall recommence at the rate provided in such participant's subscription agreement at the beginning of the first Offering Period which is scheduled to end in the following calendar year, unless terminated by the participant as provided in Section 10.

At the time the option is exercised, in whole or in part, or at the time some or all of the Company's Common Stock issued under the Plan is disposed of, the participant must make adequate provision for the Company's federal, state, foreign or other tax or social insurance withholding obligations, if any, which arise upon the exercise of the option or the disposition of the Common Stock. At any time, the Company may, but will not be obligated to, withhold from the participant's compensation the amount necessary for the Company to meet applicable withholding obligations, including any withholding required to make available to the Company any tax deductions or benefit attributable to sale or early disposition of Common Stock by the Employee.

<u>Grant of Option</u>.

On the Enrollment Date of each Offering Period, each eligible Employee participating in such Offering Period shall be granted an option to purchase on each Exercise Date during such Offering Period (at the applicable Purchase Price) up to a number of shares of the Company's Common Stock determined by dividing such Employee's payroll deductions accumulated prior to such Exercise Date and retained in the Participant's account as of the Exercise Date by the applicable Purchase Price; provided that in no event shall an Employee be permitted to purchase during each Offering Period more than a number of shares determined by dividing $12,500 by the fair market value of a share of the Company's Common Stock on the Enrollment Date, and provided further that such purchase shall be subject to the limitations set forth in Section 3(b) and 12 hereof. Exercise of the option shall occur as provided in Section 8 and shall expire on the last day of the Offering Period.

Options may be granted under the Plan from time to time in substitution for stock options held by employees of another corporation who become, or who became prior to the effective date of the Plan, Employees of the Company or a Designated Subsidiary as a result of a merger or consolidation of such other corporation with the Company, or the acquisition by the Company or a Designated Subsidiary of all or a portion of the assets of such other corporation, or the acquisition by the Company or a Designated Subsidiary of stock of such other corporation with the result that such other corporation becomes a Designated Subsidiary.

Exercise of Option. A participant's option for the purchase of shares will be exercised automatically on the Exercise Date, and the maximum number of full shares subject to option shall be purchased for such participant at the applicable Purchase Price with the accumulated payroll deductions in his or her account. No fractional shares will be purchased; any payroll deductions accumulated in a participant's account which are not enough to purchase a full share shall be retained in the participant's account for the subsequent Offering Period. Any other monies left over in a participant's account after the Exercise Date shall be returned to the participant. During a participant's lifetime, a participant's option to purchase shares hereunder is exercisable only by him or her.

Delivery. As promptly as practicable after each Exercise Date on which a purchase of shares occurs, the Company shall arrange the transfer of the shares purchased upon exercise of each participant's option in electronic form to a broker designated by the participant, or, in the discretion of the Company, the delivery to the participant of a certificate representing such shares.

Discontinuance of Payroll Deductions; Termination of Employment.

A participant may discontinue his or her payroll deductions during an Offering Period no later than 21 calendar days before the end of the Offering Period by giving written or electronic notice to the Company in the form provided by the Company. The discontinuance shall be effective with the first full payroll period following five business days after the Company's receipt of the notice of discontinuance unless the Company elects to process a given discontinuance more quickly. Although no further payroll deductions for the purchase of shares will be made during the Offering Period, all the participant's payroll deductions credited to his or her account prior to the discontinuance will be applied to the purchase of shares in accordance with Section 8. If a participant discontinues his or her payroll deductions during an Offering Period, payroll deductions will not resume at the beginning of the succeeding Offering Period unless the participant delivers to the Company a new subscription agreement.

Upon a participant's ceasing to be an Employee for any reason or upon termination of a participant's employment relationship (as described in Section 2(g)), the payroll deductions credited to such participant's account during the Offering Period but not yet used to exercise the option will be returned to such participant or, in the case of his or her death, to the person or persons entitled thereto under Section 14, and such participant's option will be automatically terminated.

In the event an Employee fails to remain an Employee for at least 20 hours per week during an Offering Period in which the Employee is a participant, he or she will be deemed to have elected to discontinue payroll deductions.

A participant's discontinuance of payroll deductions during an Offering Period will not have any effect upon his or her eligibility to participate in any similar plan which may hereafter be adopted by the Company or in succeeding Offering Periods which commence after the termination of the Offering Period during which the participant discontinues payroll deductions.

Interest. No interest shall accrue on the payroll deductions of a participant in the Plan.

Stock.

The maximum number of shares of the Company's Common Stock that may be made available for sale under the Plan is 6,000,000, subject to adjustment upon changes in capitalization of the Company as provided in Section 18. If on a given Exercise Date the number of shares with respect to which options are to be exercised exceeds the number of shares then available under the Plan, the Company shall make a prorate allocation of the shares remaining available for purchase in as uniform a manner as shall be practicable and as it shall determine to be equitable.

The participant will have no interest or voting right in shares covered by his option until such option has been exercised.

Shares to be delivered to a participant under the Plan will be registered in the name of the participant.

Administration.

The Plan shall be administered by the Board of the Company or a committee of members of the Board appointed by the Board. The Board or its committee shall have full and exclusive discretionary authority to construe, interpret and apply the terms of the Plan, to determine eligibility and to adjudicate all disputed claims filed under the Plan, and to provide or permit any notice or other communication required or authorized by the Plan in either written or electronic form. Every finding, decision and determination made by the Board or its committee shall, to the full extent permitted by law, be final and binding upon all parties. Members of the Board who are eligible Employees are permitted to participate in the Plan, provided that:

Members of the Board who are eligible to participate in the Plan may not vote on any matter affecting the administration of the Plan or the grant of any option pursuant to the Plan.

If a Committee is established to administer the Plan, no member of the Board who is eligible to participate in the Plan may be a member of the Committee.

Notwithstanding the provisions of Subsection (a) of this Section 13, in the event that Rule 16b-3 promulgated under the Securities Exchange Act of 1934, as amended (the "Exchange Act"), or any successor provision ("Rule 16b-3") provides specific requirements for the administrators of plans of this type, the Plan shall be only administered by such a body and in such a manner as shall comply with the applicable requirements of Rule 16b-3.

The Board may adopt rules and procedures relating to the operation and administration of the Plan to accommodate the specific requirements of local laws and procedures. Without limiting the generality of the foregoing, the Board is specifically authorized to adopt rules and procedures regarding handling of payroll deductions, payment of interest, conversion of local currency, payroll tax, withholding procedures and handling of stock certificates which may vary with local requirements. The Board may also adopt sub-plans applicable to Subsidiaries, which sub-plans may be designed to be outside the scope of Section 423 of the Code. The rules of such sub-plans may take precedence over other provisions of this Plan, except for Section 12(a), but unless otherwise superseded by the terms of such sub-plan, the provisions of this Plan shall govern the operation of such sub-plan.

Designation of Beneficiary.

A participant may file a written designation of a beneficiary who is to receive any shares and cash, if any, from the participant's account under the Plan in the event of such participant's death subsequent to an Exercise Date on which the option is exercised but prior to delivery to such participant of such shares and cash. In addition, a participant may file a written designation of a beneficiary who is to receive any cash from the participant's account under the Plan in the event of such participant's death prior to exercise of the option. If a participant is married and the designated beneficiary is not the spouse, spousal consent shall be required for such designation to be effective.

Such designation of beneficiary may be changed by the participant at any time by written notice. In the event of the death of a participant and in the absence of a beneficiary validly designated under the Plan who is living at the time of such participant's death, the Company shall deliver such shares and/or cash to the executor or administrator of the estate of the participant, or if no such executor or administrator has been appointed (to the knowledge of the Company), the Company, in its discretion, may deliver such shares and/or cash to the spouse or to any one or more dependents or relatives of the participant, or if no spouse, dependent or relative is known to the Company, then to such other person as the Company may designate.

Transferability. Neither payroll deductions credited to a participant's account nor any rights with regard to the exercise of an option or to receive shares under the Plan may be assigned, transferred, pledged or otherwise disposed of in any way (other than by will, the laws of descent and distribution or as provided in Section 14 hereof) by the participant. Any such attempt at assignment, transfer, pledge or other disposition shall be without effect.

Use of Funds. All payroll deductions received or held by the Company under the Plan may be used by the Company for any corporate purpose, and the Company shall not be obligated to segregate such payroll deductions.

Reports. Individual accounts will be maintained for each participant in the Plan. Statements of account will be given to participating Employees at least annually, which statements will set forth the amounts of payroll deductions, the Purchase Price, and the number of shares purchased.

Adjustments Upon Changes in Capitalization, Dissolution, Merger, Asset Sale or Change of Control.

Changes in Capitalization. Subject to any required action by the stockholders of the Company, the Reserves as well as the price per share of Common Stock covered by each option under the Plan which has not yet been exercised, shall be proportionately adjusted for any increase or decrease in the number of issued shares of Common Stock resulting from a stock split, reverse stock split, stock dividend, combination or reclassification of the Common Stock, or any other increase or decrease in the number of shares of Common Stock effected without receipt of consideration by the Company; provided, however, that conversion of any convertible securities of the Company shall not be deemed to have been "effected without receipt of consideration". Such adjustment shall be made by the Board, whose determination in that respect shall be final, binding and conclusive. Except as expressly provided herein, no issue by the Company of shares of stock of any class, or securities convertible into shares of stock of any class, shall affect, and no adjustment by reason thereof shall be made with respect to, the number or price of shares of Common Stock subject to an option.

Dissolution or Liquidation. In the event of the proposed dissolution or liquidation of the Company, the Offering Period will terminate immediately prior to the consummation of such proposed action, unless otherwise provided by the Board.

Merger or Asset Sale. In the event of a proposed sale of all or substantially all of the assets of the Company, or the merger of the Company with or into another corporation, each option under the Plan shall be assumed or an equivalent option shall be substituted by such successor corporation or a parent or subsidiary of such successor corporation, unless the Board deter mines, in the exercise of its sole discretion and in lieu of such assumption or substitution, to shorten the Offering Period then in progress by setting a new Exercise Date (the "New Exercise Date") or to cancel each outstanding right to purchase and refund all sums collected from participants during the Offering Period then in progress. If the Board shortens the Offering Period then in progress in lieu of assumption or substitution in the event of a merger or sale of assets, the Board shall notify each participant in writing, at least 10 business days prior to the New Exercise Date, that the Exercise Date for his option has been changed to the New Exercise Date and that his option will be exercised automatically on the New Exercise Date. For purposes of this Section, an option granted under the Plan shall be deemed to be assumed if, following the sale of assets or merger, the option confers the right to purchase, for each share of option stock subject to the option immediately prior to the sale of assets or merger, the consideration (whether stock, cash or other securities or property) received in the sale of assets or merger by holders of Common Stock for each share of Common Stock held on the effective date of the transaction (and if such holders were offered a choice of consideration, the type of consideration chosen by the holders of a majority of the outstanding shares of Common Stock); provided, however, that if such consideration received in the sale of assets or merger was not solely common stock of the successor corporation or its parent (as defined in Section 424(e) of the Code), the Board may, with the consent of the successor corporation and the participant, provide for the consideration to be received upon exercise of the option to be solely common stock of the successor corporation or its parent equal in fair market value to the per share consideration received by holders of Common Stock and the sale of assets or merger.

The Board may, if it so determines in the exercise of its sole discretion, also make provision for adjusting the Reserves, as well as the price per share of Common Stock covered by each outstanding option, in the event the Company effects one or more reorganizations, recapitalization, rights offerings or other increases or reductions of shares of its outstanding Common Stock, and in the event of the Company being consolidated with or merged into any other corporation.

Amendment or Termination.

The Board of Directors of the Company may at any time and for any reason terminate or amend the Plan. Except as provided in Section 18, no such termination can affect options previously granted, provided that an Offering Period may be terminated by the Board of Directors on any Exercise Date if the Board determines that the termination of the Plan is in the best interests of the Company and its stockholders. Except as provided in Section 18, no amendment may make any change in any option theretofore granted which adversely affects the rights of any participant. To the extent necessary to comply with Rule 16b-3 under the Securities Exchange Act of 1934, as amended, or under Section 423 of the Code (or any successor rule or provision or any other applicable law or regulation), the Company shall obtain stockholder approval in such a manner and to such a degree as required.

Without stockholder consent and without regard to whether any participant rights may be considered to have been "adversely affected," the Board (or its committee) shall be entitled to change the Offering Periods, limit the frequency and/or number of changes in the amount withheld during an Offering Period, establish the exchange ratio applicable to amounts withheld in a currency other than U.S. dollars, permit payroll withholding in excess of the amount designated by a participant in order to adjust for delays or mistakes in the Company's processing of properly completed withholding elections, establish reasonable waiting and adjustment periods and/or accounting and crediting procedures to ensure that amounts applied toward the purchase of Common Stock for each participant properly correspond with amounts withheld from the participant's Compensation, and establish such other limitations or procedures as the Board (or its committee) determines in its sole discretion advisable which are consistent with the Plan.

Notices. All notices or other communications by a participant to the Company under or in connection with the Plan shall be deemed to have been duly given when received in the form specified by the Company at the location, or by the person, designated by the Company for the receipt thereof.

Conditions Upon Issuance of Shares. Shares shall not be issued with respect to an option unless the exercise of such option and the issuance and delivery of such shares pursuant thereto shall comply with all applicable provisions of law, domestic or foreign, including, without limitation, the Securities Act of 1933, as amended, the Securities Exchange Act of 1934, as amended, the rules and regulations promulgated thereunder, and the requirements of any stock exchange upon which the shares may then be listed, and shall be further subject to the approval of counsel for the Company with respect to such compliance. As a condition to the exercise of an option, the Company may require the person exercising such option to represent and warrant at the time of any such exercise that the shares are being purchased only for investment and without any present intention to sell or distribute such shares if, in the opinion of counsel for the Company, such a representation is required by any of the aforementioned applicable provisions of law.

Term of Plan. The Plan shall become effective upon the approval by the stockholders of the Company. It shall continue in effect until it is terminated under Section 19.

Additional Restrictions of Rule 16b-3. The terms and conditions of options granted hereunder to, and the purchase of shares by, persons subject to Section 16 of the Exchange Act shall comply with the applicable provisions of Rule 16b-3. This Plan shall be deemed to contain, and such options shall contain, and the shares issued upon exercise thereof shall be subject to, such additional conditions and restrictions as may be required by Rule 16b-3 to qualify for the maximum exemption from Section 16 of the Exchange Act with respect to Plan transactions.

EXHIBIT A

COMPANY J INC.

1992 EMPLOYEE STOCK PURCHASE PLAN
SUBSCRIPTION AGREEMENT

Original Application Enrollment   Date:
Change of Beneficiary(ies)
Change in Rate of Payroll Deductions

1. _____ hereby elects to participate in the Company J Circuit, Inc. (the "Company") 1992 Employee Stock Purchase Plan (the "Purchase Plan") and subscribes to purchase shares of the Company's Common Stock in accordance with this Subscription Agreement and the Purchase Plan.

2. I hereby authorize payroll deductions from each paycheck in the amount of _____% of my Compensation on each payday (from 1% to 10%) during the Offering Period in accordance with the Purchase Plan. (Please note that no fractional percentages are permitted.) **If reducing to 0% you may not use this form, you must use the "Notice of Withdrawal" form**.

3. I understand that said payroll deductions shall be accumulated for the purchase of shares of Common Stock at the applicable Purchase Price determined in accordance with the Purchase Plan. I understand that if I do not withdraw from an Offering Period, any accumulated payroll deductions will be used to automatically exercise my option.

4. I have received a copy of the complete " Company J Inc. 1992 Employee Stock Purchase Plan." I understand that my participation in the Purchase Plan is in all respects subject to the terms of the Plan. I understand that the grant of

the option by the Company under this Subscription Agreement is subject to obtaining stockholder approval of the Purchase Plan.

5. Shares purchased for me under the Purchase Plan should be issued in the name(s) of: _____.

6. I understand that if I dispose of any shares received by me pursuant to the Purchase Plan within 2 years after the Enrollment Date (the first day of the Offering Period during which I purchased such shares), I will be treated for federal income tax purposes as having received ordinary income at the time of such disposition in an amount equal to the excess of the fair market value of the shares at the time such shares were delivered to me over the price which I paid for the shares.

I hereby agree to notify the Company in writing within 30 days after the date of any such disposition and I will make adequate provision for Federal, State or other tax withholding obligations, if any, which arise upon the disposition of the Common Stock.

The Company may, but will not be obligated to, withhold from my compensation the amount necessary to meet any applicable withholding obligation including any withholding necessary to make available to the Company any tax deductions or benefits attributable to sale or early disposition of Common Stock by me.

If I dispose of such shares at any time after the expiration of the 2-year holding period, I understand that I will be treated for federal income tax purposes as having received income only at the time of such disposition, and that such income will be taxed as ordinary income only to the extent of an amount equal to the lesser of (1) the excess of the fair market value of the shares at the time of such disposition over the purchase price which I paid for the shares, or (2) 15% of the fair market value of the shares on the first day of the Offering Period. The remainder of the gain, if any, recognized on such disposition will be taxed as capital gain.

7. I hereby agree to be bound by the terms of the Purchase Plan. The effectiveness of this Subscription Agreement is dependent upon my eligibility to participate in the Purchase plan.

8. In the event of my death, I hereby designate the following as my beneficiary(ies) to receive all payments and shares due me under the Purchase Plan:

NAME (Please Print): _____

                            (Last)   (First)   (Middle)

(Relationship): _____

(Address):_____

Employee's HKID Number：

Employee's Address: _____

                                  _____

I UNDERSTAND THAT THIS SUBSCRIPTION AGREEMENT SHALL REMAIN IN EFFECT THROUGHOUT SUCCESSIVE OFFERING PERIODS UNLESS TERMINATED BY ME.

_____

Signature of Employee

Employee No. _____

Dated: _____

36.Who want to be Chinese Worker ?

10 years ago, a survey of 4000 households held in Shanghai in 2007, only 1% were willing to work as workers. Some may find it strange that only 1% of people are willing to be workers. My point is the opposite: 1% of people are willing to be workers? It's incomprehensible.

2009 American Times Magazine showed the annual figures of "Chinese workers", "China continues to maintain its fastest pace in the world's major economies, and leads the world towards economic recovery, thanks in the first place to the millions of hardworking and tough ordinary workers in China."

"What is the image of "Chinese worker" after 10 years? What kind of mission does it take? Each year, the influx of people to the bustling coastal cities to sell their own labor force, the industry to other countries to transfer the risk of crisis-holders and victims-the pay cut or layoffs, for big cities to build skyscrapers, rich villas, golf courses but nowhere they have to live, saddled with "low-end population" of the famous migrant workers, they are more industrious than ants, pay less than worker bees, climbed crane claim for salary, husband and wife separated, "Left behind children" lonely & helpless.

Just a little bit checking. In the companies I served, the most analysis is how to reduce staff turnover rate.

We used more than 20 indicators to carry out a full range of statistics:

Income level, More Overtime, Shift, Labor mode, Department, Position, Rank, Supervisor, Product, Whether stand work, Home, Age, Sex, Marriage, Education level, Outside the house, Work journey and spend time, Canteen taste, Entrepreneurship, Family reasons, Handling documents, Holiday jobs.

There are doubts about the relevance and certainty of their findings, in order to prove that we have used the most authoritative black belt experts in the company to deduce the results using the most accurate method of data statistics.

Fully open to non-governmental organizations, questionnaires, in-person interviews, analysis of historical data, even send "new employees spy" to join the company for two months, let them record all the unfair treatment encountered one by one.

By the staff relations Group and the production supervisor, crosses the line leaders, personally one by one asks the employee who has the problem, we are afraid the staff answer is not true, also has carefully elaborated the question which got from interview with leavers.

Constantly collect the salary and welfare treatment of our own companies and compared to other companies, for fear of falling behind.

Arrange employee surveys, cross-region, cross-border, cross-position, and invite professional IBM statistical agencies to keep a secret from the group's level. ""It will be better If the employees know that we are so care about them, I often laugh at myself."

Just joined Company J, one SVP visited, asked about the turnover rate, I truthfully answered the monthly average of 6%, he said with a sense of blame: "We have not been 3%, how to reach 6% now?" I reported this to my direct supervisor, I also feel suffocated in the heart, why turnover rate is so high?!

Then there is a repeat of the depth of the analysis, at that time we "do not know the truth, only stay the confusion". Constantly ask myself: these people live with us every day, I do not know what are they thinking?

Today it seems that the truth is very clear:

Why are the workers leaving?

1. Wages are too low;

2. Overtime is not enough, wages can't cope with living need;

3. High working pressure;

4. A bad class leader;

5. There is no opportunity for personal development;

6. Family (e.g. children stay at home)

Can wages solve all the problems? Interpretation from the concept of "marginal diminishing law" in economics (insert a model here): In the same degree of satisfaction, the more wages a person can get, the less willing they are to give up other satisfaction in exchange for wages;

CNY 问题原因探讨—经济学的解释
- 工资能解决所有问题吗？

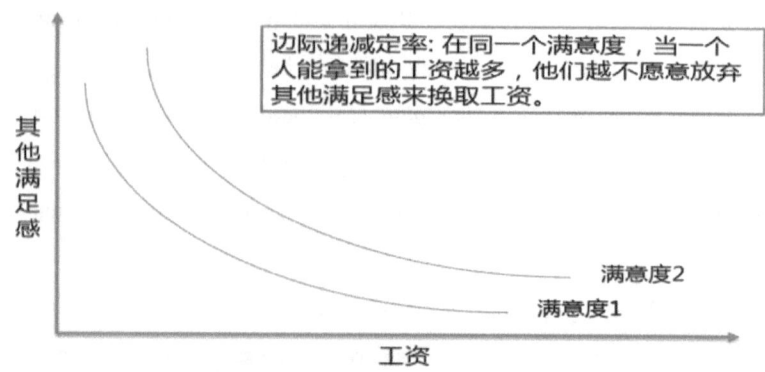

Workers in 8 hours of continuous overtime work at full load, when they are working in the work of not much money, to a certain time they will choose to give up: I do not earn much, but I also want to earn more money, so I have to go to more overtime, or my production line from the year to the end, I've made enough money. I'm going to go home and open a shop or find a cushy job, better than the money get from exhausted job.

From the boss's point of view that the company spent 8 hours of wages and overtime, the company has cost control, it is impossible to spend more than the existing costs of wages, so every time HR in the submission of analysis reports and recommendations, the boss would ask the most tricky question: you want the company to invest this large amount of cost, how many percentage of the turnover rate do you have the confidence to reduce? How much do we have to pay to meet the expectations of our employees?

From HR point of view, the factory does not know what 's the workers need? And even the workers don't know what they need? Frequently, when we ask them questions, the answers are the following:

1. Insufficient wages.
2. No career development
3. Family reasons

They are repeating what the others said. Or simply do not say anything, just quit! From Company J accounted for more than 50% turnover. Factory hasn't the plan for the manpower needs and training, after receiving the orders, the planning department think about how to buy material at the first time but never know to inform recruitment team to hire worker, order time for material is one month, but often giving only three days' notice for the recruitment of workers, always blame HR recruitment speed, But record one months to recruit 3,000 people Recruitment speed in Company J, lasted for n months. Even in the morning to recruit workers, in the evening to have the training class, in order to alleviate the staff shortage in a timely manner. such a vicious circle is not sustainable.

HR in such a big environment, on one hand, workers need to be replaced, they expect to integrate into the urban life, the hope is not to do "robot" work, they expect to have more technical expertise, they expect the management to listen to their suggestions to improve, they pay attention to fair treatment, expect to be respected, however the ideal is very good, The reality is very "bony".

On the other hand, companies face the upgrading of industry, if only rely on the advantages of the past cheap labor costs have been rapidly disappearing, gone forever. Either speed up or be eliminated, because the manufacturing competition is not China's domestic competition but the global competition, no job is easy, this is the truest words my boss told us.

How to change? Turning a crisis into an opportunity? We have developed a long-term strategy, starting with six aspects:

Standards-not only to have, but also to unify;

Reward-contribution to be rewarded, and to be fair;

Clear-Let employees know the future of the enterprise, understand the prospect of their relationship and the boss of their own expectations;

Team-is the employee proud of his or her business and can help?

Flexibility-Rules and regulations do not constrain the creativity of employees;

Empowering-giving employees the necessary authority;

In response to these six aspects, we have done:

Standards-not only to have, but also to unify;

In the past, we had inconsistent calculations of overtime payments for Labor dispatch workers and our own companies, dispatch workers only count 1.5 times overtime pay, the contractor labor did not, the monthly costs involved in the hundreds of thousands of RMB, never HR dare to touch the unequal treaties, turnover rate doubled compare with normal staff, seeing dispatch workers came and went, can't do anything.

For the line leader and the clerk took the initiative to take the lead to steal OT, stealing more overtime from the loopholes of the pay process, even idle to falsely claim overtime.

We boldly put forward the system of equal pay for dispatch workers and contractors, revise the omission of the calculation of overtime program, and catch the discipline case of cheating overtime.

There is an interesting story, our HR internal rehearsal how to persuade the boss to accept the system of equal pay, I play the role of the boss, because every time the boss proposed that you have confidence to reduce turnover rate of the number of points, is the most burning time for HR, the same problem when I asked the subordinates they were also asked to suffer a crushing defeat, mess answer, make a laugh, in the process I realized the reason: I instructed HR have the statistics over the past year turnover rate, among which I put the recruitment fee, new work clothing shoes cards, bedding, train up new workers to speed up, different turnover rate caused by different production lines of the defective cost all converted into cost, List the hidden costs to be paid by the company for each turnover percentage. I compare the income of more than 30 large manufacturing enterprises collected in the surrounding area, and listed whether they are still using the illegal overtime formula.

On the day of the demonstration, I had no reservation to show the data to the management, I asked them to imagine that the two employees working together, did the same job, but you get 0.5 times more overtime pay than I do because I am a dispatch worker? We don't know how much the loss rate will eventually fall, but we all know that the drop is going to be in exchange for the company's cost and even heavy costs and the company's management to do a series of improvements, now our pay is not to compare with other multinational companies, We are just comparing with the Taiwan factories which are often ranked the lowest in the salary and welfare, because they make the same products as we do, and the production prices are the same, what do we compare with them?!

Listen to my most sincere words, SVP questioned my immediate boss the same as he questioned my high turnover rate: "How do you put our 500-strong American company employees pay the same as Taiwan factories, where is the attractiveness of our company?" "I deeply know this will be difficult for my boss, because he knows how much of the additional cost, also know that the product price to digest the increment in this benefit, if I was him I also feel quite hard to answer, but this is a big trend, We should reflect on the fact that if other factories can do it, why can't a multinational company of the top 500 do it.

Finally GM stood up and admitted that we really need to improve it immediately.

1. Reward- The contribution has a return, and to be fair.

"3R" Respect, recognize, reward is our C&B basic principles established in Company J.

In general companies, workers are seldom considered to take the initiative to guide their employees to improve their skills and build a fair system for their skills and commitment. have been working for a long time to give a seniority award, advertised as a cooked manual, but whether it really mastered the key skills, how about the usage situation? How is the effect we never known.

In the case of workers who have built up an assessment of skills and encouraged workers to develop their own career paths by their own abilities and seniority, at Company J, we have established this successful system-we named it PWT (Perfect Work Team) management system.

2. Our concept is that our company in accordance with the customer process divided into different teams, each team is accountability, each master the essentials, a product that brings a team together of the various positions of skills and output.

We divided the entire staff of the system into 7 levels, across the three main lines of production, materials and engineering, 9 functional departments, employees from the first-level promotion must have enough seniority, pass training exams promote to the next level to enjoy the remuneration package, all levels of remuneration package is open, Encourage employees to get better treatment with skills.

We mobilized the production, materials and engineering of the three main lines under 9 functional departments, designed the training content, questionnaire, to various functional departments of the training of all employees, after the issuance of a unified booklet, employees go back to recitation.

Familiar with the requirements of the company and has enough seniority, nominated by the Supervisor, employees participate in the public regular examination, the questionnaires designed by the technical experts of various departments, we put the title and answer into the PWT test system, each exam, each person's questions are not the same, the results of the examination immediately displayed. There is no ingredient for making false. At the same time for the actual operation of the station by the Department of Technical experts to train HR trainers to understand the main points of the real exercise, let them go to the unified upgrade training, practical examination, there is no special treatment, but the same as the trainer to go through a unified examination, like a teacher's exam.

When the exam is passed, the salary is adjusted automatically.

After a trial period of time, we found that there were other problems: although the staff were tested, they did not use the skills they had learned, in order to get a higher salary, they were actively involved in training and learning, and some of the old employees mastered a number of skills, but only one skill was used in the operation, all the work station difficult to do change to the new people, so that both the time wasted in training and paid more skills costs, but also to force new employees will lose faster, so we have launched a succession of "PWG Position with Grading" positioning plan: The actual needs of each station of the required skills input into the workstation computer, employees punch badge to start Workstation Computer, the computer will connect personnel training system, search staff training skills, to ensure the skill match with working position requirement, enter into the computer of the work station, start and record production.

Staff to melted down again every six months, pass the exam can continue to enjoy the allowance, the company continued to add new process requirements into the system.

No one in the company is going to talk about how much you got the perks, how much I got, what they're talking about is you got a couple of stars in the PWT exam, I got a few stars, because passing the exams, their work clothes are clearly labeled, they are proud of getting more stars.

3. Clear-Let employees know the future of the enterprise, understand the prospect and the boss expectations on their own;

In Company J, how the business is does not have a secret, even the workers on the production line all know a loss of money, how much to earn, because every quarter, HR tell employees the financial figures, employees get the bonus accordingly, although not much: from zero to 8%, But employees pay more attention to the company. They are not very enthusiastic about how many the group earns, but they are most keen to know how much they earn, only if the company earns money will give them more bonuses.

We have a red apple every day to evaluate the system of employee performance: Each employee has a small card in every month, cards hanging in the front of the production line, every day before off working hour to assess the performance of each employee, satisfied kick on the Red Apple, not satisfied or need to improve kick on green apple, which is one of this indicator for employees each month's performance award, In addition, there are 5S, quality and lean improvement. The PWT bonuses that employees receive each month are based on the results of the public assessments and can be submitted to HR for comments.

4. Team-is the employee proud of his or her business can help each other?

The company encourages internal recommendations, employees can recommend the family and friends into the company, at the key time there are new awards. According to historical statistics, we have a colleague from the computer department who introduced 15 workers to join the company, earn the new prize more than his salary.

The company's Buddy program, New Campus, Big Brother big sister system help new employees adapt into the role of the system as soon as possible. For the new staff to focus on the day shift rather than night shifts, so that they adapt to the new environment as soon as possible before the shift. Invite the low turnover of the production line with the high turnover of the production line to visit each other, Exchange leader, so that different groups experience different management style, the department head set retention plan how to improve the turnover rate. A "Buddy Program" to assist in the introduction of the job for new employees.

The Employee clubs help employees to play a common interest, among them the voluntary association function is more obvious, they organize staff to visit the elderly homes, orphanage, to support poor villages' education, organize blood donation, clothing donation.

We set up a family fun day, inviting at least 600 families to visit the company in each year, so that employees can show their families the companies they served. In the new year, we ask our employees ' families to come to the factory for new year celebration, to make dumplings and play garden party. When Employees are sick, the first to think about the family is the company, the company's colleagues are also regular organize blood donation, do not need the company's strong call.

5. Flexibility-Rules and regulations do not constrain the creativity of employees; In Company J, HR often struggled not to punish employees, but how to reward employees, because you only know how to reward, you already know how to manage the staff. This is the culture of Company J.

The company has a lean improvement award, but the winning team is more and more sparse, because the production line is busy, no one has time to lean, at this time our GM personally to pull up to explore the opportunity and encourage the staff, one of IE technician just made a small improvement, use automatic method to move one component from one production line to another, GM was happy propaganda this outstanding deed to the whole plant, because in his opinion this is only the most ordinary technician, but he has a self-improvement heart, he promoted him to lead a group continue to make more improvements.

The company's promotion of the system unanimously open green light for outstanding contributions to the staff: Record results, PWT test Leapfrog Jump.

6. Empowerment-giving the employee the necessary authority;"3E" Project is also a successful project in Company J: Employee Voice, Empower, Engagement, pay attention to the voice of employees, empowerment and a sense of belonging. Empower and encourage employees to make decisions within their own areas of responsibility, no need to report.

The production line often change model, the production staff inform technician, wait for the technician station by station to change equipment and adjust parameters, to start the production of new model, at least to wait for half an hour, 20-30 minutes for a short time to change the model, The whole production line wait to see the technician's face.

Later we decided to use good worker change the model, the time reached 15 minutes to complete the installation of the entire production line, the production line of these products with high-speed operation, an hour can produce dozens or hundreds of parts, eventually we actually let the staff take a try?!

But we did it, the first employee to be trained by a front-line employee, after three months, the prize was awarded by me and the general manager on the spot for a promotion. If I am the worker, I will cherish this document for a lifetime, because it is my own effort obtain the company's immediate recognition!

Frequent, HR and department heads blame each other for shirking responsibility for employee turnover reasons, but this really does not need to push or blame, because everyone is the bearer of the result, all suffer from the pain. Do what you should do, the natural result will come out.

By the time I left Company J, the overall turnover rate was not more than 3%

per month, compared with the Mexican factory, they only praised and studied our share. One day, if I stay at Company J, if i drop the employee turnover rate to 0% so I could enjoy my free trip to Japan, where the group HR SVP once made a bet on me.

37.Happy life beyond 80

HR work in China manufacturing have to face two big problems:

How to control overtime of employees and make it meet CSR social responsibility system requirements: 20 OT hours/week, no more no less, have more OT hours will not pass customer audit: get red light for alarm, even if the order will be stopped, directly affect the company's business.

At the same time, if lacking of overtime, will lead to the direct increment on manufacturing costs, employees believe that overtime pay is also a part of their fixed income, the lower income will lead to the employees' intention to leave, the turnover rate will increase, affect product quality and shipping efficiency, which also directly affect the company's revenue.

20 hours/week-approximately equal to "80" hours/month overtime (4 weeks * 20 hours/week), this is dilemmic situation.

The Second Puzzle:

The new generation of employees are difficult to manage, starting from 2011 until now, China and even the whole world discussion on this topic has not stopped: frequent job-hopping, slack, challenge management ... A series of "negative" nouns are set on these "After 80s" employees.

Both big problems, I was also struggled before, but HR can't throw the problem to the boss, but to find out the problem and solve it, you give the boss answer is not what you want to do, but how to do!

I give the answer to the boss, we not only solve the problem, but also to solve the two problems at the same time, with one stone to solve two big problems thoroughly!

So that our "Happy Life Beyond 80" theme year has created, it contains a twofold meaning:

we respect "After 80" employees, we want to ensure that employees work overtime on or below "80" hours!

To respect " After 80" employees, first understand "after 80" employee specific situation, understand their values, understand their needs:

1. At Company J, we have 84% employees born in the 80 's;
2. Like new things, hate the elders of calling to mind past sufferings and think over the good times: "Do not tell me that you do not have enough to eat when you are young, you almost can't afford to pay school fees ..., you do not want us to have the same day as you do?"
3. More frequent job-hopping: In 2016, the annual report of two thousand-**Millennium** new generation, published by Deloitte accounting firm, surveyed 19 countries, 300 new generations in each country, 83% new generations resign from the existing job in the coming one year.

    In my first survey, I remember a new generation of employees who answered one of our questions: What are three major reasons to leave the company? His reply was straightforward: "I didn't even think about doing it in this company for long time!" Will you laugh or cry when you see such an answer?"
4. General education is higher than their elders, more than 90% of Company J workers are high school or above, of which 15% is a college graduate or above.
5. Do not like repetitive labor, do not want to do "robot" work.
6. Know how to get rich information quickly with Internet access, that is why employees who earn 3,000 to 4,000 yuan are willing to buy Apple phones from 5,000 to 6,000 yuan, which also reflects their expectations of mastering new technologies and information. There is data showing that the amount of information and sent mail on Earth is more than the total number of people on Earth. Remember when we sent a letter by using three days' time when we were young, to call the telephone booth to send a message?
7. Willing and quite looking forward to learning more professional knowledge,

not reconciled to the whole life on the production line. Hope to have a better accommodation and work environment, more colorful amateur activities to show their personalities.
8. Like to have their "circle of Friends" in the company.
9. Expect "motorized working hours" to fight for the balance of life and work: "If you can't believe that your employees can maneuver their work, start by not hiring" it's their creed.

Do not like excessive overtime, have the right ask for leave at any time, if the line leader not approve, they often choose to resign or even resign without prior notice.
10. They want to gain more recognition, even if it's unrelate with money. Also like the supervisor as real-time reminders, in person, rather than hindsight.
11. They like the "dolphin-type" Boss-wise, knowledgeable, skilled managers who act as advocates, supporters rather than "managers".

Why do we have so many behind-the-scenes "contents"? Because we:
1. Do the statistics, summary and sharing of the collective situation to the company's existing new generation staffs;
2. Arrange for the new generation of employees and their line management to do a corresponding detailed questionnaire survey, the results analysis and sharing;
3. Interviewed more than 100 new generation of employees and their supervisors, let two sides understand each other: The New generation of dreams, their expectations, their needs, a sentence they want to talk with the director, all included in the collection of the replay.
4. Invite the Doctor of Peasant workers and NGO to talk about how to get along with the new generation of migrant workers.
5. We have been extensively searching for insights into the global issue of new generation research.

6. We have printed the lectures in a booklet so that the new generation of migrant workers and their supervisors can read the reminders.
7. We organize a manager-level course, and they are all in attendance with the general manager to discuss their views on the management of the new generation of migrant workers, and how can they feel and improve later.
8. Joint Group headquarters to do research analysis and training:

We have designed a training course for a new generation of new employees around the world that is quite interesting:

We invite employees of all ages of the company to participate in the course so that they can open their hearts without reservation and make a questionnaire with 12 questions. Strange result appeared: the same time 1930-1945, 1946-1964, 1965-1980, 1980-2000, their concept of work, idolatry, self-determination, the way of communication, the way of entertainment has a serious sense of convergence, but also does not exclude the existence of differences, or a generational identity.

Finally, we come to the conclusion that:

1. We have no choice but to live in times of intergenerational coexistence, and we must first establish a "Don't separate" concept.
2. Each age has a personality of each age, each person has a personality, as managers should be to distinguish between adaptation rather than discrimination.
3. Finally, we have launched a "Gen C" (not gen X or Y) activity plan:

    "C" Represents
    1. Connected
    2. Community
    3. Curious
    4. Customizable
    5. Creative

6. Collaborative

A global company, maintaining connectivity is the first priority, establishing a company that equates to a social concept, giving back to society, encouraging curiosity, innovating and staying competitive, innovating, coordinating, advocating self-expression,

Connection-in order to encourage communication and connectivity, Mr. Sheetoh used weekend to visit places where young people love to go to, internet cafes, shopping malls, to understand the preferences of the youth, his own work in the production line to get the feelings of staff, he asked all managers to emulate, to feel what 's the employees' feeling.

We offer a wide range of communication/promotion channels: Corporate TV, staff radio station, emotional post, world coffee space banqueting, afternoon tea, Friday beer time ...

Community-Organization of 20 employee interest Activities Group, Volunteer Association is the hottest association: support the students, help the elder, love the little, blood donation, rice & cooking oil donation, love the environment and Love the clean environment.

Curiosity-the company encourages employees to constantly ask questions, propose improvements to the problem, set a lean improvement award every month, recognize the team and individuals.

Self-expression-the company hold monthly sport and literary activity competition, "I am talented I show", "Super skillful man", colorful activities never stop. "Work hard and play hard "is the employee's favorite company culture.

Innovation-the group's best program demonstration contest is a global showdown, a variety of new models of new methods, in addition to a good plan to pay attention to innovative packaging, innovative presentation, because each branch can come up with thousands of innovative improvement programs, a little martial arts is not strong enough, will certainly "Be defeated."

Coordination-the Company welcomes employees to participate in the management, Staff canteen Management Committee, the Dormitory Management committee has the absolute authority and ability of self-management, all activities competitions, company logo slogan, wearing clothing, holiday gifts, management problems encountered, lean improvement and so on employees all involved in.

For the second challenge: in order to control the monthly overtime in 80 hours, we:

1. Interview employees with the most overtime on a monthly basis to see why they are adding so many classes: Special for certain business group? No production plans? A lot of work? Unexpected Downtime? Is the assignment unreasonable? Is it the problem of the bottleneck of the process design? Back to the holiday time? Is there a suspicion of cheating overtime? Is the vacancy rate too slow? Lack of training?......

   Then HR will be categorized, to the field investigation: If the problem is the supervisor, let them come up with specific improvement of the plan and the time of completion. If it is a production scheduling or material problems of the Planning Department and the Department of Materials, and even responsible for suppliers, compensation for overtime losses. If it is the design department of the problem to find the design department to solve the design defects problem. If it is the staff discipline and HR support issues, HR self-accountable. From the problem of overtime analysis, HR can understand and find a lot of production management problems, from the problem of HR is also upgrading the "understand production, integrate into production" skills.

2. Brand A mobile phone often place "rash order", last for half a year, after six months full stop, even mobile phones also exist obvious production in the low season, but the electronics industry is not comprehensive time-based

enterprises in accordance labor law, can't apply for comprehensive time in the low season.

In order to solve the "fluctuation" order problem of Company J 's first major customer, we started by transferring all functional department's expert managers to support. Later found out 24 hours of day and night office and production line of the simultaneous operation of the method will drag us down: so we designed for special business group special frequency and equipped with enough staff: 3 classes 2 turn and 4 Class 3 turn out of the way, even the staff of the Office also arranges day and night reversal of the shift, Office staff were accustomed to the day shift is used to be the "King", how to make them change? Our GM and Asst GM David lead as good example have the night shift for three months, so that all staff and workers convinced. Different business groups bundled with each other staff: at the beginning of each business group to pull out the staff, each business group to support 3 to 4 staff to this business group, staff have been accustomed to the original group of work, now to be removed to join the "Irregular Army", the heart is extremely uncomfortable, so "angry", The management fight with the fire ... This time is HR show time: open to promote the General Assembly, promote company brand effect, tell employees to move to this business unit is a kind of upgrade, is also a discipline-can master new technology management method, but at the same time to achieve the world's most famous brand customer requirements is not an easy thing let them all hold the challenge, to celebrate in the success of the mass production, and secure the small results ... A year later we really have a real feeling of "Alive"!

3. To use the system monitor is the most common way to control overtime, but all the systems are artificially manipulated, which brings too much uncontrollable factors: to control overtime, the system control is not strict enough, the detail must be counted. To drive a single order, put any system

and process in the "invisible", HR often take the "top responsibility" of a department.

At Company J, I'm not a "silent lamb"! I'll "expose" the overtime status to the board!

3.1. First, I give all the bosses, managers, supervisors and employees to carry out EICC knowledge, how to schedule OT should be? I also describe it clear, at the same time, all issued a notice, let GM take the lead with the Slap printing, from top to bottom, let employees understand we are under the cruel to control overtime.

3.2. Joint IT department, to achieve "seamless" system control functions: the end of each shift immediately accumulated overtime in the month, once the time-out immediately issued a warning mail to the department head and attendance clerk.

Overtime report cut by day/week/month/quarter/year, Department supervisor and attendance clerk can cut and analyze casually.

3.3. In the time attendance system by the group unified management restrictions, we have written a plug-in procedures, the monthly director of the work of the month overtime plan, after seeking the approval of the boss, HR update system, in the month of employees to settle attendance, if not exceed the monthly plan, attendance automatically updated the attendance system, if not overrun, automatic report generation, attendance is intercepted and wages are not counted.

At this time, the Human resources department of all over-limits of the situation listed, layer by report, over 80-100 hours need to go through the business Group Operations Manager, marketing manager, the company's general manager, Asia-Pacific SVP Audit. Over 100 hours directly to the Group management Committee for review and filing.

Because of this "spicy trick", GM rare received a sharp message from the CEO of the group: "Hello!" David. I understand that the volume of business in your China office is rising sharply, but this does not mean that you can take effective control as soon as possible despite the specific requirements of EICC for overtime." David got angry, called all department heads who violated the overtime rules and order:

Production Planning department can't set seven days a week run, must be full stop on Sunday;

IE department to monitor the labor efficiency of each production line, in order to reduce the day of the situation to improve labor efficiency, or the company's manufacturing costs immediately rise;

Authorized HR continue to pay close attention to cheat overtime, once found "shoot-to-kill", so the act is tantamount: To stealing, without pains, the plot is more serious. HR from this to the end have not relaxed the regulation of this policy, before and after catching "thieves" more than 100 people!

Weekly meeting HR report the status of overtime, department head to explain overtime reasons; The department head does not report overtime plan or actual overtime plan without reasonable explanation, all responsibility will be taken by the department head, the boss will not come forward to explain.

These managers lost the "umbrella", then no one dare to violate.

In the end, the group reduced our OT total hours by 4%, and the same example of revenue assurance was presented in the case summary of the group management meeting and was invited to do a demonstration of the focus in Asia. In fact, the reason is very simple, let Gen Y employees make full use of 80 hours of overtime, increase the company production speed. As an upright HR, when knowing the most need of company: how to stand up to face the problem, with all the support, to do the right thing.

38.The employee survey just like "Look at the flowers in the flog"

In Company J, a global 160,000 headcount size company, is basically conducting a global employee survey every other year, because they have a scary data: 150,000 people leave the jobs every year! How to increase the employee's engagement degree and understand why they are leaving is the most real reason for the employee's investigation.

When I first joined the company, I received 2009 employee survey result sharing transferred to me from GM CM, the investigation of the problem separated into "customer satisfaction, quality control, people oriented" three themes to design, a total of 60 questions, the survey results show:

43% of the employees are satisfied with the company in the customer-first performance, 48% satisfied with the quality of the performance, only 41% of the staff is satisfied with the people-oriented performance, are not passed;

Compared to the global results: 64%,63%,61%, it should be said that the group's average score has been quite low, that is why the group's share price USD30/shares fell to the bottom of the USD3/stock from the peak of two years ago;

No comparison no hurt. "The group also has three of our EMS factory to correspond: The original most profitable Canton factory in the past year not only suffer the number of business decline, but also brand N mobile phone customer accounted for 60% of all production orders were withdrawn overnight, the company was forced to streamline staff quickly, Processing methods let employees feel "ruthless", people who was terminated hate the company, next to the ability of the people are "evacuated", lead to the people "Submit the complaint joint letter" to the group asked to replace the boss;

What do you think the results will be in the context of employee satisfaction surveys? The timing of the investigation will directly affect the outcome of the investigation, the right time to take investigation.

The investigation way is also quite important, 60 questions are too much, not only need to translate the topics accurately into the language of each country, but also to make employees to answer it like examination, so that HR done a lot of work for collecting data, difficult to focus on the key point.

We focus on the 10 most unsatisfactory aspects:

From the result analysis, what can you see? How to take measures to improve it? "Staff believe that management is not fully empowered, lack of communication, lack of effective incentive measures and development space." These are clearly reflected in the 10 most unsatisfactory items.

The most challenging for me-the new HR to analyze, answer and figure out solutions. To answer this GM request, I really think he is kind of feeling "A guilty person gives himself away by consciously protesting his innocence. ". In fact, he knows better than me that there are seven of these 10 unsatisfied items are against him, but if I am going to point out he is not, why should I point out this? Because I'm a newcomer? Or I'm his subordinate?

He asked me to answer, hoping that I would help him go through this "crisis" rather than pointing out his own fault. The use of investigative means "HR know that" is not the most important: how to design questionnaires and get answers, analyze the existing problems, but to make practical improvements as soon as possible, if no action taking turn everything to nothing.

So I called all HR supervisors, told them: "It is not the problem of the boss, in fact, all the problems are human problems, as we are the bridge between management and staff, HR isn't follow the staff to complaint, are we playing the specific role?!"Why does the management said day and night that the requirements didn't cascade to the most basic staff?! Why do employees feel that there is no room for development, no incentive polices?!"

Items	Number Responding	Difference Jabil Overall	Percent Responding (% Favorable / % Mixed / % Unfavorable)			Dimension
			% Favorable	% Mixed	% Unfavorable	
48. I am empowered to make appropriate business decisions	5748	10	29%	31%	39%	Commit to Customer
9. There is a clear link between my job performance and my pay	5819	8	34%	33%	33%	Focus on People
10. I have the decision-making authority I need to meet the needs of my customers	5818	8	35%	33%	32%	Commit to Customer
39. Local Management does a good job of acting on the suggestions of employees	5776	9	36%	34%	30%	Focus on People
51. Senior Management actively communicates with employees	5740	6	35%	36%	29%	Focus on People
12. Providing opportunities for advancement is a priority at Jabil	5831	4	36%	36%	28%	Focus on People
56. Local Management does a good job of recognizing employee contributions	5728	7	36%	36%	28%	Focus on People
20. I have a good understanding of Jabil's annual business goals	5835	10	34%	39%	27%	Commit to Customer
34. My performance was accurately evaluated in my most recent performance review	5806	6	37%	37%	26%	Focus on People
52. Local Management regularly communicates with employees	5745	5	37%	37%	26%	Focus on People

All HR lowered head, I continue to tell them: communication and communication, improve the effectiveness of HR work to achieve the "minimum" requirements, this is the direction of our efforts this year, do not let internal staff complaints like "overwhelming" to HR and management! Our responsibilities, 25 items of improvement immediately implemented, 25 of the measures for a company HR of "the highest turnover rate" is indeed more difficult than Climbing the sky, but I can't let them continue to do so, I must carry out "HR revolution"! As a result, we responded to the group by this, we implemented it individually.

By the year 2011, when we did not know whether or not to do the staff survey, we designed 20 questions survey, simple and clear, we got the "gratifying" answer: "I would like to recommend to the others that Company J is a worthy company to join" is the most important problem, we have 78% of the staff selected "I will"!

For management dissatisfaction: serious decreased to only "4%", but GM has been replaced by Sheetoh.

In that year, HR won the first "The Best Employer Award".

But we also see the competitiveness of remuneration, traffic services and work pressure is the most dissatisfaction with the factors:

I fully understand why employees have such a reaction:

1. Their greatest dissatisfaction is dispatch workers and contractors for the unfairness of the overtime calculation method.

2. For EMS industry, the workload is big pressure, the company earns the manufacturing fee can't support the high salary system operation, but the customer's request is not low.

3. Employees often work day and night, the company can't take care of their commute every moment of the traffic.

As HR, we can change immediately:

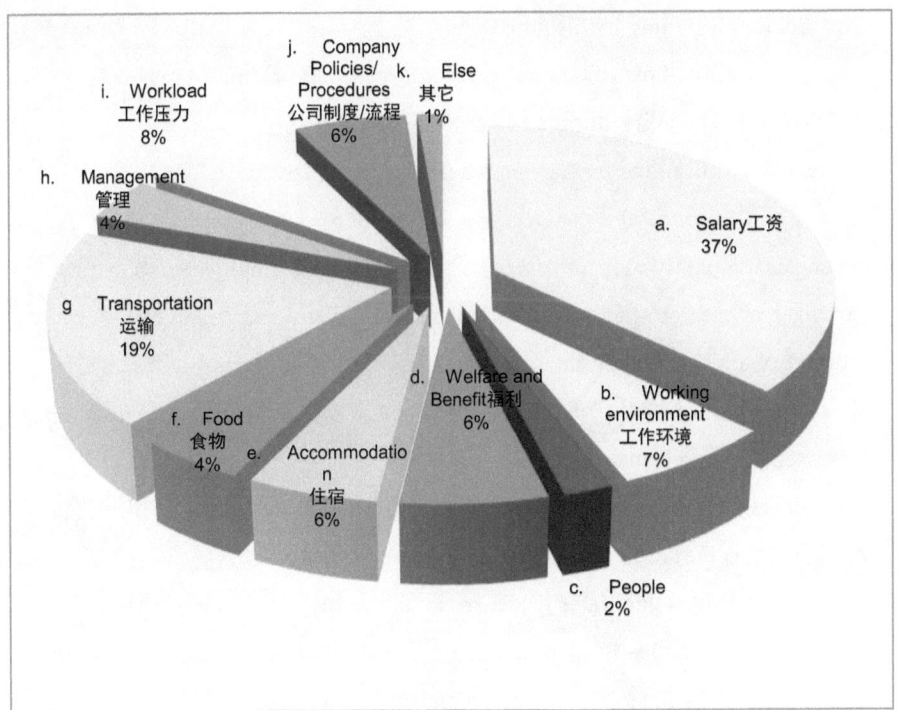

We replaced the suppliers who we used for more than 10 years with low quality service, for which I offended a VP who has been enjoying the "interests of the party", No much choice, with good faith to make a decision, easy to make judgement, this is my current 66-year-old boss share with me.

In 2012, the group CXO urged the group to organize a second staff survey, it is strange that the group HR may be afraid of offending some factories, covered the comparison of the results with the previous summary, only published the staff most dissatisfied 10 items:

We feel pity, because HR guys are gearing up to look at the results of a better, strong, and prove that the past three years of time HR has done something to improve? The investigation must have the continuity, otherwise can't see the actual effect. The goal of the survey let employees know the company cares about their feelings, took the improvement, we want to hear their feedback!

The problem we found in this time:

1. The inequality of overtime income has more impact on employees.

2. Canteen food quality, dormitory hardware and software.

3. The level of frontline management needs to be improved.

In order to improve the canteen and the service of the dormitory, we also organized a monthly random survey of 100 anonymous employees, so that they provide feedback on specific indicators, only in this way, we found that:

Dormitory has nearly thousands of rooms have different degrees of leakage;

In winter because of the quality of construction problems, the dormitory hot water temperature is insufficient;

The canteen only focused on high-priced dishes, did not focus on the cheap meals but it is the staff's most frequently eaten packages.

So we installed a solar water heater in the dormitory, when the temperature is low it can automatically start the electric heating, we also applied for the country's funding due to energy saving and environmental protection.

A large amount of maintenance money was applied and the leaking of all the rooms were repaired.

The canteen supplier is required to make a commitment to increase the employee's satisfaction to 80% or above, otherwise the evaluation will be

In 2015, we launched a global survey of "VOEE employees' voices" survey, replaced immediately.

VOEE represents employees, engagement, and voices triple meaning.

The goal is to recognize, measure, and clarify what aspects are affecting employee engagement. Focus and resources in these areas to drive better performance in your business.

The employee engagement indicator consists of three topics:

1. I rarely consider looking for another new job;

2012 Employee Opinion Survey
China - Huangpu/Guangzhou

10 Most Unfavorable Items

Items	Number Responding	% Favorable	% Mixed	% Unfavorable
59. I prefer less overtime	10,761	24%	29%	47%
56. Jabil cafeteria food is of good quality and good selection	10,832	29%	32%	39%
60. I am comfortable with current levels of overtime	10,884	33%	32%	35%
8. I feel I am fairly compensated for my job role	11,010	32%	34%	34%
42. My benefits package is comparable to others in this industry	10,836	36%	33%	31%
16. My manager/supervisor listens to me	11,036	45%	30%	25%
55. Jabil dormitories are adequate for space, cleanliness and safety	10,845	53%	26%	21%
11. I would highly recommend working at Jabil to friends and family	11,025	47%	33%	21%
35. My local management provides opportunities for advancement	10,910	49%	31%	20%
17. My manager/supervisor makes it easier for me to do my job well	11,022	51%	29%	20%

2. I am willing to do my best to help the company achieve its goals;

3. Feel that you are contributing to a great cause;

This indicator helps us measure engagement within the company, the best performing employees associate the company's business performance so that it continues to gain market share.

The employee's purely corporate promotion metrics cover only one issue:

1. I highly recommend Company J is a good company worthy of working

Employees can improve their company's performance, if they like the company, more efforts to improve customer satisfaction, production efficiency, the use of more innovative ways of innovate processes and improve services.

The results of the survey show that:

Dimensions	JABIL Norm	EMS Overall	Huangpu Heat Map	Huangpu Saturation Map
Engagement Index	75%	70%	69%	29%
NPS	68%	62%	64%	22%

Dimensions	S.No	Survey Statements	JABIL Norm	EMS Overall	Huangpu Heat Map	Huangpu Saturation Map
EE Index	1	I rarely think about looking for a new job with another company.	65%	59%	61%	29%
	2	I am willing to give extra effort to help Jabil meet its goals	83%	79%	76%	19%
	3	I feel my contributions are part of something great.	76%	73%	70%	25%
Overall	4	The senior leadership of this company has communicated a vision of the future that motivates me.	73%	68%	69%	24%
	5	I can see a clear link between my work and this company's vision.	75%	70%	75%	19%
	6	My immediate supervisor/manager has made a personal investment in my growth and development.	73%	69%	71%	21%
	7	I understand how my performance is evaluated.	73%	67%	72%	19%
	8	I have the training I need to do my job effectively.	73%	69%	73%	20%
	9	I am appropriately involved in decisions that affect my work.	75%	73%	71%	22%
	10	My immediate supervisor/manager demonstrates honest and ethical behavior	78%	73%	76%	18%
	11	I have opportunities for advancement at this company.	73%	71%	67%	23%
	12	My immediate supervisor/manager does a great job at people management	72%	67%	73%	20%
	13	I feel that I am part of a team.	79%	73%	81%	15%
	14	There is open and honest two-way communication at this company.	73%	69%	74%	19%
	15	All employees in this company are treated as individuals, regardless of their job, age, race, gender, physical capabilities, etc.	76%	73%	76%	17%
Net Promoter	16	I would recommend this company as a great place to work.	75%	71%	71%	22%

We followed up with a six-step process:

1th Step: Review the results of the VOEE survey

1. We found that the staff level, SG&A support department score is lower;

2. We found that 8-10 years, more than 10 years of staff satisfaction is low;

3. Employee-level satisfaction varies from 40% to 82%;

4. There is a higher degree of dissatisfaction with career development and promotion;

5. Lower satisfaction of small business groups;

2nd Step: Record & Measure the Leader response

What issues lead to our surprise?	What issues lead to our joy?
What issues lead to our disappointment?	Which field need the deep assessment?

3rd Step: Communication results and action planning process

Organize "full communication reports" in the form of face-to-face conversations (e.g., full meetings, departmental meetings, etc.) rather than emailing.

4th Step: Develop insights and action plans

Adjust the idea of the "Ideas for Action" section based on feedback from employees.

Based on the feedback and conversations, integrate the theme and work on (limited to) 2 to 3 areas.

5th Step: Communication Themes and actions

Communication topics:

Thanks to the staff for their participation

Use the templates from pages 10th through 13th to share a snapshot of the survey summary with your employees

A brief description of how to proceed with the "Plan of Action"

Explain general topics identified in the action planning process

Share the action items identified based on these thematic/focus areas.

6th step: Track progress and continuous communication

Track Progress:

Track action items and time ranges

Communicate with the person in charge to understand the latest progress

Operations Manager and HR Manager are fully responsible as promoters

Continuous communication:

Regularly update completed action items

Regularly update changes in the organization or at all levels

Use regular communication channels such as bulletin boards, group meetings, full-time meetings, etc.

Pass through the 7 years' time space, experienced 4 global-scale staff survey, eventually evolved to such a version, such a process, is the more satisfactory version of our HR team, but the most satisfactory is that we pay attention to the personal feelings of employees, and constantly improve their own human resources analysis and improve the implementation of capacity, To catch up with the continuous raised expectations of employees and management.

39.The unique annual gathering

To receive each visiting in the Company J, we will introduce the grand occasion, origination and history of annual gathering "Pig roast party", because it is unprecedented, comparable to the annual CCTV gala, more importantly, it represents the culture of Company J, everyone involved, attentively to enjoy, the performance draw whole attention, to enjoy the "Exhausted" and successful process, who is the last one? It must be the party organizers, I am one of them.

Pig Roast annual gathering originated 50 years ago when the company was first established, September is the start of the new fiscal year of Company J, to summarize the financial performance of the old fiscal year, after that the bosses went to the nearby forest to hunt one wild boar : Not more or less, because at that time the company's founding staff were 9 people, At this time the workman is not the workman but the boss, because only that day out of 365 days a year, it is the boss to serve the workman: Hunting, and slaughtering, but also roasting, distribute it, the boss and staff particularly enjoy such a kind of boss and workman work together, fair, interdependent, close relationship, enjoy "Annual revenue growth" fruitful results.

By the end of the development of Company J to the global 126 factories and branches, in September of each year, every factory in the world, to held the pig roast annual gathering with the country characteristics: For example, Malaysian factories held neither roast pigs nor roast "cattle", because they have faith in the Islamic staff, they also have faith in Hindu staff, they can roast sheep, roast rabbits, roast chicken. China is a secular country without religious belief, there are not so many scruples that we roast pigs. because of headcount sizing: Each evening party 8000 people, 16,000 people to be held for two consecutive nights, every night will kill 18 big pigs, 36 pockets.

At the party, the roast pig appearance ceremony is comparable to the Olympic flame lighting ceremony, has high-tech: From the mid-air fireworks show out; There are traditional: like the Pig roast Festival of the Minority Nationality, playing drums, dancing, singing songs, by a number of strong men lined up to carry out the roast pig; the large magics they are.

The bosses are going to work on that day, holding a spoon to scoop up the food for each employee, at least more than 1,000 times scoops in one night! Bosses are calling this than knocking on the keyboard or hard exercising. Some very enjoy: Only the boss to be eligible to divide the dish on that day, that is "Supreme" honor. Some heartfelt "self-inflicted": because there were one or two sessions they did not participate in sub-dishes, they were afraid of the company's pig roast culture would "Lost", the next session must be restored! They shouted.

Held the annual gathering, how can it be without good planning?

The theme for Y2010: Happy life beyond 80

The theme for 2011: my COMPANY J, my love, Lean improvement, I prefer

The theme for 2012: We are one family

The theme for 2013: "Dreams, blossoming in Jabil"

The theme for 2014: "With new blood. Creating Wonders"

The theme for 2015: "One Jabil, One dream"

The theme for 2016…

Remember that was the first year I joined, Company J be abandoned by the biggest customer N, posted negative news by NGO, all departments are immersed in a tense atmosphere, the group CEO from the United States flew in the first time, participated in our pig roast Congress, then the annual gathering has not yet begun, the United States management came early on to the venue, he looks here and there, the spirit of the party, as the commander in chief, I cannot just hang the boss over there, so I went up to chat, asked him to compare the United States headquarters pig roast party with us what is the difference? He said: "There is a big difference: The American Pig roast annual gathering more like a family-style party, everyone is drinking beer, eating barbecue, chatting, Chinese pig roast more like a wonderful party, while tasting delicious buffet."

It was a moving party, in the corner of the party, introduced our Vice president of Asia, VL who has served in Company J for more than 10 year, glorious propaganda page, we collected a lot of photos of his past 10 years of work, which recorded he help Company J from building a factory to develop the driving force of the Group Development Center, Dozens of the factory built up by him, he stood there one by one glance through, I am happy to ask him do you like it? He nodded: "Thank you very much! How did you find these precious photos?" I told him: "It is his most intimate partner TP collected all these from the various old colleagues " he deeply nodded.

Only TP, a venerable senior vice president, got Asia's first staff number, he is so called his own, the courage to retire at the height of his official career, provide the position to the young and capable successor, TP can see and read out each colleague's name, he can send the blessing to every colleague's birthday on the day of the Mail, not too late, It was on that day. I received his 7 birthday greetings from Company J in 7 years, I asked him, what day is your birthday? He never answer me.

That night we arranged a program for the Long Service Award, when CEO Tim grant the award to VL, VL in tears, he was looking back on the hard work of the past ten years, he was moved by his colleagues to recognize his contribution, he was grateful to CEO Tim give him the award of Honor, He had been choking and couldn't make a sound, all audience was impressed, all the guests stood up and applauded, the managers automatically walked to the sides of the stage and shook hands tightly with him, thanking him for his contribution to the company and comforting him for his retirement.

That episode was deeply imprinted on my mind, though I didn't work with VL Tan.

That is a unique party, a top management from British has such evaluation, we divided into four nights, more than ten thousand employees, especially after the government's top management seen, all the representatives of trade unions and HR director in the area all invited to join, let's make the most wonderful part of the play again, so we have five nights totally, why did the audience feel so special? It is because we have a "Miss pig roast" campaign, the imitation of sound like an ugly than beauty, but the actual is choosing the most beautiful female colleague among company, we put the beauty link into four phases, each night a topic: self-introduction, talent contest, answer questions, group singing and dancing performances, the award granting, Why so interesting is that the public can vote on Miss pig roast in every evening, it is a public vote, quite like super girl singing competition evaluation, we distribute 100 balls, employees can put the ball into his thought of winning candidate, funny in the end, not only the ball, oranges and apples with their own hands vote to others, the purpose is to influence the outcome of the audience and the judges scoring, but to reassure them all named champion deserved, because they have not only beauty but also has the wisdom, the questionnaire is not a fixed list, the audience VIP and employees can't imagine the questions, such as the microphone handover to me, I asked participants, what is beauty exactly? What is the standard of beauty? The common people will be stuck here, but the final winner is quite intelligent, she replied "I think confidence is the most beautiful!" I quite appreciated her confidence and wise answer, as commander in chief of the party, I took the roses on the table to the contestants, which is added a lot of points to the girl.

Our program has to be innovative in every year, Miss pig roast Competition only held for two years to stop, because we do not want the audience feel bored, then to stop.

After that we held the employee dream show, singing, dancing, magic, Allegro, talk show, martial arts acrobatics, comedy crosstalk ... Too much, through this game we know the original staff skills and performance of the dream is to rely on a large stage to show. Another five nights of full play did not affect the enthusiasm of these performers, they are excited in every night, after the performance of the company to continue the performance in the garden into a circle for the second day of the show preparation, so they do not need our HR department like catching chickens to catch them for training and performing, They are more active than anyone, the party is more exciting each day because they have to perform different things and accumulate more points in every night. In the process of these dream show, we have a dance drama called "Me and my Chasing dream", we put the action of physical challenge staffs to the stage, after the show, Asia-Pacific Human Resources senior director came over and shook my hand, praised our party made quite successful, his eyes all turned red, indeed, the program made the people have a kind of "want to cry" impulse.

The company has 20 staff clubs, we make full use of these clubs every year, or create special programs, put their works on stage, or make plans, or work out: for example, calligraphy and Painting Association draw on the spot, dance singing performances, English association is responsible for translating the speech, makeup association responsible for makeup, Photography Association is responsible for photography, it is a long & short focal camera show time....

Each year EIT college students must present a program, we hope they become the seeds of Company J culture, in the soil of Company J culture to grow, the company's "Work hard and play hard" culture spread all over the world.

People do not think that the manager just sit and watch the performance, in addition to sub-dishes, they also participate in the performance, singing and dancing, I have participated in three performances, although my performance cells are not mature but amongst a bunch of managers I still can do.

The party's participation rate in the company was the biggest, which was better than that of the CCTV gala, whose audience only applauded in unison.

The first is the pig roast shirt: The whole company from top to bottom, no difference, on that day all changed to a unified pig roast shirt, jeans, so from the platform under the stand, quite uniform, when the staff holding the Fire fly stick in the shake, it looks like a beautiful star sky, because the costumes are unified background color. In fact, this pig roast shirt style is selected and even design by the employees, a team of employees without gender sensitization, summer or fall-winter pattern? Does the employee design or use the outside professional design? It takes a heat discussion to get a verdict.

Then there is the logo of the pig roast, all design by the staff and vote, see one of the year logo, I particularly like:

Buffet supplier selection is also voted by the staff, not just eat & drink so simple, the company form a small judge group, to participate in the bidding of the major star hotels and try to taste it, to review the catering capacity of these hotels, to serve more than 2800 participants, to start cooking 18 hours early. Food can't be prepared late, nor ready to be afraid of stale. My predecessor had a painful lesson, she did not provide the meal on time, black recorded by the boss and the staff.

The choice of what kind of Long service awards are also vote to choose the right gift, gold, watches, commemorative coins and travel box, the budget range of choice.

But only one will not let employees to choose, I bear the consequences alone, that is to continue the annual five-night performance, or move the venue to the development Zone Performing Arts Center-world-class standard venues and audio equipment, I must make the final decision, do a good job of the company's annual meeting up a grade, messed up is my responsibility, So far, I see the number of the factory has risen to an uncontrollable level, the pressure and load of the actors have risen to an uncontrollable level, the same performance for 6 nights, who can bear it?!

I work with the team to estimate what obstacles we will encounter? The team immediately listed a large basket of questions:

1. How can 10,000 people be transported to the venue within 1.5 hours with 80 buses and backward to the company?

2. The rental of the venue cost the party a large budget.

3. Cooking is not allowed on the site, how to carry out the buffet service?

4. The scope large that we can't find the direction!

5. The show must be strong enough to fight alone because the audience sits on the "mountain" position will not be visible!

Oh, my God! Always living in the river stream is really difficult to know the broad sea, but me - a small fish too yearning for the sea, I want to try, with my team members, I want to take them together to experience difficulties to solve them one by one to do a high-style high-level difficult to make their own unforgettable party!

The host is an important part of the annual meeting, a perfect speech makes the party icing on the cake. The selection of the party host is quite harsh, from different departments, even from the production line to find them out, asked them to use three days change to the moderator: their own string of the opening ceremony of the annual meeting, speech and concluding remarks, candidates have to brain storm, in order to write a satisfactory host speech, Do not know that how many brain cells died, from which you will know which one should be the perfect one.

Three months before the party's performance, we organized a dance competition, karaoke contest, the selection of elite talent.

Even hostesses have to be set up early, because they have to perform on other programs.

Do not rely on the program submitted by the departments, do not rely on the collection outside the performance of the program, depends on the external professional mentor, cooperate with the creation of songs, dances, stories, lighting choreography and so on.

I fully believe the performance of the performers, to the rehearsal time, the actors were most afraid of the most eager thing: "Cindy is coming, you do not perform in the good way will be scolded." "I played a red-faced role: detailly correct their shortcomings, they perform like elementary school pupil, seriously listen to my advice, I only teach once, they know their own problem, I let them record their performances of the fragments, repeat to adjust, the program played over and over again, Until they feel satisfied.

I need to seek the support of that department in this department because I need their support. I find IE help to calculate 80 buses drive into the factory space, I find the procurement to re-find various services and the previous requirements of a complete different list supplier: The stage layout, Lighting, Music, Actor's clothing makeup supplier, Photographic video arrangement, even cooked food bags, the bus use for traffic, They also help me to negotiate this price or that price, to ensure that the budget is spent per planning, I will find the production department to mobilize staff to ensure the delivery of goods, stage layout, delivery time, I have to find all the department heads to arrange the holiday and production plan, because it can't affect production, I find the government department to give the green light Because so many employees and vehicles will block the road, worry about material transport and weather effects. None of this has ever happened, because the performance of the venue is in the factory, take something, it is not easy? But not now, even take a hammer from the factory to the venue of the show, the equipment must be counted and packed.

The annual meeting is a multi-sectoral collaborative work, a meticulous and perfect process is necessary, but also to ensure the smooth progress of the annual meeting. Thanks to all the staff, they gave me the best support:

They can make the opening music for this successful party to lost sleeping overnight in the audio-visual room, they can move 2000 chairs and tables on the truck, they can be ready for five hours, in order to prepare a variety of food into the food bag, They can instruct more than 80 buses within 1.5 hours for the employees with no stop, let them sit in the bus, then sit in the party on their own seat without any delay.

The time and process of the meeting was just right and the employees arrived at the venue 15 minutes early.

Rang up the music, lit up the light, we ushered the moment in the life of the most eager to show ....

The Word from My Husband

Although you were one Superman/Superwoman, there were existing the gap to be one qualified HR head.

Perhaps you will think will it go into heroics? Being life partner of one HR head, sympathize with the sufferings. I still remember one time we traveled to Philippine together, we found out the biggest expense wasn't accommodation, it was telephone fee! Because in the whole journey, the call from her company never stop.

Allow me to use what 's Liu Xiaoqing (one Chinese film star) saying, it is tough to take HR role, it will be much more tough to be one MNC HR, it must be the most tough to be HR head of MNC.

You should first try to acquaint yourself with labor law from country to country. Because the subdivision located worldwide, you need to understand with different cultural of different location, You need to understand different manner, different religion, different habit people, you can work over night, because the different time zones amongst different division, you need to have zest, because nobody know when will happen what the issues, you need to work no matter day and night, it is your working hour, You need to be master of professional skill, because you have to settle the business, you need to know lyra-playing, chess, calligraphy and painting, sport and entertainment, Because you need to face different level people, Either to be elegant or to be Fierce, Neither to satisfy the employees by forgetting company benefit, not to be servile boss without justice.

Compare with Superman, one qualified HR head must have a great faculty can be qualified this role.

www.ingramcontent.com/pod-product-compliance
Lightning Source LLC
Chambersburg PA
CBHW021809170526
45157CB00007B/2515